Profane Illumination

Weimar and Now: German Cultural Criticism

Martin Jay and Anton Kaes,
General Editors

Profane Illumination

Walter Benjamin and the Paris
of Surrealist Revolution

Margaret Cohen

UNIVERSITY OF CALIFORNIA PRESS
Berkeley · Los Angeles . London

University of California Press
Berkeley and Los Angeles, California

University of California Press
London, England

Library of Congress Cataloging-in-Publication Data

Cohen, Margaret.
    Profane illumination: Walter Benjamin and the Paris of surrealist
revolution / Margaret Cohen.
        p.   cm.—(Weimar and now; 5)
    Includes bibliographical references and index.
    ISBN 0–520–08023–8 (alk. paper)
    1. Benjamin, Walter, 1892–1940.   2. Philosophy, Marxist.
3. Surrealism.   4. Paris (France)—Intellectual life—20th century.
5. Philosophy, German—20th century.   I. Title.   II. Series.
B3209.B584C64   1993
838'.91209—dc20   92–36861
                                                          CIP

Printed in the United States of America

1   2   3   4   5   6   7   8   9

Contents

Illustrations

Abbreviations

R   Benjamin, *Reflections*
V   Breton, *Les Vases communicants*

Acknowledgments

My thanks go first of all to Peter Brooks for his perspicacious advice when this project began as a dissertation at Yale. I am grateful for the generosity of the Whiting Foundation, which permitted me to complete a first draft of the manuscript in dissertation form. I appreciate greatly the patient responses of Marguerite Bonnet, Gary Smith, and Claude Pichois to my queries about Breton, Benjamin, and Baudelaire. Subsequent thanks go to all my colleagues at New York University—particularly to Michael Taussig, whose interest in the project helped it through the difficult metamorphosis from dissertation to book; to Richard Sieburth, for insights on nineteenth-century Paris and Benjamin; and to Timothy Reiss, for his support of my research and writing. NYU offered welcome aid in defraying the costs of obtaining illustrations. I would also like to thank my readers at the University of California Press, notably Martin Jay, for comments that proved invaluable in refining my thought. Edward Dimendberg has given judicious guidance through the stages of the publication process. Finally, I could not have completed this work without multiple acts of kindness and insight from family and friends. April Alliston, Leslie Camhi, Anne Higonnet, and Barbara Vinken provided thoughtful commentary on the manuscript at various moments in its production. Above all, thanks go to Daniel Klotz, who has seen the project through from beginning to end and whose influence, incalculably diffusive, is on every page.

GUIDE DE
PARIS
MYSTÉRIEUX

LES GUIDES NOIRS
Tchou, éditeur

1. Title page to the *Guide to Mysterious Paris* (*Guide de Paris mystérieux*). Courtesy of Tchou Publishing House.

CHAPTER 1

Gothic Marxism

Some years ago a French publishing house put out a series of guides to the Gothic sides of familiar places. The series called itself *Guides Noirs,* punning on the touristic *Guides Bleus* through allusion to the *roman noir,* the French equivalent of the Gothic novel. *Guide to Mysterious France, Guide to Mysterious Provence, Guide to Mysterious Paris* ran the titles of its volumes devoted to the irrational, illicit, inspired, passional, often supernatural aspects of social topography obscured in the bustle of ordinary life and the monumental litanies of standard guides. The *Guides Noirs* classified sites with a series of categories indicating the scope of their concerns: "Legendary History," "Prehistoric Enigmas," "Pagan Myths and Monuments," "Sacred Spots and Christian Miracles," "The *Illuminati,*" "Mores and Customs," "Fantastic Bestiary," "Marvelous Creatures," "Devil, Sorcerers, Ghosts," "Strange Stones and Constructions," "Uncanny Landscapes," "Underground Passages, Treasures," "Imaginary Museums," "Tragedies and Bizarre Deeds."[1]

Profane Illumination constitutes a title in a still uncatalogued series of *Guides Noirs* to Gothic Marxism. This series charts the contours of a Marxist genealogy fascinated with the irrational aspects of social processes, a genealogy that both investigates how the irrational pervades

---

1. *Guide de Paris mystérieux,* n.p. Unless otherwise noted, all translations are mine.

existing society and dreams of using it to effect social change. Gothic
Marxism has often been obscured in the celebrated battles of main-
stream Marxism, privileging a conceptual apparatus constructed in narrowly Enlightenment terms. The Enlightenment, however, was always
already haunted by its Gothic ghosts, and the same can be said of
Marxism from its inception. An archaeology of Gothic Marxism entails
not only reclaiming obscured texts for the Marxist repertoire but attending to the darker side of well-known Marxist topoi, starting with
the writings of Marx himself; the *Guides Noirs* often focus on the
hidden life of sites familiar from the seemingly rational daylight business of production.

My concern in this book will be to reconstruct early attempts to
theorize Gothic Marxism: the first efforts to appropriate Freud's seminal twentieth-century exploration of the irrational for Marxist thought.
In France these efforts were initiated by surrealism, that avant-garde
movement generally responsible for introducing psychoanalysis into
French intellectual circles.[2] They were most extensively elaborated by
the movement's leader, André Breton, in the course of what Micheline
Tison-Braun characterizes as the "ballet of surrealism and the revolution last[ing] from 1925 to 1935, abundantly commented on by Breton,
more and more peremptory and perplexing."[3] While "vulgar Marxism"
has undeniably become an "overdetermined and mythically hypos-
tatized category," the anguished tone of Breton's writings as he strug-
gled with his relation to the French Communist Party speaks eloquently
to the pressure it once exerted, both in France of the time and on him.[4]

It was in the process of trying to accommodate surrealism to this
Marxism that Breton devised his "bold" attempt to "reconcile Engels
and Freud."[5] Breton modified practical Marxist notions of subjectiv-

2. As Helena Lewis puts it, "Freud was almost unknown in France until the Surrealists 'discovered' him and became fascinated with his theory of dreams." See *The Politics of Surrealism*, x.

3. Micheline Tison-Braun, *La Crise de l'humanisme*, II, 153. Lewis provides a detailed history of Breton's difficulties with practical Marxism. See also Anna Balakian's
account in *André Breton, Magus of Surrealism*.

4. Lawrence Grossberg and Cary Nelson, introduction to *Marxism and the Interpretation of Culture*, 3. Tison-Braun's figure of the ballet is a bit dismissive; as Leslie Camhi
writes of Breton's subsequent engagement with the politics of revolution: "For the man
who spent weeks with Trotsky in Mexico writing 'For an Independent Revolutionary
Art,' just months before the exiled Soviet's assassination, both esthetic and political questions were clearly matters of life and death." Leslie Camhi, "Extended Boundaries," 43.

5. André Breton, *L'Amour fou*, 31. I cite verbatim from *Mad Love*, trans. Mary Ann
Caws, 23. Caws has recently provided impressive translations of the two hermetic Breton
prose texts central to my argument, *Mad Love* and *Communicating Vessels*, the latter
with Geoffrey T. Harris, from which I have profited greatly and which I in large part

ity, historical process, causality, praxis, and event with psychoanalytic concepts and content while he wandered through a landscape reworking nineteenth-century representations of *Paris noir* (Gothic Paris). My exploration of Breton's Gothic Marxism thus proceeds through motifs remarkably similar to the categories of classification found in the *Guides Noirs* (the trajectory of Breton's *Nadja* is moreover among the promenade routes that the *Guide to Mysterious Paris* recommends).[6] Uncanny landscapes, ghosts and sorcerers, strange stones and constructions, *illuminati*: to these will be added such surrealist concepts as objective chance, intersubjective desire, the lucky find, the encounter, the dream, bohemian resistance, the social unconscious, and the capillary tissue connecting the communicating vessels of psychic and material life. Breton called his unholy brew "modern materialism," an appellation borrowed from Friedrich Engels's nineteenth-century critique of mechanical materialism.[7]

"Profane illumination" was how Walter Benjamin formulated the kernel of surrealist Marxism in an essay that remains arguably the most important assessment of the political and theoretical objectives of the movement to date: "The true, creative overcoming of religious illumination . . . resides in a *profane illumination,* a materialist, anthropological inspiration."[8] I have a second pressing stake in using Benjamin to reconstruct surrealist Marxism: to elucidate modern materialism's formative but neglected role in shaping Benjamin's thought. My concern will be with its vital contribution to Benjamin's writings that take pride of place in the corpus of Gothic Marxism. These are the unfinished ruins of the *Passagen-Werk,* the arcades project. Centerpiece of the "Parisian production cycle," as Benjamin called the critical work that was to preoccupy him from his turn to Marxism in the later 1920s, the *Passagen-Werk* was to serve both as *Guide Bleu* and *Guide Noir*

---

follow. I hence reference both the French original and the published translation in every citation from these texts. I also cite in this fashion to help the non-French-speaking reader follow my argument. When I use the English translations unmodified, as here, I will so indicate in a footnote. *L'Amour fou* will subsequently be abbreviated as *AF* and *Mad Love* as *ML*.

6. David Macey comments that the surrealists' "interest in mysticism and the occult" is "inseparable from their interest in Freud, whose discovery of the unconscious will help them to go beyond the limitations of conventional thought." See David Macey, *Lacan in Contexts,* 51.

7. Breton cites from Engels in the *Second Manifesto of Surrealism* in André Breton, *Manifestoes of Surrealism,* 141. Referred to hereafter as *M.*

8. Walter Benjamin, "Surrealism," in *Reflections,* 179. Referred to hereafter as *R.* I have changed Jephcott's "materialistic" to "materialist." For the German original, see *GS,* II, 1, 297.

to the nineteenth-century Paris that Marx had termed "the new capital of the new world."[9] In it Benjamin set out to capture the psychological, sensual, irrational, and often seemingly trivial aspects of life during the expansion of industrial capitalism which such monolithic Marxist categories as base and superstructure tend to obscure. Seeking nonetheless to integrate his preoccupations with the concerns of Marxist theory, Benjamin brought Marxism together with all manner of paradigms for grasping the irrational, ranging from the high tragic narratives of Jewish mysticism to the tawdry spiritism of nineteenth-century Parisian mass culture and the surrealist profane illumination.[10]

The importance of modern materialism to the *Passagen-Werk* can be summed up by a quote from Breton included in the *Passagen-Werk*'s Konvolut N, where Benjamin collects his epistemological and methodological musings in densest form. " 'I can't stress enough that, for an enlightened materialist like Lafargue, economic determinism is not the "absolutely perfect instrument" that "might become the key to all the problems of history," ' " runs the citation.[11] Benjamin takes the quote from the 1935 *Political Position of Surrealism (Position politique du surréalisme)*, a text originally given as a lecture in Prague, when

9. I take the term "production cycle" from one of Benjamin's letters at the arcades project's inception: "When I have finished the work with which I am occupied at the moment, carefully, provisionally . . . then the *One-Way Street* production cycle will be closed in the same way that the tragic drama book brought the Germanist one to a close," Benjamin wrote to Scholem, Berlin, 30 January 1928, *Briefe*, I, 455 (referred to hereafter as *B*). Benjamin identified this "production cycle" with Paris from its opening work, *One-Way Street*. "It was in Paris that I found the form for that notebook," Benjamin told Hugo von Hoffmansthal from Pardigon on March 17, 1928, *B*, I, 446. The Marx citation is from a letter to Arnold Ruge, Kreuznach, 1843, in *The Marx-Engels Reader*, 12.

10. On this hybrid aspect of Benjamin's thought, Christine Buci-Glucksmann comments:

> In his attempt to make the irrational dialectical and to let it be seen . . . Benjamin was constrained to put into play *two languages* and *two worlds*. One, political and Marxist, derives from the dialectic as the site of confrontation where the perspective, the praxis of the vanquished, is in perpetual opposition to the governing and oppressive rule of the victors. . . . The other, the complementary world of Kafka or Klee, that of the "theological dwarf," that of the Angel, is not dialectical: it indicates the interruption of history, catastrophe, the inhuman, and the dehiscence-dwindling of the subject.

Christine Buci-Glucksmann, *La Raison baroque de Baudelaire à Benjamin*, 99.

11. *Das Passagen-Werk*, I, 585 (N 6, 4) (designated hereafter *PW*). The pagination and text of this edition are identical with volumes V, 1 and 2 of Benjamin's *Gesammelte Schriften*. In citing from Konvolut N, I will hereafter identify the fragments simply by N and their number enclosed in parentheses. I do so to facilitate their location by readers using either the German text or the English translation of Benjamin's epistemological Konvolut by Leigh Hafrey and Richard Sieburth, published first in *The Philosophical Forum* and then included in Gary Smith et al., *Benjamin—Philosophy, Aesthetics, History*. This translation is invaluable and I use it with only occasional modifications throughout my citations from Konvolut N.

Breton's struggles with pragmatic Marxism were culminating in despair. Benjamin found Breton's modern materialism useful in working through his own difficulties with pragmatic Marxism. One of the arcades project's central methodological concerns was to free Marxist theory from its immersion in the nineteenth century, "which produced not only imperialism but also the Marxism that has such useful questions for it," as Benjamin put it in "Brecht's *Threepenny Novel*" (*R*, 202). "Every presentation of history must begin with awakening; in fact it should deal with nothing else," Benjamin comments in Konvolut N.[12] "This one deals with awakening from the nineteenth century" (N 4, 3). Awakening Marxist theory was necessary if Marxism was to offer a critical representation of the moment in which this body of thought itself first took shape.

Benjamin muses on how to free Marxism from the conceptual limitations of its nineteenth-century origins throughout the epistemological Konvolut N. Stating that "one of the methodological objectives of this project [the *Passagen-Werk*] can be considered the demonstration of historical materialism which has canceled out the idea of progress in itself," he announces the need to free Marxist historiography from a notion of historical process dear to the nineteenth century's ruling bourgeoisie (N 2, 2).[13] Benjamin also asks, "by what route is it possible to attain a heightened graphicness (*Anschaulichkeit*) combined with a realization of the Marxist method," as he speculates on how to avoid the "historical vulgar naturalism" that Marxist historiography all too often shares with the contemplative bourgeois historiography it should critique (N 2, 6).[14] And throughout his notes and essays from the *Passagen-Werk*, Benjamin is concerned with revising Marxism's "classicist" view of art, as he puts it in the 1937 "Eduard Fuchs," as well as the deterministic and simplistically reflective way in which vulgar Marxism posits base-superstructure relations, with its attending consequences for conceptualizations of ideology and praxis.[15]

12. I modify what is doubtless a typo in how Hafrey and Sieburth render the opening clause of the sentence: "Every presentation is history must begin with awakening . . ."

13. Benjamin designates his own Marxist allegiance with slippage among various terms, notably historical materialism, materialism, and Marxism. In this slippage he expresses his simultaneous discomfort with orthodox Marxism and his interest in aligning himself with a Marxist project. A similar discomfort with the term Marxism runs through Breton's writings.

14. Hafrey and Sieburth translate this phrase as "the vulgar naturalism of historicism." The original German runs (I cite the phrase in context): "mit dem historischen Vulgärnaturalismus zu brechen."

15. Walter Benjamin, "Eduard Fuchs, Collector and Historian," in *One-Way Street and Other Writings*, 361 (referred to hereafter as *OWS*).

In a 1937 letter to Max Horkheimer, Benjamin placed the application of psychoanalysis to orthodox Marxism at the core of the *Passagen-Werk*'s methodological concerns: "I imagine that the definitive and binding plan of the book . . . would have to emerge from two fundamental methodological investigations. One would have to do with the critique of pragmatic history on the one hand and of cultural history on the other, as it presents itself to the materialist; the other with the significance of psychoanalysis for the subject of materialist historiography." [16] I argue here that modern materialism provides Benjamin with fertile speculation for these concerns. We will see Benjamin particularly provoked by (1) the modern materialist appeal to the fissured subject of psychoanalysis to modify the conscious and rational subject dear to practical Marxism; (2) its application of psychoanalytic notions of history to collective history in order to displace a linear or mechanically causal vision of historical process and to break down the base-superstructure distinction with appeal to libidinal forces permeating both; (3) its use of psychoanalytic formulations of determination and representation to complicate a reflective model for the relation between superstructure and base; (4) its psychoanalytically informed interest in the everyday, which it uses to revise orthodox Marxist notions of the stuff of history as well as to open possible reservoirs for recuperative experience in damaged life; and (5) its application of psychoanalytic notions of therapy to an Enlightenment view of critique, notably as this application pertains to the dialectical image. Finally, we will see Benjamin provide historical justification for the affinity of Breton's modern materialism with nineteenth-century *Paris noir*. My concluding chapter is devoted to Benjamin's speculations on Marx himself as a denizen of this Paris, in pursuit of what Konvolut N proposed as the *Passagen-Werk*'s crucial contribution to Marxism: "First, it will explore the way the environment from which Marx's teachings arose influenced the latter through its expressive character, and not just through its causal relationships; and secondly, it will show those features that Marxism shares with the expressive character of the material products that are contemporary with it" (N 1a, 7).

RESCUING CRITIQUE

Theodor Adorno was the first critic to recognize the potential importance of modern materialism to Benjamin, although Adorno's general

16. Benjamin to Horkheimer, Paris, 28 March 1937, *PW*, 1158.

hostility to surrealism did not allow him to develop this recognition beyond rather skeptical surprise. In a 1934 letter Adorno drew Benjamin's attention to *Communicating Vessels,* a text that, as Mary Ann Caws notes, is "among Breton's works . . . the most 'philosophical' and 'political' in the strong senses of those terms":[17]

> Moreover, it is just now that an important impetus from outside seems to be transmitted to the arcades. I read in an English film journal a review of the new book by Breton (*Communicating Vessels* [Paris 1932]), that, if I am not mistaken, approaches our intentions very closely. Thus, it turns against the psychological interpretation of the dream and advocates one oriented towards objective images; and seems to accord them importance as historical key. The whole thing lies much too near your concerns not to make a radical turnabout probably necessary precisely in the most central point (where, I can't tell from the review); but by triggering this turnabout, it could become of great importance, perhaps as important as, *what a parallel!,* Panoffsky and Saxl for the Baroque book![18]

Adorno's comments remain an isolated instance of critical interest in the importance of Benjamin's relation to Breton, however, both in his own work and in readings of the arcades project to come.

That the *Passagen-Werk* has an affinity to surrealism is clear, for Benjamin asserted in no uncertain terms the centrality of high surrealism to the arcades project from its inception. Indeed, it was rather the "all too ostentatious proximity" of the movement that disturbed him; so he told Gershom Scholem in November 1928:

> In order to lift the work [the *Passagen-Werk*] out of an all too ostentatious proximity to the *mouvement surréaliste* that could become fatal to me, as natural and well-founded as it is, I have had to expand it more and more in my mind, and make it so universal in its most particular, tiniest frameworks that it would enter upon the *inheritance* of surrealism even in a purely chronological respect and precisely with all the absolute powers of a philosophical Fortinbras. In other words: I am mightily deferring the time for composing the thing.[19]

17. Mary Ann Caws, "Linking and Reflections: André Breton and His *Vases Communicants,*" in *Dada/Surrealism,* no. 17, 92.
18. Theodor Adorno to Walter Benjamin, Oxford, 6 November 1934, *PW,* 1106–7 (emphasis added). In a letter found in the Bibliothèque Nationale Benjamin archive, dated 20 March 1935 from Merton College, Oxford, Adorno pursues the subject of the importance of surrealism to the arcades project: "Do you actually know Max Ernst? I have never met him, but it would be easy for me to procure your acquaintance through Lotte Lenya, who is a close friend of his. And I can imagine that in the current state of the arcades project, the meeting with the surrealist who, it seems to me, has achieved the most, would be quite *à propos.*"
19. Walter Benjamin to Gershom Scholem, Berlin, 30 October 1928, *B,* I, 483.

Benjamin was to continue asserting the *Passagen-Werk*'s intimate relation to surrealism throughout the twelve years of its unfinished composition. In 1935 he described one of his project's two central aims as a conceptual liquidation of the surrealist inheritance. He wrote to Scholem: "The work represents both the philosophical utilization of surrealism—and with that its sublation—as well as the attempt to seize the image of history in the most insignificant fixations of existence, in its refuse as it were." [20] But from the time of Adorno's first ambivalent letters taking apart "Paris, Capital of the Nineteenth Century," this philosophical utilization has been read as Benjamin's effort to transmute surrealist aesthetics to philosophy, notably surrealism's fascination with the debris of bourgeois society and the movement's shocklike method of montage. [21] In the standard Marxist readings of this relation, informed by the Marxism either of the Frankfurt School or of Brecht, Benjamin's use of psychoanalytic language, notably dream language, has been considered the place where he substitutes the smoke and mirrors of writerly technique for critical analysis.

That surrealist Marxism has long remained illegible in the works of Benjamin owes much to its own ill repute. As Peter Wollen observes in one of the first recent writings to engage the theoretical content of surrealist Marxism, "Historians of Western Marxism have tended to discount Breton, seeing him as 'off-beat'(!) or lacking in 'seriousness.'" [22] When the interest of surrealism to twentieth-century Marxist thinking has been recognized, it has generally been credited to the renegade surrealists, who were themselves dubious that high surrealism could for-

20. Benjamin to Scholem, Paris, 9 August 1935, quoted in *PW*, II, 1137.
21. On surrealism's contribution to Benjamin's work, see Ernst Bloch's "Revue Form in Philosophy," in *Heritage of Our Times,* Theodor Adorno's "Benjamins 'Einbahnstraße,'" in *Über Walter Benjamin,* Susan Buck-Morss's *The Origin of Negative Dialectics* and *The Dialectics of Seeing,* and Richard Wolin's *Walter Benjamin, An Aesthetic of Redemption* as well as "Expérience et matérialisme dans le Passagen-Werk de Benjamin" in *Walter Benjamin et Paris,* subsequently reprinted in English translation as "Experience and Materialism in Benjamin's *Passagenwerk*" in Smith et al., *Benjamin.* See also Elizabeth Lenk and Rita Bischof's "L'Intrication surréelle du rêve et de l'histoire dans les Passages de Benjamin" and Jacques Leenhardt's "Le Passage comme forme d'expérience: Benjamin face à Aragon," both of which are found in *Walter Benjamin et Paris.* The reader may, in addition, wish to consult Joseph Furnkäs's "La 'Voie à sens unique' weimarienne de Walter Benjamin" in *Weimar ou l'explosion de la modernité* and his later book on the same subject, *Surrealismus als Erkenntnis.* Furnkäs is above all interested in the contribution of surrealism to the construction of Benjamin's "characteristic and specifically avant-garde short prose writings" (p. 2).
22. Peter Wollen, "The Situationist International," 78. This statement is on the same page as a footnote speculating on the importance of surrealist Marxism to Benjamin: "Within the Western Marxist tradition, Walter Benjamin was also greatly indebted to surrealism."

mulate political philosophy worthy of the name.[23] "It is regrettable, we say, that nothing can enter into M. Breton's confused head except in poetic form. All of existence, conceived as *purely* literary by M. Breton, diverts him from the shabby, sinister, or inspired events occurring all around him," Georges Bataille writes in his 1929–30 "The Old Mole and the Prefix *Sur*," an essay that takes its title from Marx's *Eighteenth Brumaire* but that owes as much to the polemical energy of *The Holy Family*.[24] Bataille's opinion has been shared not only by detractors of high surrealism but also by its friends.[25] In the same year that Bataille was engaged in the heat of avant-garde polemic, however, Benjamin was formulating the materialist content to the profane illumination. "To win the energies of intoxication for the revolution—this is the project about which Surrealism circles in all its books and enterprises. This it may call its most particular task," Benjamin writes in "Surrealism— The Last Snapshot of the European Intelligentsia" (*R*, 189). "Only the Surrealists have understood . . . [the] present commands" of the *Communist Manifesto*, the essay concludes (*R*, 192). In my discussion, I will be concerned with the serious Marxist content of what may be considered Breton's own Parisian production cycle, the three major prose works from the period of his engagement with French communism

23. On Bataille's own links to Marxism, see Denis Hollier's comments in his foreword to *The College of Sociology*: "Bataille had never been a communist. But he played what he claimed was a Marxist card against Breton. Work would be to society as sexuality was to the individual—the part that is damned, a center of unbridled energies that are uncontrollable and unassimilable, a locus of expenditures that are inconceivable in terms of a rationalist economy. The proletariat is the abject of private property, family and State." In Denis Hollier, ed., *The College of Sociology (1937–39)*, xix. See also observations throughout *Yale French Studies* no. 78, *On Bataille*.

24. Georges Bataille, "The 'Old Mole' and the Prefix *Sur* in the Words *Surhomme* [Superman] and *Surrealist*," in *Visions of Excess*, ed. Allan Stoekl, 41.

25. Thus, Marie-Claire Banquart: "Breton does not hesitate to use Lenin as reference to predict and preach the proletarian liberation. But is the city any less magical for it? No, it teaches rather that the becoming of man is subjective before all. . . . in the development of the Parisian dream, is the Leninist revolution any more important for Breton than the system of Joseph de Maistre for Baudelaire?" To her rhetorical question Banquart offers the expected no. See Marie-Claire Banquart, *Paris des surréalistes*, 122–123. See also the writings of Michel Carrouges, Anna Balakian, Jean Gaulmier, and Yvette Gindine, to mention but a few of the more well-known critics with this opinion. Fredric Jameson's brief discussion of the subject in *Marxism and Form* is an exception to this reception. In contrast to the Anglo-French reception of surrealism, the German reception takes much from Benjamin's understanding of this movement's serious materialist content. Peter Bürger's *Der französische Surrealismus* opens with the following declaration: "If a *parti pris* underlies the work, it is solely that of grasping surrealism here not according to its weakness, its magical irrationalism, but rather according to its strength, its reaction to alienation" (p. 18). Bürger's opposition between a magic irrationalism and a rational Marxist project does not appreciate, however, the extent to which surrealist Marxism attacks this very distinction.

(1926–35), *Nadja, Communicating Vessels,* and *Mad Love,* which Breton saw as forming a unified prose trilogy.[26] In a recent issue of *Dada/ Surrealism* devoted entirely to Breton, Anna Balakian comments on these latter two works: "Breton's narratives . . . have been with the exception of *Nadja* mostly neglected in scholarship."[27] I suspect this neglect owes much to the fact that Breton's bold effort to reconcile Engels and Freud is central to these texts; they yield their significance above all to a reader taking this effort seriously.

In my project to salvage previously illegible aspects of Benjamin and Breton's Gothic Marxisms, I pursue the Benjaminian imperative of "rescuing critique."[28] For Benjamin this rescue is effected by reading: "The historical index of the images doesn't simply say that they belong to a specific time, it says above all that they only *enter into legibility* at a specific time" (N 3, 1, emphasis added). Speculating on what factors determine the legibility of images at one moment and not another, Benjamin links such legibility to how these images mediate between the critic's present and their own: "Every Now is determined by those images that are synchronic with it: every Now is the Now of a specific recognizability," Benjamin suggests (N 3, 1). And: "It isn't that the past casts its light on what is present or that what is present casts its light on what is past; rather, an image is that in which the Then and the Now come together into a constellation like a flash of lightning" (N 3, 1).[29]

What Now and Then come together in *Profane Illumination?* I

26. *Mad Love* was published in 1937 but is composed of essays written largely in the period 1933–35. Marguerite Bonnet tells us that "Breton moreover himself wanted to make the unity of the three works palpable: on December 2, 1939, he writes to Jean Paulhan that he would have liked to unite in one volume *Nadja, Communicating Vessels,* and *Mad Love,*" although Gaston Gallimard refused to accept this project because *Mad Love* was not yet out of print. See Marguerite Bonnet, notes to *Nadja* in André Breton, *Oeuvres complètes,* 1560. Because there exists at the moment only one volume, I have hereafter abbreviated the text as OC.

27. She continues, "Haim Finkelstein and I . . . found fifteen comprehensive commentaries on *Nadja* within a single decade but total neglect of the other two books of the trilogy." See Anna Balakian, "Introduction," 3.

28. For a discussion of this concept in all its complexities, see notably Irving Wohlfarth, "On the Messianic Structure of Walter Benjamin's Last Reflections." See also Jürgen Habermas, "Walter Benjamin: Consciousness-Raising or Rescuing Critique," in *On Walter Benjamin,* ed. Gary Smith.

29. I situate my study under the aegis of rescue as conceptualized in Konvolut N rather than in the "Theses on the Philosophy of History" because the urgency regulating my project does not approach the terrifying pressure of fascism leading Benjamin to rearticulate the flash of historical recuperation in 1940: "To articulate the past historically . . . means to seize hold of a memory as it flashes up at a moment of danger." See Walter Benjamin, "Theses on the Philosophy of History," in *Illuminations,* 255 (hereafter referred to as *I*). I return to Benjamin's use of surrealist rhetoric to describe historiographical rescue in chapter 7, "Benjamin Reading the *Rencontre.*"

would suggest two answers to the question. Jean Baudrillard has observed that "revolution is the spectacle of the changes that have already occurred"; in the past few years, we have witnessed the spectacle of the demise of Revolution itself. The recent collapse of the rusted-out Iron Curtain has monumentalized (albeit as debris) a problem that has periodically troubled Marxist thinkers throughout the twentieth century: How is Marxism to be salvaged from failed attempts to translate its theory into political practice? If, as Ernesto Laclau and Chantal Mouffe put it several years before, "we are now situated in a post-Marxist terrain," this is a terrain with which Gothic Marxists have long been familiar, and Benjamin and Breton are no exception.[30] Indeed, the problem of salvaging Marxism from the disillusionment provoked by the political systems it generated was particularly acute at the time that Benjamin and Breton wrote, in the wake of the Stalinist turn taken by the Russian Revolution.

The recent critical popularity enjoyed by Benjamin confirms that the pressures of post-Marxism have helped bring the conjuncture of Benjamin and Breton's Gothic Marxisms into view. In the time it has taken me to frame this book, I have been hard-pressed to keep up with the proliferation of work attempting to appropriate Gothic Marxist aspects of Benjamin's musings for cultural theory across the disciplines. I too offer my elaboration of Benjamin and Breton's Gothic Marxisms in response to post-Marxist pressures; if images from the past spring to legibility in the present, it is because they speak to its concerns. The most suggestive material rescued here includes: (1) the valorization of the realm of a culture's ghosts and phantasms as a significant and rich field of social production rather than a mirage to be dispelled; (2) the valorization of a culture's detritus and trivia as well as its strange and marginal practices; (3) a notion of critique moving beyond logical argument and the binary opposition to a phantasmagorical staging more closely resembling psychoanalytic therapy, privileging nonrational forms of "working through" and regulated by overdetermination rather than dialectics; (4) a dehierarchization of the epistemological privilege accorded the visual in the direction of that integration of the senses dreamed of by Marx in *The 1844 Manuscripts*: "... the complete *emancipation* of all human senses and qualities ... The *senses* have therefore become directly in their practice *theoreticians*"; accompanying this dehierarchization, a practice of criticism cutting across tradi-

30. Ernesto Laclau and Chantal Mouffe, *Hegemony and Socialist Strategy*, 4. The work of Slavoj Žižek exemplifies the Gothic strain in some of the best post-Marxism.

tionally separated media and genres as well as critical attention to how and why these separations came to be;[31] and (5) a concomitant valorization of the sensuousness of the visual: the realm of visual experience is opened to other possibilities than the accomplishment and/or figuration of rational demonstration.

The present flaring to view of surrealist Marxism is also generated by its encounter with a second aspect of our Now. Not only Breton's modern materialism but high surrealism more generally has been a dead letter in the theoretical ferment of the past thirty years. Above all, high surrealism was dismissed by the French theoretical avant-garde that came to dominance in the sixties and seventies and that has been so influential in shaping the current critical scene. When surrealist theory (like surrealist Marxism) has been noticed, interest has focused on the renegade surrealists around Bataille. As David Macey puts it, "The structuralists forget or simply repress their historic debt," and Macey notes "the belligerent tone of the criticisms addressed to Breton."[32] But with the aging of the French theoretical avant-garde, the time has come to look critically at its claims. The imperative can be put in stronger terms: The moment when this avant-garde falls back into history is the moment to define its place there, to detail how, despite its absolute language, it (like all avant-gardes) did not spring full blown from the heads of some important men and a few women. High surrealism must be included as an intellectual pressure to which the French theoretical avant-garde responded, a movement that reigned with crushing authority over the very notion of the avant-garde during the youth of this generation.[33]

31. Karl Marx, *Economic and Philosophic Manuscripts of 1844,* 139.

32. Macey, *Lacan in Contexts,* 49. Macey refers specifically here to the summer 1971 issue of *Tel Quel.* Macey's book provides an illuminating contribution to the neglected story of surrealism's importance for postwar theory. In particular, Macey stresses the importance of surrealism for Lacan, pointing out that Lacan is as unstraightforwardly straightforward about his debt to surrealism as he is about anything. Macey writes, "Of the forty or so French literary authors included in the name index [of *Ecrits*], more than half belonged to the surrealist group at one time or another, or were claimed by the surrealists as their forbears. Surrealism is the only identifiable 'school' to which Lacan refers so consistently. . . . The frequency with which Lacan alludes to surrealism is all the more striking in that it is not a major reference for the post-war avant-garde to which received opinion would have him belong" (p. 45).

33. Wollen remarks of Breton: "French culture is unthinkable without him. Not only did he develop a theory and practice of art which has had enormous effect (perhaps more than any other in our time), but he also introduced both Freud and Hegel to France, first to non-specialist circles, but then back into the specialized world through those he influenced (Lefebvre, Lacan, Bataille, Lévi-Strauss)" (p. 78). With the aging of the generation tyrannized by high surrealism, official recognition of the movement is returning. Visitors to Paris in the summer of 1991 may remember that its landscape was punctuated with posters of Breton sporting a leather jacket, an advertisement for a massive exhibit of his

One of my aims is thus to draw attention to the subterranean but vital presence of surrealism in subsequent key moments of twentieth-century French thought. In keeping with this study's focus on the Marxist dimensions of surrealism, I am interested here above all in the importance of surrealism for the Marxist wing of the French theoretical avant-garde: that the schizophrenic strolls into Gilles Deleuze and Felix Guattari's *Anti-Oedipus* from surrealism's politicized treatment of madness, above all Breton's *Nadja*; or what Michel de Certeau's work on tactics and everyday life owes to Breton's social application of psychoanalytic models for expression in situations of repression and censorship.[34] Because my discussion of Benjamin and Breton's Gothic Marxisms is already quite detailed, I have by and large relegated these links to the margins of my argument. But I also wanted to give at least one in-depth example of how the French theoretical avant-garde incorporated the tenets of surrealist Marxism into its thought.[35] In "The Questions of Modern Materialism," I discuss the ways in which Louis Althusser reworks modern materialism through the intermediary of Lacan.

I focus on Althusser for reasons pertaining to my own procedure in rendering legible Benjamin and Breton's work. Phenomena "are rescued by exhibiting the discontinuity that exists within them," Benjamin declares in one of his many meditations on "rescuing critique" from Konvolut N (N 9, 4). In the cases of Benjamin and Breton, this discontinuity is often egregious; if these texts can be shown to diverge from their received interpretations, it is because they are profoundly divided against themselves. Benjamin observed, the "profane illumination did not always find the Surrealists equal to it," and the same might be said of Benjamin's reworking of it as well (R, 179). In such a situation, an appeal to theoretical work that carries on the project of the texts in some measure can be helpful; that modern materialism was reworked by French structural and poststructural Marxism has been invaluable to

---

private collection at the Pompidou Center. See Camhi's previously mentioned article, "Extended Boundaries," which considers the actuality of surrealism as it emerged from the exhibit.

34. The importance of surrealism to the Marxist wing of the French avant-garde is also visible in the debt to surrealism owed by Jameson.

35. In many cases, the transmission of surrealism to the French theoretical avant-garde of the sixties and seventies is far from straightforward. Besides owing much to Bataille and the renegade surrealists, the legacy of surrealism sometimes passes, as Wollen's article makes clear, through situationism. The hostile but engaged relation of existentialism to surrealism is also of importance.

me in this regard. Because both Benjamin and Breton were preoccupied with using psychoanalytic categories to recast the base-superstructure distinction, I found Althusser's writings particularly useful in clarifying their discontinuous musings.

One last word on a road not taken: I would have liked to supplement a textual discussion of Benjamin and Breton's Marxisms with biographical material. How did these men's paths cross in the Paris of the late 1920s and 1930s, might their personal intercourse provide some clue to their textual exchange? Information on this subject (at least publicly accessible) is, however, absent, tantalizingly untraceable, as Gershom Scholem comments in his introduction to the published selections from Benjamin's correspondence: "Of the letters to Benjamin's French correspondents, the letters to André Breton are for example either lost or are not traceable." [36] Gary Smith confirms that there is no letter between the two men in either the unpublished Frankfurt or Berlin archives.[37] On the west side of the Rhine, Marguerite Bonnet, Breton's editor, finds no mention of Benjamin in any Breton correspondence.[38] Certainly, one can speculate on the basis of suggestive details from Parisian intellectual life of the time. Pierre Klossowski recalls, "I met Walter Benjamin in the course of one of the meetings of *Contre-Attaque,* the name adopted by the ephemeral fusion of the groups surrounding André Breton and Georges Bataille in 1935." [39] So too Breton and Benjamin were both at the opening of a show of Gisèle Freund's photographs at Adrienne Monnier's bookstore in March 1939.[40] But there is no more vivid record of Benjamin's biographical relation to Breton.

My argument for Breton's importance to Benjamin must hence proceed through textual examination alone. And the discontinuous nature of the texts under examination does not facilitate the critic's task. I will not try to recuperate this discontinuity as strategically important (although this argument could and has been made), nor to make whole

36. Gershom Scholem, introduction to *B*, I, 9.

37. Gary Smith, personal letter, Berlin, 24 September 1989.

38. Marguerite Bonnet, personal letter, Paris, 19 September 1989.

39. Pierre Klossowski, "Between Marx and Fourier," in *On Walter Benjamin,* ed. Smith, 368. Klossowski also emphasizes that Benjamin's position in the Parisian intellectual landscape of the 1930s was with the renegade surrealists opposing the high surrealism of Breton. "Later, Benjamin was an assiduous auditor at the Collège de Sociologie," Klossowski continues, "an 'exoteric' emanation of the closed and secret group *Acéphale,* which crystallized around Bataille soon after his break with Breton." Klossowski, in *On Walter Benjamin,* 368.

40. Gary Smith brought my attention to this event. The name of the bookstore is La Maison des Amis des Livres.

systems that never were.[41] Rather, the measure of Benjamin and Breton's work lies not in the evaluation of its success or failure but in a criterion whose very ambivalence rendered it dear to Benjamin and surrealism alike. That criterion is fascination.[42] As Benjamin stated of artifacts from the past in a rather different context, "we believe the charm they exert on us reveals that they still contain materials of vital importance to us—not, of course, for our architecture, the way iron trusswork anticipates our design; but they are vital for our perception, if you will, for the illumination of the situation. Materials of politically vital importance at any rate; the Surrealists' fixation on these things proves it, as does their exploitation in contemporary fashion" (N 1, 11).

41. See Irving Wohlfarth's articles on Benjamin for acute characterizations of Benjamin's brooding mode of critical reflection. On Benjamin as brooder, see also Richard Sieburth, "Benjamin the Scrivener," first printed in *Assemblage,* no. 6, and then reprinted in Smith et al., *Benjamin—Philosophy, Aesthetics, History.*

42. On Benjamin and fascination, see Ackbar Abbas, "On Fascination: Walter Benjamin's Images." Abbas comments: "He sees in fascination not a will-less affect, not the response of last resort, but a willingness to be drawn to phenomena that attract our attention yet do not submit entirely to our understanding" (p. 51).

2. Anonymous. *Passage de l'Opéra*. Courtesy of the Musée Carnavalet.

CHAPTER 2

Benjamin's Marxisms

What is *une psyché*? [1]
　　—Benjamin, *Pariser Passagen I*

"THE MATERIAL RELATIONSHIPS OF PRODUCTION AND THE REMOTER REALMS OF THE SUPERSTRUCTURE, INCLUDING ART"

In the 1937 essay "Eduard Fuchs, Collector and Historian," Benjamin raised a question that has preoccupied Marxist aestheticians throughout the century. "It is well known that Marx nowhere really divulged how the relationship between superstructure and infrastructure should be conceived in individual cases. All that can be said with confidence is that he envisaged a series of mediations, as it were transmissions, interpolated between the material relationships of production and the remoter realms of the superstructure, including art (*OWS*, 368)." [2] The problem of how to characterize the relation that Benjamin termed mediation or transmission was central to the Parisian production cycle from its opening *One-Way Street* to the last "Theses on the Philosophy of History."

If Benjamin's dissatisfaction with existing Marxist theory of art is evident ("now swaggering, now scholastic" is how he qualified it in Konvolut N), so too is his dissatisfaction with orthodox critique of ideology (N 4a, 2). [3] To understand the effects of the superstructure as

---

1. The words are in French in Benjamin's German text. The term *psyché* designates a swing mirror.
2. The German runs "Vermittlungen, gleichsam Transmissionen" (*GS* II, 2, 486).
3. On this point, see Jürgen Habermas, "Walter Benjamin: Consciousness-Raising or Rescuing Critique," in *On Walter Benjamin*, ed. Smith.

directly reproducing the causal agency of the base is to evince the vul-
garity that Marx denounces in other contexts: "With regard to political
economy, Marx characterizes its 'vulgar element' as above all 'that element in it that confuses the mere reproduction of appearance with its
conceptualization' . . . This vulgar element should also be denounced in
other sciences" (N 16, 3). But what alternative Benjamin proposed to
existing Marxist aesthetic theory has been the subject of critical debate.
Benjamin approaches the mediations between "the material relationships of production and the remoter realms of the superstructure, including art," in the maverick fashion characteristic of his Gothic Marxism more generally, by attempting to fuse Marxism with all manner of
non-Marxist discourses (OWS, 368).

Benjamin's less than orthodox treatment of the base-superstructure
problematic has been used as evidence for his lack of interest in it,
dismissed as his engaging in radical talk against his inclination, to
satisfy his more tendentiously Marxist friends. I leave the unstated
political undercurrents informing such dismissal to chroniclers of the
current critical scene. I only note that Benjamin's failures have proved
an important ongoing source of his critical appeal (although also danger; stories are told of critics who, like Benjamin's collector among
his books, disappear into his musings, never to emerge). Benjamin is
not afraid to pose problems in all their difficulty, sketching gestures of
solution where the most precious intellectual moment is perhaps the
point where the gesture breaks down. No one more than he displays
the mood of the essay as Lukács once characterized it: a form of longing
for an idea not yet born.

I am rather concerned with the critical lineage that takes seriously
the interest of the Parisian production cycle in base-superstructure relations, a lineage inaugurated by Adorno's ambivalent response to the
excerpts from the arcades project sent to him by Benjamin. To open a
discussion of Benjamin's Gothic Marxism, I want to examine this response, particularly Adorno's reaction to what he perceived as a major
conceptual weakness of the arcades project: Benjamin's suggestion that
the expressions of the superstructure can be understood with recourse
to a psychoanalytic model for how repressed forces come to expression
in dreams. I do not negate the value of many Frankfurt objections to
Benjamin's thinking, but it must be made clear that Adorno treats as
conceptual weakness what is in fact a rich aspect of Benjamin's thought.
Benjamin turns to psychoanalytic vocabulary to conceptualize a revision of base-superstructure relations which he both grounds in Marxist

theory but finds Marxism unable to describe because of its own immersion in Enlightenment concepts of representation and causality.

Benjamin himself stressed that he found coherence in what others considered aberration: "Comparison of others' attempts to setting off on a sea voyage in which the ships are drawn off course by the magnetic north pole. Discover *that* North Pole. What for others are deviations, for me are data by which to set my course. I base my reckoning on the differentia of time that disturb the 'main lines' of the investigation for others" (N 1, 2). In 1928 Benjamin used a similar image to signal the coherence of the course laid out for the arcades project by surrealism's seeming deviations: "Gradually, I encounter passages in young French authors ever more frequently that . . . betray the influence of a magnetic north pole unsettling their compass. And I am steering towards it." [4] It is my argument that Benjamin's deviation from Frankfurt Marxism follows the trajectory that his rhetoric maps out. I have chosen to discuss Benjamin's reworking of surrealist Marxism before I characterize the theory in its own right or argue for its links to him. I do so because a surrealist approach to Benjamin has led me to understand his reflections on Marxist issues in a fashion differing substantially from prevalent critical assessment. It thus seems important to render palpable this alternative Marxism, neither Frankfurt nor Brechtian nor vulgar, before speculating on the textual genealogies responsible for its existence.

THE "SHIFTING GROUND" OF BENJAMIN'S ARCADES

Before turning to the Parisian production cycle, a word about the pitfalls of reading theoretical content out of the *Passagen-Werk* is in order. The task entails speculating on meditations that are in many ways failures, in any case contradictory, and, moreover, incomplete; Wolin speaks of the "shifting ground" of the arcades project.[5] Adorno observed (although with a bad conscience?): "That Benjamin's work

4. Benjamin, letter to Scholem, Berlin, 1 August 1928, *B*, I, 479.
5. Wolin, "Expérience et matérialisme dans le Passagen-Werk de Benjamin," in *Walter Benjamin et Paris*, 669. This image is not retained in Wolin's English rewriting of the essay. Buck-Morss observes, "It must not be forgotten that there is no *Passagen-Werk*. We are in a real sense confronting a void." Susan Buck-Morss, *The Dialectics of Seeing*, 47 (referred to hereafter as *DS*). Wohlfarth asks, "In what sense was the *Arcades Project* not to be? *Was* it inherently unrealizable? Or rather did it go unrealized? . . . even if the *Arcades Project* cannot be fully pieced together, to what extent can it nevertheless be rendered less incomplete?" See Irving Wohlfarth, "Re-fusing Theology. Some First Responses to Walter Benjamin's Arcades Project," 7.

remained fragmentary is thus not simply to be ascribed to his adverse fate; rather, it is implicit from the start in the structure of his thought." [6] This does not mean, however, that Benjamin's texts cannot be approached with critical rigor.

Confronting the ruins of the Jamf Ölfabriken Werke AG, in the light that breaks "some night at too deep an hour to explain away," Thomas Pynchon's Enzian reaches an "extraordinary understanding. This serpentine slag-heap . . . is *not a ruin at all. It is in perfect working order.*" [7] An Enzianlike epiphany is one way to do justice to the fragmentary quality of Benjamin's thought. I, however, will take a somewhat different tack, following the interpretive protocol laid out by Buck-Morss. [8] "To say that the *Passagen-Werk* has no necessary narrative structure so that the fragments can be grouped freely, is not at all to suggest that it has no conceptual structure, as if the meaning of the work were itself totally up to the capriciousness of the reader," Buck-Morss writes (*DS*, 54). [9] Articulating why the *Passagen-Werk* uses psychoanalytic vocabulary to discuss base-superstructure relations, I too seek a conceptual structure implicit in Benjamin's fragments, although one where narrative progression plays a role. For Benjamin concepts are dynamic entities constantly in the process of elaboration, as sentences show up in revised form from one text of the Parisian production cycle to the next. It is to his own "Parisian pictures" (*tableaux parisiens*) that Benjamin's observation on Baudelaire's method could best be applied: "In general he appears to have suffered the compulsion to return to each of his motifs at least once. One can compare this with the compulsion which continually draws the criminal to the scene of the crime. . . . Baudelaire was a poor philosopher, a good theoretician, but he was incomparable only as a *Grübler* (brooder)." [10]

6. Theodor Adorno, "Introduction to Benjamin's *Schriften*," in *On Walter Benjamin,* ed. Smith, 6.

7. Thomas Pynchon, *Gravity's Rainbow,* 520.

8. Wohlfarth allies possible interpretive strategies with specifically Benjaminian notions of hermeneutics: "We can either train on it [the *Arcades Project*] the withering gaze of the baroque allegorist who further immobilizes an already petrified landscape; or else we can contemplate it with the longing eyes of the 'angel of history' who yearns to piece the débris together." Wohlfarth, "Re-fusing Theology," 7.

9. Buck-Morss's work on Benjamin's Paris writings first appearing as essays in *New Left Review* and *New German Critique* and then rewritten into *The Dialectics of Seeing,* has been helpful throughout my project, both for its historical information as well as its detailed interpretations of Benjamin's texts grappling with Marxism throughout the 1920s and 1930s. I have also found useful her translations of fragments from the *Passagen-Werk*.

10. Walter Benjamin, "Central Park," 40–41 (abbreviated hereafter as "CP").

ADORNO'S POINT OF DEPARTURE

"Let me take as my point of departure the motto on p. 159, *Chaque époque rêve la suivante* [Every epoch dreams its successor]," wrote Adorno in his August 1935 Hornberg letter, finally responding to "Paris, the Capital of the Nineteenth Century" after a tense silence of some three months.[11] "This seems to me an important key in that all those motifs of the theory of the dialectical image which underlie my criticism, crystallize around it as an *undialectical* sentence whose elimination could lead to a clarification of the theory itself" (*AP*, 111). Adorno's point of departure locates the focus of his critique. In this exposé Benjamin drew an analogy between products of the superstructure from the inception of industrial production, what he called "wish-images," and the Freudian model for the dream. Suggesting that these products came into contact with deep-seated collective desires, Benjamin proposed that they could be put to socially transformative ends. To get at the potentially transformative forces, however, it was necessary to mediate them by theory, for the forces were hidden in a realm whose inaccessibility he likened to that of the unconscious understood in psychoanalytic terms. Benjamin glossed his epigraph from Michelet in this context, speculating:

> In the dream in which, before the eyes of each epoch, that which is to follow appears in images, the latter appears wedded to elements from prehistory [*Urgeschichte*], that is, of a classless society. Its experiences, deposited in the unconscious of the collective, interpermeate with the new to create the utopia that has left its traces in thousands of configurations of life.[12]

The task of the cultural critic, then, became to discover the proper analytic protocol transforming collective dreams into what Benjamin called

---

11. Theodor Adorno to Walter Benjamin, Hornberg, 2 August 1935, in *Aesthetics and Politics* (hereafter *AP*), 111. I have replaced the definite article dropped from the essay's standard English translation ("Paris, Capital of the Nineteenth Century") to differentiate the 1935 "Paris, *die* Hauptstadt des XIX. Jahrhunderts" from the 1939 "Paris, capitale du XIXème siècle" (emphasis added). When Benjamin drops the definite article in his 1939 essay, he responds to a comment in the Hornberg letter: "As a title, I should like to propose *Paris, Capital of the Nineteenth Century*, not *The Capital*" (*AP*, 115).

12. Benjamin, "Paris, the Capital of the Nineteenth Century," in *R*, 148 (referred to in this chapter as "PC"). I have modified Jephcott's translation of the beginning of the second sentence, which runs, "Intimations of this, deposited in the unconscious of the collective, mingle with the new to produce etc." The German original is in *PW*, 47. For a discussion of how nature and history relate in Benjamin's conception of the dreaming collective, see Buck-Morss's comments in *The Dialectics of Seeing*. Buck-Morss's discussion of Benjamin's interest in applying the metaphor of an individual's growth to the collective body also sheds light on this passage.

"dialectical images," able to "awaken the world from the dream of itself," as Marx put it in an 1843 letter to Ruge that Benjamin took as epigraph to the arcades project's Konvolut N (*PW*, 570).[13]

In challenging Benjamin's citation of Michelet, Adorno voiced his skepticism of the redemptive potential that Benjamin found inhering in the dreams of the superstructure. In particular, Adorno noted that Benjamin thereby suggested "a conception of the dialectical image as a content of consciousness, albeit a collective one" (*AP*, 111). Now the dream is not the only characterization of products of the superstructure that "Paris, the Capital of the Nineteenth Century" proposes. Benjamin also describes these products with a term borrowed directly from Marx. And Adorno had little quarrel with this alternative formulation, taken from *Capital*.

" 'This fetishism of commodities has its origin . . . in the peculiar social character of the labor that produces them . . . It is only a definite social relation between men that assumes, in their eyes, the phantasmagorical form of a relation between things,' " writes Marx in a celebrated passage discussing commodity fetishism as a dominant structure of subjective experience in capitalist society.[14] Following Marx, Benjamin describes how the commodities displayed within the Universal Exhibitions manifest themselves in phantasmagorical terms: "The phantasmagoria of capitalist culture reaches its most brilliant display in the Universal Exhibition of 1867" ("PC," 153).[15] In addition, he suggests that intellectual reflection in the nineteenth century takes on a phantasmagorical cast. Benjamin writes of "the phantasmagoria of 'cultural history,' in which the bourgeoisie savors its false consciousness to the last," and the phantasmagorical illusions of the proletariat: "The Commune puts an end to the phantasmagoria that dominates the freedom of the proletariat. It dispels the illusion that the task of the proletarian revolution is to complete the work of 1789 hand in hand with the bourgeoisie" ("PC," 158, 160).

13. For an interpretation of the dialectical image stressing this concept's debt to German aesthetic theory, see Michael Jennings, *Dialectical Images: Walter Benjamin's Theory of Literary Criticism*.

14. I quote Benjamin quoting this passage from Otto Rühle's *Karl Marx: Leben und Werke* in Konvolut G, *PW*, 245. See Karl Marx, *Capital*, I, 83. When Benjamin rewrites his sketch of the arcades project in 1939, his interest in phantasmagorical representation will have increased to the point that he drops the dream model for products of the superstructure. In the final chapter I consider the possible epistemological motives dictating Benjamin's turn away from a description of the superstructure as dream.

15. I modify Jephcott's translation of "Weltausstellung" as World Exhibition in light of these shows' French name that Benjamin uses in the 1939 essay: *exposition universelle*. For the German, see *PW*, 51.

From the exposé's unconceptualized use of phantasmagoria it seems that Benjamin applies this term to those products of the superstructure where negative ideological mystification prevails. Benjamin does not, however, explicitly position the dream in relation to the phantasmagoria. His failure to explain the relationship between these two forms of manifestation taken by the superstructure is characteristic, indicative of an uncommented slippage throughout his Parisian production cycle. When discussing ideology, the *Passagen-Werk* often collapses the question of how ideology mystifies material relations into the question of how the superstructure transforms the base. Such, for example, is the case in the following statement from Konvolut K: "Concerning the doctrine of the *ideological superstructure*. At first it seems as if Marx here wanted only to establish a causal relation between superstructure and base. But the observation that *the ideologies of the superstructure* reflect the relations in a false and distorted manner already goes beyond this" (*PW*, 495, emphasis added). In this passage Benjamin speaks of an ideological superstructure, implicitly opposing this superstructure to other superstructures. But in the phrase "the ideologies of the superstructure" he also treats the superstructure as the producer of ideology or alternatively as itself having ideological modes of existence. Such slippage derives from Benjamin's uncertainty as to whether an experience of the superstructure is possible outside the experience of ideological distortion. We will see this uncertainty run throughout Benjamin's thought, notably in his musings on the dialectical image as a content of consciousness.

When Benjamin designates the ideological experiences of the superstructure as phantasmagorias, he extends Marx's figure from the specific experience of the commodity to Parisian cultural products as a whole.[16] But the extension remains close to Marx (in 1935, at least; my final chapter returns to Benjamin's increasingly recuperative approach to the phantasmagoria as the Parisian production cycle progresses). This use of the phantasmagoria is familiar from *The Eighteenth Brumaire*, a way for Marx to characterize the ghostly objectivity that ideological products possess. Thus, commenting on the failure of the 1848 Revolution to put a liberal-republican ideology into practice, Marx writes:

> The Constitution, the National Assembly, the dynastic parties, the blue and
> red republicans, the heroes of Africa, the thunder from the platform, the

16. On this matter, see Buck-Morss, as well as Rolf Tiedemann, "Dialectics at a Standstill," in *On Walter Benjamin*, ed. Smith.

sheet lightning of the daily press, the entire literature, the political names
and the intellectual reputations, the civil law and the penal code, the *liberté,
égalité, fraternité* and the second Sunday in May 1852—all has vanished like
a phantasmagoria before the spell of a man whom even his enemies do not
make out to be a sorcerer.[17]

Benjamin's description of the constructions of the superstructure as
dream echoes another figure for ideological delusion employed by
Marx, although the figure derives rather from the earlier Marx of the
letter to Ruge and *The German Ideology*. But in this case Benjamin
echoes Marx's rhetoric to modify its sense. Marx uses dream rhetoric
to emphasize that ideological representation is subjective distortion. As
Althusser comments on this use, "Ideology is conceived as a pure illusion, a pure dream, i.e. as nothingness. All its reality is external to it.
Ideology is thus thought as an imaginary construction whose status is
exactly like the theoretical status of the dream among writers before
Freud." [18] When Benjamin, in contrast, characterizes the products of the
superstructure as dream, he brings to collective constructions what,
echoing Althusser echoing Lacan echoing Freud, we might call Freud's
Copernican Revolution (Benjamin too conceives of his historiographical enterprise as a Copernican revolution).[19] Asking how socially constitutive forces permeate seeming ideological detritus, Benjamin trans-

17. Karl Marx, *The Eighteenth Brumaire of Louis Bonaparte*, 20. It is significant that
Adorno did not take issue with the parts of "Paris, the Capital of the Nineteenth Century"
which described ideological projection in this fashion following Marx. The Hornberg letter commented only that Benjamin should provide more details on the theory underwriting his adaptation of Marx's rhetoric: "Of course, a great definition and theory of phantasmagoria belong on p. 165f." (*AP*, 116–117).

18. Louis Althusser, "Ideology and Ideological State Apparatuses," in *Lenin and
Philosophy*, 159.

19. On Lacan's relation to Freud's Copernican figuration of the discovery of the unconscious, Macey comments that

in 1955 Lacan refers to this revolution as "worthy of the name of Copernicus," and
later alludes to the "so-called Copernican revolution to which Freud himself compared his discovery" and to "what Freud in his doctrine articulates as constituting a
'Copernican' step." Lacan often appeals to a concept of scientificity which owes a
great deal to the French rationalist school of epistemology associated with Bachelard,
Canguilhem and Koyré (his overt references are usually to the latter), and the Copernican revolution is a classic paradigm for its history of the sciences. Freud does on a
number of occasions compare himself to Copernicus, but the key terms in this description of the Freudian discovery—"revolution in knowledge" and "Copernican step"—
are Lacan's, and do not figure in Freud.

The effect, if not necessarily the intention, of Lacan's formulations is to lend Freud
the discourse and accents of an epistemology which is quite alien to him and, at the
same time to induce a certain misrecognition of the role played by the name "Copernicus" in Freud's imaginary (p. 112–113).

forms this detritus into an index of vital social energy. Benjamin concludes his essay by allying the theoretical procedure releasing the positive potential of ideological projections with what he called "awakening," a standpoint which he is careful to differentiate from the habitual waking world. "The arcades and interiors, the exhibitions and panoramas," he proposes, "are residues of a dream world. The utilization of dream elements in waking is the textbook example of dialectical thinking.[20] For this reason dialectical thinking is the organ of historical awakening. Each epoch not only dreams the next, but also, in dreaming, strives toward the moment of waking" ("PC," 162).

"I'm going to take up Freud in the near future. Does anything in him or his school having to do with a psychoanalysis of awakening come to mind?" Benjamin asked Adorno in a letter written shortly after he sent "Paris, the Capital of the Nineteenth Century" off for Adorno's perusal (PW, 1121). "I am not acquainted with any psychoanalytic literature about awakening, but I shall look into this," answered Adorno in the Hornberg letter. "However, is not the dream-interpreting, awakening psychoanalysis which expressly and polemically dissociates itself from hypnotism (documentation in Freud's lectures) itself part of Art Nouveau with which it coincides in time?" (AP, 118). In this question Adorno makes evident one of his main objections to Benjamin's application of the dream to collective historical processes. If, as Adorno suggests, aspects of psychoanalysis are enmeshed in the ideological assumptions of bourgeois art nouveau, the science cannot provide, unmodified, a guide to conceptualizing the collective realm. Rather, psychoanalysis itself must be interrogated as one of the ideological products whose grounding in objective conditions Benjamin's study should reveal.

Consonant with this comment, Adorno repeatedly voices concern that Benjamin's collective application of psychoanalysis simply transfers a form of experience articulated on the bourgeois subject intact from the individual to the social sphere. Adorno asks:

> If the disenchantment of the dialectical image as a "dream" psychologizes it, by the same token it falls under the spell of bourgeois psychology. For who is the subject of the dream? In the nineteenth century, it was surely only the individual; but in the individual's dream no direct depiction of either the fetish character or its monuments may be found. (AP, 112–113)

20. Jephcott translates the opening of this sentence as "The realization of dream elements . . . " See PW, 59.

Adorno reads Benjamin's invocation of collective consciousness as an
attempt to resolve this problem. In proposing such a concept, Adorno
asserts, Benjamin attempts to retain the dream without the bourgeois
dreamer. But in fact, Adorno continues, Benjamin's notion of collective
consciousness raises more difficulties than it solves.

> Hence the collective consciousness is invoked, but I fear that in its present
> form it cannot be distinguished from Jung's conception. It is open to criti-
> cism on both sides; from the vantage point of the social process, in that it
> hypostasizes archaic images where dialectical images are in fact generated
> by the commodity character, not in an archaic collective ego, but in alienated
> bourgeois individuals; and from the vantage point of psychology in that, as
> Horkheimer puts it, a mass ego exists only in earthquakes and catastrophes,
> while otherwise objective surplus value prevails precisely through individual
> subjects and against them. (*AP,* 113)

From the "vantage point of psychology," Adorno criticizes the notion
of collective consciousness because it makes the bourgeois subject the
measure of society. "The 'individual,'" Adorno reminds Benjamin, "is
a dialectical instrument of transition that must not be mythicized away,
but can only be superseded" (*AP,* 119). From the "vantage point of the
social process," Adorno criticizes the collective psyche for drawing Benjamin dangerously near to the mythicizing thought of Jung and Klages.
Threatening to return history to the realm of myth, Benjamin blurs the
specific relations of production subtending ideological forms.[21]

Seen from the side of the subject or the object, collective consciousness blurs the fundamental dialectic operative in capitalist society: between alienated individuals and alienating objective conditions. Adorno
states: "The notion of collective consciousness was invented only to divert attention from true objectivity and its correlate, alienated subjectivity. It is up to us to polarize and dissolve this 'consciousness' dialectically between society and singularities, and not to galvanize it as
an imagistic correlate of the commodity character" (*AP,* 113). Adorno
concludes his admonition by pointing out how far the notion of collective consciousness takes Benjamin from a Marxist theory of class. "It
should be a clear and sufficient warning that in a dreaming collective
no differences remain between classes" (*AP,* 113).

If Adorno was suspicious of the dream language Benjamin used to

21. For a discussion of what Adorno's own work may owe to the thought of Klages,
see Axel Honneth, "'L'Esprit et son objet'—Parentés anthropologiques entre la 'Dialec-
tique de la raison' et la critique de la civilisation dans la philosophie de la vie," in *Weimar
ou l'explosion de la modernité,* ed. Gérard Raulet (Paris: Editions Anthropos, 1984).

describe products of the superstructure, he was even more suspicious when such language entered into Benjamin's discussion of cultural critique. "Ambiguity is the imagistic appearance of dialectics, the law of dialectics at a standstill," Benjamin writes of the dialectical image.[22] "This standstill is utopia and the dialectical image therefore a dream image" ("PC," 157).[23] To Benjamin's statement, Adorno responds:

> If you transpose the dialectical image into consciousness as a "dream" you not only take the magic out of the concept and render it sociable, but you also deprive it of that objective liberating power which could legitimize it in material terms. The fetish character of the commodity is not a fact of consciousness; rather, it is dialectical, in the eminent sense that it produces consciousness. This means, however, that consciousness or unconsciousness cannot simply depict it as a dream, but responds to it in equal measure with desire and fear. (*AP*, 111)

When Benjamin associates the dialectical image with consciousness, whether collective or individual, Adorno points out, he mires dialectics in that murky realm between objective forces and subjective experience. Against Benjamin, Adorno sees the dialectical image as a fragment of objective relations: "Dialectical images are as models not social products, but objective constellations in which 'the social' situation represents itself. Consequently, no ideological or social 'accomplishment' can ever be expected of a dialectical image" (*AP*, 115–116). In recognizing the dialectical image as a chunk of objective conditions, Adorno argues, Benjamin will simultaneously clarify the way in which objective conditions in fact produce the ideological dream. He will therefore not only clarify the objective content of the dialectical image but the objective content of subjective experience as well: "In its dialectical construction the dream should be externalized and the immanence of consciousness itself be understood as a constellation of reality" (*AP*, 112). Adorno's view of the dialectical image thus differs substantially from that proposed by Benjamin. For Benjamin repeatedly associates the dialectical image with some form of subjectivity: first with collective consciousness, as dream image, and then with the critic's work of construction, as this dream's demystification.

Adorno's letter is a curious document, interspersing acute insights with petty quibbling and at times displaying strangely willful blindness to the broader stakes of Benjamin's project; Adorno himself apologized

---

22. I modify here Jephcott's translation, which runs: "Ambiguity is the pictorial image of dialectics, the law of dialectics seen at a standstill." See *PW*, 55.
23. Jephcott translates this phrase as "dialectic image." See *PW*, 55.

for the letter's "carping form" (*AP*, 120).[24] In any case, the letter has been tremendously influential, as much a part of critical discussion on the Marxist Benjamin as "Paris, the Capital of the Nineteenth Century" itself. Largely within the parameters established by the Hornberg letter, critics have either defended Benjamin's Marxism or taken it to task.

The importance of these parameters becomes evident in two contrasting accounts of Benjamin's interest in base-superstructure relations, both concerned with a passage that has become a *locus classicus* in Benjamin interpretation, from Konvolut K, "Dream City and Dream House, Dreams of the Future, Anthropological Nihilism, Jung." This passage is intimately related to Benjamin's discussion of the collective dream in "Paris, the Capital of the Nineteenth Century," modeling the shape taken by expressions of the superstructure with the language of dream. Benjamin's psychoanalytic description of expression runs:

> Concerning the doctrine of the ideological superstructure. At first it seems as if Marx here wanted only to establish a causal relation between superstructure and base. But the observation that the ideologies of the superstructure reflect the relations in a false and distorted manner already goes beyond this. The question is, namely: if the base somehow determines the superstructure in the material of thought and experience, but this determination is not one of simple *reflection,* how is it then to be characterized, leaving aside the question of the cause for its emergence? As its *expression.* The superstructure is the expression of the base. The economic conditions of a society's existence come to expression in the superstructure, just as the over-filled stomach of someone who is sleeping, although it may causally determine the dream content, finds there not its reflection but its expression. (*PW*, 495, emphasis added)

The reading of this passage by Habermas may be situated on one end of the critical spectrum.[25] Habermas cites it in the context of interrogating Benjamin's Marxism, opposing "Adorno who, in comparison

24. The tone could also be qualified as condescending, for the letter includes disparaging statements about Benjamin's critical powers. Calling for always more dialectics, Adorno also suggests that dialectics are not Benjamin's forte: "I would surmise that the greatest interpretative results will be achieved here if you unhesitatingly follow your own procedure, *the blind processing of the material.* If, by contrast, my critique moves in a certain theoretical sphere of abstraction, that surely is a difficulty, but I know that you will not regard it as a mere problem of 'outlook' and thereby dismiss my reservations" (*AP*, 114, emphasis added).

25. See Habermas, "Walter Benjamin: Consciousness-Raising or Rescuing Critique," in *On Walter Benjamin,* ed. Smith. Other texts in this spectrum include Tiedemann's "Dialectics at a Standstill," in Smith et al., *Benjamin,* as well as Wolin's chapter on the Benjamin-Adorno debate in *Walter Benjamin, An Aesthetic of Redemption* and "Experience and Materialism in Benjamin's *Passagenwerk,*" in Smith et al., *Benjamin.* See too Gary Smith, "Thinking through Benjamin," in *On Walter Benjamin,* ed. Smith. Also crucial to this discussion are Buck-Morss's writings, to which I will shortly return.

with Benjamin was certainly the better Marxist" to "his friend [who] was never prepared to give up the theological heritage." [26] Disregarding the dream language in which Benjamin describes the products of the superstructure, Habermas uses the passage to echo Adorno's opinion that Benjamin's interest in ideological "expression" takes him from the realm of materialism to the realm of myth. "Benjamin also deceived himself about the difference between his manner of proceeding and the Marxist critique of ideology," Habermas suggests, and he goes on to propose that "Expression, for Benjamin, is a semantic category that is more akin to what Kassner or even Klages intended than to the base-superstructure theorem." [27]

When Buck-Morss interprets the fragment from Konvolut K, she, in contrast, uses it to refute Adorno's attack on Benjamin's Marxism. Specifically, she applies it to a charge from the Hornberg letter mentioned above. "Class differentiations were never lacking in Benjamin's theory of the collective unconscious," Buck-Morss contends, pointing out that "even in his earliest formulations he considered [it] an extension and refinement of Marx's theory of the superstructure. The collective dream manifested the ideology of the dominant class" (DS, 281). Endowing the dreaming collective with the materialist kernel that Adorno deemed it to lack, Buck-Morss finds evidence for the class content of Benjamin's collective consciousness in, among other places, the citation from Konvolut K.[28] She writes about the corporeal description that Benjamin gives of the repression resulting in the products of the superstructure: "It is of course the bourgeoisie, not the proletariat, whose dream expresses the uneasiness of an overly full stomach" (DS, 282). Buck-Morss goes on to suggest that Benjamin adopts psycho-analytic language to describe the bourgeoisie's relation to its cultural products because psychoanalysis well describes the contradictory affect with which the bourgeoisie charges such products: "If one takes the bourgeois class to be the generator of the collective dream, then the socialist tendencies of that industrialism which it itself created would seem to catch it, unavoidably, in a situation of ambivalent desire" (DS, 282).

26. Habermas, "Walter Benjamin," in On Walter Benjamin, ed. Smith, 117.
27. Habermas, "Walter Benjamin," in On Walter Benjamin, ed. Smith, 116.
28. More generally, Buck-Morss suggests that Benjamin and Adorno's "disagreement [in the controversy over 'Paris, the Capital of the Nineteenth Century'] was in fact limited to their evaluation of the collective's utopian desire (and hence the degree to which mass culture could be redeemed). Benjamin affirmed this desire as a transitory moment in a process of cultural transition. Adorno dismissed it as irredeemably ideological" (DS, 121).

Buck-Morss's discussion is complex and persuasive, and her argument for a class-bound unconscious is supported by multiple passages in Benjamin's notes.[29] But what happens if the materialist stakes of Benjamin's psychoanalytic vocabulary are oriented toward a different challenge to vulgar Marxism than the dialectics of the Frankfurt School? This is surrealist Marxism, although my initial approach to it will be as it has marked the thought of Althusser. I proceed in such fashion because to introduce an alternative reading of Benjamin's discontinuities through the extremely resistant texts of Breton would make for cumbersome exposition. And if, as I show in chapter 5, Althusser works through the base-superstructure problematic with the help of modern materialism, Althusser, in contrast to Breton, submits to standards of logical argument. Significantly, the reader of Benjamin most sensitive to his alternative application of psychoanalysis to Marxism at issue in this chapter is Christine Buci-Glucksmann, a thinker who was initially influenced by Althusser.[30] Buci-Glucksmann comments, "Benjamin's archaeology might be defined as an *archaeology of the imaginary of and in history*."[31] She continues, "Does not such a privileging of the 'logic of dislocation' over that of sublation stage a radical uncanny to reinscribe in the Freudian text, able to explode Marxisms of progress to the benefit of a torn [*déchiré*] Marxism, a Marxism of tearing apart?"

This is not to suggest that Benjamin's interest is as a precursor to Althusser; as many differences separate the two thinkers as bring them together. But Benjamin's divergence from Frankfurt School Marxism must be read as his orientation toward another recognizable Marxist position rather than as his turn away from Marxist thought.

BENJAMIN AND ALTHUSSER

I'm in the Arcades—"it seems to me like in a dream,"
"like it was a piece of me"
                    —Benjamin to Siegfried Kracauer

29. Thus, Buck-Morss also grounds her notion of the class-bound unconscious in an observation from an early draft of the arcades project (0° 67): "Did not Marx teach us that the bourgeoisie can never come to a fully enlightened consciousness of itself? And if this is true, is one not justified in connecting the idea of the dreaming collective (i.e., the bourgeois collective) onto his thesis?" (*DS*, 285; *PW*, 1033).

30. Wolin too observes that Benjamin has much in common with recent revisions of Marxism and suggests in passing the centrality of surrealism to this aspect of Benjamin in "Experience and Materialism in Benjamin's *Passagenwerk*," in Smith et al., *Benjamin*.

31. Buci-Glucksmann, *La Raison baroque de Baudelaire à Benjamin*, 31.

Summing up Marx's "immense theoretical revolution" in *Reading Capital*, Althusser draws attention to the radically new way in which Marx posits the relation between economic phenomena and other forms of social production. Althusser finds this relation elaborated in the context of Marx's critique of "Political Economy [which] thought the economic phenomena as deriving from a planar space governed by a transitive mechanical causality, such that a determinate effect could be related to an object-cause, a different phenomenon; such that the necessity of its immanence could be grasped completely in the sequence of a given." [32] Striving to formulate an alternative to this notion of causality, Althusser argues, Marx describes a situation where economic processes act as causal agents in overdetermined rather than linear fashion. As Althusser writes, "If the field of economic phenomena is no longer this planar space but a deep and complex one . . . the concept of linear causality can no longer be applied to them as it has been hitherto. A different concept is required in order to account for the new form of causality required by the new definition of the object of Political Economy, by its 'complexity', i.e., by its peculiar determination: *the determination by a structure.*" [33]

While Marx implements this concept "'in the practical state,'" Althusser also points out that he fails to produce "*the concept* of it in a philosophical *opus* of the same rigor." [34] Althusser attributes this failure in part to the vocabularies of determination which Marx had at his disposal. Althusser writes: "The age Marx lived in did not provide him, and he could not acquire in his lifetime, an adequate concept with which to think what he produced: *the concept of the effectivity of a structure on its elements.*" [35] But if structural causality was difficult to conceptualize using the terms either of classical economics or Hegelian dialectics, Althusser suggests that twentieth-century thought provides the vocabulary missing to Marx. He appropriates for Marxism the account of the bond linking *langue* (language) and *parole* (speech) in Saussurean linguistics as well as that joining unconscious thoughts and their conscious manifestation in psychoanalysis. Of particular importance to Althusser is the work of Lacan, who is attentive to ways in which the concepts of structural linguistics resonate with the thought of Freud. Althusser thus describes structural causality as "'metonymic

32. Louis Althusser and Etienne Balibar, *Reading Capital*, 182.
33. Althusser and Balibar, *Reading Capital*, 184.
34. Althusser and Balibar, *Reading Capital*, 186.
35. Althusser and Balibar, *Reading Capital*, 29.

causality,' " glossing this term in a footnote as "an expression Jacques-Alain Miller has introduced to characterize a form of structural causality registered in Freud by Jacques Lacan."[36]

Important to refocusing Benjamin's Marxist orientation is not only that Althusser has recourse to psychoanalysis to describe base-superstructure determination but also that he uses this paradigm to describe the form in which the superstructure manifests the base. The manifestation of structural determination, Althusser argues, cannot be captured with the realist rhetoric framing representation as visual depiction employed by orthodox Marxism, starting with Marx himself. "The economic is *never clearly visible,* does not coincide with the 'given' in them [primitive societies] any more than in any other reality (political, ideological, etc.)," Althusser writes.[37] Rather, the economic appears disfigured in the "given," taking a shape resembling the dream disfiguration that Freud describes. This sentence makes evident a further transformation that Althusser's structural causality works on the base-superstructure relationship as it has traditionally been posed. Instead of considering the superstructure to be the appearance of the hidden essence of the base, Althusser accords the practices included under this rubric a material reality of their own. Like the forces of the base, these practices manifest themselves in their phenomenal form only symptomatically, and like the base too, their "real" state is available as construction: "The identification of the economic is achieved by *the construction of its concept.*"[38]

Let us now return to the celebrated quote from Konvolut K. Benjamin opens by taking his distance from the causal link drawn by Marxism between superstructure and base, suggesting instead his interest in the link of "expression."[39] Expression is a charged term within Benjamin's critique of Marxism, repeatedly employed when he takes to task a functional model for base-superstructure relations. Statements such as the following run throughout the Parisian production cycle: "Marx describes the *causal* connection between economic system and culture. The *expressive* relationship is what matters here" (N 1a, 6, emphasis added). When Benjamin goes on to explain what he means by expression, he suggests a relationship both indicated by Marx's vo-

36. Althusser and Balibar, *Reading Capital,* 188.
37. Althusser and Balibar, *Reading Capital,* 179.
38. Althusser and Balibar, *Reading Capital,* 178.
39. While I limit myself to Benjamin's materialist interest in expression, a full investigation of the concept would need to start with his earliest linguistic theory and continue through Benjamin's treatment of expression in his work on the German baroque.

cabulary and transgressing the base-superstructure model that Marx simultaneously proposed. "At first it seems as if Marx here wanted only to establish a causal relation between superstructure and base. But the observation that the ideologies of the superstructure reflect the relations in a false and distorted manner already goes beyond this," Benjamin writes. How to describe the relation which Marx intimated but which he also failed to articulate as such? Benjamin solves this question by recasting social processes in the language of dream.

If we read the theoretical gains of Benjamin's recourse to psycho-analytic vocabulary through the lens of Althusser, we find that this vo-cabulary enables Benjamin to correct precisely the vulgar way in which much Marxism links superstructure and base. When Benjamin describes "the economic conditions of a society's existence" which "come to ex-pression in the superstructure" as the dream of an overfed sleeper, he makes the products of the superstructure a result of the social body's hyperstimulated material processes. He thus posits a model for social processes that eliminates a linear and/or mechanistic link between base and superstructure as well as a notion of the superstructure as the direct reflection of the base. Rather, the causal link between base and super-structure becomes one of complex overdetermination, while the "ideol-ogies of the superstructure" express the base in disfigured products of repression.

Benjamin's psychoanalytic modification of Marx is difficult to per-ceive here because he introduces it through comparison rather than through an explicit conceptual statement. The modification is also obscured because Benjamin posits his theoretical contribution to Marx-ism in terms belonging to a conceptual paradigm he invokes psycho-analysis to replace. Suggesting that he is interested in the *expressive* relation between base and superstructure, Benjamin employs language that might, as Althusser points out, be allied with a Hegelian model for totality rather than with psychoanalytic overdetermination. The He-gelian model presupposes "that the whole in question be reducible to an *inner essence,* of which the elements of the whole are then no more than the phenomenal forms of expression." [40] But, as Althusser states too, terminological uncertainty is characteristic of a text answering a question that it cannot formulate as such: "We cannot but hear behind the proffered word the silence it conceals, see the blank of suspended rigor, scarcely the time of a lightning flash in the darkness of the

40. Althusser and Balibar, *Reading Capital,* 186.

text."[41] That Benjamin simultaneously insists on dream determination as adequate to his displacement of a vulgar Marxist base-superstructure model indicates that "expression" is a misleading phrase for the complexity of the concept toward which he strives.

Benjamin's mapping of base-superstructure relations with appeal to dream topography is not limited to the celebrated fragment discussed above. Throughout Konvoluts K, L, and N, as well as in the earliest draft of the arcades project, *Pariser Passagen I* (*Parisian Arcades I*), Benjamin likens the relation between the economic and superstructural processes of the nineteenth-century collective to that between repressed processes, both somatic and psychic, and their expressions in dreams. The fourth entry in Konvolut K speaks of the sleeper who "undertakes the macrocosmic journey through his body" and brings it to representation in dream pictures (*PW*, 491). Benjamin then compares this situation to the sleeping nineteenth-century collective representing material processes of the social body in its cultural constructions: "This happens also to the dreaming collective, that in arcades becomes absorbed in its interior. We must investigate it, in order to interpret the nineteenth century in fashion and advertising, buildings and politics as the consequences of its dream face" (*PW*, 491–492).

An early passage from the short Konvolut R entitled "Mirror" asks:

> Could there spring from the repressed economic contents of the consciousness of a collective, similar to what Freud maintained concerning the sexual contents of an individual consciousness, a poetry [*Dichtung*], a fantasy-conception, then we would have before our eyes in this representation the consummate sublimation of the arcades. (*PW*, 669)

Benjamin describes the literary superstructure here as the sublimation of the contents of collective consciousness, which he qualifies not as libidinal impulses but rather as economic activity. While this repressed economic content could, as Buck-Morss suggests, be read as a class's repressed wishes that focus on economic matters, it could also be read as the realm of economic production itself. For Benjamin proposes the repressed economic contents of collective consciousness not as the realm where a collective's desires are situated but rather as *the collective equivalent* to individual desire. And he goes on to give as an example of this content the activity of economic circulation. My reading of this passage is in keeping with Benjamin's reflections on the difference between the contents of individual and collective consciousness running

41. Althusser and Balibar, *Reading Capital*, 143.

throughout Konvolut K. Meditating on how one might transfer the model of consciousness from the individual to the collective realm, Benjamin writes: "Naturally, much is internal to it which would be external to the individual, architectures, fashions, yes, even the weather are in the interior of the collective what organ sensations, the feeling of sickness or health are in the interior of the individual" (*PW*, 492).

Benjamin's methodological speculations challenging vulgar Marxism with the help of Marxism support such a reading of the theoretical questions underwriting Benjamin's interest in the dream. Benjamin repeatedly cites well-known Marxist texts attacking precisely those aspects of vulgar Marxism which are at issue in his recasting of base-superstructure relations in psychoanalytic terms. These texts, moreover, are often the passages in Marx where Althusser finds the notion of structural causality described but not named. Benjamin and Althusser are, of course, not alone in invoking these celebrated passages, for they have been the disputed terrain of Marxist discussions of ideology throughout the century. But Benjamin and Althusser can be singled out for the way in which they use psychoanalytic concepts to resolve their difficulties.

The multiple citations from Karl Korsch on Marx in Konvolut N exemplify Benjamin's interest in undermining vulgar Marxism with the help of Marxism. Thus, Benjamin reflects on the "theory of the superstructure" in the following fragment:

> Theory of the superstructure according to Korsch: "To determine the specific kind of relationships and connections between the economic 'base' and the juridical and political 'superstructure' and the 'corresponding [*entsprechenden*]' forms of consciousness . . . neither the philosophical concept of 'dialectical' causality, nor 'causality' as conceived by the natural sciences and supplemented by the notion of 'reciprocal effects' can suffice." (N 17)

Here Korsch asserts that the form of base-superstructure determination at issue in Marxism challenges not only vulgar Marxist economic determinism but also the dialectical causality so important to Adorno. Korsch goes on to suggest that Marx's own ability to conceptualize the nature of this determination was in part hampered by the architectural rhetoric that Marx employed: "One should not cling too anxiously to the phraseology, often intended only metaphorically, that Marx used to describe specific existing connections as a relation between 'base' and 'superstructure,' as 'correspondences,' etc." (N 17). Korsch's distinction between "the philosophical concept of 'dialectical' causality" and causality as conceived by the natural sciences of interest to Benjamin is

not unlike Althusser's distinction between expressive (Hegelian) and
mechanistic causality, neither of which Althusser finds adequate to the
notion of historical process elaborated by Marx. Althusser too will
make the point that Marx is hampered by his rhetoric to justify his appeal to psychoanalytic vocabulary.

In the remainder of the citation Benjamin interjects comments speculating on how an alternative to mechanistic and Hegelian causality may
be derived from the vocabulary of Marx himself. Benjamin pays specific
attention to the celebrated concept of the "unequal development" mentioned in Marx's 1857 *General Introduction* to the *Grundrisse.* "The
most significant results . . . achieved by Marx and Engels do not lie in
theoretical formulations of the new principle, but in its specific application to a series of questions," writes Korsch as cited by Benjamin, and
Benjamin observes in brackets:

> [To these belong, for example, questions touched upon at the end of the
> 1857 Introduction pp. 779 ff. and which deal with the 'unequal develop-
> ment' of different fields of social life: the unequal development of material
> production vis-à-vis artistic production (and of the various arts among them-
> selves), the level of education in the United States vis-à-vis that of Europe,
> the unequal development of conditions of production as legal conditions,
> etc.]. (N 17)

For Althusser too the "unequal [uneven] development" is one of the
concepts where Marx most directly articulates the overdetermined notion of causality that Althusser finds sketched in fragmentary form
throughout Marx's work. Indeed, Althusser considers this term important enough to employ in naming the alternative to expressive and
mechanistic causality that Marx implies. This is a causality that is—"if
you will forgive me the astonishing expression—complexly-structurally-unevenly determined. I must admit, I preferred a shorter term:
overdetermined." [42]

NONSENSUOUS CORRESPONDENCES

While Althusser helps to clarify the materialist potential of Benjamin's psychoanalytic rhetoric, it is important not to oversimplify the
substantial differences between these thinkers. Benjamin is neither so
concerned as Althusser with the historical debates of Marxist theory
nor with a close and rigorous reading of Marx. Another obvious differ-

42. Louis Althusser, "On the Materialist Dialectic," in *For Marx,* 209.

ence is the extensive historicizing concern of Benjamin's project. While both Benjamin and Althusser investigate those aspects of Marxism that implicate it in nineteenth-century conceptual paradigms, Althusser considers this implication primarily to understand how it limits the ability of Marxism to articulate the radical content of its conclusions. His aim is to free Marxism of its ideological component, thereby contributing to the solidification of Marxism as a science. His highly abstract and technical manner of writing provides a stylistic correlate to this aim. The content of Benjamin's interest in the nineteenth-century character of Marxism, to say nothing of his manner of discussing it, is more ambiguous. On the one hand, he is interested in freeing Marxism from the ideological vestiges of its nineteenth-century origin. On the other hand, he often treats Marxism not as a science but as an important nineteenth-century form of *expression* whose relation to other contemporary forms of expression it becomes one of the *Passagen-Werk*'s central projects to define.

Another significant difference is Benjamin's marked interest in the therapeutic potential of the application of psychoanalytic notions to the base-superstructure problematic. The status of agency for Althusser is, of course, a disputed issue—his theory has been criticized as ending in the grim despair of an overdetermination precluding the possibility of action, with the notion of determination in the last instance by the economic (whose lonely hour never comes) trying desperately to stave off this situation. But even if we accept that there is space for human action in Althusser's model of social processes, the content of this action, within his own writings at least, remains within recognized Marxist parameters. Its privileged foci are rigorous critical constructions clarifying the structure of social relations veiled in mystifying immediacy and relatively orthodox Marxist strategies of intervention valorizing, even if not always happily, the organ of the party. Benjamin, in contrast, speculates on how the psychoanalytic recasting of the base-superstructure problematic may not only diagnose the complexity of current social relations but also provide models for socially transformative activity. He is particularly interested in the therapeutic treatment of irrational and symptomatic phenomena, the fact that psychoanalysis values such phenomena as rich forms of expression and seeks their significance with a battery of tactics that are not encompassed by the activity of rational critical construction (this vision of social activity separates the surrealists as well as Benjamin from Althusser). Benjamin's fascination with the wish images of a collective is exemplary of the therapeutic dimension to his notion of praxis. This therapeutic dimension also manifests itself in his notion of "the dialectical image" that is a "dream image" disturbing to Adorno ("PC," 157).

Benjamin's more eclectic battery of conceptual paradigms with which to take his distance from Marxism constitutes another obvious difference from Althusser. Benjamin appeals not only to psychoanalysis but to Jewish theology, Romantic aesthetic theory, baroque allegory, and the poetic practices of Baudelaire (although both Althusser and Benjamin share an important debt to the Brechtian formulation of the relation between ideology and aesthetics, with its attendant polarities of empathy, naturalization, and narrative opposed to disruption, defamiliarization, and montage). In addition, and related to this eclecticism, Benjamin's own linguistic theory, primarily from the period predating his Parisian production cycle (from 1915 to *The Origin of German Tragic Drama*), evinces a notion of signification suffused with theology and very different from the structural causality that Althusser took from linguistics as well as from psychoanalysis and applied to other forms of social production. The distance between these two conceptions of signification can be measured in such essays as "On Language as Such and on the Language of Men." Nothing seems farther from French structuralism than Benjamin's statements contrasting the prelapsarian happy infinity of language naming only itself with the language of men. "The proper name is the communion of man with the *creative* word of God," Benjamin writes, while "the Fall marks the birth of the *human word,* in which name no longer lives intact, and which has stepped out of name language, the language of knowledge, from what we may call its own immanent magic, in order to become expressly, as it were externally, magic. The word must communicate *something* (other than itself)" (*R*, 324, 327).

But I wonder if the Althusserian and Benjaminian notions of signification are not so different from each other as to amount to mirror images in a linguistic instance of spleen and ideal. To put this speculation in terms of the relation between Benjamin's own linguistic theory and his meditations on the base-superstructure problematic: could the psychoanalytically informed causality regulating the dyspeptic dreaming collective be read as the dystopia of the signifying relations obtaining in paradise? The effectivity of a structure in its elements, with that structure nowhere visible except as a process of critical reconstruction: is this not spleen to the glowing ideal of the absolute self-sufficiency and self-evidence of prelapsarian language? In that case, and consonant with the utopian hopes that Benjamin continued to place even in fallen language throughout the 1930s, it would be the language of men that mediates between the two states.

Such a relation is confirmed by the way in which Benjamin reworks his account of linguistic signification after his immersion in the Parisian production cycle. In the 1933 "On the Mimetic Faculty" Benjamin devises the notion of nonsensuous similarity, which, if one of his most hermetic concepts, is concerned with the traces left by divine language in the postlapsarian world. As Wolin writes, "the nonsensuous correspondences of language are closer to reconciliation, to the sacred as Benjamin calls it, insofar as they come nearest to the divine origins of things in the creative language of God." [43] In what does this "com[ing] nearest" consist? I am interested in Benjamin's introduction of psychoanalysis into his battery of conceptual paradigms when he discusses the manifestation of nonsensuous similarities in "the observable world of modern man" (R, 334).

"On the Mimetic Faculty" turns to psychoanalysis following Benjamin's speculation that nonsensuous similarity is like the relations among parts in a structuring whole. "For if words meaning the same thing in different languages are arranged about that thing as their center, we have to inquire how they all—while often possessing not the slightest similarity to one another—are similar to what they signify at their center," Benjamin asks, reworking his figure of languages as the fragments of a lost vessel from his "Task of the Translator" written ten years earlier (R, 335). But in his subsequent representation of the content of this bond Benjamin appeals to a paradigm challenging the unified and visible model of totality which the 1933 description shares with the image of the vessel. Benjamin continues:

> It is nonsensuous similarity that establishes the ties not only between the spoken and the signified but also between the written and the signified, and equally between the spoken and the written.
>
> Graphology has taught us to recognize in handwriting images that the unconscious of the writer conceals in it. It may be supposed that the mimetic process that expresses itself in this way in the activity of the writer was, in the very distant times in which script originated, of utmost importance for writing. Script has thus become, like language, an archive of nonsensuous similarities, of nonsensuous correspondences. (R, 335)

43. Wolin, *Walter Benjamin*, 244.

As Miriam Hansen observes, "At this juncture, psychoanalysis enters through the backdoor of graphology."[44] In the figure of graphology, nonsensuous similarity is suggested as the bond of repression, the relation between manifest and latent content.[45] While this form of relation differs from the way in which signs signify in their conventional social use, it depends, like the bond of repression, on that use for its manifestation. "The mimetic element in language can, like a flame, manifest itself only through a kind of bearer. This bearer is the semiotic element. Thus the coherence of words or sentences is the bearer through which, like a flash, similarity appears" (R, 335).

Benjamin's psychoanalytic figuration of nonsensuous correspondence substantially complicates the nature of the totality structuring these bonds, for their previous characterization was as the bonds between words in different languages arranged around the thing. If these bonds are also akin to the bonds of repression, the linguistic totality becomes fissured by some *other* dimension that is certainly not immediately accessible. Whatever the content of this alterity, my point here is that Benjamin's notion of language now includes an overdetermination reminiscent of the structural causality at issue in his musings on nineteenth-century Paris. The relation of nonsensuous correspondence is not only the residue of the divine language of paradise but also points forward to the complexities of modern capitalist society.

The two-faced character of nonsensuous similarity helps to clarify a terminological slippage which has generally been passed over in this obscure text: the use of two words in "On the Mimetic Faculty" to describe the charged relationship at issue—similarity and correspondence (*Korrespondenz*). From his opening discussion Benjamin associates similarity with "nature," "time immemorial," some primitive sacred that in the 1933 rewriting of his earlier linguistic theory replaces any mention of a prelapsarian world (R, 333, 334). In correspondence, in contrast, Benjamin elects a word oriented in part toward nineteenth-century Paris that resonates with the poetic practices of Baudelaire and symbolism.[46] Might it also look forward to the Marxist notion of cor-

44. Miriam Hansen, "Benjamin, Cinema, and Experience: 'The Blue Flower in the Land of Technology,'" 197.

45. One might expect Benjamin to invoke as example of this bond the more orthodox psychoanalytic example of dream expression that he privileges elsewhere; perhaps he turns to the model of graphology for its link to written script, which constitutes such an important dimension to his conception of language.

46. "Only a thoughtless observer would deny that there are correspondences [*Korrespondenzen*] between the world of modern technology and the archaic symbol-world of mythology," Benjamin comments in Konvolut N (N 2a, 1).

respondence (*Entsprechung*) as the privileged relation structuring relations among different forms of social practice? As Hansen observes, Benjamin's concept of mimesis "has to be distinguished . . . from contemporary Marxist theories of reflection (*Widerspiegelung*); it was actually in explicit opposition to [them] . . . that the writers of the Frankfurt School endorsed and redefined the idea of mimesis."[47] Indeed, when I read Althusser citing Marx's groping to describe this relation for which he lacked the terms, I am reminded of nothing so much as Benjamin on how nonsensuous correspondences become manifest:

> It is on this problem that Marx is attempting to focus in the tentative sentences we can read in the *Introduction*: "In all forms of society it is a determinate production and its relations which assign every other production and its relations their rank and influence. It is a general illumination (*Beleuchtung*) in which all the other colors are plunged and which modifies their special tonalities. It is a special ether which defines the specific weight of every existence arising in it."[48]

Benjamin's rhetoric for the way in which relations of nonsensuous similarity manifest themselves provides a further index of this concept's Janus-faced character. He uses the surrealist-informed rhetoric of profane illumination, employed throughout the Parisian production cycle to characterize the therapeutic potential of the dialectical image but absent in such early texts as "On Language as Such and on the Language of Men." We have seen him write in "On the Mimetic Faculty," "Thus the coherence of words or sentences is the bearer through which, like a flash, similarity appears." He continues, "For its production by man—like its perception by him—is in many cases, and particularly the most important, limited to flashes. It flits past" (*R*, 335). Multiple passages in Konvolut N may be compared to this statement, most celebrated from its late reworking in the "Theses on the Philosophy of History": "The true picture of the past flits by. The past can be seized only as an image which just flashes up at the instant of its recognizability and is never seen again" (*I*, 255).[49]

47. Hansen, "Benjamin, Cinema, and Experience," 195.
48. Althusser and Balibar, *Reading Capital*, 187.
49. Zohn translates the first part of the second sentence as "The past can be seized only as an image which flashes up at the instant when it can be recognized . . . " (*I*, 255). I change the translation to emphasize that Benjamin uses here the same phrase that he previously used to designate "'the Now of *recognizability*,' in which things put on their true—surrealist—face" (N, 3a, 3). For the German original see Walter Benjamin, *Gesammelte Schriften* (hereafter GS), I, 2, 695. In the quote from Konvolut N, Hafrey and Sieburth translate "surrealistische" as "surrealistic."

OVERDETERMINING THE
COLLECTIVE UNCONSCIOUS

If we now return to Benjamin's use of dream vocabulary in "Paris, the Capital of the Nineteenth Century," we are better equipped to foreground its theoretical stakes. These stakes emerge most explicitly in "the earliest surviving draft of the 1935 exposé," at the moment that Benjamin introduces his notion of the collective dream (*PW*, 1223). Similar to the more polished version sent to Adorno, the early draft of "Paris, the Capital of the Nineteenth Century" proposes the notion of collective dream (or wish image) to describe products of the superstructure belonging to the inception of industrial production. "To the form of the new means of production, that in the beginning is still ruled over by the old (Marx), there correspond in the social *superstructure* wish images in which the new interpermeates with the old in fantastic fashion," Benjamin writes (*PW*, 1224–1225, emphasis added). It is in the context of this discussion that Benjamin demonstrates his ambition to resolve an important problem in Marxist theory:

> The reflections of the base through the superstructure are thereby inadequate not because they are consciously falsified by the ideologists of the ruling class, but rather because the new, in order to give itself imagistic form, joins its elements unceasingly with those of classless society. The collective unconscious has more part in them than the consciousness of the collective. (*PW*, 1225)

Here Benjamin explains why a functional model for base-superstructure relations is insufficient by mapping the collective according to psychoanalytic topography. If the products of the superstructure take the distorted form of dreams, Benjamin suggests, it is because they are doubly determined, not only by material forces but also by a nonmaterial collective agency that Benjamin names the collective unconscious. Benjamin ties the collective unconscious to some form of buried libidinal experience when he relates it to classless society from prehistory (*Urgeschichte*). At the same time, however, Benjamin describes the transformations undergone by the new as responding to other than purely libidinal forces. Benjamin isolates a collective symbolic need: the need to give the new imagistic form. Freud termed a similar need "considerations of representability" in *The Interpretation of Dreams*.

In the version of "Paris, the Capital of the Nineteenth Century" sent to Adorno, Benjamin deleted the sentence making explicit the Marxist dialogue in which his collective dream intervenes. Nonetheless, he retains his use of psychoanalytic vocabulary to revise a vision of the superstructure as reflecting the base. As before, Benjamin describes base-superstructure relations with a rhetoric of repression rather than reflection. And, as before, he hypothesizes the existence of a collective unconscious to explain why this rhetoric applies.

In the later version, however, Benjamin's conception of the collective unconscious has grown somewhat more complex. In part, Benjamin follows the earlier version, suggesting that the collective unconscious transforms material reality because of a collective symbolic need: to shape the new and unknown forces with the help of "elements from prehistory [*Urgeschichte*]" ("PC," 148).[50] But in part he suggests the collective unconscious to transform material reality in accordance with a historically specific ideological need, the drive to modernity so important in the nineteenth century: "In addition, these wish images manifest an emphatic striving for dissociation with the outmoded—which means, however, with the most recent past. These tendencies direct the imagistic imagination, which has been activated by the new, back to the primeval past" ("PC," 148).[51] Most importantly, and this is in keeping with psychoanalysis, Benjamin expands the libidinal component to the collective unconscious.[52] "These images are wish images and in them the collective seeks both to sublate and to transfigure the incompleteness of the social product and the deficiencies in the social order

50. For a somewhat different reading of the passage, see *DS*, 118.

51. In this citation, Jephcott translates "Bildphantasie" as "visual imagination" and "Wunschbilder" as "wish-fulfilling images." See *PW*, 47.

52. Was Benjamin interested in finding a vocabulary to characterize the constitution of the collective unconscious in its makeup both as symbolic and libidinal reservoir when he referred to an article by Doctor Pierre Mabille published in the 1936 surrealist-influenced review, *Minotaure*? The reference is found in a fragment from Konvolut K, when Benjamin invokes Mabille's notion of a double social unconscious, the distinctions between "the visceral unconscious" and "the unconscious of forgetting." While Mabille associates the first primarily with the unconscious of the individual, he suggests the second as comprising social life, the external world: "made of the mass of things learned in the course of ages or life, which were conscious, and which through circulation have fallen into oblivion . . . The passional elements of individuals are withdrawn, extinguished. All that remains are the givens drawn from the exterior world more or less transformed and digested. This unconscious is made of the exterior world . . . Born from social life, this mulch belongs to societies" (*PW*, 501). Mabille then, however, goes on to formulate this unconscious as a repository of archaic symbols, sounding rather like the antihistorical Jung from whom Benjamin was careful to dissociate himself. Benjamin speaks of "the clearly reactionary function that the doctrine of archaic images serves for Jung"; he goes on to comment that "the esoteric theory of art amounts to an attempt to make archetypes 'accessible' to the 'spirit of the age'" (N 8, 2).

of production," Benjamin writes ("PC," 148).[53] Responding to the insufficiencies of material conditions, the collective unconscious produces images where unsatisfactory material conditions are set to right.

Benjamin explains how collective dreams distort material conditions, then, by suggesting that these dreams are not determined by the base alone. He sees them also determined by multiple nonmaterial imperatives that he characterizes in libidinal, symbolic, and ideological terms. This modification is not merely additive, for in proposing such an explanation for the distortions of the superstructure, Benjamin starts to dismantle the base-superstructure distinction itself.[54] Making the dreams of the superstructure in part determined by a symbolic component, Benjamin understands them as the effects of forces that orthodox Marxism would ally with the superstructure. The same can be said of the libidinal and ideological imperatives that Benjamin posits as informing the collective dream. But that Benjamin sees these forces to play a fundamental role in shaping the collective dream simultaneously differentiates them from the superstructure in its orthodox Marxist depiction. These forces are not effects of the base, and they cannot be identified with recognizable superstructural institutions like law, the arts, or education.

How to map noneconomic forces of determination while retaining Marxism's topographic model for social processes? Benjamin's notion of the collective unconscious is in part an attempt to resolve this problem. Once again, I am struck by the similarity between Benjamin's translation of psychoanalytic overdetermination into a discussion of base-superstructure relations and the way in which Althusser uses this paradigm to facilitate his symptomatic reading of Marx. Althusser includes among the consequences of his structural causality the fact that the distinction between material processes and their phenomenal appearance occurs not only at the economic level but in "each of the other

53. I have modified Jephcott's translation of this sentence, which runs "these images are wishful fantasies and in them the collective seeks both to preserve and to transfigure the inchoateness of the social product and the deficiencies in the social system of production." See *PW,* 46–47.

54. Benjamin also works this disintegration when he discusses the noneconomic composition of the base. In a note that Tiedemann dates between 1934 and 1935, Benjamin speculates that the base is not the realm of sheer productive processes: "The [x] of the productive forces of a society is not only determined through its raw materials and tools, but also its environment, and the experiences that it makes in it" (*PW,* 1217). Extending the base from the processes of production to the environment, Benjamin associates it with "the experiences" of the collective, a category that does not fit into a neat divide between superstructure and base.

'levels' that belong to the mode of production: the political, ideological, etc." [55]

Why these determining noneconomic forces are subject to collective repression is, however, a question that Benjamin does not address. His only explanation for collective repression occurs when he discusses how the phantasmagorias of the superstructure distort the base. Likening phantasmagorical distortion to psychical processes of repression, Benjamin writes in the earliest version of the exposé, "The enthronement of the commodity and the glitter of distraction [*Zerstreuung*] surrounding it is the *unconscious* theme of Grandville's art," although in the version sent to Adorno he attenuates the psychoanalytic overtones of this relation by changing the word "unconscious" to "secret" (*PW*, 1228, emphasis added; "PC," 152). [56] In both versions too he characterizes the "conscious shaping" of the private man's interior as a way for the private man to "repress" his business concerns (*PW*, 1229). But Benjamin's explanation for the repression of the base is of little help in elucidating the repression at work masking determining noneconomic forces. For in this explanation Benjamin respects the very determination of the superstructure by the base that he simultaneously introduces the collective unconscious to dissolve. If the commodity is the unconscious theme of Grandville's art, this situation arises because commodity fetishism masks the real relations between social products. And if the private man represses material relations, he does so to avoid confronting the contradictions between his class position and his class ideology. "False consciousness," Benjamin explicitly calls this state in the version offered for Adorno's perusal, when he discusses how the phantasmagoria of cultural history distort the material processes that produce them ("PC," 158).

To explain why Benjamin suggests the forces of the superstructure as repressed, we could once again turn to the more extensive elaboration of the consequences of structural causality for the base-superstructure relationship proposed by Althusser. But in this context Althusser's

55. Althusser and Balibar, *Reading Capital*, 183. As we have seen, Benjamin also expresses this overdetermination in more traditional Marxist terms. He has recourse to the concept of the unequal development as well as to passages, notably from Engels, on the superstructure working back on the base. In a fragment from the middle period of Konvolut N, Benjamin writes: "Historical materialism strives neither for a homogeneous nor for a continuous presentation [*Darstellung*] of history. As the superstructure works back on the base, it turns out that a homogeneous history, say of economics, exists as little as does one of literature or jurisprudence" (N 7a, 2).

56. I substitute "distraction" for Jephcott's "amusement." See *PW*, 51.

discussion of the matter rather creates difficulties than clarifies Benjamin's thought. Althusser both explains this repression as the necessary way in which a structure is perceived in its effects and links it to the phenomenon of ideological misrecognition, which he develops in the essay on ideological state apparatuses. We return, that is, to Adorno's query concerning how Benjamin proposes to apply psychoanalytic concepts to the collective realm but we do so with a substantially more complex notion of his project's theoretical potential than Adorno allows. Benjamin does not employ "the notion of collective consciousness . . . to divert attention from true objectivity and its correlate, alienated subjectivity" (*AP*, 113). Rather, he devises it to propose a link between base and superstructure going beyond either linear or dialectical causality as well as to differentiate the appearance of the superstructure from its material workings. Benjamin seeks to use this notion to explain how the forces of the superstructure can have an obscured effect beyond the phenomenal forms in which they appear. In addition, he opens up the possibility for therapeutic formulations of social intervention.

AMBIGUITY, UTOPIA, DREAM

Understanding the theoretical concerns leading Benjamin to cast the base-superstructure problem in psychoanalytic terms allows us to defend his celebrated notion of the dialectical image against Adorno's attack. "Ambiguity is the imagistic appearance of dialectics, the law of dialectics at a standstill. This standstill is utopia and the dialectical image therefore a dream image," Benjamin asserts ("PC," 157). To which Adorno responds: "Dialectical images are as models not social products, but objective constellations in which 'the social' situation represents itself" (*AP*, 115–116). And also: "Ambiguity is not the translation of the dialectic into an image, but the 'trace' of that image which itself must first be dialecticized by theory" (*AP*, 119). "Your 'dream' impetus—as the subjective element in the dialectical image" is how Adorno qualified the point under dispute in a letter cited by Benjamin in Konvolut N written several days after the Hornberg letter (N 5, 2).

But Benjamin's association of the dialectical image with subjective processes, and notably the dream, is theoretically consequent with his psychoanalytic mapping of social processes previously discussed. Thus, he models critical construction on the psychoanalytic method for bringing repressed overdetermination to expression. Such modeling comes as no surprise, given Benjamin's explicit likening of his vision of critical construction to the work of the psychoanalyst confronting the dream. When "humanity, rubbing its eyes, suddenly recognizes the dream image as such," Benjamin writes in Konvolut N, "the historian takes on the task of dream interpretation" (N 4, 1).

Benjamin's dialectical image resembles the constructions of analysis in the curious objectivity that Benjamin attributes to it. Analytic constructions have an objectivity far from that of "objective constellations in which 'the social' situation represents itself" (*AP*, 115–116). If this objectivity has long been the subject of psychoanalytic speculation, let me, for the purposes of the current argument, designate its problematic status only with a quote from the late Freud. "His task [the analyst's] is to make out what has been forgotten from the traces which it has left behind or, more correctly, to *construct* it," Freud equivocates in the 1937 "Constructions in Analysis," undecided whether analysis reconstructs the traces of the past or constructs from them something new.[57] The gauge of the accuracy of the new construction is not only its faithfulness to what has been forgotten but also its therapeutic effectiveness in the present; Freud simultaneously stresses that this gauge is far from confirming that the construction ever existed as such. The problem is further complicated by the fact that the construction is the product of subjects, the analyst and the analysand, and bears the mark of the dynamic between them. The objectivity of these constructs must hence also be measured in reference to questions of transference and countertransference.

Benjamin's conclusion to "Paris, the Capital of the Nineteenth Century" at first seems to posit the dialectical image as the accurate reconstruction of the material forces producing the nineteenth-century world of dreams. When Benjamin writes, "Balzac was the first to speak of the ruins of the bourgeoisie. But only Surrealism exposed them to view. The development of the forces of production reduced the wish symbols of the previous century to rubble even before the monuments representing them had crumbled," he suggests his interest as that of an archaeologist confronting the ruins of a time gone by ("PC," 161).[58] But the essay also differentiates critical construction from reconstruction when Benja-

57. Sigmund Freud, "Constructions in Analysis," XXIII, 258–259.
58. The analyst as archaeologist is a trope familiar from Freud, also found notably in "Delusion and Dream in Jensen's *Gradiva*." This text was dear to Breton and in 1937 he assumed management of an art gallery by that name (see fig. 3). See Henri Béhar, *André Breton*, 304.

min places his dialectical image in an oddly utopian realm. Benjamin asserts, "ambiguity is the imagistic appearance of dialectics, the law of dialectics at a standstill. This standstill is utopia." In these sentences Benjamin differentiates his critical constructions from historical process, if we read the word "dialectics" in the phrase "the imagistic appearance of dialectics" as referring to the dialectical processes of history at work. Terming the place where dialectics appear as a nonplace, utopia, Benjamin both associates it with an alternative to the place where these dialectical processes work and a place saturated with wishful affect: utopia is not only a nonplace but a nonplace where wishes are fulfilled. Psychoanalysis too places its construction in an oddly utopian realm, whose peculiar nonplace can once more be designated in passing with a suggestive passage from Freud. Writing of transference manifestations, Freud describes them in paradoxical, impossible terms. They "do us the inestimable service of making the patient's hidden and forgotten erotic impulses immediate and manifest. For when all is said and done, it is impossible to destroy anyone *in absentia* or *in effigie*," Freud writes, as he asserts the literal reality of the imaginary transference, simultaneously denying it the very power to act in absentia that he in fact has just shown it to have.[59] For psychoanalysis the site of this impossible activity is of course language, and Benjamin too assigns his dialectical images to the linguistic realm: "Only dialectical images are genuine (i.e., not archaic) images; and the place one meets them is language" (N 2a, 3).[60] It should be added, however, that for Benjamin, as for psychoanalysis, the boundary between linguistic and visual media ultimately disappears. The two media signify an unconscious content in a fashion that is neither linguistically nor visually specific, and in designating this form of representation an image (*Bild*), Benjamin chooses a term central to Freud's discussion of that *other* form of representation as well, notably in *The Interpretation of Dreams*.[61] Following psychoanalysis, Benjamin proceeds to make clear that the accuracy of the dialectical image is in part measured by its effect: "The utilization of dream elements in waking is the textbook example of dialectical think-

59. Sigmund Freud, "The Dynamics of Transference," XII, 108.

60. I substitute "meet" for Hafrey and Sieburth's "happens upon."

61. In an essay appearing in a recent issue of *Diacritics* devoted to Benjamin, Anselm Haverkamp comments: "Like Wittgenstein's 'picture,' Benjamin's 'image' is a schema of thought ['Denken'] and 'Bild' is its most common, and, at the time, fashionable denominator." Anselm Haverkamp, "Notes on the 'Dialectical Image': How Deconstructive Is It?"

ing. For this reason dialectical thinking is the organ of historical awakening" ("PC," 162).

If critical construction then helps us to wake from the world of our
parents, it seems in part to be as the wish image of our own age. And
such a libidinal notion of critical construction is consonant with Benjamin's tendentious representation of critique throughout the Parisian
production cycle. Statements like the following from Konvolut K per-
vade the *Passagen-Werk*: "It is said that the dialectical method is concerned with doing justice to the specific concrete-historical situation of
its object. But this is not sufficient. For it is just as much concerned with
doing justice to the concrete-historical situation of the *interest* for its
object" (*PW*, 494). Or as Benjamin writes in a passing definition of the
montage that he suggests as a model for his own "dialectical" process:
"Wiertz as the forerunner of montage (realism plus tendentiousness
[*Tendenz*])" (*PW*).

Benjamin's association of the dialectical image with ambiguity can
best be understood as a function of his interest in applying a psychoanalytic notion of therapy to the collective realm. For Adorno am-'
biguity has no place in the negation and supersession of dialectical
thought. Rather than a tool of theoretical construction, it is a phenomenal appearance that dialectical process seeks to dissolve. But in
analytic construction ambiguity is not just a phenomenal mask that will
be removed once the structure of objective processes at work is made
clear. It is also inherent in the workings of the unconscious, a way for
Benjamin to designate the structural causality that critical analysis seeks
to bring forth. In this suggestion I follow Althusser on the distinction
between contradiction as understood in Hegelian dialectics and contradiction as it emerges in his symptomatic reading of Marx, contradiction "under the sway of the great law of unevenness." [62] In this latter
model Althusser states that "contradiction can no longer be univocal
(categories can no longer have a role and meaning fixed once and for
all) since it reflects in itself, in its very essence, its relation to the unevenness of the complex whole." [63] Althusser is also useful in explaining,
however, the strategic error that Benjamin makes when he describes

62. Althusser, "On the Materialist Dialectic," in *For Marx*, 210.
63. Althusser, "On the Materialist Dialectic," in *For Marx*, 209. In Konvolut K Benjamin relates the visible appearance of ambiguity to Marx on the fetishism of commodities and points out "how ambiguous the economic world of capitalism appears—an
ambiguity, that is greatly heightened through the intensification of capitalist economy"
(*PW*, 499).

overdetermination as ambiguity. Ambiguity is a theoretically flimsy term, one whose empirical vagueness gives the sense that Benjamin is still in a pre-theoretical state:

> We must add that, while no longer univocal, it has not for all that become "equivocal" [ambiguous], the product of the first-comer among empirical pluralities, at the mercy of circumstances and "chance" . . . it reveals itself as determined by the structured complexity that assigns it to its role, as—if you will forgive me the astonishing expression—complexly-structurally-unevenly determined. I must admit, I preferred a shorter term: over-determined.[64]

Althusser here makes an opposition between Hegelian and "complexly-structurally-unevenly determined" or "overdetermined" contradiction which Benjamin would seem to refuse. Throughout his discussion Benjamin fuses Hegelian-Marxist vocabulary with a language of dream. He describes his psychoanalytic concept of critical construction both as "dialectical" and as "dream"; he suggests also that the wish image transforms material relations in a process of sublation: "These images are wish images and in them the collective seeks both to sublate and to transfigure the incompleteness of the social product and the deficiencies in the social order of production" ("PC," 148). But in reading Marx, Althusser makes the point that the slippage between expressive causality and structural causality works to the displacement of the former. And I wonder if Adorno's hostility to Benjamin's description of the "dialectical image" in part derives from its unstated challenge to his privileged method of critique.

I have suggested Benjamin's dialectical image to be thoroughly consistent with the way in which psychoanalysis explains construction in a situation of repressed overdetermination. My position could also be put the other way around: Benjamin's psychoanalytic model for social processes has consequences not only for his understanding of base-superstructure determination but also for his understanding of critical praxis. Psychoanalysis provides Benjamin with a conceptual solution to

> a central problem of historical materialism, which ought finally to be seen: must the Marxist understanding of history necessarily come at the cost of graphicness (*Anschaulichkeit*)? Or: by what route is it possible to attain a heightened graphicness combined with a realization of the Marxist method?

64. Althusser, "On the Materialist Dialectic," in *For Marx*, 209.

The first stop along this path will be to carry the montage principle over into history. (N 2, 6)

Or, as Benjamin observed in one of the scattered fragments that Tiedemann dates from around this time: "What type of graphicness the presentation [*Darstellung*] of history should possess. Neither the lax and cheap graphicness of bourgeois history books nor the meager Marxist one. What it has to fix in graphic form, that is the images originating in the collective unconscious" (*PW*, 1217).

WHY AWAKENING?

If Benjamin works on a model for social processes using psychoanalytic concepts, he evidently does not bring this model to completion. And while his reflections take on some coherence once we understand the implicit aim of his project, their difficulties are by no means resolved. We remain with Adorno's questions as to what is meant by collective consciousness in such a situation and how this collective consciousness relates to individual consciousness.[65] How too does the collective unconscious relate to the material unconscious, and what are the specific details of the relation between the collective dream and the phantasmagoria? Does the collective unconscious play a role in the way in which the phantasmagorias repress the base, and if not, why not? In addition, questions persist concerning the historical specificity of the psychoanalytic map for base-superstructure relations proposed by Benjamin. Benjamin suggests that we too are caught up in collective dreams; are they to be constructed following the nineteenth-century model? And how does our awakening from the world of our parents relate to our implication in our own collective dreams and phantasmagorias? Similar questions resonate in "Fundamental Questions," a fragment that Tiedemann dates from the time that "Paris, the Capital of the Nineteenth Century" was composed:

the historical significance of appearance
{What are the ruins of the bourgeoisie?}

65. Benjamin grapples with this problem in the early notes to the arcades. On the relation of individual dream to the collective historical dream, for example, he writes: "We grasp the dream (1) as an historical (2) as a collective phenomenon. To try[?] [sic] to shed light on the dreams of the individual through the doctrine of the historical dreams of the collective" (*PW*, 1214).

In the new, where does the border between reality and appearance
   run
Prehistory [*Urgeschichte*] of the nineteenth century
Relation between false consciousness and dream consciousness. Reflection takes place in dream consciousness. Collective dream consciousness and superstructure.
(*PW*, 1217)

While it would be possible to consider how Benjamin explores these
problems throughout the arcades project, I want here to ask only one
last question: How does our awakening from the world of our parents
relate to our own implication in a collective dream? More specifically,
given Benjamin's libidinal notion of critique, why does he describe the
critical moment with a vocabulary of awakening at all? The rhetoric of
awakening, after all, traditionally characterizes a state more akin to the
objective vision demanded by Adorno. Within Enlightenment metaphorics, the waking world is the one where relations are contemplated
in complete clarity, where the subject accedes to things as they are.
Awakening is hence entering into this world, as the following lines from
such harbingers of Enlightenment rationality as the three youths in
Mozart's *The Magic Flute* suggest:

> Soon, heralding the morning,
> The sun will shine forth on its golden path.
> Soon superstition shall vanish,
> Soon the wise man will triumph.[66]

That Benjamin applies a vocabulary of awakening to his concept of
theoretical insight can be explained in two ways. In part, Benjamin appropriates the vocabulary from surrealism's utopian representations of
individual and social transfiguration, and we will soon explore their
details. For the moment, however, I am rather interested in a second
issue informing Benjamin's interest in awakening. Benjamin's suggestion of critique as awakening is a consequence of his representation of
the products of the superstructure as dream: awakening is the dream's
binary opposition within traditional epistemological discourse.
   I have suggested that Benjamin's characterization of products of the
superstructure as dream is but the symptom of a more ambitious theoretical project: his effort to use psychoanalytic concepts to clarify aspects of base-superstructure relations implicit in Marx but which Marx

66. Emanuel Schikaneder, libretto to *The Magic Flute*, n.p.

lacked the terms to describe. Benjamin focuses specifically on the language of dream in this endeavor in part because it seems to provide an elegant pivot from materialism to psychoanalysis. This language, central to psychoanalysis, is also one that Marx employs from time to time. But Benjamin's choice of pivot turns out to be marred by a contradiction between the rhetorical function of dream language within Marxist theory and the theoretical problem that Benjamin invokes it to solve.

Benjamin employs the rhetoric of dream as a tool in the Freudian-Copernican revolution that he works on Marxist thought. As a consequence, however, he uses dream rhetoric in substantially different fashion from Marxism. The use of dream rhetoric in Marxism is thoroughly Enlightenment, underwritten by precisely the conceptual project that Benjamin invokes dream language to dislodge. Althusser comments on Marx's Enlightenment use of dream rhetoric: "The dream was the imaginary, it was empty, null and arbitrarily 'stuck together' (*bricolé*), once the eyes had closed, from the residues of the only full and positive reality, the reality of the day. This is exactly the status of philosophy and ideology . . . in *The German Ideology*." [67] And that twentieth-century Marxism continues to employ dream rhetoric in Enlightenment fashion is evident from Adorno's response to Benjamin's use of it. Thus, Adorno objects to Benjamin's transposition of the fetish character of the commodity into consciousness as a dream: "Consciousness or unconsciousness cannot simply depict it as a dream, but responds to it in equal measure with desire and fear" (*AP,* 111). But from the Freudian perspective, the dream response is hardly simple. Rather, it is loaded with affect and precisely the ambivalence of desire and fear that Adorno describes.

Benjamin attempts to get around the Enlightenment notions embedded in Marxist dream vocabulary by making clear the psychoanalytic concepts underwriting his interest in the dream. In addition, he reiterates that he understands the states of dream and waking in a post-Enlightenment way. Repeatedly, he emphasizes that while he uses the concepts of dream and awakening to discuss critique, he simultaneously refuses the binary opposition between waking and sleeping that the Enlightenment rhetoric of dream assumes. This emphasis is visible, for example, in the reflections that Tiedemann dates from the time of "Paris, the Capital of the Nineteenth Century," where Benjamin sug-

---

67. Althusser, "Ideology and Ideological State Apparatuses," in *Lenin and Philosophy,* 160.

gests that awakening is not waking but rather a moment that, in its access to repressed processes, must be conceived of as close to the form
of experience that reigns in the world of dream. One fragment mentions
his "polemic against Jung who wants to keep the dream away from
awakening" (PW, 1212). And he also writes: "To grasp all insight
according to the schema of awakening. And shouldn't the [']not yet
conscious knowledge' have the structure of a dream?" (PW, 1213). The
following early speculation included in Konvolut K also belongs to Benjamin's deconstruction of the distinction between sleeping and waking:

> It is one of the silent assumptions of psychoanalysis that the antithetical
> contrast of sleeping and waking has no validity for the empirical form of
> human consciousness, rather it yields to an infinite variety of concrete states
> of consciousness, that are conditioned by all conceivable gradations of
> awakened-hood in all possible centers. The condition of the consciousness
> that is diversely patterned, and checkered with sleep and waking needs only
> to be transferred from the individual to the collective. (PW, 492)

Buck-Morss writes, "In 1939, with World War imminent, the In-
stitut für Sozialforschung requested a new exposé of the Passagen-Werk
in hopes of getting outside funding for it. Benjamin produced a French
version in a lucid, descriptive style, with a totally new introduction and
conclusion, in which the dream theory is strikingly absent." [68] If Benjamin turns from the language of dream to describe collective ideological
projections, it may be because he comes to realize that, given Marxism's
persistent association of dream language with Enlightenment notions,
this use of dream language turns out to be a contradiction in terms. Despite Benjamin's qualifications, his rhetoric maintains the very conceptual paradigm that he invoked it to displace.

But if Benjamin turns away from dream language as a way to import
psychoanalytic concepts into a discussion of base-superstructure relations, he does not abandon the project altogether. Rather, at the end
of the 1930s, Benjamin pursues it using two alternative vocabularies for
ideological representation that he has been employing throughout the
Parisian production cycle. The first is the vocabulary of the phantasmagoria. This vocabulary attains preeminence in Benjamin's 1939 version of "Paris, the Capital of the Nineteenth Century." The second is
the vocabulary of shock, as the moment making the overdetermination
regulating social processes accessible to the individual subject. This vo-

68. Buck-Morss, "Benjamin's Passagen-Werk: Redeeming Mass Culture for the Revolution," 238.

cabulary, visible in embryonic form already in *One-Way Street*, reaches full development in Benjamin's late work on Baudelaire.

We come then to the question of what Benjamin's application of psychoanalysis to base-superstructure issues owes to his reading of Breton. But let us let Benjamin make the bridge between his dream vocabulary and surrealism himself. Describing the surrealist content of his notion of awakening, Benjamin wrote: "Can it be that awakening is the synthesis whose thesis is dream consciousness and whose antithesis is waking consciousness? Then the moment of awakening would be identical with the 'Now of recognizability' in which things put on their true—*surrealist*—face" (N 3a, 3; emphasis added).[69] The "Now of recognizability": in this moment the strolling surrealist recognizes repressed experience surging from the shock encounter that transfigures a drab Parisian street.

69. I substitute "waking consciousness" for Hafrey and Sieburth's "consciousness." The German original is "Wachbewußtsein."

3.   André Breton in front of the gallery Gradiva. Illus. in *L'Aventure surréaliste autour d'André Breton*. By José Pierre. Courtesy of Artcurial.

CHAPTER 3

"Qui suis-je?"

Nadja's Haunting Subject

WHAT DOES SURREALISM WANT?

André Breton's interest in psychoanalysis dates to his twentieth year and his experience in the First World War. His medical studies interrupted by the draft, Breton found himself working in the latter half of 1916 at the neuropsychiatric center of Saint-Dizier under Raoul Leroy, one of Charcot's former assistants for whom Breton felt, as he put it to his friend Théodore Fraenkel, "an extra-medical admiration."[1] Leroy introduced Breton to Freud's writings before their translation into French, bringing to his attention the summaries of Freud's method in circulation in the medical establishment of the time. These works included the *Précis de psychiatrie* by Doctor Régis and *La Psychoanalyse* by Doctors Régis and Hesnard, "from which . . . [Breton] copie[d] out entire pages" for Fraenkel (*OC*, xxxiv).[2]

When Breton left medicine for poetry, he took with him the new science, but just what he did with it was less than clear. Breton returned disappointed from his visit to Berggasse 19 in 1921, while on his hon-

---

1. From Bonnet's chronology in Breton, *Oeuvres complètes,* xxxiv (hereafter *OC*).
2. On the seriousness of Breton's interest in psychoanalytic theory despite his imperfect access to the Freudian corpus, David Macey comments: "When Breton began to study psychoanalysis towards the end of the First World War, Freud's work was in a state of flux and he was very much an unknown quantity in France. The discrete corpus now known as 'Freud' did not exist. If it is relevant to point out that Binet and Janet used automatic writing as a therapeutic method long before Breton transformed it into an *ars poetica,* it is also relevant to point out that related notions of automatism feed into French psychoanalysis itself." See Macey, *Lacan in Contexts,* 50–51.

eymoon, and described his disappointment in "Interview du Professeur Freud."[3]

> I find myself in the presence of a little old man without any style, who receives in his shabby office of a neighborhood doctor. Oh! he does not much like France, the only country to have remained indifferent to his work. Nonetheless, he shows me with pride a pamphlet which just appeared in Geneva and which is nothing less than the first French translation of five of his lessons. I try to make him talk by throwing into the conversation the names of Charcot, of Babinski, but whether I appeal to memories which are too far away, or whether he maintains a prudent reticence with a stranger, all I get from him are generalities like: "Your letter, the most touching that I have received in my life" or "Happily, we are expecting a lot from the new generation." (*OC*, 255–256)

Sigmund Freud was equally dubious. Upon receiving an inscribed copy of *Communicating Vessels* (*Les Vases communicants*) from Breton a decade later, Freud wrote back:

> And now a confession, which you will have to accept with tolerance! Although I receive so many testimonies of the interest that you and your friends show for my research, I am not able to clarify for myself what surrealism is and what it wants. Perhaps I am not made to understand it, I who am so distant from art.[4]

Insisting on his distance from art, Freud provides a plausible reason for his discomfort with a movement that enlists the unconscious for creative rather than curative ends. His assertion nonetheless rings rather snide and it is far from true. Appealing to two thousand years of literature as he investigates the workings of the unconscious, Freud not only is close to art but particularly to an artistic current important to the surrealists. Like them, his understanding of psychic activity owes a great deal to the Romantic exploration of the imagination, notably the Romantic interest in the close relation between nonrational mental activity and artistic creativity as well as to Romantic formulations of the sublime.

But surrealism wants more than an aesthetic application of Freudian

---

3. Breton went to visit Freud on 10 October 1921. Bonnet tells us that "Simone Collinet (who was Simone Breton) has told us that Breton came back from this visit sad and disappointed, unwilling to speak of it" (*OC*, 1276). "Interview du Professeur Freud" appeared first in *Littérature*, new series, no. 1, 1 March 1922, 19. It was later included in *Les Pas perdus.*
4. Sigmund Freud to André Breton, 26 December 1932, in André Breton, *Les Vases communicants*, 176 (hereafter abbreviated as *V*). The English translation is in André Breton, *Communicating Vessels*, 152 (abbreviated hereafter as *CV*).

theory, and the remainder of Freud's correspondence with Breton indicates that it is these other things that Freud may find distasteful. The letter musing on "what surrealism wants" is the third letter responding to *Communicating Vessels,* preceded by two letters where Freud extensively answers a reproach brought against *The Interpretation of Dreams* by the opening of *Communicating Vessels.* Discussing the importance of Volkelt's work on dreams for Freudian dream theory, Breton takes Freud to task for his failure to cite Volkelt in his bibliography and speculates on the possible bad faith motivating this omission. Freud responds by defending his own bibliographical thoroughness, pointing out that he does indeed cite Volkelt in the German edition and that the omission noticed by Breton derives from the negligence of his French translator. Despite the ease with which he answers Breton's objections, Freud's tone in restoring what was lost in translation is curiously one of vehemence, and, more curiously yet, Freud writes a follow-up letter the next day continuing to defend himself against Breton's seemingly trivial charge.[5] Freud himself notes the strangeness of the energy that he devotes to this defense: "Forgive me for returning once more to the Volkelt business. It may not mean much to you, but I am very sensitive to such a reproach."[6]

Surprised by Freud's concern with his comment, Breton calls it "*symptomatic,*" speculating, not very convincingly, on the deeper professional anxieties the criticism may have sparked (*V,* 179; *CV,* 154). Nonetheless, Breton expresses a plausible hypothesis for the strangeness of Freud's response. And I wonder if the concerns of which it is a symptom may not manifest themselves in the remainder of the passage from *Communicating Vessels* to which Freud objects. Couched in the characteristically convoluted syntax that represents Breton's inheritance from Mallarmé, the passage opens: "Freud himself, who seems, when it concerns the symbolic interpretation of the dream, just to have taken over for himself the ideas of Volkelt, an author about whom the definitive bibliography at the end of his book remains rather significantly mute . . ." (*V,* 18; *CV,* 11). But this accusation of Freud is only an introductory clause, subordinate to the main clause of the sentence. "Freud," continues Breton,

> for whom the whole substance of the dream is nevertheless taken from real life, *cannot resist the temptation of declaring that the 'intimate nature of*

5. Caws notices the strangeness of this epistolary exchange in "Linking and Reflections," in *Dada/Surrealism,* no. 17.
6. Sigmund Freud to André Breton, 14 December 1932, in *V,* 174; *CV,* 150.

the unconscious [essential reality of the psychic] is as unknown to us as the
reality of the exterior world,' giving thereby some support precisely to those
whom his method had almost routed. (V, 18; CV, 11; emphasis added)

If Freud, as he tells Breton, does not make it beyond the tenth page of
Communicating Vessels where the sentence occurs, it may more indicate Freud's sensitivity to the political appropriation that Breton works
here on the intimate nature of the unconscious than his sensitivity to
slights on his scholarly integrity. In the sentence that so disturbs Freud,
Breton, if in typically oblique fashion, turns his attention to statements
by Freud that pivot suggestively to Marxist theory. He shows his interest in the fact that Freud accords the libidinal unconscious of psychoanalysis an alterity drawing it near the forces of external determination studied by Marxism. For Freud here suggests that the unconscious
forces determining the subject resemble, in their radical unavailability,
the processes of the external world, and "thereby," Breton construes,
gives "some support precisely to those whom his method had almost
routed" (*V*, 18; *CV*, 11). Breton speculates on the nature and consequences of this support throughout his Parisian prose trilogy. As we will
see, he pursues not only how the Marxist and Freudian forces of determination in the last instance are susceptible to apprehension by each
other's methodologies but also the possibility that they communicate
closely (thus the notion of communicating vessels) and may in fact
ultimately be indistinguishable.

The following chapter examines Breton at work on a materialist displacement of psychoanalysis from the opening sections of the first text
of his Parisian prose trilogy, *Nadja*. These sections of *Nadja* decenter
the subject into a differentiated self that is the effect of unconscious processes, what Breton calls his "haunting" self, and simultaneously displace a psychoanalytic account of the unconscious toward the forces of
material determination at issue in Marxism. I also open my discussion
of modern materialism with the opening of *Nadja* in order to emphasize
Breton's extraordinarily elusive manner of setting forth his ideas.[7]
Answering question with question, dissolving answers by qualifying
them until their content is no longer recognizable, putting words of uncertain significance into key explanatory position, Breton translates his

---

7. Such emphasis is particularly useful for an English-speaking audience, since this
quality of the text occasionally gets lost in Richard Howard's almost too elegant English
translation.

thematized challenge to the Cartesian subject onto the plane of style.[8] The mode of exposition might well be called "haunting" too, for it turns every statement into the ghost of itself.

THE HÔTEL DES GRANDS HOMMES
AND THE GHOSTLY SELF

Breton's hotel at the opening of *Nadja,* the Hôtel des Grands Hommes opposite the Panthéon, still stands today. While no longer seedy, its tacky gentrification is appropriate homage to someone who claimed that "amid the bad taste of my time I strive to go further than any one else."[9] The ignorance of the hotel staff about the literary past of their place of employment (which is certainly not the case at Proust's Grand Hôtel in Cabourg) is also in keeping with Breton's challenge to the monumentalization of the *grand homme* in *Nadja.* Breton throws down this challenge when he chooses this equivocal hotel as his "point of departure," rather than starting from the grand structure opposite containing the tombs of the nineteenth century's great men: "To the great men from the grateful country" (*OC,* 653).[10] Still, one would like to know the room where Breton resided, if only to check what view his window now affords. Would the statue of Jean-Jacques Rousseau (see fig. 4)—"whose statue I could see from behind and two or three stories below me"—that is still standing opposite the hotel produce its uncanny effect today: "I withdrew suddenly, gripped with fright" (*OC,* 658; *N,* 27).

Viewed from the front, the statue looks very much like Rousseau's pictorial figuration of his autobiographical project: the "portrait of a man, painted exactly after nature and in all its truth."[11] In transforming Rousseau's representation into the locus of uncanny experience, Breton gives visible form to the psychoanalytic transformation that *Nadja* works on the autobiographical project associated with Rousseau. While

8. For an excellent elaboration of the elusive quality of this text, see Michel Beaujour's "Qu'est-ce que *Nadja?*"
9. André Breton, *Manifesto of Surrealism,* in *M,* 16.
10. André Breton, *Nadja* (hereafter *N*), trans. Richard Howard, 23. I have generally provided my own translations of *Nadja* but have benefited from Howard's translation throughout. As with the two latter works in the Parisian prose trilogy, I give both a reference to the French original which appears in Breton's *OC* and to the published translation. Here I cite Howard verbatim.
11. Jean-Jacques Rousseau, *Les Confessions,* I, 3.

4.   J.-A. Boiffard. "My point of departure will be the Hôtel des Grands Hommes . . ." (*Je prendrai pour point de départ l'hôtel des Grands Hommes . . .*). Illus. in *Nadja*.

Rousseau's *Confessions* purport to mirror in discourse a preformed and self-knowing subject, to tell us "ce que je fus," *Nadja* opens with Breton calling into question both the extratextual existence of the subject as well as its presence to itself.[12] The content of this transformation has much to do with the uncanny, understood in psychoanalytic terms as the return of something familiar that has been repressed.

"Who am I?" asks Breton as the opening words in his text (*OC*, 647; *N*, 11).[13] Translating the Rousseauian past into the present of the narration, Breton also places Rousseau's assured declaratives in interrogative form. Breton's response to the opening question heightens the uncertainty concerning the content of the autobiographical self still more. To this question, Breton gives the following circuitous response that is no answer at all: "if this once I were to rely on a proverb: in fact why would everything not come down to knowing whom I 'haunt'?" (*OC*, 647; *N*, 11).

Alluding to the French adage "Dis-moi qui tu hantes et je te dirai qui tu es" (tell me whom you haunt, in the sense of *frequent*, and I will tell you who you are), Breton seems to invoke it to refer his subjectivity to the influence of his friends and environment. His first move in defining his identity is to suggest himself as a product of the social conditions in which he lives. But the hypothetical and ambiguous tone of Breton's questioning response undercuts a reading of this term according to its proverbial meaning, as does his use of quotation marks, which unhinge a word from accepted use. In the fourth sentence of the paragraph, Breton makes explicit that he appropriates the colloquial expression in other than its colloquial sense:

> I must admit that this last word [haunt] is misleading, tending to establish between certain beings and myself relations that are stranger, less avoidable, more disturbing than I intended. It says much more than it means, it makes me play while still alive the role of a ghost, evidently it alludes to what I must have ceased to be in order to be *who* I am [*suis*]. (*OC*, 647; *N*, 11)

Here Breton goes from suggesting that haunting is related to the places and persons that one frequents to reflecting on how this dependence starts to undermine the integrity of the *I* itself. Punning on the simul-

12. Jean-Jacques Rousseau, *Les Confessions*, I, 5. Deconstructive readers of the *Confessions* have argued that Breton's dissolution of the self-present subject may already be found in Rousseau's autobiographical practice. I am interested here, however, more in the content of Breton's polemic against Rousseau than in its accuracy.
13. I cite Howard's translation verbatim. This sentence also places Breton in an autobiographical tradition going back to Montaigne's essays. For a discussion of this tradition particularly illuminating in relation to *Nadja*, see Michel Beaujour's *Miroirs d'encre*.

taneously ontological and sequential significance of the first person singular of the verb to be, *être,* Breton posits this identity as a sequence of temporally differentiated moments. The *I* becomes a series of ghosts of its contiguous experience rather than a centered self.

In the following sentences Breton associates his displacement of haunting from its colloquial usage with the psychoanalytic notion of repression. He proposes this association when he describes the relation of ghostly self to the realm that it haunts. Rather than the companions at a local café, he starts to frequent an obscure and unknown field:

> Hardly distorted in this sense, it [the word *haunt*] leads me to understand that what I regard as the objective manifestations of my existence, manifestations that are more or less deliberate, is merely what passes, in the limits of this life, from an activity whose true field is completely unknown to me. (*OC,* 647; *N,* 11–12)

Breton obscures the content of the constitution of this field by using qualifying phrases to empty his statements of their immediate evidence ("hardly distorted in this sense"; "leads me to understand") and by linking as similar two conflicting ways that this field manifests itself, as the "objective manifestations of my existence" and the "more or less deliberate manifestations." While the first description gives to these manifestations objective content, the second formulation suggests that they take place in the realm of subjective experience, even if the content of this subjective activity is somewhat unclear. "Délibérées" contains a range of meanings from deliberated to deliberate.[14]

When Breton goes on to describe this unknown field from which both his objective and subjective self-manifestations come, he underscores its resemblance to the Freudian unconscious. He associates his various forms of self-present, visible manifestations with the hidden motivation of an obscured field that is also himself: "It is possible that my life is only an image of this kind, and that I am condemned to retrace my steps while I believe that I am exploring, to try to know [*connaître*] what I should recognize [*reconnaître*] all too well, to learn only a small part of what I have forgotten" (*OC,* 647; *N,* 12). Making the haunting subject the obscured residue of familiar but forgotten material, Breton describes it in distinctly psychoanalytic terms. Breton heightens his allusion to a Freudian schema of repression by casting its effect on the subject in the language of ghosts. Ghost language con-

14. As well as a pun on *dé-libéré* which will resonate with Breton's later use of "désenchaînement" as a description of surrealist unchaining.

stitutes one of Freud's privileged tropes for the uncanny persistence of repressed material.[15] "In an analysis . . . a thing which has not been understood," writes Freud in *Little Hans,* "inevitably reappears; like an unlaid ghost, it cannot rest until the mystery has been solved and the spell broken."[16] At the same time, however, Breton initially derived his ghostly representation of the self from the French proverb making the subject an effect of his environment. Breton's ghostly description of subjectivity points then both to psychoanalytic theory and to the constitutive effect of externally motivated forces on the subject.

Breton's remaining opening exposition of the haunting self continues to emphasize its fissured and fundamentally constructed identity. Breton writes of the repressed account of his haunting: "This view of myself only seems to me false to the extent that it presupposes me to myself, that it situates arbitrarily at a prior moment a completed image of my thought which has no reason to be reconciled with time, and insofar as it implies in this same time an idea of irreparable loss, of penitence or of a fall" (*OC,* 647–648; *N,* 12). Here he emphasizes that the deconstructed psychoanalytic subject is not to be recuperated by being projected into the past, its temporally differentiated content remedied by the suggestion of some lost primal moment of self-presence. "I strive, in relation to other men, to know in what my differentiation consists, if not what is responsible for it," he continues (*OC,* 648; *N,* 13). While Richard Howard, the English translator of *Nadja,* renders differentiation as "difference," a post-Derridean reader of *Nadja* cannot help but be attuned to the fundamentally differentiated vision of the self that Breton suggests with the word "différenciation," meaning not only Breton's difference from other men but also the *différance* that constitutes his self (*OC,* 648; *N,* 13).[17]

15. In displacing haunting from its meaning as frequenting to its meaning as ghostly return and then to a psychological meaning, Breton follows the etymology of the word. To haunt, and the French *hanter,* come from the Anglo-Saxon *hametan,* to house, from *ham,* abode, as in hamlet, only subsequently used as ghostly recurrence, as to Hamlet, and finally as the spontaneous recurrence of something to the mind.

16. Sigmund Freud, "Analysis of a Phobia in a Five-year-old Boy," X, 122.

17. The closest French equivalent that Derrida finds for différance is "differentiation," of which he writes: "Could not this (active) movement of (the production of) *différance* without origin be called simply, and without neographism, *différenciation?* Such a word, among other confusions, would have left open the possibility of an organic, original, and homogeneous unity that eventually would come to be divided, to receive difference as an event. And above all, since it is formed from the verb "to differentiate," it would negate the economic signification of the detour, the temporizing delay, 'deferral'." Jacques Derrida, "Différance," in *Margins of Philosophy,* 13. The objections Derrida raises to the word "differentiation" resemble the distance Breton establishes between the ghostly model of haunting and his own, as Breton makes clear that there is no prior mo-

The psychoanalytic character of Breton's haunting subject is further reinforced by the form of textual practice Breton proposes as suitable to represent it. This practice differs markedly from Rousseau's description of autobiographical representation as the portrait of an already formed, extratextual subject. In his account of autobiographical writing Breton borrows heavily from the psychoanalytic notion of how analytic (re)construction of the self proceeds. Breton's subjectivity is not anywhere fully present but rather must be constructed through narrative; his textual act of representation resembles the process of self-construction characteristic of the Freudian talking cure. "What matters is that the particular aptitudes that I discover slowly down here distract me in no way from the search for a general aptitude, which would be my own and which is not given to me," writes Breton (*OC*, 648; *N*, 12). He also suggests that this text proceeds through free association and within the time period of the analytic session: "I will speak of these things without pre-established order and according to the whim of the hour which lets survive whatever survives" (*OC*, 653; *N*, 23). Like an analysand's discourse, Breton's narration acquires significance not from the accuracy of any event represented but rather "dans son ensemble," from the relation among the memories narrated, as the narration becomes itself the event that generates meaning: "It is of little importance if an occasional error or a minimal omission, indeed some confusion or a sincere oversight, throws a shadow on what I tell, on what, in its entirety, cannot be unreliable (*OC*, 653; *N*, 23–24). Similar in another way to an analysand's discourse, Breton's text lacks a metalanguage that will comment with authority on the events he recounts. Asserting that his self is constituted by a series of haunting *I*'s, he refuses to grant to any one *I* a privileged status as the real Breton.

In his opening presentation, then, Breton suggests the subject as the ghost of some sort of unconscious realm, simultaneously implying that this unconscious is individual and that it is related to objective factors. Breton emphasizes the objective character of this realm increasingly as his reflections on its content proceed. By the time Breton concludes his text, he has opened up a realm of alterity powerful enough not only to turn the subject into a series of ghosts but to dissolve its identity en-

---

ment of self-presence from which the haunting self falls off and that this self consequently cannot be thought outside of temporal mediation. That Derrida's concept of *différance* echoes in Breton's definition of identity does not result from my imposition of late twentieth-century theory on an earlier time. The Freud and Nietzsche used by Derrida in "Différance" are of great importance for Breton, and Derrida reads a Nietzsche and Freud who have been filtered through the surrealist-influenced writings of Bataille and Lacan.

tirely, in a version of subjectivity fissured beyond any division proposed by Freud. This point can be well summarized by considering the transformation Breton's opening "qui suis-je" has undergone by the end of his adventures with Nadja:

> If these were sophisms at least it is to them that I owe having been able to throw at myself, at he who from farthest away comes to meet me, the cry, always pathetic, of "Who goes there [*Qui vive*]?" Who goes there? Is it you, Nadja? Is it true that the *beyond,* that all the beyond is in this life? I cannot hear you. Who goes there? Is it only me? Is it myself? (*OC*, 743; *N*, 144)

"Who goes there," Breton interrogates the ghosts, using the words of a sentinel on the haunted ramparts of a Danish castle or of Hugo's Enjolras on the barricades of 1832. Alienating the *I* as the objective *myself* and then dissociating this objectified self from himself, turning it to "he who from farthest away comes to meet me," Breton raises the uncertainty of his being able to reconstitute such alien material as a unified self at all. With the introduction of an objective dimension into the subject, the possibility exists that the boundary between subject and object will crumble in the direction of contingency rather than recuperation, and this problem echoes in the final question, "Is it myself [*moi-même*]?" Playing with the ambiguity of "même," Breton asks if under such conditions it is possible to talk of a "moi" anymore, is it even me myself? As Breton also puts it, looking back on surrealism in his subsequent preface to *Nadja* written in 1962, "Subjectivity and objectivity fight, in the course of a human life, a series of battles with each other from which most often the first rather quickly emerges badly off" (*OC*, 646).[18]

The challenge Breton proffers to a self-present subject is an aspect of surrealism condemned with great vehemence by Sartre in *What Is Literature?* The negative tone of Sartre's reaction, I suspect, plays a role in the neglect of this aspect of surrealism by postwar French and Anglo-American literary criticism; rather than investigating the interest of Breton's gesture, these critics more often defend surrealism against Sartre's attack.[19] Michel Carrouges, for example, quotes from this attack at length:

> "The subjective enters in indeed when we recognize that our thoughts, our emotions, our willing comes from us in the moment they appear to us and

18. Howard's translation was done before Breton published a revised version of *Nadja* in 1963, which contained, among other changes, this preface.
19. Martin Jay emphasizes the stature of Sartre's postwar reading of surrealism in *Marxism and Totality.*

when we deem both that it is certain they belong to us and only probable
that the exterior world regulates itself by them. The surrealist has taken a
hatred for this humble certitude on which the stoic based his ethics. . . . Automatic writing is above all else the destruction of subjectivity. When we
attempt it, spasmodic clots rip through us, their origin unknown to us; we
are not conscious of them until they have taken their place in the world of
objects and we have to look on them with the eyes of a stranger. It is not
a matter, as has too often been said, of substituting their unconscious subjectivity for consciousness, but of showing the subject to be like an inconsistent
illusion in the midst of an objective universe." [20]

To defend surrealism against Sartre, Carrouges asserts Sartre's limited
understanding of the surrealist concept of subjectivity, claiming that
surrealism exalts rather than limits the freedom of the subject. But such
a defense of surrealism, tacitly accepting the existentialist valorization
both of the subject and of freedom, rejects the validity of Sartre's reading, its hostile tone not withstanding.

Sartre reacts with venom to the surrealist representation of the subject because such a subject is ill-suited to carry out the praxis an existentialist protocol of *engagement* demands. But in his reaction Sartre un-
erringly points to one important account of subjectivity that Breton
constructs *Nadja*'s haunting self to refute. This is the conscious and
controlled subject of political praxis, the subject demanded of surrealism by the French Communist Party. It may well be asked what kind
of agency the haunting subject can have; Breton struggles with this
question throughout his discussion of surrealist praxis. "Have they
bound revolt to revolution?" is how Benjamin put the problem of surrealist politics (*R*, 189). At moments Breton yearns for some reinte-
grated realm of replenished subjectivity beyond alienation, as is visible
in lyrical passages exalting love and stirring declarations of revolutionary faith, although over and over again this yearning fails to materialize.
At other moments, however, as we will see, Breton uses his haunting
notion of subjectivity to ground the dispersed and bohemian praxis that
he terms "unchaining" (*OC*, 687; *N*, 69).

AUTOBIOGRAPHICAL PORTRAITURE: "HE
ENTERED, FOLLOWED BY HIMSELF AND HIMSELF"

"It is possible that my life is only an *image* of this kind," Breton
writes when he explains his haunting vision of subjectivity (*OC*, 647;

20. Jean-Paul Sartre, quoted in Michel Carrouges, *André Breton and the Basic Concepts of Surrealism*, 225. The Sartre passage is taken from "Situation de l'écrivain en
1947," in *Qu'est-ce que la littérature?*, published as *Situations II* (Paris: Gallimard,
1948), 215–216.

N, 12, emphasis added). He provides a visual analogue to this form of subjective existence in the way that *Nadja* plays with the relation between photographic image and text. Placing his photoportrait at the opening of his text's third section, Breton juxtaposes to it the third section's opening sentence: "I envy (in a manner of speaking) every man who has the time to prepare something like a book" (*OC*, 743; *N*, 147) (fig. 5). While in a standard documentary photo Breton's portrait would illustrate the sentence to which it is juxtaposed, Breton constructs this sentence in such a way that he problematizes establishing a one-to-one correspondence between photograph and the textual passage whose extraliterary existence it documents. There are, after all, two parts of the sentence to which the photograph could refer. The subject of the photograph could be identical with the subject of the sentence, "I." It could also, however, refer to the object of the sentence from which Breton's subject here differentiates himself, "every man who has the time to prepare something like a book." Breton reiterates his refusal of this formal public persona in other writings from the time. "I am not: a *littérateur*, a public man," Breton stated in a 1925 letter to Artaud.[21]

While we know from extratextual documents that this photo does represent the subject of the sentence who signs *Nadja,* its formal makeup implies that it refers rather to "every man who has the time to prepare something like a book." Its traditional composition and lighting as well as Breton's formal pose and expression suggest its subject to be a public person, an author, rather than the private "I" narrating his Parisian peripeteias. The public aspect of the photo is confirmed by the resemblance it bears to the publicity photo preceding it in the text, that of actress Blanche Derval by the same photographer, Henri Manuel.

If the photo referring to both the subject and the object of the sentence documents the existence of the referential Breton, then it infuses both terms to which it applies with Breton's presence or conversely displaces Breton's self-presence from association with any one representation. The power of the photographic image to capture the curious self-differentiation of the haunting subject is, moreover, thematized in this opening section, when Breton mentions a cinematic trick employed in an appealing second-rate film: "A Chinese who had found some way to multiply himself invaded New York by means of several million copies of himself. He entered followed by himself, and himself, and

21. André Breton, letter to Antonin Artaud, Paris, 27 March 1925, in *Bureau de recherches surréalistes,* vol. 1 of *Archives du surréalisme,* 125.

5.   Henri Manuel. "I envy (in a manner of speaking) every man who has the time to prepare something like a book . . ." (*J'envie [ç'est une façon de parler] tout homme qui a le temps de préparer quelque chose comme un livre* . . .). Illus. in *Nadja*.

himself, and himself into the office of President Wilson, who removed his *pince-nez*" (OC, 663; N, 36–37). This mention of how cinematic reduplication captures a differentiated subject points to a more general similarity between Breton's ghostly definition of subjective manifestation and what numerous theoreticians of photography have characterized as the ghostly nature of the photographic sign. The photograph can be considered ghostly in its indexical relation to its object, the trace of something's existence in a given place at a given time, "its blind submission to certain contingencies of time and place," as Breton notes of his ghostly subject (*OC*, 646; *N*, 12).[22] In a text bearing the marks of his own close reading of *Nadja*, Roland Barthes implicates photography in a ghostly process of subjective differentiation: "In the realm of the imaginary, the Photograph . . . represents this very subtle moment where, to tell the truth, I am neither a subject nor object, but rather a subject who feels itself become object: I then live a micro-experience of death (of parenthesis): I become truly a ghost."[23]

We might term the ghostly mode of presence that Breton's haunting subject shares with the photographic image *tracelike,* borrowing from Nadja's own description of how she will haunt Breton. (It is significant that Nadja, who is able to formulate her own tracelike nature, is also the only important character in this text who never appears in full portrait format. Max Ernst refused to paint her portrait, Breton tells us, warned off the project by the clairvoyante, Madame Sacco. Instead, Breton includes a sequence of four identical horizontally formatted photos of a woman's eyes stacked one on top of the other, as in a film strip. As caption he places under this sequence a phrase used to designate Nadja in the text of the book: "her eyes of fern" [*OC*, 714; *N*, 111].) Breton cites Nadja proposing the formulation of herself as a trace at the moment when he abandons the journal format he has hitherto used to narrate his adventures with her, explaining that the technique does not capture the most important features of these adventures.[24] Rather, Breton states, he will enumerate significant memories, as he returns to his initial narrative format modeled on psychoanalytic practice from which the journal might seem to have distanced him:

> I no longer wish to remember, as the days go by, any but a few of her sentences, spoken or written spontaneously in my presence by her, sentences

22. I follow Howard's translation of this sentence verbatim. For a discussion of the spectral ambitions of photography, see notably Philippe Dubois, "Le Corps et ses fantômes." Rosalind Krauss discusses surrealism's interest in the indexical character of the photographic sign in "Nightwalkers," 35. I elect the word *trace* over *index* in the remainder of this section because of the Freudian overtones of the relation Breton suggests between the text of *Nadja* and the experience to which it refers.

23. Roland Barthes, *Camera Lucida,* 13–14. I modify Howard's translation of this passage. For the original French, see Roland Barthes, *La Chambre claire,* 30.

24. Beaujour points out that *Nadja*'s pastiche of the journal format in fact undermines the journal's usual claim to documentation, arguing that it performs in the realm of language a process similar to the pictorial deconstruction of documentation I have been describing. See "Qu'est-ce que *Nadja*?"

which are those where I best recapture the tone of her voice and whose
resonance within me remains so great:
  "With the end of my breath, which is the beginning of yours."
  "If you wanted, for you I would be nothing, or merely a trace [*trace*]."
(*OC*, 719; *N*, 115–116)

In describing herself as a trace, Nadja chooses a term characterizing the
relation of self to representation throughout Freud's writing on memory
and repression, a term used by Freud in multiple ways but notably in
discussing his prime example of a text of repression, the dream text.
For Freud the term designates a sign that represents the subjective activity that produced it in distorted rather than mimetic fashion:

> That product, the dream, has above all to evade the censorship, and with
> that end in view the dream-work makes use of a *displacement of psychical
> intensities* to the point of a transvaluation of all psychical values. The
> thoughts have to be reproduced exclusively or predominantly in the material
> of visual and acoustic memory-traces, and this necessity imposes upon the
> dream-work *considerations of representability* which it meets by carrying
> out fresh displacements.[25]

Extending the term from dream to waking experience, Breton uses *trace*
to designate the indexical fashion in which the ghostly subject haunts
the tracks of his own experience.

THE OBJECT OF ONE OF
THOSE PERPETUAL SOLICITATIONS

  How to characterize the composition of the obscure realm of which
the subject is a ghostly manifestation: the body of *Nadja*'s narrative
pursues the question by investigating specific instances of events where
this realm surges into view. Representing the affect of this surging as
distinctly uncanny, Breton speculates on its cause in terms reminiscent
of its psychoanalytic explanation. When Breton compares himself to
Huysmans, he writes: "He too, is the object of one of those perpetual
solicitations which seem to come from outside, which stop us for a few
moments before one of those chance arrangements, of a more or less
new character, and whose secret it seems we might find in ourselves by
questioning ourselves closely" (*OC*, 650; *N*, 17). Attributing the cause
for haunting experiences to secrets contained "in us," Breton suggests
these moments as the return of something obscurely familiar which has

---

25. Sigmund Freud, *The Interpretation of Dreams*, V, 507.

been repressed. If Breton did not know "The 'Uncanny'" when he wrote *Nadja,* he certainly had read the closing sentences of *The Psychopathology of Everyday Life*: "But there is one thing which the severest and the mildest cases all have in common, and which is equally found in parapraxes and chance actions: *the phenomena can be traced back to incompletely suppressed psychical material, which, although pushed away by consciousness, has nevertheless not been robbed of all capacity for expressing itself.*" [26]

Consonant with the obscure subjective-objective source that Breton posits for his haunting, however, Breton also stresses that the explanation for these events' uncanny effect cannot come from psychoanalysis alone. Breton has the following to say concerning the possible cause for his uncanny experience of the place Maubert:

> I would like finally . . . that if I say, for example, that in Paris the statue of Etienne Dolet, place Maubert, has always simultaneously attracted me and caused me unbearable discomfort, that it will not immediately be deduced that I am merely ready for psychoanalysis, a method I respect and which I consider to aim for nothing less than the expulsion of man from himself, and from which I expect other exploits than those of a bailiff. (*OC,* 653; *N,* 24)

In this passage Breton invokes a radically dislocated subject to take his distance from orthodox psychoanalytic modes of explanation. He also indicates a central reason for his uneasiness with the new science so dear to surrealism. This uneasiness derives from the failure of psychoanalysis to pursue its potential to bring about "the expulsion of man from himself"; instead, as Breton puts it, psychoanalysis all too often acts as bailiff. Breton's choice of metaphor is expressive; he likens the disappointing aspect of psychoanalysis to those characters from nineteenth-century melodramas who come along to assert the interests of the ruling classes and further dispossess the socially disempowered. Instead of using psychoanalysis in the service of the ruling bourgeois order, Breton is interested in pressing it into the service of revolution, although the distance between his conception of this notion and the event as understood by orthodox Marxism remains to be defined.

In another of Breton's opening discussions on the composition of the uncanny experiences his text will enumerate, he provides a clue as to what aspect of the surrealist uncanny escapes a psychoanalytic mode

26. Sigmund Freud, *The Psychopathology of Everyday Life,* VI, 279.

of explanation.[27] He does so in a characteristically difficult paragraph and in characteristically elusive fashion:

> It is a question of facts which, even if they were on the order of pure observation, present on each occasion all the appearances of a signal, without our being able to say precisely what signal; and which have the result that, in complete solitude, I uncover in myself implausible complicities, which convince me of my illusion each time I think myself alone at the helm of a boat. (OC, 652; N, 19–20)

Stating that the "complicities" may not be explicable in terms of the subject alone, Breton does so in allusive language which functions to link these complicities to the post-Romantic experience of subjectivity. His metaphor of the subject at the helm refers to one of Baudelaire's celebrated *Parisian Pictures* (*Tableaux parisiens*) dealing with uncanny Parisian haunting: Baudelaire's "Seven Old Men." [28] When Baudelaire describes his flight from the frightening repetition of seven old men into the solitude of his room and his attempt to make sense of it, he represents his reason with the figure of the tiller to which Breton alludes:

> Vainement ma raison voulait prendre la barre;
> . . . Et mon âme dansait, dansait, vieille gabarre
> Sans mâts, sur une mer monstrueuse et sans bords! [29]

Unable to resolve this repetition on a Parisian street into either "mystery" or "absurdity," Baudelaire ends with his reason adrift on a Parisian sea.

27. Krauss points to the importance of the uncanny for *Nadja* and *L'Amour fou* in her Freudian reading of surrealist photography, "Corpus Delicti." Rather than asking, however, how Breton may modify the Freudian uncanny, and particularly Freud's subordination of collective to individual experience, Krauss uses Freud's explanation of the uncanny to demystify the surrealists' attempts to collapse the distinction interior/exterior. Krauss writes: "The collapse of the distinction between imagination and reality—an effect devoutly wished by surrealism, but one that Freud analyzes as the primitive belief in magic—animism and narcissistic omnipotence are all potential triggers of that metaphysical shudder that is the uncanny." See Rosalind Krauss, "Corpus Delicti," in Krauss and Livingston, *L'Amour fou: Photography and Surrealism*, 85.

28. The tendency of repressed material to become confused with external phenomena is also evident in Freud's essay on the uncanny. Freud locates two possible sources for uncanny experience, one in the personal past of the individual, the other in the way in which the individual has interiorized a collective past. He writes: "An uncanny experience occurs either when infantile complexes which have been repressed are once more revived by some impression, or when primitive beliefs which have been surmounted seem once more to be confirmed. Finally, we must not let our predilection for smooth solutions and lucid exposition blind us to the fact that these two classes of uncanny experience are not always sharply distinguishable." See Sigmund Freud, "The 'Uncanny,'" XVII, 249.

29. Charles Baudelaire, "Les Sept Vieillards," in *Oeuvres complètes*, I, 88. Baudelaire originally planned to entitle this poem "Parisian Ghosts" (*Fantômes parisiens*). A literal translation runs: "In vain my reason wanted to take the tiller; / . . . And my soul danced, danced, old scow / Without masts, on a monstrous sea without bounds!"

If Breton alludes to Baudelaire in the course of expressing the insuffi-
ciency of subjective causes to exhaust the psychoanalytic content of the
uncanny, I interpret this allusion as a way for Breton to gesture to a
Parisian field his own differentiated subject may haunt. In chapter 4 I
will be interested in how Breton's ghostly subject haunts the traces of
the Parisian past. For the moment, however, I want to return to the
opening of *Nadja* where Breton intimates an objective, Parisian source
to his haunting self when asking that seemingly most subjectively
oriented of questions, who am I? On an idle afternoon at a sale of used
French books in New York, I came across a less monumental but
specifically Parisian source to this statement whose relation to *Nadja*
must be approached through the closing lines of Breton's 1924 *Soluble
Fish*.

While much more dreamlike than *Nadja*, *Soluble Fish* already demonstrates Breton's interest in those uncanny encounters when the subject opens itself to experiences from an obscurely subjective and objective field. The work is full of moments when Breton and a Parisian
cityscape fuse, and the text indeed ends with this fusion: "The walls of
Paris, what is more, had been covered with posters showing a man
masked with a black domino, holding in his left hand the key of the
fields [*la clé des champs*]: this man was myself" (*M,* 109).[30] At this
used-book sale, then, I came by chance (so surrealism contaminates its
students) across a card advertising the services of one Eugène Villiod,
private eye, dressed in a Fantomas outfit and holding a key (figs. 6 and
7). Under the image with which *Soluble Fish* closes, the detective has
placed the phrase Breton uses as the opening lines in his subsequent text
of Parisian prose wandering, *Nadja*: "Qui suis-je?" Villiod asks.

---

30. *Prendre la clé des champs* means to run off or away.

qui suis-je?

6–7. Parisian Private
Detective's Card, c. 1920.
Author's collection.

Qui je suis? c'est ma
19 ème année

Villiod Eugène
Détective

Officier de l'Instruction publique
Titulaire de la Médaille d'Honneur

Je suis l'Auteur de :

"Comment on nous vole, comment on nous tue"
"La Machine à voler"
"Les Bandes noires"
"Comment on nous vole au jeu"

Je me charge avec succès de toutes
Enquêtes recherches et surveillances
pour mariages – successions – divorces – vols –
abus de confiance – etc ....

Écrivez-moi : 37, Boulevard Malesherbes, Paris
Télégraphiez-moi : Détecville Paris
Téléphonez-moi : Central 79-85

IMPRIMERIES ALLIN - ÉPINAL

CHAPTER 4

The Ghosts of Paris

Every step, on a bridge, on a square, recalls a great past—at
each corner of the street, a fragment of history unfolded.
— Goethe, quoted by the
Guide pratique à travers le vieux Paris

In his admirable *Entomological Memories,* Mr. Fabre proves
to us that it is almost impossible to lift a pebble without disturbing some insects; is it not equally true to affirm that in
Paris it is impossible to move a stone without evoking some
ghosts?
— Georges Cain, *Le Long des rues*

MONUMENTAL PARIS

Visitors to Paris know its monumental litany, the historic structures
that punctuate the city in the panorama offered on nice days from the
escalator of the Centre Pompidou. The Eiffel Tower, the Trocadéro, the
Madeleine, the Sacré Coeur as one looks out to the west of the city,
and the Louvre, Notre-Dame, the Panthéon to the city's south. Running
down the tourist's "musts," the reliable 1924 *Guide Bleu* singled out
similar spots (fig. 8). Charles Henny's 1923 *Guide de Paris* condenses
the monuments that matter in even more abbreviated form:

> It is on the banks of the Seine and on its bridges that the soul of Paris can
> best be communed with. *All the history of France* is evoked when, from far
> or near, one sees there the Hôtel de Ville, Saint-Gervais, the Tour Saint-
> Jacques, here Notre-Dame and the spire of the Sainte-Chapelle, the Con-
> ciergerie and the Pont-Neuf.[1]

The tourist's itinerary, the guide's conception of all French history,
belong to a form of historiography which Nietzsche termed monumental when he described the nineteenth century's veneration of its triumphal past. In Paris such historiography was written in part by its poets.
Reading Victor Hugo's *Notre-Dame de Paris,* we might almost think

---

1. Charles Henny, *Guide de Paris, abrégé esthétique et pratique avec un plan,* 17 (emphasis added).

8.   Parisian Panorama. Illus. in *Les Guides Bleus: Paris et ses environs*. Paris: Hachette, 1924.

Nietzsche coined his phrase for official history with its chapter entitled "A Bird's Eye View of Paris" in mind. There Hugo uses each Parisian monument to embody a different moment in the development of the French state:

> There is the Paris of Catherine de Medicis at the Tuileries, the Paris of Henri II at the Hôtel de Ville, both structures still in the best of taste; the Paris of Henri IV at the place Royale: brick façades with stone corners and slate roofs, tricolored houses; the Paris of Louis XIII at Val-de-Grâce: a crushed and squat architecture with arches like the handles of a basket, and some-

thing pot-bellied in the column and hunchbacked in the dome; the Paris of
Louis XIV at the Invalides: a tall rich man, gilded and cold; the Paris of
Louis XV at Saint-Sulpice: volutes, bows, clouds, spaghetti, and chicory, the
whole thing in stone; the Paris of Louis XVI at the Panthéon: Saint Peter's
of Rome badly copied (the edifice has settled clumsily, which has not
mended its lines); the Paris of the Republic at the Ecole de médecine: an im-
poverished Greek and Roman taste which resembles the Coliseum or the
Parthenon like the constitution of the year III resembles the laws of Minos,
in architecture, it is called *Messidorian* taste; the Paris of Napoléon at the
place Vendôme: this one is sublime, a bronze column made out of canons;
the Paris of the Restoration at the Stock Exchange: a very white colonnade
supporting a very smooth frieze, the whole thing is square and cost twenty
million francs.[2]

Breton's *Nadja* offers no such monumental vision of Parisian historical grandeur. Rather than encompassing the city in a panoramic glance,
Breton wanders in among its streets, catching enigmatic glimpses of
scenes from daily life or dwelling on places singularly tangential to the
great structures of collective memory.[3] The place Maubert, the Porte
Saint-Denis, the wide faceless boulevards in the second, ninth, and tenth
arrondissements are not eloquent with tradition, and when Breton nears
a monumental spot, he brushes by it obliquely. At the Panthéon he
shows us not its familiar beehive dome but rather his own equivocal Hôtel des Grands Hommes opposite, and though he mentions the
Colonne Vendôme, he refuses its evocation of Napoleonic glory. "The
magnificent light in Courbet's paintings is for me that of the place Vendôme, at the hour when the column fell," he writes, identifying the
square and the column with the destruction of the column under the
Paris Commune attributed to Courbet (*OC*, 649; *N*, 14–15).

Restored in 1874, the Vendôme column at the moment that *Nadja*
takes place displays no visible trace of its turbulent past. Instead, the
column looks to the casual viewer immutable, one more image of the
bourgeois state's eternal reign. That the history of the Paris Commune
is no longer visible where it once most spectacularly occurred makes
clear one challenge facing anyone who would use the content of daily

2. Victor Hugo, *Notre-Dame de Paris,* 156.
3. *Nadja*'s refusal of the panoramic glance exemplifies surrealism's more general
critique of Western ocularcentrism elaborated by Jay. "In the case of Surrealism," Jay
comments, "it is readily apparent that speculative reason, bathing in the light of clear
and distinct ideas mirrored in the mind's eye, and mimetic observation, trusting in the
reflected light of objects apparent to the two physiological eyes, were both explicitly
scorned. It is no less evident that the third tradition, that of visionary illumination, was
elevated in their place to a position of honor." Martin Jay, "The Disenchantment of the
Eye: Surrealism and the Crisis of Ocularcentrism," 23.

Parisian life to write nonmonumental historiography. Such historiography cannot rely on realist methods of representation. As Barthes has suggested in *S/Z*, these methods privilege visual aspect as the bearer of meaning; we think, for example, of Balzac's celebrated description of the Pension Vauquer which opens that text oft-cited as exemplary of Parisian realism, *Le Père Goriot*.[4]

In an article discussing how paradigms of visual representation have informed the narrative structures of historiography, Michael Ann Holly quotes Hayden White's confident assertion that "there have been no significant attempts at surrealistic, expressionistic, or existentialist historiography in this century."[5] The question of significance aside, the following discussion suggests that in *Nadja* Breton explores the possibility of writing surrealist historiography by applying a Freudian paradigm of memory to collective events. In *Nadja*'s uncanny moments of Parisian *encounter,* objective history effaced in the manner of repressed material flashes momentarily to view through its contact with the strolling surrealist and his concerns (here turning around the problems of "la révolution surréaliste"). "The substitution of a political for a historical view of the past" is how Benjamin describes *Nadja*'s treatment of the past in his essay on surrealism (*R*, 182). Benjamin's comments on *Nadja*'s strange photos in the essay grope, I think, toward the way in which the text uses its images to dismantle the illustrative function of visual representation assumed by realist paradigms. "In such passages in Breton, photography intervenes in a very strange way. It . . . draws off the banal obviousness of this ancient architecture to inject it with the most pristine intensity toward the events described" (*R*, 183).[6] And *Nadja*'s treatment of the Parisian past is central to Benjamin's own surrealist historiography in a project whose significance, if not success, is indisputable.

---

4. Surrealism's polemical stance toward realism is exemplified by the *Manifesto of Surrealism*: "By contrast, the realist attitude, inspired by positivism, from Saint Thomas Aquinas to Anatole France, clearly seems to me to be hostile to any intellectual or moral advancement. . . . It constantly feeds on and derives strength from the newspapers and stultifies both science and art by assiduously flattering the lowest of tastes; clarity bordering on stupidity, a dog's life" (*M*, 6). I modify the translation which renders "réaliste" as "realistic." See *OC*, 313.

5. Michael Ann Holly, "Past Looking," 371.

6. Dawn Ades comments on *Nadja*'s use of photography: "There are signs, then, in the 'dumb' photographs, which may be read if they are taken in conjunction with the text. And yet they can never be fully 'interpreted.' The photographs convey only parts of the cryptogram in which Nadja's life was hidden." See Dawn Ades, "Photography and the Surrealist Text," in Krauss and Livingston, *L'Amour fou: Photography and Surrealism*, 165.

Reflecting from the viewpoint of Benjamin, I have provisionally termed this treatment surrealist historiography, but it also constitutes a psychoanalytically informed contribution to the lineage of textual remembrance which Beaujour defines as the "self-portrait." This historiography is indissociable from Breton's previously discussed revision of the autobiographical project following Freud.[7] "It is a type of memory both very archaic and very modern through which the events of an individual life are eclipsed by the recollection of an entire culture, thus bringing about a paradoxical forgetting of the self," Beaujour writes of the simultaneously individual and collective acts of remembering that the self-portrait's open-ended creation of the subject performs.[8]

PARISIAN PANORAMAS
AND PARISIAN GHOSTS

That *Nadja* is a haunted text has been amply observed.[9] But to recognize the identity of the ghosts hovering around Breton and Nadja's uncanny strolls is no easy task. While Breton mentions the power of phantoms throughout the work, only Nadja's vague hallucinations ally these phantoms with any recognizable dead. On the place Dauphine, notably, "She is disturbed by the thought of what has already occurred in this square and will occur here again. Where only two or three couples are at this moment disappearing into the shadows, she seems to see a crowd. 'And the dead, the dead!'" (*OC*, 695; *N*, 83). For the contemporary reader such evocations of the Parisian dead are too vague to prove historically revealing. But was this always the case? Could Breton have been addressing a contemporary Parisian historical imagination for which the content of the dead frightening Nadja would be clearer than it is for readers distanced in time and space? To initiate discussion of *Nadja*'s Parisian uncanny, I have sought to reconstruct the Parisian ghosts associated with *Nadja*'s uncanny sites at the time that Breton wrote, speculating that there then existed a horizon of expectation concerning the Parisian past with which Breton could play.

7. Michel Leiris's *L'Age d'homme* is another important work of surrealist autobiography where the distinction between autobiography and historiography disappears.
8. Beaujour, *Miroirs d'encre*, 26.
9. See, most recently, Alina Clej's "Phantoms of the *Opera*: Notes Towards a Theory of Surrealist Confession—The Case of Breton." I differ from Clej, however, who situates the origin of Breton's melancholia in his medical experience in the First World War. I understand it, in contrast, as deriving from his ambivalent relation to the tradition of "revolution."

Any history of Paris from the ten years following the First World War would provide an index not only of the events that had left visible reminders but also of events of which little observable trace remained. But because I am interested in those memories that would have been accessible to an educated but not specialized readership, I have chosen to reconstruct this horizon using works that display the range of historical commonplaces associated with Parisian places, even at the expense of historical accuracy.[10] These works belong to the minor genre Benjamin identified in "Paris, the Capital of the Nineteenth Century" as panoramic literature. Nonfictional, descriptive writing on Paris often full of errors and fanciful embroidery, the panoramic texts range from the extraordinarily naive to the strangely eloquent and apt. The haphazard quality of these texts, however, well suits them to our purposes.

It was with some trepidation that I confronted the thousands of panoramic texts estimated by the editor of the 1924 *Guide Bleu* to exist on Paris. But by the time I had completed my perusal of three excellent collections, those of the Bibliothèque Nationale, the Bibliothèque Historique de la Ville de Paris, and the Sterling Library at Yale University, it became clear that an exhaustive consultation of Parisian panoramic literature of the time was redundant. Repeatedly, the same historical associations were identified with Breton's charged Parisian sites, confirming the hypothesis that there did indeed exist a contemporary reservoir of Parisian phantoms that Breton could invoke. Once having acquired some familiarity with the Parisian ghosts hovering around Breton's favorite sites, we will see their traces flare up in Breton's descriptions of his experiences there, albeit in oblique form.

It may be objected that this way of reading *Nadja* is overreading, that Breton could not have intended to endow his offhand mention of Parisian details with the resonances of the Parisian past.[11] My reading, however, not only follows Benjamin's use of Breton but also the hypothesis Breton himself subsequently proposed as explanation for the strange sensation that some Parisian places inspire. Mentioning "the steps that, without exterior necessity, take us back to the same points of a city" in the 1952 "Pont-Neuf," Breton writes:

> When it is a question of a city as old and with a past as rich as Paris, it seems to me impossible to maintain that these [each person's privileged]

10. I cite above all from texts from the 1920s, but I have occasionally referred to somewhat earlier texts (from the time of the surrealists' youth) which I found particularly eloquent (Billy, Cain).

11. For economy of argument I leave the thorny problem of authorial intention aside, all the thornier in a text whose author valued so highly the unconscious lucky find.

structures are only physical. Their interest is that they arise to a large extent from *what has taken place* here or there and that, if we tried to see our way clearly through the matter, they would make us more conscious of what makes us tremble as well as of what gives us back our balance.[12]

The uncanny effects of Parisian places, Breton suggests, derive from effaced historical memories that continue to cluster around the place of their occurrence in invisible but perceptible form. The notion of Paris as a city haunted by ghosts, above all the ghosts of violent death, is, moreover, familiar from a lineage of Parisian representation important to Breton (thus his allusion to Baudelaire's "Seven Old Men").[13] This lineage of Parisian representation was also one with which the master theoretician of the uncanny himself was familiar. When Freud went to Paris to study with Charcot, he wrote to his fiancée's sister, Minna Bernays, of his contact with Parisian streetlife:

> I am under the full impact of Paris and, waxing very poetical, could compare it to a vast overdressed Sphinx who gobbles up every foreigner unable to solve her riddles. But I will save all this for verbal effusions. Suffice it to say that the city and its inhabitants strike me as uncanny [*unheimlich*]; the people seem to me of a different species from ourselves; I feel they are all possessed of a thousand demons; instead of "Monsieur" and "Voilà l'Echo de Paris" I hear them yelling "A la lanterne" and "A bas" this man and that. . . . They are a people given to psychical epidemics, historical mass convulsions, and they haven't changed since Victor Hugo wrote *Notre-Dame*. To understand Paris this is the novel you must read; although everything in it is fiction, one is convinced of its truth.[14]

PARISIAN PROMENADE:
"THE MIND'S NETHER REGIONS"

Finally reaching the platform, the surprised eye is able
to grasp Paris. From the summit of the Tour [Saint-
Jacques], it appears, not neat, classified, methodical,
as in a guide, not readable, as in a map, but confused,

12. André Breton, "Pont-Neuf," in *La Clé des champs,* 229–230 (Breton's emphasis).
13. In an article written at the height of surrealism, Roger Caillois observes that literary representations of Paris have created a myth where "the Paris that the reader knows is not the only, nor even the true city, but rather a brilliantly lit décor, all too *normal . . .* and which hides another Paris, real Paris, a ghostly Paris, nocturnal, elusive, all the more powerful as it is the more secret, and which at every site and at every moment comes to mix itself dangerously with the other Paris." Roger Caillois, "Paris, mythe moderne," in *La Nouvelle Revue Française,* 25th year, no. 284, May 1937, 687.
14. Sigmund Freud, *Letters of Sigmund Freud,* 187–188. "Voilà l'Echo de Paris" suggests a newspaper seller's cry, while "A la lanterne" and "A bas . . . " mean "String him/her up" and "Down with. . . . "

tangled, inextricable, the superimposition of twenty
cities, the amalgam of one hundred worlds which
chance in turn brings together or separates.

—Paris au hasard

In a charming sally, Mme de Girardin one day said that for
the Parisian, walking is not taking exercise—it is search-
ing . . . The Parisian truly seems an explorer, always ready
to set off again, or, better, like some marvelous alchemist
of life.

—F. Bloch, *Types du boulevard*

Examining Parisian panoramic literature for the collective past of
Breton's favorite haunts reveals first of all the commonplace of historical Paris itself. Consistently presenting Paris as the place where past
and present harmoniously mix, the guides represent the city's relation
to history in a fashion specific to the beginning of the twentieth century.
During the second half of the nineteenth century Haussmann's reconstruction of Paris was under way, and panoramic literature took sides.
When this literature did not exalt the beauty and efficiency of the new
Paris, it lamented the historical Paris that seemed about to be forever
lost.[15] The end of the nineteenth and the first quarter of the twentieth
century, in contrast, were characterized by renewed interest in preserv-
ing the Parisian past.[16] In 1935 Le Corbusier might lament, "Paris fills
me with despair. That once admirable city has nothing left inside it but
the soul of an archaeologist. No more power of command. No head.
No powers of action."[17] But the consensus of the panoramic literature
from the first quarter of the century was somewhat different. For Parisians describing their city, past and present had achieved an almost ideal

15. So Louis Veuillot's 1867 *Les Odeurs de Paris* complains: "New Paris will never
have any history and it will lose the history of old Paris. Every trace of it is already erased
for men of thirty years of age . . . City without a past, full of minds without memories,
hearts without tears, souls without love!" (pp. 10–11).

16. While guidebooks in both the nineteenth and the twentieth centuries placed
ghosts in the streets of Paris, Norma Evenson, in her *Paris: A Century of Change, 1878–
1978*, points out that the end of the nineteenth and first quarter of the twentieth century
were characterized by renewed interest in the Parisian past. Such interest, a reaction to
the tremendous urban and modernizing expansion in the second half of the nineteenth
century, resulted in a series of laws protecting historic buildings against demolition, notably a national preservation law in 1913. See Norma Evenson, *Paris: A Century of
Change, 1878–1978*.

17. Le Corbusier, *La Ville radieuse*, quoted in Evenson, *Paris: A Century of Change*,
175.

equilibrium. As Henry Frichet's 1925 *Paris et ses merveilles* tells us: "But if Paris is the past with all its artistic, literary, and scientific treasures, Paris is also the future, undergoing everyday the imprint of new discoveries, recent *moeurs,* adapting itself to all types of progress." [18]

Sometimes the nature of this equilibrium is more complex than simple spatial coexistence. When the editor of the 1924 *Guide Bleu, Paris et ses environs,* considers the persistence of the past in the present, he treats it as something hidden and mysterious, to be sought with the energy of a detective if not created with the imagination of a poet:

> It is simply necessary to saunter about, in reaping according to your fantasy the tragic or grandiose memories which meet each other at each step. . . . And how many ghosts stroll here! What people lived before you under this ceiling? What secrets have these walls heard? What scenes of crime, of seduction, of joy or of despair have these mirrors reflected? The flagstones of this dark walk echoed under the steps of Molière; on this iron banister the hand of Voltaire rested; in front of this small mirror of a cramped house on the rue Saint-Honoré, Robespierre knotted his tie the morning of 9 Thermidor; from the top of these stone stairs, the Pope gave his benediction to the prostrated crowd. . . . Let this retrospective amusement not be made fun of; the great soul of Paris is made of these reminiscences. [19]

André Billy's 1909 *Paris vieux et neuf* not only asserts the mysterious and hidden way past Paris appears in the present but resituates the interpenetration of past and present in the soul of the Parisian inhabitant. Standing on the Pont-Neuf Billy tells us:

> *Unconsciously* and little by little, a *rêverie* rises in you, like the humming of a foreign and distant voice which melts at first into the background noise of surrounding life, the rumble of vehicles on the cobblestones of the bridge. And then you realize that *this voice is in fact yours,* that it is the voice of your profound being, the voice of your Parisian and French soul. It sings of confused and forgotten things that your skepticism is astonished to find alive, old general ideas fallen into disuse but which our moral organism never eliminates. This square du Vert-Galant, this statue of King Henri, this historic strip of ground where the volunteers of 1792 signed up, this place Dauphine inhabited by Mr. Josse, the goldsmith, and Madame Roland . . . what is more suited to awaken this complex sensibility that is ours, French of the twentieth century, so often incomprehensible to ourselves? [20]

Mentioning the unconscious power of a strange and distant voice from your "deep being" which proves to be familiar, Billy links uncanny

18. Henry Frichet, *Paris et ses merveilles,* avant-propos, n.p.
19. *Les Guides Bleus: Paris et ses environs,* xviii (first ellipsis mine, second ellipsis in the text).
20. André Billy, *Paris vieux et neuf,* II, 60–63 (emphasis added).

events not only to forgotten material that is in some way familiar but also to forgotten material from a collective past that has now been surmounted.[21]

Such language strangely prefigures Freud's conclusions ten years later on the uncanny effect of experiences seemingly testifying to the performative power of thought. "An uncanny experience occurs either when infantile complexes which have been repressed are once more revived by some impression," Freud writes, "or when primitive beliefs which have been surmounted seem once more to be confirmed. Finally, we must not let our predilection for smooth solutions and lucid exposition blind us to the fact that these two classes of uncanny experience are not always sharply distinguishable."[22] Freud goes on to link these experiences to collective but abandoned beliefs from prescientific society, beliefs that resemble Billy's "old general ideas fallen into disuse but which our moral organism never eliminates."

If, in less uncanny fashion, Billy's Pont-Neuf bears a strong resemblance to Breton's 1952 "Pont-Neuf," Breton's earlier *Nadja* contains no explicit hypothesis for what induces disequilibrium at certain privileged Parisian sites. Rather, guides in hand, we must reconstruct the possible source of their haunting power ourselves.

1. PLACE MAUBERT

The first Parisian place that *Nadja* singles out as inspiring an uncanny feeling is a site important for Breton's relation to psychoanalysis. "In Paris the statue of Etienne Dolet, place Maubert, has always simultaneously attracted me and caused me unbearable discomfort," Breton writes (*OC*, 653; *N*, 24). Guides concur in allying the place Maubert with two differing but not always distinct sets of ghosts. Because this square provides an entrance into the commonplaces of Parisian panoramic literature, it is useful to quote from several guides' representations of it to make the point that this literature provides a set of commonplaces which do recur. *Paris et ses merveilles* notes:

21. The association of the historical experience of Paris with a collective unconscious is found in nineteenth-century panoramic literature on the city as well. In the afterword to one of the mid-nineteenth century monuments in the genre, *Le Diable à Paris*, the editor, Hetzel, comments: "The history of a great city like Paris can thus only be the unconscious result of a kind of common action. . . . Everything must enter into the composition of this work. . . . Types, characters, portraits, genre pictures, taken from both private and public life, the street and the home, from old Paris and modern Paris." Hetzel, "Post-face" to *Le Diable à Paris*, II, 191.
22. Freud, "The 'Uncanny,'" XVII, 249.

During the Middle Ages, it [the place Maubert] was the true forum of the
university quarter, the meeting-place of students, jugglers, and gossips, as
well as the center of low-class language; it was said of a crude man that he
had learned his *compliments at the place Maubert*. . . . This celebrated crossroads was the theater of tumultuous scenes and executions. It is there that
the printer, Etienne Dolet, was burned as a heretic. It is there that the Guises
erected their first barricades against Henri III, that those of the Fronde were
raised as well. It is at two steps' distance that Voltaire and Crébillon began
in life as attorney's clerks.[23]

The center of past bohemian activity, the square was also the place of
insurrectional ferment, and it is a statue of a figure from this insurrectional history, Etienne Dolet, which so frightens and attracts Breton.[24]
The links of this statue with insurrection extend from the figure it represents to the circumstances of the statue's erection. It was put up in
1889 to commemorate the insurrectional past, the only visible trace of
this past that remains. So the *Guide historique et anecdotique de Paris*
concludes after running through similar details:

It was formerly the site where students gathered and a site of execution.
There, Alexandre d'Evreux in 1533, Claude Lepeintre in 1540, Etienne
Dolet in 1546, were burned as heretics . . . this last, a printer, philologist and
philosopher, martyr to his daring and aggressive ideas. During the Fronde
and in 1848, barricades were set up there. The square was also the haunt
of cut-throats and hooligans before the opening of the boulevard Saint-
Germain and the rue Monge. In 1889 the statue of Etienne Dolet was erected
there, in memory of certain riots.[25]

While the insurrectional past comes down only as a memory of "certain riots" vaguely collected around Etienne Dolet's statue, guides concur that the square's bohemian past lingers on as visible in the present.
Frichet's unpretentious text and *Paris et ses environs*, a coffee-table
book bound in leather and lavishly illustrated, both isolate the same
"picturesque" detail that makes the present square worthy of notice.
"In the center of the place Maubert, a statue has been put up of Etienne

23. Frichet, *Paris et ses merveilles*, 61.
24. In applying the term *bohemian* to pre-nineteenth century society, I use it loosely,
for nineteenth-century Paris coined the word to describe its own time. Such usage is, however, consonant with that of its popularizers. "Nineteenth-century writers were quick to
claim a long pedigree for Bohemia. Murger would trace its ancestors back into classical
Greece, and follow the family tree through the whole of French cultural history. If some
of that genealogy seems fanciful, other parts of it deserve to be taken seriously: medieval
figures like François Villon did share features with modern Bohemians, while poor writers
like the young Diderot and lesser eighteenth-century literary hacks and gutter poets were
still closer in character as well as in time." See Jerrold Seigel, *Bohemian Paris*, 25.
25. *Le Guide historique et anecdotique de Paris*, 189.

Dolet. On this square, which has kept its popular physiognomy, the picturesque market of 'cigarette butts' is still held on certain days," writes Frichet.[26] *Paris et ses environs* comments: "In the center of the square stands the proud statue of *Etienne Dolet,* burned there in 1546. Despite its embellishments, the place Maubert has remained a very picturesque and popular center; it has a clientele of regulars who have nothing in common with the aristocracy. For a long time, one met there dealers in the ends of cigars, who transformed these *butts* into a tobacco savoured by smokers who practiced thrift."[27] When *La Fleur des curiositez de Paris* dwells on the seamy aspect of this place, it singles out the low-class prostitution found there, providing a list of the square's bohemian inhabitants worthy of Marx's *The Eighteenth Brumaire*:

> Day and night, there is drinking, singing, bickering, and sometimes blows. Prowlers, ragpickers, collectors of cigarette butts, pimps and a whole lousy, ragged, pitiable, wretched population haunt the *Père Lunette,* where they find alcohol "stronger than anywhere else" and women of all ages, who like to find a companion for the moment who will buy them a drink.[28]

Nonetheless, the guides insist, this picturesque state is nothing like the squalor that used to reign: "Now embourgeoisified and nicely laid out, adorned, if I dare to call it that, with a deplorable statue of Etienne Dolet who was burned there in 1546, it only vaguely recalls to us this 'plac' Maub'' still visible six or seven years ago, notorious, narrow, lined with old houses with pointed roofs, the haunt of robbers, full of suspicious nooks where the police could throw its nets and be almost sure of catching someone."[29]

When the guides associate the square with the dangerous classes, they summon up a collective representation of the site closer to the square's association with previous insurrectional history than first might seem. The dangerous classes weighed heavily on the imagination of the nineteenth-century bourgeoisie, which viewed them as nefarious instigators of working-class insurrection. Indeed, the Haussmannization of Paris, cleaning up, among other sites, the plac' Maub', was in part motivated by the bourgeoisie's efforts to remove the criminal classes from visible position in the center of Paris.[30] If past political in-

26. Frichet, *Paris et ses merveilles,* 61.
27. Fernand Bournon and Albert Dauzat, *Paris et ses environs,* 53.
28. Charles Fegdal, *La Fleur des curiositez de Paris,* 151.
29. Georges Cain, *Coins de Paris,* 176–179.
30. On this subject see Louis Chevalier's *Classes laborieuses et classes dangereuses.* In "Paris, the Capital of the Nineteenth Century" Benjamin makes a similar observation.

surrection persists only in stone, the dangerous classes persist in living form, although their menace to the social order has been tempered. In the guides' descriptions, they are transformed from dangerous criminals into abject prostitutes and collectors of society's debris.

2. THE SKULL OF JEAN-JACQUES ROUSSEAU, PLACE DU PANTHÉON

After remarking on the power of the place Maubert, Breton's haunting Parisian itinerary takes him to the statue of Rousseau on the place du Panthéon. Previously I emphasized the literary reasons leading Breton to dwell on the uncanny terror that the statue of Rousseau incites. But perhaps historical considerations play a role in Breton's fascination with the statue as well. Rousseau is allied with the radical social aspirations of the French Revolution, and Parisian panoramic literature makes the point that the Panthéon next to Rousseau's statue summons up not only the Republic's veneration of its great men but revolutionary struggles over what relics this structure should contain:

> In 1791, the Constituent Assembly decided that the Panthéon would be consecrated, with the name that it bears today, to receiving the remains of great citizens and had placed on the ornamental front the inscription: *To the great men from the grateful Fatherland,* which the Restoration effaced in order to turn the edifice back over to worship. It became the Panthéon after 1830, Sainte-Geneviève in 1851; finally, since 1885, on the occasion of Victor Hugo's funeral, it has taken back the function and the name which the Constituent Assembly gave to it.[31]

Or, as Cain puts it, "the Panthéon is certainly the Parisian monument which has been the most often baptized, debaptized and rebaptized."[32] These baptisms were mostly by fire, in response to the changing way in which the successive governments that assumed power during France's long century of revolutions monumentalized the transcendent authority providing the ideological basis of their state.

3. THE PORTE SAINT-DENIS AND THE GRANDS BOULEVARDS

After recounting uncanny experiences at his own seedy equivalent to the Panthéon, the Hôtel des Grands Hommes standing opposite, Breton

31. *Les Guides Bleus: Paris et ses environs,* 202.
32. Cain, *Coins de Paris,* 116.

takes us on to something, rather unclear, around the Grands Boulevards, and particularly at the Porte Saint-Denis:

> Meanwhile, you can be sure of meeting me in Paris, of not spending more
> than three days without seeing me come and go, toward the end of the after-
> noon, along the boulevard Bonne-Nouvelle between the *Matin* printing
> office and the boulevard de Strasbourg. I do not know why it should be pre-
> cisely there that my feet take me, that I go almost always without specific
> purpose, without anything decisive but this obscure data, namely that *it*
> [*cela*] (?) will happen there. I hardly see, in this quick trajectory, what could
> constitute for me, even without my knowing it, a magnetic pole in either
> space or time. No: not even the very beautiful and very useless Porte Saint-
> Denis. (*OC*, 661–663; *N*, 32)

The guides make clear that the Porte Saint-Denis was not always useless: "Erected in 1673. In 1830, during the days of 27, 28, and 29 July
which cost Charles X the throne, cobblestones were thrown from the
top of the monument onto the cuirassiers of Maréchal Marmont, and,
during the Revolution of 1848, the June days began by the attack on
the barricades surrounding the gate." [33] The political and often explicitly revolutionary resonance of this monument had, interestingly, long
been encoded in the history of its visual representation, for it served as
backdrop either for a challenge to official power or occasionally for this
power's display throughout the nineteenth century (figs. 9–11).[34]

Insurrectional memories once again haunt a site that disturbs and
fascinates Breton without his being able to state why. This past is a
political past of nineteenth-century class struggle including both the
bourgeois consolidation of 1789 in the revolution of 1830 and the
working-class revolt against the bourgeoisie on the barricades of 1848.
Once again, too, little visible reminder of this past persists in the present, even less reminder, indeed, than at the place Maubert. There Breton
found the statue of Etienne Dolet on which to focus his uncanny sensation. Here Breton's malaise can find no point of reference beyond the
site itself.

In dwelling on the area around the Porte Saint-Denis, Breton displays, as at the place Maubert, his preference for "that little *déclassé*
something we like so much" (*OC*, 670; *N*, 42). He frequents an area

---

33. *Le Guide historique et anecdotique*, 192.
34. As examples I include Prieur's *Alerte de la nuit du 14 au 15 juillet 1789* (Alert
on the night of 14–15 July 1789); the anonymous *Entrée de Louis XVIII à Paris le
3 mai 1814* (Entrance of Louis XVIII into Paris, 3 May 1814); and Lecomte's painting,
Combat de la Porte Saint-Denis, le 28 juillet 1830 (Combat at the Porte Saint-Denis,
28 July 1830). For other examples, see *Les Grands Boulevards*, 228 ff.

9. Prieur. *Alert on the night of 14–15 July 1789 (Alerte de la nuit du 14 au 15 juillet 1789)*. Courtesy of the Musée Carnavalet.

10. Anonymous. *Entrance of Louis XVIII into Paris, 3 May 1814 (Entrée de Louis XVIII à Paris le 3 mai 1814)*. Courtesy of the Musée Carnavalet.

11. Hippolyte Lecomte. Combat of the Porte Saint-Denis, 28 July 1830
(*Combat de la Porte Saint-Denis, le 28 juillet 1830*). Courtesy of the Musée
Carnavalet.

where the insurrectional past has been replaced by a bohemian present,
a fact that *Comment et où s'amuser à Paris* makes evident. A slim text
devoted to a single question, where to find prostitutes in Paris, this
guide narrates the adventures of a young man from the provinces who
inherits a small fortune and comes to Paris to squander it. His worldly-
wise Parisian friend Jean takes him on a tour of the city and, stopping
in a "small street near the Grands Boulevards and the Porte Saint-
Denis," comments on the relatively high-class prostitutes associated
with this site. "The rooms above . . . are comfortably furnished," explains Jacques, and he goes on to tell of the pedicures, manicures, good
food, good linen, day off, and "amant de coeur" the women in these
brothels enjoy.[35]

The degenerate state of the Porte Saint-Denis exemplifies the more
general decay of the surrounding boulevards where Breton wanders,
strangely unnerved and waiting for "it," and where he will eventually

35. Jacques Darys, *Comment et où s'amuser à Paris,* n.p. The style of the text's illustrations and typography locate its time of publication during the 1920s.

have *the* uncanny meeting that crystallizes his text: the encounter with
Nadja. Like the Porte that Breton uses as their emblem, the Boulevards
are currently associated with that prurient term, *pleasure.* If the visitor
"seeks the center of pleasures," *L'Art de circuler dans Paris* tells us, "he
will choose a lodging in that part of the boulevard between the rue
Saint-Denis and the rue Royale."[36] This guide goes on to show, however, that here, as in Breton's other uncanny spots, the bohemian present hides memories of the area's troubled political past and, more precisely, the nineteenth-century consolidation of bourgeois power:

> The Grands Boulevards which before the annexation of 1860 were called
> the interior boulevards measure, from the Bastille to the Madeleine, 4,600
> meters and include the boulevards Beaumarchais, des Filles-du-Calvaire, du
> Temple, Saint-Martin, Saint-Denis, Bonne-Nouvelle, Poissonnière, Mont-
> martre, des Italiens, des Capucines and de la Madeleine.
>
> Each part of this long line of boulevards recalls a historical fact which
> interested the entire world. It is, to speak only of what is close to us: Louis
> XVI going to the place de la Révolution to be guillotined; the passage of
> the allied troops in 1814 and 1815; the funeral rites of general Lamarque
> which opened the Revolution of 1830; the pistol shot before the Ministry
> of Foreign Affairs, boulevard des Capucines, which determined the fall of
> Louis-Philippe; the coup d'état of 1851; the review of Général Trochu before
> 1870, and finally all the events which have left a mark in our history since
> the Franco-Prussian War.[37]

In addition, the Boulevards impel the guidebook writers to summon up
a Parisian topos already encountered at the place Maubert. There the
square's current seedy state was represented as the degraded remnant
of its once formidable criminal past. At the Boulevards, too, the seedy
present is not glossed as the traces of a revolutionary past but rather
lamented as the decline of past celebrity. This glory, however, is of a
rather different sort, for it is that of nineteenth-century chic Paris:

> If the truth be told, only the stores have remained, for the elegant hotels have
> taken themselves elsewhere, the majority of famous cafés have been replaced
> by banks and the theaters do not enjoy the same vogue as before, or at least
> have shared it with movie theaters that purvey "artistic" films which narrate
> adventurous lives and extraordinary crimes.
>
> It was in the nineteenth century and above all towards its middle, that
> the success of the Boulevards was indisputable.[38]

36. *L'Art de circuler dans Paris,* 21. "Or in Montmartre," the guide continues, listing
the area where Breton himself dwells.
37. *L'Art de circuler dans Paris,* 26.
38. *Paris-Guide: Le Guide de la vie à Paris 1925,* 56–57.

As if to illustrate his fondness for sites of decline, Breton ends his section
on the Grands Boulevards by narrating his visits to movie theaters offering precisely the sort of films which elicit the guide's sighs. *The Grip
of the Octopus* is the title of the movie he discusses in some detail, and
while this phrase may evoke Hugo's *Les Travailleurs de la mer,* its lurid
scenario in the flier included among *Nadja*'s visual artifacts is of a different sort. "Fifth episode: The Eye of Satan," the text begins, and continues, "What a horrible situation was that of Ruth and Carter both
carried along towards the abyss in the car uncoupled from the train!"
(*OC,* 665; *N,* 35).

4. LE THÉÂTRE MODERNE, PASSAGE DE L'OPÉRA

In the remainder of the prologue Breton uses the city as backdrop
rather than as the focus of the uncanny sensation itself. Nonetheless,
with a proliferation of guides at hand I cannot resist reconstituting the
historical condition of these subsequent sites at the moment Breton
visited them. While such reconstitution digresses momentarily from the
next step in our reconstructive quest, a consideration of how Parisian
panoramic literature represents the past ghosts associated with Breton's
uncanny experiences of Parisian places in his adventures with Nadja,
it is not tangential to the argument. Already, we have seen Breton's
fondness for sites not only with an insurrectional past but also with a
bohemian past and present. A consideration of the historical specificity
of the remainder of the uncanny sites collected in the prologue shows
that they too exhibit "that little *déclassé* something we like so much"
(*OC,* 670; *N,* 42). And Breton's fascination with bohemian activity is
a crucial component to *Nadja*'s attack on orthodox Marxist notions of
praxis.

Moving west on the boulevards, Breton takes us inside an adjoining
liminal structure in what constitutes his homage to Aragon's *The Paris
Peasant.* "The 'Théâtre Moderne,' located at the end of the now destroyed Passage de l'Opéra, aside from the fact that the plays put on
there had still less importance, corresponded perfectly to my ideal [of
"the nether regions of the mind"], in this sense" (*OC,* 663; *N,* 37–38).
The guides consider the arcades a *ne plus ultra* of degeneration, infinitely more decrepit than the boulevards, for certain boulevards to the
west of the city retain something of their elegance (these are *not* the
boulevards frequented by Nadja and Breton): "The boulevards des
Italiens, des Capucines and de la Madeleine have remained, whatever

one may say, very Parisian. Without a doubt the vogue of the arcades, where society liked to meet as at the Palais-Royal, is finished, without a doubt the Café Riche, the ice-cream parlor Tortoni, the Maison Dorée, the Cafés Anglais and Helder are only memories." [39]

If all guides concur on the defunct and highly bohemian state of the arcades in general, the "passage without passerbys," as an early twentieth-century guide put it, specific discussion of the Passage de l'Opéra at the time that Breton wrote was hard to find (leaving aside its eloquent representation by Aragon).[40] The only nonfictional description of the Passage de l'Opéra available was written ten years after the arcade's demolition in 1924. Rather than supplementing literature with nonliterary conceptions of Parisian reality, Charles Fegdal's 1934 *Dans notre vieux Paris* bears witness to the documentary function of Aragon's description of the arcades in *The Paris Peasant*. This text mentions precisely those aspects of the arcade Aragon preserves; Fegdal writes of the Théâtre Moderne:

> I leave Mr. Gélis and his historic boutique. The *Galerie du Baromètre* is il-luminated by one thousand electric lights. There, in its depths, sparkles the luminous sign for the *Théâtre Moderne*. A large sign announces to us that *Fruit d'amour* is being played there; we read these suggestive lines: *With the prettiest girls of Paris. The exciting girls* [in English]. I do not know if the English words defy honesty; but, not trusting words, we will not enter the *Théâtre Moderne*.[41]

5. MONTMARTRE: THÉÂTRE DES DEUX-MASQUES, RUE FONTAINE, AND THE CHAT NOIR

Early on in *Nadja* Breton moves his residence from the rue Soufflot next to the Panthéon to the Montmartre area. Breton's next stop in his prologue's itinerary of unsettling Parisian places is the area that he has chosen as home. "But for me really to descend into the mind's nether regions [*les bas-fonds de l'esprit*] where it is no longer a question of night's falling and rising again (and is that day?) means to follow the rue Fontaine back to the 'Théâtre des Deux-Masques'" (*OC*, 668–669; *N*, 39–40). Breton goes on to describe a play staged at this theater, *Les Détraquées*, evocative of Lautréamont.[42] When *The American Guide to*

39. *Paris-Guide: Le Guide de la vie à Paris*, 58. The abandoned state of the arcades is well-captured by the photograph that introduces my second chapter (see fig. 2).

40. Hector-Hogier, *Paris à la fourchette: Curiosités parisiennes*, 24.

41. Charles Fegdal, *Dans notre vieux Paris*, 156.

42. Bonnet comments: "The author of the play was the actor Pierre Palau, advised by the eminent neurologist Joseph Babinski, who had been briefly in 1917 Breton's teacher" (*OC*, 1535).

Paris lists the "Théâtre des Deux-Masques," it gives ample evidence that Breton's description is rooted in historical fact. Placing it under the rubric "*Speciality Theaters,*" the guide writes: "These theaters are of a very special character, giving plays that are unsuitable for children or very young people, as well as for people who are easily shocked."[43]

Breton allies the Montmartre area not only with representations of the *bas-fonds de l'esprit* but also with the early surrealist interior explorations to discover what these *bas-fonds* contain. He situates there Robert Desnos's heroic sleep-talking, which was later to be "discredited" as a faked effect. "It is evening, in my studio over the Cabaret du Ciel," he writes in a section sandwiched between the uncanny place du Panthéon and the Grands Boulevards. "Outside, someone is shouting: 'Come one, come all, come to the Chat Noir!' And Desnos continues to see what I do not see, what I see only as he gradually shows it to me" (OC, 661; N, 31).

When guides mention the current state of Montmartre, they confirm not only that it is bohemian but that it is a version of bohemia in decline. In elegiac tones the guides point out sadly that the authentically artistic and socially alternative ambiance of the late nineteenth century has turned into prostitution, crime, and cheap thrills. The dilapidated state of current Montmartre extends even to the syntax of the description of the *Chat Noir* in English guides of the time:

> The name it bears was once mode by illustrious its founders [sic] who were no less than Rodolphe Salis Sapeck, Maurice Donnay, Edmond Haraucourt, Georges d'Esparbès, André Gill, Moréas, Alphonse Allais, etc. In this cabaret, then situated in the rue Victor-Massé, passed most of our contemporary poets and writers. It is still present in the memory of those who saw it in its splendor.[44]

The Pleasure Guide writes of the 1927 *Cabaret du Ciel* above which Breton lives:

> The door opens, quite luminous and white, decorated with a colossal plaster angel.
>   A beadle introduces you beneath the vaults of a gothic cathedral resounding now with the strumming of a piano, now with the sounds of organs.
>   Seraphs in curly golden wings, crowned with roses, having light wings fastened to their backs, their legs in pink tights and their feet in sandals, invite you to sit down to the "celestial banquet", a long table at which you are served with the "sacred cup", the "*divine chalice*", the "nectar", the

43. *The American Guide to Paris,* 25.
44. *Pleasure Guide to Paris,* 105.

"ambrosia" of the gods in the shape of glasses of beer, syrup, or brandy-cherries.

Father Onésime, in a velvet jerkin, with a holy-watersprinkler in his hand, officiates as the beadle.

He it is who rings the wooden bell (Joséphine), who cuts short the preaching of the praying father with irreverent jokes; who leads round the idol of the Golden Calf (the god Porcus), and exhorts the faithful to lie prostrate at the foot of the Swine set up like an altar at the further end of the church.

After sundry burlesque ceremonies, the "faithful" who have "purified their souls" are at last permitted to witness the *celestial visions*: houris, bayadères, almees, and at last to go up to Heaven.

Heaven is *on the first floor.*

Saint Peter, impersonated by a robust fellow armed with a long key, heads the procession of the elect, and a policeman, an angelic . . . [sic] guardian of the peace, closes it.

You step into a wide grotto from the gilt vault of which hang myriads of gold stalactites.

Angels appear suspended in space. Unexpected and charming transformations take place before your eyes. You really seem to be carried away far from this gloomy earth of ours, into ethereal and serene regions where all women are angels! (The show lasts about 30 or 45 minutes).[45]

6. SAINT-OUEN: LE MARCHÉ AUX PUCES

Breton's final site of uncanny experience in the prologue is a place of marginal social practice: "Again quite recently . . . I went with a friend one Sunday to the 'flea market' at Saint-Ouen (I go there often, in search of those objects that can be found nowhere else, outmoded, fragmented, useless, almost incomprehensible, *perverse* in short, in the sense that I give to the word and that I like)" (*OC,* 676; *N, 52;* emphasis added). The flea market at the time that Breton writes is not only known for its socially marginal character but is itself at a particularly marginal moment in its history. In 1926 the market threatened to become a thing of the past because the fortifications where it was situated were being demolished to make room for Parisian urban sprawl. André Warnod tells us:

"The End of the Flea-Market"—the demolition of the fortifications is under way. The embankments covered with grass are disemboweled and on the banks is a whole litter of rails and tip-trucks. The first result of these projects has been to oblige the flea-market, which took place at the Porte Clignan-

45. *Pleasure Guide to Paris,* 102–103.

court every Sunday morning, to move out and go install itself somewhere else.[46]

THE PLACE DAUPHINE:
"'THE DEAD, THE DEAD!'"

Strolling through *Nadja*'s prologue with the guides reveals Breton to experience his uncanny sensations at sites where ghosts of past insurrectional activity cluster, sites frequented by bohemians both in the present and in the past. In addition, Breton's narrator associates his uncanny sensations with contemporary aspects of the site where the obscured past persists in disfigured form. At the place Maubert Breton fixates on the statue of Etienne Dolet, the only visible reminder of "certain riots"; at the Panthéon he turns to Jean-Jacques Rousseau. What particularly frightens Breton in the latter case is the superimposition of pieces of chopped wood on his skull. Once we remember that the Panthéon is a Parisian monument associated with revolutionary violence, the association of hacked wood with heads conjures up the guillotine. When Breton discusses the attractions of the Boulevards and the Porte Saint-Denis, he can find no visible detail on which to fixate. It is important to note, however, that in his very failure to locate the source of his uncanny sensation, Breton confirms, albeit negatively, that the haunting power of these sites may come from their relation to temporal passage and spatial location: "I hardly see . . . what could constitute for me, even without my knowing it, a magnetic pole, in either space or *time*" (*OC*, 663; *N*, 32; emphasis added). Is this invisible, haunting "it" the magnetic north pole toward which Benjamin steers?

The traces of the insurrectional past in the uncanny present are rather oblique and would probably not even be noticed, were it not for Breton's subsequent adventures with his surrealist muse. We turn to the evening on the place Dauphine, adjacent to the Pont-Neuf, which is *Nadja*'s most extended narrative of the Parisian uncanny. "This place Dauphine is certainly one of the most profoundly secluded places I know, one of the worst wastelands in Paris. Whenever I have happened

46. André Warnod, *Les Plaisirs de la rue,* 33. For a more contemporary history of the flea market, see Jean Bedel: "During the last days of 1925, the 26th of December more precisely, a decree declares the old zone of the fortifications unhealthy. 1926 will not be a good year for the junk sellers. The police conduct new expulsions. Once more, the marginal ragpickers disperse, seeking new locations on the sidewalks of the rue des Rosiers, the rue Paul Bert, and the rue Jules Vallès." Jean Bedel, *Les Puces ont cent ans,* 85.

12.   J.-A. Boiffard. "We have our dinner served outside by the wine
seller . . ." (*Nous nous faisons servir dehors par le marchand de vins . . .*).
Illus. in *Nadja*.

to be there, I have felt the desire to go somewhere else gradually abandon me, I have had to argue with myself to get free from a very gentle
embrace, that is too pleasantly insistent, and, finally, crushing" (*OC,*
695; N, 80). For Nadja, closer to the things than Breton, the frightening
lure of this spot is clear. "She is disturbed by the thought of what has
already occurred in this square and will occur here again. Where only
two or three couples are at this moment disappearing into the shadows,
she seems to see a crowd. 'And the dead, the dead!' " (*OC, 695; N,* 83).

Parisian panoramic literature on the place Dauphine suggests that
these dead possess a precise historical identity. The guides comment,
first of all, on the square's melancholy atmosphere, which contrasts
markedly with its once lively past. Despite its deserted quality, however,
the guides stress that memories of this past have not entirely disap-
peared. André Billy makes the point most eloquently: "The place
Dauphine, like the place des Vosges, seems to doze and relive, in a
dream, its former life. Its melancholy is accentuated when the leaves of
its chestnut trees fall around its benches where no one ever sits" (Breton
and Nadja go there in October, and Breton includes a photo of the site
making evident its abandoned quality; see fig. 12).[47] After luxuriating
in the deserted atmosphere reigning at the square, Billy, like later
guidebook writers, proceeds to describe the colorful events the square
once witnessed. He mentions the 1314 burning of the Knight Templar
Jacques de Molay; he notes the bohemians who congregated there, the
charlatans, *badauds,* sellers of dubious wares, and the generally motley
crowd who enjoyed the performances of Tabarin and Mondor.

The guides link this place not only to protorevolutionary figures like
Jacques de Molay but also to shades directly connected with the Revolution, with "these two houses which are one of the jewels of Paris, one
of which was inhabited by Madame Roland."[48] When they discuss the
remainder of the island, they associate the Conciergerie primarily with
the condemned Marie-Antoinette and Madame Roland, although they
sometimes also mention other illustrious revolutionary dead who were
both perpetrators and victims of the Terror: Desmoulins, Danton,
Hébert, Fabre d'Eglantine, and Robespierre.[49] Multiple ghosts of revolutionary violence moreover descend on the place Dauphine from
all sides, from the Pont-Neuf, where "the Revolution tore down the

47. Billy, *Paris vieux et neuf,* II, 96.
48. Billy, *Paris vieux et neuf,* II, 95–96.
49. See texts ranging from the 1907 *Coins de Paris* to the 1924 *Les Guides Bleus: Paris et ses environs.*

bronze statue of King Henri IV" to the Palais de Justice burned by the Commune.[50]

Armed with this knowledge, let us examine more closely the seemingly trivial incidents that inspire Breton and Nadja with such dread.

> Nadja's gaze now surveys the surrounding houses. "Do you see that window over there? It's black, like all the rest. Look hard. In a minute it's going to light up. It will be red." The minute passes. The window lights up. There are, in fact, red curtains. (I am sorry, but I am unable to do anything about the fact that this may exceed the limits of credibility . . . I confine myself to *granting* that this window, being black, then became red, that is all.) I confess that here fear grips me, as it also starts to grip Nadja. (*OC*, 695; *N*, 83)

Breton suggests that the explanation for his uncanny experience may be sought in the fact that Nadja once lived opposite the house, in the Hôtel Henri-IV, "which faces the house just discussed," he comments, "this still for those who like easy solutions" (*OC*, 695; *N*, 84). But for those who like more difficult solutions, might not the uncanny derive from the lurking ghosts of the place who start to come alive under Nadja's gaze? The color of the window that so frightens Nadja and Breton is red, the color of revolutionary violence, and it flares up at the site where a victim of the Terror and revolutionary, Madame Roland, once lived.

Nadja then starts to recall a moment when she might have committed suicide by falling from her window in the Hôtel Henri-IV: "There was also a voice saying: 'You will die, you will die'" (*OC*, 697; *N*, 84). Referring to the guides, we discover that the name of her hotel evokes not so much a king as his image that the 1789 revolution destroyed. It may once again seem far-fetched to associate Nadja's fear of death with the surfacing of past Parisian revolution. But what of the events that follow?

"I think it is high time to leave this site," declares Breton, as Nadja's bizarre behavior disturbs him more and more (*OC*, 697; *N*, 84). They walk along the quais: "The length of the quais, I feel her trembling all over. She is the one who wanted to go back toward the Conciergerie" (*OC*, 697; *N*, 84). In front of this structure Nadja allies herself and Breton with those who, like Madame Roland, were put to death during the Terror: "It's not there . . . But, tell me, why do you have to go to prison? What will you have done? I have been to prison too. Who was I? It was centuries ago. And you, then, who were you?" (*OC*, 697; *N*,

50. Fegdal, *Dans notre vieux Paris*, 146.

84). Nadja makes her identification with those condemned by the Revolution even more precise on the following page: "She wonders who she might have been, in Marie-Antoinette's circle. The footsteps of passers-by make her shudder at length. I am concerned, and taking her hands away [from the iron railing] one after the other, I end up making her follow me" (*OC*, 697; *N*, 85).

But Breton's fear does not disappear, and neither does Nadja's strange behavior. Thinking to calm Nadja by leading her away from the places that so frighten her, Breton's subsequent choice of route rather stumbles once more on the ghosts the uncanny place Dauphine evoked: "The bridge crossed, we head toward the Louvre. Nadja continues to be distracted. To bring her back to me, I recite a poem by Baudelaire but the inflections of my voice frighten her again" (*OC*, 697; *N*, 85). If Breton's Baudelaire so alarms Nadja, it may be because the recitation of Baudelaire at the Louvre continues to call up the suppressed ghosts hovering around the place Dauphine. What other poem would better suit this site than Baudelaire's "Le Cygne" (The Swan), a poem Breton explicitly quotes in the last section of *Nadja*, although he does not acknowledge its source. "I am not one," he tells us, "to meditate on what becomes of 'a city's form' " (*OC*, 749; *N*, 154). This phrase comes from the famous lines of "Le Cygne" in which Baudelaire laments Haussmann's reconstruction of a site of bohemian and insurrectionary activity following the revolution of 1848: "Old Paris is no more (a city's form / Changes more quickly, alas! than a mortal's heart)."[51]

The final instance of Nadja's fear around the place Dauphine responds yet again to traces of past social disruption associated with the square, although it is the disruption worked by bohemians rather than political revolutionaries. Already on the right bank, leaning on a balustrade by the Seine, Nadja looks out over the river in the direction of the left bank and the Ile de la Cité from which she has just come. Distraught, she asks: "That hand, that hand on the Seine, why that hand which is flaming over the water? It's true that fire and water are the

51. Charles Baudelaire, "Le Cygne," in *Oeuvres complètes*, I, 85. For a more realistic description of the former life of this place, see Balzac's *La Cousine Bette*, or Jules Champfleury enumerating "sellers of engravings, picture sellers, sellers of old books, conjurers, sellers of all kinds of birds. The spot was marvelous for minds who, liking life, movement, curios and curiosities, chat in browsing in front of prints, mechanically open old books, and do not want to be idle with their hands, ears or eyes." From *Grandes figures d'hier et d'aujourd'hui* (1861), quoted in Pierre Citron, *La Poésie de Paris dans la littérature française de Rousseau à Baudelaire*, II, 312. Breton follows his citation of Baudelaire with a reference to Flaubert's *L'Education sentimentale*, which represents some of the events of 1848 evoked above.

same thing. But what does that hand mean? How do you interpret it? Let me look at that hand. Why do you want us to leave? What are you afraid of? You think I'm very ill, don't you? I'm not ill" (*OC*, 697; *N*, 85–86). While Breton's fear at Nadja's hallucination might again be linked to its sheer bizarreness, the hallucination is also rich with literary allusion. Fixating on a demonic hand over the Seine, Nadja evokes Gérard de Nerval's post-Revolutionary fantastic tale of long-ago bohemian life set on the place Dauphine, "La Main enchantée," which takes a demonic dismembered hand as its central conceit.

Nadja's oblique contact with the ghosts of Parisian insurrection continues throughout her strolls in the company of Breton. Repeatedly experiencing hallucinations that recall Parisian revolution, Nadja usually identifies herself and Breton with forces across the political spectrum that lost out. These hallucinations include her subsequent association of Breton, on the night at the place Dauphine, with "le dauphin," the crown-prince, after she has associated herself with Marie-Antoinette; her strange adventures at the subway stop bearing the name of one of the Revolution's first martyrs (Lepeletier); her perception of evil energy at the quai that was home to the Enlightenment thinker apotheosized by revolutionary ideology, Voltaire; and her final appearance in Breton's narrative of their joint adventures as the *frondeuse*, Madame de Chevreuse.

CLOSED FOR REPAIRS

Although Nadja is "closer to the things" than Breton, the repressed reality she touches would not seem to be one fusing dream and waking life into a future utopian state of surrealist revolution. Indeed, this reality does not belong to the future of revolutionary transformation at all. In *Pariser Passagen I* Benjamin assessed surrealism's relation to revolutionary activity in the following terms: "Surrealism—wave of dreams—new art of strolling. New past of the nineteenth century—Paris its classic site. . . . Its [Fashion's] tall loutish clerk, death, measures the century by the ell and, in order to economize, himself serves as the mannequin and personally leads the 'clearance sale' that in French is called 'revolution'" (*PW*, 1000). Breton's and particularly Nadja's contact with Parisian ghosts is in keeping with Benjamin's assertion. From Madame Roland to Madame de Chevreuse, Nadja contacts figures testifying to failed scenarios of violent revolution.

Breton turns against violent revolution not only when he contacts

13.   J.-A. Boiffard. "The *Humanité* bookstore . . ." (*La librairie de* L'Humanité . . .). Illus. in *Nadja.*

the distant Parisian past but also when he remarks in *Nadja*'s concluding section on his disappointment with the unfulfilled promise of his
earlier uncanny sensation at the Porte Saint-Denis: "While the boulevard Bonne-Nouvelle, after having—unfortunately during my absence
from Paris, in the course of the magnificent days of riot called 'Sacco-
Vanzetti'—seemed to come up to my expectations in showing itself
truly as one of the great strategic points that I seek in matters of disorder and about which I persist in believing that references are obscurely
given me . . . while the boulevard Bonne-Nouvelle, the façades of its
movie-theaters repainted, has subsequently become immobilized for
me, as if the Porte Saint-Denis had just closed" (*OC*, 748; *N*, 152–154).
In associating his turn away from the Porte Saint-Denis with the failure
of the 1927 Sacco and Vanzetti riots, Breton allies this turn with an
event produced by orthodox Marxism, as part of its program of social
change. The failed demonstrations in support of the condemned American workers were organized by the French Communists, although they
also exhibited much spontaneous participation, and were to have been
the spark that ignited a more general social revolt.

   In the conclusion to *Nadja*, then, Breton adds Communist praxis to
his text's clearance sale of an insurrectional tradition.[52] And the status
of Communist praxis was fraught with urgency for him at the time he
wrote *Nadja*. After reading Trotsky's *Lenin* in August 1925, Breton
gave much thought to the compatibility of orthodox Marxist notions
of revolution and the "révolution surréaliste." Breton's interest in practical Marxism was also encouraged by surrealism's solidarity with the
Communists in opposing the 1925 Moroccan war. In late 1925 and
1926 the surrealists debated whether to join the Communist party.
While some members of the group coauthored Communist political
tracts appearing in *L'Humanité* and collaborated with the Communist
group around the periodical *Clarté*, others were vehemently opposed
to what they considered a tendentious politicization of the surrealist
program. Matters came to a head in a series of heated discussions occurring late in the fall of 1926 and resulted in the voluntary emigration of
Antonin Artaud and the exclusion of Philippe Soupault. Of Breton's
political position in this debate, Bonnet writes: "Agreement with the
Communist program of political and social revolution, the will to main-

52. Theoreticians across the political spectrum argue that the history of Parisian insurrection provides a crucial model for traditional Marxist protocols for revolutionary
change. See François Furet, *Marx et la Révolution française*, as well as Laclau and
Mouffe's use of Furet in *Hegemony and Socialist Strategy*.

tain the independence of surrealist research in the area it claims as its own—the mental realm, language—, hesitation over joining the Party" (*OC*, 1717).

Breton finally did sign up in January 1927, despite suspicion on both sides. The experience was brief and bitter. Throughout the spring he attempted to participate in the gas cell to which he had been assigned, but by the time he sat down in the summer of 1927 to write *Nadja*, he had abandoned this attempt at orthodox Communist praxis (although he continued his efforts to find some common ground between the French Communist Party and the surrealist movement until his exclusion from the International Congress of Writers for the Defense of Culture in 1935): "I was asked to make a report on the Italian situation to this special committee of the 'gas cell,' which made it clear to me that I was to stick strictly to the statistical facts (steel production, etc.) *and above all no ideology.* I couldn't." [53]

"I couldn't": *Nadja*'s collective uncanny may be read as Breton's implicit defense of this impossibility. For in these experiences Breton finds confirmation for a haunting notion of subjectivity which calls into question the possibility of establishing an enlightened and conscious subject outside of ideology in several ways. Posing the problem of whether there exists a self-present subject at all, Breton also suggests the conscious subject as the locus where the reigning ideology reproduces itself. Ghosts endowed with powers of resistance only surge up in moments when the subject's conscious experience is disrupted by forces coming from a mysterious unconscious realm. In addition, the collective uncanny suggests that history is composed of temporal strata layered as in the situations of individual psychic repression at issue in psychoanalysis. This layering substantially complicates the linear notion of historical process that underwrites the teleologically oriented praxis of the French Communist Party. In Breton's theoretical exposition in the remainder of his Parisian prose trilogy, he will explicitly brandish the uncanny *rencontre* against these aspects of orthodox Marxism.

THE RAGPICKER AS REVOLUTIONARY

Nadja turns against a Communist notion of praxis not only in Breton's close-out sale of revolution but also through direct attack. Breton

53. *Second Manifesto of Surrealism*, in *M*, 143. I have altered Seaver and Lane's translation of the ending to this passage which runs: "*and above all not get involved with ideology.* I couldn't do it." See *OC*, 795–796, for the original French.

makes the following comments on the dreary aspect of the street at the end of the working day: "The offices and workshops were beginning to empty out, from the top to the bottom of buildings doors were closing, people on the sidewalk were shaking hands, already there were more people in the street. I observed without meaning to faces, clothes, ways of walking. No, it was not yet these who would be found ready to make the Revolution" (OC, 683; N, 63–64). When Nadja defends the working class as "good people," Breton grows vehement: "I know that at a factory furnace, or in front of one of those inexorable machines which all day long, at a few seconds' interval, impose the repetition of the same gesture, or anywhere else under the least acceptable orders, in a cell or before a firing squad, one can still feel free, but it is not the martyrdom one undergoes which creates this freedom" (OC, 687; N, 68–69). Rather, against the Marxist interest in mobilizing the proletariat, Breton stresses the need for individual, tactical disruptions of reigning social orders in what he calls "unchaining." In doing so Breton disqualifies the class from which orthodox Marxism expects revolution, for he suggests as precondition to praxis the subject's being freed from the material conditions of industrial production. Socially transformative activity becomes instead the province of subjects who no longer define themselves according to their work:

> It is, I mean, a perpetual unchaining [désenchaînement]: yet for this unchaining to be possible, constantly possible, chains must not crush us, as they do many of those you mention. But it is also, and perhaps, in human terms, much more, the relatively long but marvelous series of steps which man is allowed to make unchained. Do you suppose these people are capable of taking these steps? Have they even the time for them? Have they the heart? Good people, you said, yes, good like those who get themselves killed in wars, isn't that what you mean? Enough talk of heroes: a lot of unhappy people and a few poor imbeciles. (OC, 687; N, 69)

Associating these moments of disruption with what he terms the "marvelous," Breton transfers to the realm of politics a prime interest of surrealism from its inception, an interest that surrealism itself took over from the Gothic tradition. In the first Manifesto Breton comments on the marvelous that "it partakes in some obscure way of a sort of general revelation only the fragments of which come down to us: they are the romantic ruins, the modern mannequin. . . . In these areas which make us smile, there is still portrayed the incurable human restlessness, and this is why I take them into consideration" (M, 16).

When Breton chooses the word désenchaînement for social praxis, he makes clear the polemical thrust of his vision of revolutionary activity. He plays on the word *chaîne,* in French at once assembly line and chain, to twist Marx's revolutionary call to the workers at the end of the *Manifesto of the Communist Party.* For Breton the proletarians cannot rise up and cast off their chains because of the *enchaînement* in which they are caught. In addition, Breton uses this word's polysemia to give a conceptual turn to his dislocating twist on an orthodox Marxist revolutionary schema. *Enchaînement* is a word resonating not only on the material level but also on the conceptual level, as the *enchaînement* of ideas; the disruption of dominant conceptual structures is an oft-stated goal of surrealist revolution.

If Breton appropriates the Marxist liberatory language of "unchaining," then, it is to displace Marxism's vision of the working class rising up and casting off its chains. And throughout *Nadja* Breton is on the trail of activities of unchaining which will unleash powers hidden in the humdrum of daily life. The text's privileged example of surrealist unchaining is Breton and Nadja's marvelous series of steps, instigated by the unchained subjectivity of Nadja. This promenade defies logic, convention, and the workday world and stumbles on objects of startling beauty. In addition, in an aspect of Breton's unchaining important for Benjamin, marvelous steps encounter ghosts of the past associated with revolution and bohemia.

Why bohemia as well as revolution? The answer to this question helps explain Breton's fondness for sites where bohemia has persisted from the past down to *Nadja*'s present, which is not the case of the revolutionary tradition. Breton, moreover, draws attention to this fondness by filling his texts with bohemia's subjects.[54] Nadja, the mad woman-prostitute-drugseller-clairvoyante-artist, is only one among the novel's cast of bohemian characters that includes avant-garde artists, theatrical and cabaret performers, a drunk, a seller of illicit pornographic postcards, a clairvoyant, and a mysterious *femme de lettres.* Living on the margins of society and engaging in activities that do not conform to the processes of production valorized by Marxist theory, bohemians have long had a dubious status in orthodox Marxism, starting with Marx's celebrated representation:

> Alongside decayed *roués* with dubious means of subsistence and of dubious origin, alongside ruined and adventurous offshoots of the bourgeoisie, were

54. For a discussion of Bataille's interest in bohemia, see Peter Stallybrass, "Marx and Heterogeneity: Thinking the Lumpenproletariat."

> vagabonds, discharged soldiers, discharged jailbirds, escaped galley slaves, swindlers, mountebanks, *lazzaroni*, pickpockets, tricksters, gamblers, *maquereaus*, brothel keepers, porters, *literati*, organ-grinders, ragpickers, knife grinders, tinkers, beggars—in short, the whole indefinite, disintegrated mass, thrown hither and thither, which the French term *la bohème*; from this kindred element Bonaparte formed the core of the Society of December 10.[55]

Marx did not trust this fragmented, non-productive, and displaced social group to ally itself in stable fashion with an existing class interest, and it was dubious that bohemia constituted a class of its own.[56] But precisely its marginal relation to capitalist processes of production endears bohemia to Breton. In its *Lumpen* constitution and practices, bohemia embodies the unchaining of social hierarchies that surrealism seeks.

It is important that the only designated revolutionary in *Nadja* is a bohemian, the flea-market seller, Fanny Beznos. When Breton first meets Beznos, "a very merry young woman," at Saint-Ouen, he observes her talking to a worker "who listens to her, it seems, with delight," and he remarks:

> Extremely cultivated, she has no objection to discussing her literary tastes with us, which tend towards Shelley, Nietzsche and Rimbaud. Spontaneously, she even speaks to us of the surrealists, and Louis Aragon's *The Paris Peasant*, which she has been unable to finish, the variations on the word Pessimism having stopped her. All her remarks indicate a great revolutionary faith. (*OC*, 676–679; *N*, 55)

The disruption worked by the flea market is to some extent economic. Sellers who support themselves through buying and selling used goods refuse to engage in the productive activity of the *chaîne*. The flea marketplace is situated outside the institutionalized paths of economic exchange as well. But flea-market objects particularly attract Breton for the conceptual *désenchaînement* they work. Breton tells us that they are "objects that can be found nowhere else, outmoded, fragmented, useless, almost incomprehensible, perverse in short, in the sense that I give to the word, and that I like" (*OC*, 676; *N*, 52). By emphasizing perversion, from the Latin *pervertere*, to overturn, Breton chooses a word that

55. Marx, *The Eighteenth Brumaire*, 75.
56. For a historical discussion of bohemia's political affiliations, see Seigel's *Bohemian Paris*, particularly his chapters on the relation between bohemia and the revolutions of 1848 and 1871. The bohemian involvement, Seigel suggests, was ambivalent: "To Marx, the real, the working-class, Paris of the Commune was not Bohemian. So it was not. . . . Yet in fact there was a Bohemian side to the Commune" (p. 185).

more closely approaches his flea-market vision of social change than
does the word *revolution*. In a practice encapsulating his more general
flânerie, Breton in both *Nadja* and *L'Amour fou* visits the flea market
to find objects freed from the drudgery of being useful, hoping that in
this state they will give access to forces hidden from daily life. The flea
market becomes one of the dream sites within the everyday; "the objects that, between the lassitude of some and the desire of others, go
off to dream at the antique fair" is how Breton puts it in *L'Amour fou*
(*AF,* 41; *ML,* 28).[57]

The attraction of bohemia for surrealism derives in addition from
another of the features of surrealism which made the movement distasteful to orthodox Marxists. From its opening *Manifesto* surrealism
is fascinated by the socially transformative potential of repressed libidinal forces; one of its rallying cries is to unleash such forces on existing
social orders. Bohemia has had privileged links to society's erotic, often
illicit urges throughout its history.[58] In keeping with these links, Breton
represents many of the bohemian subjects that attract him throughout
his Parisian trilogy as agents of libidinal unchaining with socially disruptive effect.

Given Breton's assertive heterosexuality, most of the subjects are
women, and this use of feminine representation constitutes one notorious ideological blind spot that Breton shares with many of his male surrealist cohorts. While he privileges women's representations as embodiments of socially disruptive libidinal energy, this embodiment is too
often inseparable from an exploitation and misogyny all the more ob-
jectionable given women's marginalization within the actual workings
of the movement.[59] An appreciation of the Marxist stakes of high surrealism allows us to put surrealism's treatment of women into historical
perspective in two ways.[60] One looks backward: Surrealism's marginalization of women from its own activity at the same moment that it con-

57. I follow Caws here verbatim.
58. In Breton's subsequent theoretical writings he will try to reconcile Marxism with
his interest in unchaining libidinal forces, speculating that the seemingly differentiated
fields of libidinal and economic production may in fact turn out to be one.
59. In *Subversive Intent* Susan Suleiman explores the problems posed by women and
the feminine in modern avant-garde movements. Suleiman's insightful discussion of
Nadja and *Nadja*'s feminist rewriting by Marguerite Duras in *The Ravishing of Lol V.
Stein* are particularly relevant here. See also Mary Ann Caws, "Ladies Shot and Painted:
Female Embodiments in Surrealist Art," in *The Female Body in Western Culture,* ed.
Susan Suleiman. On women's experience in the surrealist movement, see Mary Ann Caws
et al., *Surrealism and Women.*
60. Other than by taking account of the gender ideology of the time; it is sometimes
forgotten, for example, that women could not vote during the heyday of surrealism.

stitutes them as emblems of its power has been characteristic of a Jacobin-inspired revolutionary tradition from the moment the Jacobins themselves first threw women out of the political arena. The other perspective looks forward, to the historical legacy of surrealism's politicized unchaining even for feminist theory. To speak of this legacy entails first a brief comment on the contribution of surrealism to the notion of subversion, which recently has enjoyed such popularity in the American academic left.

After over a decade, subversion is losing its prestige; touting it as a political practice all too often seems like prescribing snakeoil for gaping social wounds. The pressing critical questions, we have started to feel, are elsewhere (nothing is so profoundly anti-erotic as the recently outmoded, Benjamin remarks), for example in exploring the complex relation of the aesthetic to other forms of social production rather than in denying its specificity or simplistically exalting its effect. I suspect moreover that the death-knell of subversion has, at least for the moment, been sounded with the fracturing of the Reagan-Bush right. Alleviating in some measure the academic left's sense of social and political marginalization, this fracturing removes a key factor in the appeal of subversion to the politically engaged wing of American critical postmodernism throughout the 1980s. In the context of discussing Bretonian unchaining, the point to be made is that postmodern articulations of subversion owe a debt to surrealism's use of psychoanalysis to devise unorthodox strategies of political resistance. These efforts have been transmitted to politicized postmodernism through a genealogy that is far from straightforward, including, first and foremost, the French theoretical avant-garde of the sixties and seventies (as well as the American reception of surrealism by the Beats—Breton lived in Greenwich Village during the Second World War). Thus, for example, surrealism's politicized application of psychoanalysis comes down to postmodern accounts of subversion through Michel de Certeau's reworking of surrealism in his own interest in the borderline between psychoanalysis and Marxism. De Certeau's links to surrealism have been appreciated as his obvious debt to the Collège de Sociologie, and above all to Bataille. But in the case of tactics de Certeau's view more resembles Bretonian unchaining than the equivalent therapeutic unleashing of the forces of the unconscious onto existing social order prescribed by Bataille. For Bataille this unleashing takes the form of a radically transgressive sublime. As, most famously, "The Notion of Expenditure [*dépense*]" makes clear, Bataillean subversion extols complete negation, the encouraging of a generalized collapse of economies. Both Breton and de Certeau, in contrast, privilege shifting and individual or small-scale moments of intervention modeled on psychoanalytic accounts of how material comes to expression in situations of repression and censorship: jokes, dreams, parapraxes.

De Certeau nods to the surrealist genealogy of tactics in his rhetoric, which echoes high surrealism's privileged rhetoric of profane illumination.[61] Writing of one example of tactics, "the art of dealing blows," de Certeau asserts: "By procedures which Freud clarifies in speaking of the joke, it combines elements boldly brought together [*rapprochés*] to insinuate the flash [*l'éclair*] of something else in the language of a site and to strike the receiver. Zig-zags, bursts, cracks, and lucky finds [*trouvailles*] in the grid of a system, consumers' practices of everyday life are the practical equivalents to the joke."[62] In this statement he prefaces a mention of the *trouvaille* dear to high surrealism with an echo of Breton's most celebrated figure of light and encounter, the description of the surrealist image in the first *Manifesto*: "It is, as it were, from the fortuitous juxtaposition [*rapprochement*] of the two terms that a particular light has sprung, *the light of the image,* to which we are infinitely sensitive. . . . This is the most beautiful night of all, the *lightning-filled night* [*la nuit des éclairs*]: day, compared to it, is night" (*M,* 37–38; *OC,* 337–338).

Surrealism also transmits its disrupted subjectivity to the mobile subject positions valued by politicized postmodernism through the Marxist wing of the French theoretical avant-garde. I think, for example, of Deleuze and Guattari's "molecular multiplicities of desiring-production," which owe much to *Nadja*'s haunting subjectivity; the trajectory here runs from unchaining to deterritorialization.[63] High surrealism is certainly a conspicuous absence in *Anti-Oedipus,* a text replete with references to the renegade surrealists and to the Beats. Nonetheless, as opening paradigm for a positively valorized dispersed subjectivity, *Anti-Oedipus* proposes a strolling schizophrenic reminiscent of Breton's mad

61. When de Certeau discusses high surrealism's links to psychoanalytic theory, he waffles over its importance. In "Psychoanalysis and Its History," he can both imply the insignificance of Breton's thought to psychoanalysis: "The introduction of psychoanalysis in France was originally the work of men of letters (the first favorable article was written by Albert Thibaudet); [and] André Breton (who was not taken seriously by Freud)," and claim, one page later, that "inscribing personal destinies within a more general genealogy still has some relevance; for example, there is relevance . . . in recognizing Lacan's links to Surrealism." In *Heterologies,* 13, 14.
62. Michel de Certeau, *Arts de faire,* 87–88.
63. Gilles Deleuze and Félix Guattari, *Anti-Oedipus,* 380.

flâneuse, Nadja. "In the street, for her the only field of valid experience" is how Breton puts it in *Nadja* (*OC*, 716; *N*, 113). "A schizophrenic out for a walk is a better model than a neurotic lying on the analyst's couch. A breath of fresh air, a relationship with the outside world," Deleuze and Guattari comment.[64]

Surrealism's regressive treatment of gender relations also did not stop the feminist wing of the French theoretical avant-garde from refunctioning its attempts to apply psychoanalytic concepts to social praxis. When Hélène Cixous calls for *écriture féminine* in her famous manifesto, she speaks of the need for disruptive unchaining, identifying women with the unconscious forces that all manner of avant-garde practices are to bring forth. While this eruption is occasionally figured in the rhetoric of illumination or encounter borrowed from high surrealism, however, the explicit debt that Cixous repeats throughout her manifesto is to Bataille. Sentences directly echoing "The Notion of Expenditure" proliferate in "The Laugh of the Medusa": "Woman unthinks [*dé-pense*] the unifying, regulating history that homogenizes and channels forces"; "this is an 'economy' that can no longer be put in economic terms," and so on.[65]

THE APORIAS OF REVOLUTIONARY UNCHAINING

Discussing the degraded life of the urban proletariat, Breton points out that to make the worker into an agent of social change is to aestheticize the social realities of the worker's life. One can certainly argue, however, that Breton's interest in bohemian practices lends glamour to the dirty business of sifting through society's trash. Unlike Fanny Beznos, many of the merchants at the flea market were ragpickers, engaged in this activity because they could not find more profitable means of subsistence. Living in abject and degrading poverty, they were persecuted by urban authorities who linked them to crime and to the spread of disease. It could equally be objected that Breton glamorizes prostitution and madness. *Nadja*'s marvelous series of steps consist of Breton on the trail of Nadja's streetwalking; that any authentic social disruption results from this pursuit is dubious. Breton has an affair, hardly a revolutionary thwarting of social convention. If Nadja's haunting subjectivity allows her to produce objects of surrealist beauty and contact a hidden realm of ghosts, it also destroys her. In the time Breton knows

64. Deleuze and Guattari, *Anti-Oedipus*, 2.
65. Hélène Cixous, "The Laugh of the Medusa," 252, 264.

her (and with his encouragement), she passes from prostitution, poverty, and mental instability to the straitjacket of a mental institution.

To condemn Breton's affair with Nadja as wishful aestheticization of sordid and trivial experience is, however, to mistake the most haunting aspect of Breton's own practice in writing *Nadja*, marvelous in the sense that Breton formulates this concept in the first *Manifesto*: "There is still portrayed the incurable human restlessness" (*M*, 16). *Nadja* is not merely a manual for would-be surrealist *flâneurs*. Rather, Breton simultaneously narrates his encounters with Nadja in a fashion undoing the bohemian suggestions for revolutionary practice that he proposes. Finally, in a self-consuming example of the surrealist pessimism discouraging to the revolutionary Fanny Beznos (see Aragon's variations on the word *Pessimism* in *The Paris Peasant*), Breton's clearance sale of revolution extends to the possibility of revolutionary intervention at all.

Nadja dismantles the social power of Bretonian unchaining through Breton's manipulation of nineteenth-century traditions of representing social reality. Breton constructs the plot of *Nadja* through a little literary ragpicking of his own. The details of Nadja's life link her with a character familiar from the nineteenth-century social novel.[66] A young, poor, unskilled and mentally unstable woman who comes to Paris with a troubled past, including an illegitimate child, Nadja cannot find work, attempts to smuggle drugs, and falls into prostitution: "the one who *fell*" (*OC*, 716; *N*, 113). She continues to look for work in bakeries and butcher shops where men offer her laughable salaries accompanied by ambiguous advances: "One boss of a bakery who promised her seventeen francs a day, after having glanced at her a second time, corrected himself: seventeen or eighteen. And she, very animatedly: 'I told him: seventeen, yes; eighteen, no'" (*OC*, 688; *N*, 70). In this desperate state, she meets a bored, young, married aesthete. Fascinated by her fragile mental health, the aesthete seduces her, driving her to madness; repelled by the sordid details of her life, he eventually abandons her. Later learning that, utterly destitute and alone, she has been institutionalized, he does nothing to help her but only abstractly bemoans her fate.

The social writer represents social reality in all its squalor in order to promote change: in the hands of Eugène Sue Nadja's story would

66. There did exist a historically verifiable woman who provided the model for Nadja, although her psychiatric records will not become available for years to come. See Bonnet's notes to *Nadja*, OC, 1509.

solicit sympathy, in the hands of Emile Zola disgust. But Breton complicates an understanding of his text as a social novel, for he associates Nadja not only with the clichés of this tradition but also with the commonplaces of the post-Romantic prose poem. Nadja speaks the language not of Nana but rather of Nerval, Baudelaire, and Rimbaud. Breton tells us: "About to leave her, I want to ask a question which sums up all the others, a question which only I would ever ask, doubtless, but which, at least once, has found a reply worthy of it: 'Who are you?' And she, without hesitating: 'I am the wandering soul'" (OC, 688; N, 71). Her answer echoes Baudelaire's description of the streetwalking Parisian poet in "Crowds":

> The poet enjoys this incomparable privilege, that he can, as he pleases, be himself and others. Like those wandering souls who seek a body, he enters, when he wants to, into each person's role . . .
> What men call love is most paltry, most limited and most weak, compared to this ineffable orgy, to this holy prostitution of the soul which gives itself entirely, in poetry and charity, to the unforeseen which shows itself, to the stranger passing by.[67]

Breton's allusion to Baudelaire, like his multiple allusions in Nadja's speech to Nerval and Rimbaud, grounds his heroine in a tradition in which the writer's province is aesthetic unchaining. The post-Romantic prose poem does not represent social reality with a view toward social transformation but rather turns toward innovative aesthetic practice, valuing marginal social activity in its freedom from the standards of bourgeois morality. In valorizing the prostitute, for example, Baudelaire's prose poem redeems as aesthetically fertile her availability to chance and to the unknown as well as her refusal to engage in the forms of behavior which bourgeois morality defines as work. As Breton later states in "Political Position of Surrealism": "Pétrus Borel, Flaubert, Baudelaire, Daumier or Courbet. These five names alone would point to a common will not to compromise in any way whatsoever with the reigning class, which from 1830 to 1870 is ridiculed and stigmatized by artists for its morals above all else" (M, 217).

In Nadja's moment of glory Breton seems to espouse the post-Romantic redemption of Parisian mud. Placing Nadja's deviance from everyday habits in a visionary lineage, he provokes reflection on the fact that when writers such as Sue and Zola portray the life of the prostitute in brutal and sordid fashion, they may not only represent the reality of

67. Baudelaire, "Les Foules," in Oeuvres complètes, I, 291.

the prostitute's life but also a certain ideological necessity.[68] Such representations of prostitution are too immersed in bourgeois morality to show the prostitute's life as containing any positive experience outside the moral redemption that Marx found so odious in *The Mysteries of Paris*. But in Nadja's decline Breton also provokes reflection on the price of such flight from bourgeois morality. When Breton translates Baudelaire's figure for the poet in "Crowds" from the narrow space of a prose poem to a narrative of daily life in the Parisian streets, he shows that Nadja's poetic capability does not dispel the social novel's ugly truths. Breton demonstrates the impossibility of replacing the social Nadja with the aestheticized Nadja when he asks:

> Who is the real Nadja . . . the always inspired and inspiring creature who enjoyed being nowhere but in the street, for her the only field of valid experience . . . or (why not admit it?) the one who *fell*, sometimes, since after all others had felt authorized to speak to her, had been able to see in her only the most wretched of women, and of all the least protected? Sometimes I reacted with terrible violence against the over-detailed account she gave me of certain scenes of her past life, concerning which I decided, probably quite superficially, that her dignity could not have survived entirely intact. (*OC*, 716–718; *N*, 112–113)

Nadja's prostitution is not "holy" but rather sordid, and her schizophrenia leads her not into the souls of others but rather into an insane asylum. Seeking disruption through bohemian unchaining, Breton runs up against the depressing materiality of an order that writerly alchemy does not have the power to transform.

While the encounter of the social novel with the post-Romantic prose poem in *Nadja* exemplifies Breton's perverting juxtaposition of separate traditions of representing Parisian reality, it also demonstrates the minor mode in which such perversion occurs. Breton's generic disruption does not offer transcendence or liberation but rather throws the reader into impasse, aporia, and specifically the aporia of oppressive material conditions which destroy the efforts at ideological unchaining necessary to change them. Indeed, Breton's narrative of his relation to Nadja repeatedly stresses this aporia. Thus, while Nadja is strong in her revolutionary ideal, she also demonstrates its fragility at the very moment that she poses it in radical terms. When Nadja asserts that she has decided to refuse logic ("the most detestable of prisons"), living instead according to pure contiguity, Breton applauds her bravery but

68. Marx makes a similar point in *The Holy Family*, a text dear to Breton, when he discusses Sue's portrait of the prostitute in *Les Mystères de Paris*.

also appends the following footnote: "Does this not approach the extreme term of surrealist aspiration, its most powerful *limiting idea*" (*OC*, 741, 690; *N*, 143, 74). Nadja's fate makes these limitations painfully apparent. Recaptured by logic, she is placed into another and certainly hateful prison, the insane asylum. While Breton initially posits Nadja's ability to resist *enchaînement* even within the insane asylum, he then recognizes that her marvelously fragile revolutionary activity is no match for the thickness of its walls:

> The essential thing is that for Nadja I do not think that there can be much difference between the inside of a sanitarium and the outside. There must, alas, be a difference all the same, on account of the grating sound of a key turning in a lock, or the wretched view of the garden, the impudence of the people who question you when you would not even want them to shine your shoes, like Professor Claude at Sainte-Anne . . . on account of the effort necessary to adapt oneself to such a milieu, for it is after all, a *milieu* and as such, it requires a certain degree of adaptation. (*OC*, 736; *N*, 136–139)

Nadja's fate raises the possibility that surrealist *désenchaînement* may not only fail to undermine the superior force of the ruling order; it may exist only as an effect of the order it thinks to challenge.

Breton's representation of his own relationship to Nadja partakes of his disruptive synthesis of topoi from the post-Romantic prose poem and the social novel as well. In the same passage where Breton praises Nadja's imaginative potential, we see him simultaneously condemn the sordid side of Nadja's life, calling her, in highly moralizing tones, she who sometimes "fell." The paragraph describing the detrimental effect of the madhouse on Nadja makes the bourgeois morality of *Nadja*'s narrator even more explicit. He valorizes the concept of *milieu*, favored by Balzac and Zola in their more positivist moments as well as by nineteenth-century deterministic social science to describe the subject's subordination to material conditions. And in subsequent discussions of the madhouse, he surprises us by taking a condescending position toward its inmates despite his interest in conceptual unchaining. He objects to the "apparatuses of so-called social conservation which, for a peccadillo, some initial superficial lapse in convention or common sense, throw a subject among other subjects whose association can only be harmful to him and, above all, systematically deprive him of relations with everyone whose moral or practical sense is better established than his own" (*OC*, 739; *N*, 139). Rather than valuing the unchaining worked by madness, Breton points here to the debilitating effect of madness on the relatively sane person; the moral terms found in this passage smack of condescension, echoing, like *milieu,* the attitude of bourgeois social reformers to social institutions they deplore. As Peter Brooks writes of Sue, Breton's attitude "is tinged with bourgeois paternalism; it never wholly ceases to resemble Clémence d'Harville's condescension to the wretched of Saint-Lazare who are capable of redemption, but only within limits." [69]

For someone interested in ideological unchaining, Breton's narrator seems surprisingly pleased with his own implication in the existing social order. After valuing Nadja's ability to live outside bourgeois morality, he goes on to lament that Nadja, unlike the surrealists, lacked a certain "instinct of self-preservation . . . which has as effect that after all my friends and myself, for example, *behave ourselves*—confining ourselves to turning our heads—when a flag goes by . . . that we do not give ourselves the unparalleled joy of committing some splendid 'sacrilege', etc." (*OC,* 741; *N,* 143). But what is left of the "marvelous series of steps" in such a simple turn of the head?

Many readers have expressed disappointment that Breton does not present his and Nadja's adventures as heady and intoxicating transcendence. Condemning Breton for his final betrayal of Nadja, they link it to his betrayal of the marvelous series of steps the text sets out to take. It seems to me, however, that such betrayal does not mark the failure of the text's disruptive power but instead its accomplishment. The disruptive force of the betrayal can indeed best be gauged by readers' persistently negative reactions to it, which bear witness to their own unexamined needs for texts presenting optimistic schemas of social change.[70] I have called the content of Breton's unchaining aporia; Breton terms it perversion. But perhaps the best description of how Breton rewrites the old rousing scenario is contained in one of *Nadja*'s footnotes describing the (de)compositional techniques of a strangely scrupulous artist trying to represent the setting sun:

> Thus I remarked, while idling on the quay of the Vieux-Port in Marseille, shortly before sunset, a strangely scrupulous painter struggling with skill and

69. Peter Brooks, *Reading for the Plot,* 167.
70. On the ideologically dislocating potential of such disruption, Franco Moretti comments: "What we may call the dominant 'ironic' mode of modernist literature is subversive of the modern bourgeois worldview. There is no doubt that 'open' texts contradict and subvert organicistic beliefs, but it remains to be seen whether, as is now widely and uncritically assumed, in the past century the hegemonic frame of mind has not in fact abandoned organicism and replaced it with openness and irony." See "The Spell of Indecision," in Grossberg and Nelson, eds., *Marxism and the Interpretation of Culture,* 339.

speed on his canvas against the fading light. The spot of color corresponding
to the sun gradually descended with the sun. Finally, nothing remained. The
painter suddenly discovered that he was far behind. He obliterated the red
from a wall, painted over one or two gleams lingering on the water. His
painting, finished for him and for me the most unfinished in the world,
looked to me very sad and very beautiful. (*OC*, 744–746; *N*, 148)

CHAPTER 5

The Questions of Modern Materialism

If you are a Marxist . . . you have no need to be a surrealist.
—Michel Marty, quoted by Breton in the
Second Manifesto of Surrealism

MODERN MATERIALISM

The fusion of psychoanalysis with Marxism becomes Breton's central thematized concern in the two remaining texts of the Parisian prose trilogy, *Communicating Vessels* and *Mad Love*. Designating this fusion modern materialism, Breton chooses an expression according his brand of surrealist Marxism a rightful place within the landscape of Marxist thought. He proposes the designation when he surveys definitions of chance by Aristotle, Cournot, and Poincaré and then proceeds to "its definition by the modern materialists, according to whom *chance is the form of manifestation of exterior necessity which traces* [se fraie] *its path in the human unconscious* (boldly trying to interpret and to reconcile Engels and Freud on this point)" (*AF*, 31; *ML*, 23). As Breton already indicated in the *Second Manifesto of Surrealism*, he coins the phrase modern materialism with Engels's help: "'In the course of the evolution of philosophy, idealism became untenable and was repudiated by *modern materialism*.'" [1]

In selecting the expression *modern materialism*, Breton directs the very designation of his form of surrealist Marxism against its principal opponents. Engels used the term in the *Anti-Dühring* to assert that Marxism repudiates idealism, also differentiating Marxism from "the simple metaphysical and exclusively mechanical materialism of the

1. Breton, *Second Manifesto of Surrealism*, in *M*, 141 (emphasis added).

eighteenth century."² Against eighteenth-century materialism, "modern materialism is essentially dialectical," Engels states.³ For Breton the mechanical materialism at issue is no longer eighteenth-century materialism but rather the Marxism of the French Communist Party, which repeatedly attacked surrealist Marxism for its idealism. Breton calls this Marxism "simplistic materialism" when he inveighs against it in the *Second Manifesto of Surrealism,* repudiating "attacks which stem both from those who by base conservatism have no desire to clarify the relations between thought and matter and from those who, because of a revolutionary sectarianism only partly understood, confuse, in defiance of what is required, this materialism with the materialism that Engels basically distinguishes from it" (*M*, 141). Breton reacted most bitterly to the polemic directed against surrealism by

> certain intellectuals I know whose moral qualities are at best subject to close scrutiny, having tried their hand at poetry or philosophy, fall back on revolutionary agitation and, thanks to the general confusion rampant within the revolutionary movement, manage to convey some vague impression that they are doing something, and then, for convenience' sake, turn right around and disown as loudly as they can something such as surrealism. (*M*, 143)⁴

In *Communicating Vessels* Breton will charge that the French Communist Party in its vision of praxis subscribes to an unexamined idealism of its own: "A severe rule, like the one that requires from individuals an activity strictly appropriate to an end such as the revolutionary one, proscribing to them any other activity, cannot fail to replace [*replacer*] this revolutionary end under the sign of the abstract good" (*V*, 144; *CV*, 123).⁵

Breton's identification of surrealism with a term bashing idealism intervenes on a second polemical front. The charge of idealism was also leveled against Breton by the renegade surrealists around Bataille.⁶

---

2. Friedrich Engels, *Herr Eugen Dühring's Revolution in Science (Anti-Dühring)*, 31. See also Friedrich Engels, *Socialism Utopian and Scientific.*

3. Engels, *Anti-Dühring*, 31.

4. While Breton's attack on the Marxism of the French Communist Party is more vehement here than in *Nadja,* its target is substantially the same: orthodox Marxism's narrow view of what activity can serve the revolution. Breton continues, "To say that this production [artistic and literary] can or must reflect the main currents which determine the economic and social evolution of humanity would be offering a rather vulgar judgment, implying the purely circumstantial awareness of thought and giving little credit to its fundamental nature: both unconditioned and conditioned, utopian and realistic, finding its end in itself and aspiring only to serve, etc." (*M*, 155). I modify the translation slightly. For the French original see *OC*, 804.

5. I follow Caws's translation here verbatim.

6. The renegade surrealist side of this debate was carried out in the review *Docu-*

Thus, in the *Second Manifesto of Surrealism,* Breton accused Bataille of being an "excrement-philosopher" (the term is Marx's):

> In M. Bataille's case, and this is no news to anyone, what we are witnessing is an obnoxious return to old anti-dialectical materialism, which this time is trying to force its way gratuitously through Freud. "Materialism," he says, "direct interpretation, *excluding all idealism,* of raw phenomena, so as not to be considered as materialism in a state of senility, ought to be based immediately on economic and social phenomena." (*M,* 183; *M,* 185)

Bataille's own polemical gusto is exemplified by "The Old Mole and the Prefix *Sur.*"[7] "Since 'all that does not aim at the annihilation of being in an interior and blind radiance' is *vulgar* in his eyes, M. Breton seeks only, in sluggish confusion, raising on occasion some sad shreds of grandiloquence, to provoke a panic capable of justifying his willful aberrations. . . . Servile idealism rests precisely in this will to poetic agitation rather than in a strictly juvenile dialectic."[8]

This chapter examines the primary tenets of modern materialism, showing Breton to hold a substantially more complex position than the polemic on either front allows. An attack on the very distinction material/ideal is constitutive of Breton's surrealist Marxism, part of surrealism's thorough-going war on the founding binary oppositions of Western thought and the binary opposition itself. "Everything tends to make us believe that there exists a certain point of the mind at which life and death, the real and the imagined, past and future, the communicable and the incommunicable, high and low, cease to be perceived as contradictions": thus Breton describes the surrealist ambition in the *Second Manifesto of Surrealism* (*M,* 123). In some ways, then, Breton's concerns are not as opposed to those of Bataille's during the same period as their heated exchanges might suggest; as Krauss points out, "Bataille was careful to characterize himself as surrealism's 'old enemy from within.'"[9] Dismantling the dialectic as it has been rigidified by historical materialism is central to Breton's modern materialism, and

---

ments, whose first issue appeared in April 1929. As Bonnet comments, "A good number of former surrealists . . . clustered around it: Boiffard, Desnos, Leiris, Limbour, Masson, Vitrac. . . . Bataille cuts the figure of a sort of 'anti-Breton' or, more exactly, a 'Gothic [*noir*]' Breton, in the sense that the author of the *Anthology of Black Humor* [*humour noir*] himself understood this chromatic adjective" (*OC,* 1586–1587).

7. While accepted by *Bifur,* the review "ceased publication . . . before 'The "Old Mole"' could see the light of day" (Bataille, *Visions of Excess,* 259). The article had to wait until after Bataille's death, when it appeared in *Tel Quel* 34 (Summer, 1968).

8. Bataille, "The 'Old Mole' and the Prefix *Sur,*" in Bataille, *Visions of Excess,* 41.

9. Krauss, "Corpus Delicti," in Krauss and Livingston, *L'Amour fou,* 64.

Bataille's writings focus on this project as well.[10] For both thinkers, too, the psychoanalytic paradigm of the unconscious is crucial in this dismantling, although in differing ways. Bataille turns to the unconscious and the drives for a model of radical negation.[11] Breton, in contrast, is interested in the complex perspectives on mediation that the unconscious opens up.[12]

In taking seriously the theoretical content of *Communicating Vessels* and *Mad Love,* I diverge from their standard reception as lyrical outpourings focused first and foremost on love. Moreover, as Balakian has pointed out, these texts have generally been neglected in the voluminous literature on Breton.[13] Reading them as theory, however, is difficult because they flout the logical exposition and rhetorical moves familiar to rational argument. While Breton repeatedly invokes Marxist and psychoanalytic concepts (as well as the major names of Western philosophy), he refuses to employ them in logical or reliable fashion. Sliding unrigorously between charged binary oppositions and dislocating their terms, he links propositions that do not follow one another, plucks conclusions from the air, and couches his whole discussion in a tortuous syntax reminiscent of Mallarmé. In addition, he repeatedly intercuts his theoretical discussion with the most trivial details from his private life. Such practice has been read as Breton employing theoretical terminology and the metalanguage of logical argument for aesthetic effect rather than demonstrative force. Nonetheless (as any reader of Benjamin knows), to discuss theoretical issues eccentrically is not necessarily to invoke theory in empty fashion.

THE DREAM

"*Communicating Vessels*—dreams, their workings [*action*], their danger, their usefulness" runs an advertisement for this text in the front

10. Wollen comments on Breton's assessment of Hegel's contribution to the dialectic: "For Breton, Hegel provided the philosophical foundation for a rejection of dualism—there was no iron wall between subject and object, mind and matter, pleasure principle and reality principle, dream (everynight life, so to speak) and waking everyday life." Wollen, "The Situationist International," 81.

11. See, for example, Bataille's "The Critique of the Foundations of the Hegelian Dialectic" from 1932, the year *Communicating Vessels* was published, reprinted in *Visions of Excess.* Bataille is also interested in Freud for his "representation of matter," as he puts it in "Materialism," in Bataille, *Visions of Excess,* 15–16.

12. Bataille's "base" interpretation of Freud's view of matter can be opposed to Breton's interest in the power that Freud accords desire; just what Breton means by desire is a problem to which we will return.

13. See Balakian, "Introduction," *Dada/Surrealism,* 2.

of *Le Surréalisme au service de la révolution* (*Surrealism in the Service of the Revolution*), number 5. In this second work of his Parisian prose trilogy, Breton sets out to attack the material/ideal distinction through Freud's discussion of the dream. The dream is a psychological experience of long-standing interest to surrealism, providing the kernel of the 1924 *Manifesto*'s enunciation of the movement's new credo: "I believe in the future resolution of these two states, dream and reality, which are seemingly so contradictory, into a kind of absolute reality, a *surreality*, if one may so speak" (*M*, 14). Already in the first surrealist *Manifesto*, Breton designates his imagined conceptual upheaval with the emancipatory vocabulary familiar from Marxist theory. But this text, written before Breton's 1925 turn to Marxism, employs such vocabulary for its vaguely radical resonance. It does not engage a specific theoretical model for practicing social change.

Between writing the *Manifesto of Surrealism* and *Communicating Vessels*, however, Breton entered into the complexities of surrealism in the service of the revolution.[14] When Breton returns to the dream in *Communicating Vessels*, it constitutes a linchpin in his defense of surrealist praxis against the French Communist Party. Breton turns the psychoanalytic notion of the dream against the version of the material/ideal opposition underwriting the French Communist Party's refusal to admit that surrealist imaginative activity might have practical social consequences. This is the separation that vulgar Marxism draws between material praxis, teleological activities focusing on the realm of facts and the politico-economic sphere, and surrealism's "ideal" dwelling in the land of aesthetics, subjectivity, desire, dream.

Breton opens his attack on the material/ideal opposition by seeming to accept a "simplistic materialist" view of the dream. Placing the dream on the side of ideal experience, Breton describes it as a conservative social force with a compensatory relation to the shortcomings of material life. Because the dream enables the subject to make up for material deficiency in the ideal realm, it blocks rather than catalyzes "practical action." Breton writes:

> The dream . . . here has the role of liquidator. It tends to take off our hands, cheaply, everything we think we will no longer use. . . . It literally bars me from practical action. . . . The dialectical balance sees its equilibrium dis-

14. Although *Communicating Vessels* appeared in 1932, Breton wrote it in the period between 1930 and 1932; some fragments were initially published in independent form.

turbed to the benefit of the subject who, tired of depending on what is exterior to him, seeks, by all means possible to make what is exterior depend on him instead. (*V*, 132–133; *CV*, 112)

Breton underlines his negative assessment of the dream's manner of overcoming material reality by equating it with suicide. He states of this gesture, "I refuse to see anything else there than the expression of the personal discouragement of one man" (*V*, 134; *CV*, 113).

Proceeding to ally this view of dream with the Marxist critique of idealism, Breton summons up Marx on idealism against Bruno Bauer and Eugène Sue. "We are still in the presence of the same schoolmaster with his eyes put out, the one of Eugène Sue's *Mystères de Paris*, whom Marx considered the prototype of the man isolated from the exterior world," Breton writes, alluding to *The Holy Family* (*V*, 134; *CV*, 114). In such a circumstance, Breton continues:

> The cloistered individual, whether he wishes to or not, becomes in all his doings a factor of this world that exists only as a function of the other and lives on the level of the real as a parasite of it. As Marx showed, furthermore, in his fourth thesis on Feuerbach, the fact of the splitting of the secular basis of the religious world into its antagonistic parts can only have meaning if it is established that "God" is not the totally abstract creation of man and the conditions of existence ascribed to him the reflection of the conditions of existence of man. (*V*, 134–135; *CV*, 114–115)[15]

That this passage bolsters its discussion by allusion to Marx's celebrated attack on idealism in the "Theses on Feuerbach" might be considered redundant, an example of surrealism's overdone citation of a theoretical tradition that it refuses to work with in sustained form. But Breton's move from Marx on the *The Holy Family* to Marx on Feuerbach could also be viewed as displacing the concepts that he invokes. With this move Breton shifts to a passage in Marx facilitating an attack on the "old antinomy" materialism/idealism he has just seemed to accept. Marx's fourth thesis on Feuerbach runs: "That the secular basis detaches itself from itself and establishes itself as an independent realm in the clouds can only be explained by the cleavages and self-contradictions within this secular basis."[16] Marx not only opposes ideal and ma-

15. In French, this final clause runs: "à la condition qu'il soit établi que 'Dieu' n'est pas la création toute abstraite de l'homme et les conditions d'existence qui lui sont prêtées le reflet des conditions d'existence de l'homme" (*V*, 135).

16. Karl Marx, "Theses on Feuerbach," in Marx and Engels, *The German Ideology*, 122.

terial worlds but links them closely. Despite their seeming independence, the same material factors are at issue in the secular basis and the clouds: "The secular basis detaches itself from itself," Marx writes.

Breton goes on to liken Marx's treatment of the ideal/material opposition to the Freudian distinction between waking and sleeping life:

> But, in the same way that the dream draws all its elements from reality and implies beyond that the recognition of no other or new reality, so that the splitting of human life into *action* and *dream,* which people try equally to make us consider as antagonistic, is a purely formal division, a fiction—so, all of materialist philosophy, backed up by the natural sciences, bears witness to the fact that human life, conceived *outside* its strict limits that are birth and death, is to real life only what the dream of one night is to the day that was just lived. (*V,* 135; *CV,* 115)

In his comparison of the psychoanalytic opposition dream/waking and the Marxist couple ideal/material, Breton depends on an unstated similarity between the two bodies of thought. Both Marx and Freud attribute similar causes to the mechanisms of subjective distortion in their respective discussions of ideology and dream. In his fourth thesis on Feuerbach Marx proposes that the distortions of ideology result from a material situation of contradiction, cleavage, impasse. Psychoanalysis explains dream distortion as a result of similar factors, as Breton indicates when he states that the dream compensates the subject for the material obstacles he cannot resolve.

But when Breton parallels the Freudian opposition between dream and waking and the Marxist opposition between ideal and material, he does not merely find points of contact between Marxist and psychoanalytic accounts of hallucinatory psychic activity. In addition, he pursues his use of psychoanalysis to dislocate the opposition between material and ideal realms central to orthodox Marxism. Repositioning the Marxist distinction between material and ideal worlds according to the psychoanalytic opposition waking/dreaming, he transforms this distinction into "a purely formal division" (*V,* 135; *CV,* 115). For Marx in *The German Ideology* the valorized bottom line of material experience is the realm of primarily economic *Verkehr* (commerce), which the secondary processes of ideological work transfigure and distort. Freud, in contrast, accords no privileged status to the waking world. Rather, both waking and sleeping worlds are different psychological expressions of some other "essential reality of the psychic," as Breton calls it citing Freud at the opening to the *Communicating Vessels* (*V,* 18; *CV,* 11).[17]

17. Whether this reality can be located in a specific place is a matter of debate, for it is questionable that the radical negativity of the unconscious can be encompassed by positive notions such as location. At the end of the *Manifesto of Surrealism* Breton qual-

When Breton fuses Marx and Freud on the forces structuring experience, then, he makes both material and ideal activity two different expressions of an obscured realm. The usefulness of this notion in justifying surrealist praxis against orthodox Marxism is evident. As Breton states in the *Second Manifesto of Surrealism*: "The problem of social action, I would like to repeat and to stress this point, is only one of the forms of a more general problem which surrealism set out to deal with, and that is *the problem of human expression in all its forms*" (M, 151). As Breton also noted, rewriting another thesis of Marx on Feuerbach: "So we manage to conceive a synthetic attitude in which the need to *transform* the world radically and to *interpret* it as completely as possible are reconciled" (V, 148; CV, 127; emphasis added). Once Breton transforms material practice and ideal construction to two different forms of expression of an obscured third realm, surrealism's exploration of ideal activity becomes as much concerned with this hidden realm as practical Marxism's attention to statistics and facts.[18] Indeed, the value of surrealism to the revolution can be put in stronger terms. If both these states are different forms of "expression" of some "elsewhere," surrealism does more than just study a realm of equal value to what Marxism considers material reality. In its urgent concern with "expression," the movement becomes essential to understanding the relation between material and ideal practices and the obscured realm of forces they transform.

The nature of the obscured forces underwriting both material and ideal practices is a problem with which Breton struggles throughout his thought. In the discussion of the dream in *Communicating Vessels* Breton hypothesizes two different unconscious realms, a material and a psychic unconscious. The work of modern materialism becomes to describe the exchanges between the two. This text, Breton explains, studies

> a *capillary tissue*, without which it would be useless to try to imagine mental circulation. The role of this tissue is, we have seen, to guarantee the constant exchange which must occur in thought between the exterior and the interior worlds, an exchange that requires the continuous interpenetration of the activity of waking and that of sleeping.[19] My entire ambition has been to give here a glimpse of its structure. (V, 161; CV, 139)[20]

---

ified it with a vague "elsewhere," associating it with the metonymical displacements of desire.

18. The notion of the politics of form is central to much avant-garde activity; Benjamin develops this notion against vulgar Marxism in his essay on Eduard Fuchs.

19. See Benjamin's statement from Konvolut K on "the consciousness that is diversely patterned, and checkered with sleep and waking" (PW, 492).

20. Breton plays on the similarity in etymology of the words *text* and *tissue* to give a scientific cast to his surrealist vision of this exchange.

At other moments in the same text, however, Breton speculates that the distinction between material and psychic unconscious must itself be dissolved. Breton puts forth this position when he considers Freud's retreat into idealism. While psychoanalysis questions the Cartesian mind/body distinction, Breton takes his distance from what he views as its reassertion in the last instance of the separation of psychic from material world:

> More depressing still is the fact that Freud, after having experimentally found again and expressly valorized in the dream the principle of the reconciliation of opposites . . . that Freud the monist should have finally let himself make a declaration, ambiguous to say the very least, that "psychic reality" is a specific form of existence *that must not be confused* with "material reality." Was it really worth it to have attacked, as he did previously, the "mediocre confidence of psychiatrists in the solidity of the causal link between the body and the mind?" (*V*, 20; *CV*, 13)

But Breton also considers how to use psychoanalysis against its own idealist assumptions, as, for example, when he reflects on the implications of Freud's statement that "the intimate nature of the unconscious [essential reality of the psychic] is as unknown to us as the reality of the exterior world" (*V*, 18; *CV*, 11). "Perhaps," Breton goes on to speculate, "more is at stake than we believed—even, who knows, the great key which should permit the reconciliation of *matter* with the rules of formal logic, which have shown themselves until now incapable of determining it [matter] by themselves, to the great satisfaction of reactionaries of every stripe" (*V*, 18; *CV*, 12).[21]

"I read in an English film journal a review of the new book by Breton (*Communicating Vessels* [Paris 1932]) that, if I am not mistaken, approaches our intentions very closely," Adorno wrote to Benjamin (*PW*, 1106–1107). As Adorno noticed, evident parallels exist between Breton's efforts to redeem the dream in *Communicating Vessels* and the arcades project's interest in the fantasy projections of the nineteenth century.[22] Like Breton, Benjamin uses psychoanalysis to redeem the

21. "Of course, the material existence of the ideology in an apparatus and its practices does not have the same modality as the material existence of a paving-stone or a rifle. But, at the risk of being taken for a Neo-Aristotelian (*NB* Marx had a very high regard for Aristotle), I shall say that 'matter is discussed in many senses', or rather that it exists in different modalities, all rooted in the last instance in 'physical' matter," writes Althusser in "Ideology and Ideological State Apparatuses," in *Lenin and Philosophy*, 166.

22. Because I have already considered Benjamin's interest in dream language in some detail, I do not engage in extensive comparison between Benjamin and Breton here. I have saved an explicit confrontation of Breton's modern materialism with Benjamin's fusion of psychoanalysis and Marxism for my discussion of another key surrealist concept in the material/ideal problematic of importance to Benjamin: the encounter.

aberrational realm of subjective representation from its status as mere detritus.[23] Benjamin also uses psychoanalytic concepts to break down the Marxist opposition of material to ideal and its hierarchical ranking of economic and political reality over a culture's representations and desires. In addition, Benjamin speculates on an obscured reality informing both visible material and ideal practices, and he associates this reality with a historical collective unconscious that he characterizes in libidinal, symbolic, and economic terms. A somewhat better Marxist than Breton, Benjamin does not assert the equality of material and ideal practices with quite the same vigor. He emphasizes that ideological wish images are distortion and he seeks to reconcile the forces that produce them with a Marxist version of the real. Simultaneously, however, Benjamin remains fascinated by the wish images' curious materiality.

"A TRUE *DIALECTIZATION* OF THE DREAM THOUGHT"

We have seen Breton break down the Marxist opposition material/ ideal by recasting it in psychoanalytic terms in order to assert what Marxism would call the "material" content to psychic reality. But Breton also puts the gains of this breakdown in reverse: as confirmation that Marxism's realm of the material may be similar to the psychic realm studied by Freud. In this case, Breton speculates, the overdetermined form of causality which psychoanalysis understands to regulate psychological expression may apply to external processes, economic, social, and political life; dialectical causality becomes indissociable from psychoanalytic overdetermination. Breton bolsters this speculation with narratives of strange experiences occurring on the streets of Paris which suggest a similar logic to rule in waking and sleeping life; as Wollen puts it, "Breton describes how his dreams re-organize events of everyday life ('day's residues' in Freudian terms) into new patterns, just as everyday life presents him with strange constellations of material familiar from his dreams."[24]

Breton elaborates the consequences of this hypothesis in theoretical discussion, comparing the logic of social processes isolated by Marx

23. Benjamin's project to redeem the realm of subjective representation also owes much to Georg Lukács's attack on the subject/object dichotomy in "Reification and the Consciousness of the Proletariat," notably Lukács's dismantling of the category of objectivity.

24. Wollen, "The Situationist International," 80–81.

and Freud. He pursues a comparison around the problem of contradiction:

> It is well known, for one thing, that the dream possesses no term to express either alternatives or contradiction ("Even in the unconscious," Freud notes, "every thought is tied to its opposite") and, for another, that even in waking, from the dialectical viewpoint which must at any price surmount the viewpoint of formal logic, "the notions of cause and effect are concentrated and entwined in that of the universal interdependence at the heart of which cause and effect unceasingly change place" (Engels). (*V*, 60; *CV*, 46–47)

Likening Freud on the representation of contradiction in dreams to Engels on the mobility of cause and effect in both dialectical thinking and the dialectical processes of history, Breton suggests that Marxist dialectics and dream representation may well be on the track of a similar form of causality. Breton writes of the dream within the dream:

> It is a question . . . of a real memory of the sort to block the realization of desire which then undergoes a necessary depreciation, destined to permit this realization in the best of conditions. That is the formal negation of an event which took place, but which must be overcome at all costs, the product of a true *dialectization* of the dream thought which, hastening to arrive at its ends, gets away with breaking the last logical frameworks (*V*, 74; *CV*, 59).

Passages in *Communicating Vessels* not only liken dialectics and dream thought but suggest that dream representation is closer to dialectical processes than the mechanical model in orthodox Marxist circulation. Breton proposes that the dream gives an experience of negation endowed with the lived immediacy that rational argument finds only in the opening moment from which dialectical mediation starts. "This completely intuitive faculty of immediate determination of the negative (tendency to escape in the dream, in love)," Breton writes of the processes by which the dream in particular and the unconscious more generally "negates" external reality, "sees to it that a particularly colorful and exciting series of lived facts is maintained in its framework of *natural* sequence [*enchaînement*]" (*V*, 154; *CV*, 133). At other moments Breton asserts the superiority of dream representation over dialectics by reformulating dream reality in utopian revolutionary terms. He stresses that the obscure unconscious forces informing the opposition between material and ideal praxis constitute not only the hidden reality of social relations but also the new reality that will appear in a future moment of radical social upheaval. Describing the new reality with a Marxist language of revolution, Breton simultaneously asserts that this reality cannot be encompassed with the measures of reality habitually accepted as objective. Breton declares, "Time and space in the dream are thus real time and space: 'Is chronology obligatory? No!' (Lenin)" (V, 62; CV, 48).[25] The declaration takes aim, among other targets, at the rationalistic praxis Breton had encountered in his own bout with French communism: just the statistics, Monsieur, and please, no ideology.

We have seen a similar interest run through Benjamin's project to map objective processes in dreamlike terms. For Benjamin the project culminates in the controversial crossover notion of the dialectical image that *is* a dream image.

LA RENCONTRE (THE ENCOUNTER);
LE HASARD (CHANCE)

Chaos and chance are never excuses for confusion, but
the token of the irruption of the real.
                                        —Pierre Macherey

When Breton returns to the communication between psychic and material reality in *Mad Love,* he turns away from the dream. He does so in part because, as Breton puts it, in the dream "the dialectical balance sees its equilibrium disturbed to the benefit of the subject" (V, 132; CV, 112). Despite efforts to redeem the dream for revolution, *Communicating Vessels* never entirely refutes the dream's overwhelming link to the subjective world. The text concludes not with praise of the dream but rather with the statement that "the poet to come will surmount the depressing idea of the irreparable divorce between action and dream" (V, 170; CV, 146).[26] If the dream can only lead Breton so far along the path to studying exchanges of subjective with objective forces, *Mad Love* rather pursues another nonrational psychological experience dear to surrealism. This experience is the encounter (*rencontre*), when the divorce between objective and subjective activity is surmounted through no conscious action on the subject's part. At the moment of the encounter "natural necessity agrees with human necessity in such an ex-

25. I follow Caws and Harris here verbatim.
26. I follow Caws and Harris here verbatim. In this statement Breton echoes Baudelaire's nostalgic glance back at a world where "action is the sister of dream," but he projects his glance into the future. Benjamin too reworks Baudelaire's formulation when he considers how to wake the world from the dream of itself.

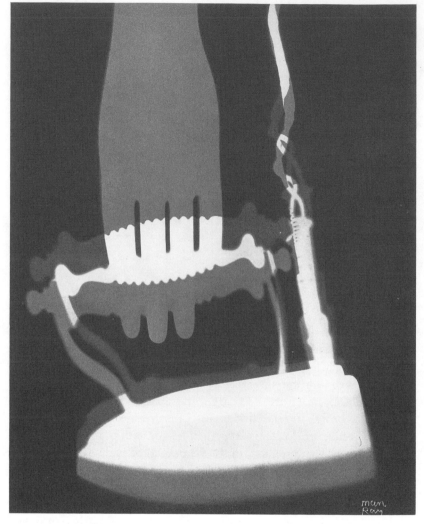

14. Man Ray. *Lingerie.* Courtesy of the National Museum of American Art,
Smithsonian Institution.

traordinary and disquieting way that the two determinations are indis-
cernible" (*AF,* 28; *ML,* 21).

Like the dream, the encounter is a concept central to surrealism from
its early days. And like the dream, this concept is initially explored by
the movement in primarily aesthetic terms. "It is, as it were, from the
fortuitous juxtaposition of the two terms that a particular light has
sprung, *the light of the image,* to which we are infinitely sensitive," Bre-

ton writes in the *Manifesto,* as he echoes an image from Lautréamont dear to surrealism: the fortuitous encounter of a sewing machine and umbrella on a dissection table (*M,* 37). When surrealism explores the aesthetic importance of the encounter, it concentrates on the fact that the encounter, like the dream, presents an alternative to the assumptions about representation inherent in realist aesthetic codes.

Surrealism objects, among its other criticisms, to the way in which realist aesthetics privilege notions of representation modeled on visual reflection.[27] Despite claims to accuracy, surrealism charges, in this model the subject remains alienated from the world represented. Against an understanding of representation as visual reflection, surrealism proposes that the artist enters into direct contact with the reality to be captured. The entrance occurs in the moment of encounter, as surrealism gives even a tactile quality to the act of vision (hence the fondness of the surrealists for that most indexical of visual media, photography).[28] The surrealists place such emphasis on the indexical relation of an object to its representation because surrealism's fundamental project is to release unconscious forces that leave their imprint on the visible world but that nowhere appear as such. The kernel of the surrealist act of tracing might be called "A Decalcomania of Desire" (in French, *décalquer* means *to trace*), a title Breton uses to preface a collection of surrealist images in *Minotaure,* number 8, although, as we have seen, Breton does not understand the unconscious only in libidinal terms.

The encounter structures surrealist practices of representation across the visual and linguistic spectrum. The encounter is visible in the sparks of surrealist metaphor construction as well as in the movement of automatic writing where attention is drawn to tracing letters on the page. It is manifested by Breton's interest in the indexical nature of photography, by Max Ernst's *frottages, grattages,* and *decalcomanias,* by Dali and Ernst's visit to a blind man's house where the art objects were tactile, the walls lined with fur, by Meret Oppenheim's fur teacup. One of the most celebrated forms of the encounter as representation is Man Ray's rayographs, where photographic images are produced by the direct contact of objects with light-sensitive photographic paper. Fittingly, rayographs figured heavily in a series of photos commissioned from Man Ray by the Parisian electric company in 1931 (fig. 14).[29] It

27. Jay discusses surrealism's objections extensively in "The Disenchantment of the Eye."
28. On this aspect of surrealist photography, see Krauss's essays on surrealism in Krauss and Livingston, *L'Amour fou: Surrealism and Photography.*
29. "In recognition of Man Ray's stature as an artist and innovator, the Paris electric

is almost as if this commercial agency sought to extract its representational due from the important figurative role played by electricity in surrealism's descriptions of the encounter. In the practice of the encounter, the paradigmatic surrealist act of representation is not to hold a mirror up to the world. Rather, the surrealist presents the world with a yielding substance where traces can be left. Breton's Parisian prose trilogy makes the central yielding substance the surrealist subject himself (I use the masculine pronoun advisedly).

Mad Love, the last work of the Parisian prose trilogy, theorizes the significance of the encounters Breton has spent so many pages narrating. Breton introduces his theorization by discussing a survey that he and Eluard first published in *Minotaure* numbers 3–4.[30] "Can you say what was the encounter of capital importance in your life? To what extent did this encounter give you, and does it give you now, the impression of being fortuitous? necessary?" asks Breton at the opening to the second chapter of *Mad Love* (AF, 27; ML, 19). When Breton explains the theoretical issues informing this discussion, he returns to the unseen interpenetration of material and psychic determination of *Communicating Vessels*. In this survey, Breton states, he and Eluard sought to "emphasize the links of dependence which unite these two causal series (natural and human), links which are subtle, fleeting, and disquieting in the present stage of knowledge, but which sometimes throw on the most faltering of human steps an intense light" (AF, 32; ML, 24).

To conceptualize the nature of the interdependence between seemingly independent causal series, Breton appeals to a concept that would seem to challenge the notion of determination itself. He raises the age-old problem of chance, which, like the dream and the encounter, is of long-standing importance to surrealism. *Le hasard* (chance) was central to the surrealists before they were even surrealists, for it played a role in their fascination with Dada. "When will one give the arbitrary the

---

company in 1931 commissioned the deluxe portfolio *Eléctricité*. Printed in an edition of five hundred, with an imaginative text by Pierre Bost that describes the 'wizardry' of Man Ray, the ten-print folio was intended to be given as a gift to the company's top customers. The futuristic looking images used experimental techniques that combined traditional elegance, such as the classically posed nude torso of his assistant Lee Miller with the new 'beauty' of electric power." Text to International Center of Photography exhibit, *Man Ray in Fashion*, September 7–November 25, 1990.

30. Professor C.-G. Jung responded to the survey as follows: "It was doubtless my birth. The other encounter of capital importance will be my death, an experience that I have not yet had. Between these two, there are events whose value is difficult to estimate. . . . I think my existence was necessary since doubtless it was inevitable." In *Minotaure*, nos. 3–4, 110.

place that falls to it in the formation of works or of ideas," Breton asked in the 1920 "Pour Dada" (For Dada), and he praised the Dadas for getting the project underway (*OC,* 236).

If the Dadas called spectacular attention to the value of chance, they did so in negative fashion, as a force capable of destroying habitual conceptual order. Surrealism, in contrast, with the help of psychoanalysis, understands chance in more positive terms. From the aesthetics of surrealist image-making to Parisian *flânerie,* chance becomes the moment when the habitual veil of repression is rent, allowing a true hidden order of things to surge forth. In its initial discussion of the revelation that chance permits, surrealism views not only the structure but also the content of the chance revelation in predominantly psychoanalytic terms. But *Nadja*'s collective uncanny suggests that the chance encounter also brings repressed collective experience to view. In *Mad Love* Breton explicitly proposes chance as a moment giving privileged access to the repressed but imbricated forces of psychic and material determination.

"Chance having been defined as 'the encounter [*rencontre*] of an external causality and an internal finality,'" Breton writes (*AF,* 28; *ML,* 21).[31] Here Breton proposes chance not only as an exemplary encounter but as a meta-encounter, an encounter not between causal factors from two different orders but rather between the two differing forms of causality structuring these orders. That the chance encounter manifests a form of causality challenging what we habitually experience as causal is a point reiterated throughout Breton's narratives. "Causality was for me that morning a slippery and particularly suspicious thing," Breton writes of one of his strange experiences of Parisian encounter in *Communicating Vessels* (*V,* 111; *CV,* 93).

What is this new form of causality that Breton forges from the collapse of external necessity and the human unconscious? "*Chance is the form of manifestation of exterior necessity which traces* [*se fraie*] *its path in the human unconscious* (boldly trying to interpret and to reconcile Engels and Freud on this point)," Breton proposes when he rewrites chance in modern materialist terms (*AF,* 31; *ML,* 23). In this statement specific Marxist and psychoanalytic models of determination are at stake. When Breton designates chance as a moment when the forces of "exterior necessity" mark the human unconscious, he alludes to Engels on the causal structure of historical process in *Ludwig Feuerbach and the Outcome of Classical German Philosophy.* There Engels uses the

31. I follow Caws verbatim.

term "external necessity" to suggest that objective historical processes are at work in events that individual subjects experience as accident, chance. Describing the materialist dialectic, Engels writes:

> We comprehended the concepts in our heads once more materialistically—as copies [*Abbilder*] of real things instead of regarding the real things as copies of this or that stage of development of the absolute concept. Thus dialectics reduced itself to the science of the general laws of motion—both of the external world and of human thought—two sets of laws which are identical in substance, but differ in their expression in so far as the human mind can apply them consciously, while in nature and also up to now for the most part in human history, these laws assert themselves *unconsciously* in the form of *external necessity* in the midst of an endless series of seeming accidents.[32]

Breton finds here a statement from the heart of the Marxist corpus authorizing his psychoanalytic repositioning of Marx's fourth thesis on Feuerbach. Human conceptual processes and the laws of the external world are hypothesized as different expressions of "laws which are identical in substance." Using the term *unconscious* to designate these laws, Engels read after Freud can be understood to suggest that structures similar to those regulating psychic processes are common to both.

True, Engels seems to use the term *unconscious* in nonpsychological fashion, to describe laws of history and nature beyond individual human control. But, asking how the individual historical subject has access to the objective forces structuring history, Engels goes on to speculate on the possible psychological composition of historical process itself. Engels points out that if historical process is objective, it nonetheless simultaneously arises from the interplay of individual psychic acts: "The conflict of innumerable individual wills and individual actions in the domain of history produces a state of affairs entirely analogous to that in the realm of unconscious nature."[33] Rather than viewing these acts as simply immaterial to historical process, Engels asks how they contribute to objective history at work. He thus calls for the need to develop a psychological science of ideology that will clarify the exchange between objective material factors and psychological impulses. Engels writes:

> To ascertain the driving causes which here in the minds of acting masses and their leaders—the so-called great men—are reflected as conscious mo-

---

32. Friedrich Engels, *Ludwig Feuerbach and the Outcome of Classical German Philosophy*, 44 (emphasis added). I modify the translation, which renders "Abbilder" as "images."
33. Engels, *Ludwig Feuerbach*, 48.

tives, clearly or unclearly, directly or in ideological, even glorified form—
that is the only path which can put us on the track of the laws holding sway
both in history as a whole, and at particular periods and in particular lands.
Everything which sets men in motion must go through their minds.[34]

When Breton gives his modern materialist definition of chance, then,
he is interested in an orthodox Marxist text linking historical and
psychological processes in one circuit of energy. Engels, of course, never
himself came to any solutions about the nature of this circuit, and his
formulations raise more difficulties than they solve. His mapping of determination as it stands, for example, degenerates easily into mechanical materialism; notably, he assumes precisely the homology between
individual psychology and collective social forces that Breton invokes
psychoanalytic models of determination to displace. Nonetheless, despite the numerous problems with Engels's formulations on the subject,
Breton is not the only thinker working on a psychoanalytic critique of
deterministic Marxism to find them provocative. I think, notably, of
Althusser, who devotes the appendix of "Contradiction and Overdetermination" to reading a late Engels text speculating on the relation between "individual wills" and objective history.

The text is Engels's letter to Joseph Bloch, London, 1890, a "*decisive
theoretical document for the refutation of schematism and econo-
mism.*"[35] In reading the letter Althusser cites extensively from Engels's
discussion of how the relation between material and psychological factors determines history. His long citation begins: "*History is made in
such a way that the final result always arises from conflicts between
many individual wills, of which each again has been made what it is
by a host of particular conditions of life. Thus there are innumerable
intersecting forces, an infinite series of parallelograms of forces which
give rise to one resultant—the historical event.*"[36] Althusser's approach
to Engels's text is characteristically deconstructive, showing how Engels's posing of the problem of historical causality itself inscribes the
antinomies of bourgeois ideology from its constitutive opposition between historical event and nonhistorical forces. But the deconstruction
derives from Althusser's own interest in the matter; in reading this text

34. Engels, *Ludwig Feuerbach*, 50. When Engels mentions the crossing of individual
wills as responsible for the movement of history, he appeals to a lineage of German
philosophy all the more justifying Breton's interest in appropriating this aspect of Engels's
thought for modern materialism. Engels's discussion of the link between the will and
world history recalls the thought of Schopenhauer and Nietzsche central to Freud.
35. Althusser, "Contradiction and Overdetermination," in *For Marx*, 117.
36. Althusser, "Contradiction and Overdetermination," in *For Marx*, 120.

Althusser remains attentive to Engels's "genial theoretical intuitions" as well as Engels's "step backwards from the Marxist critique of all *'philosophy.'*"[37]

I will soon return to the trajectory linking Althusser's Marxism to Breton's. It remains to elaborate, however, the details of Breton's synthesis of Engels and Freud. For Engels's passage on individual wills particularly provokes Breton because it resonates with a specific textual moment in Freud. In describing the path of exterior necessity into the human unconscious with the verb *frayer,* Breton alludes to Freud's account of psychic forces in *Beyond the Pleasure Principle,* a text to which he refers throughout *Mad Love. Frayer* is the verb that Jankélévitch uses (*trajet frayé* is Jankélévitch's precise term) to render Freud's concept of *Bahnung* in the translation of *Beyond the Pleasure Principle* published in the 1927 Payot collection, *Essais de psychanalyse.* At issue in the Freudian concept of "facilitation" (*Bahnung*) is the process by which alien forces mark the psyche. "Becoming conscious and leaving behind a memory-trace are processes incompatible with each other within one and the same system" runs Freud's key hypothesis in its English version. "It may be supposed that, in passing from one element to another, an excitation has to overcome a resistance, and that the diminution of resistance thus effected is what lays down a permanent trace of the excitation, that is, a *facilitation.*"[38] Freud's principal concern in developing the notion of facilitation is to explain how unbounded psychic energy leaves its traumatic effects on the subject. Nonetheless, the source of this energy remains uncertain throughout his text.

Repeatedly Freud hovers between conceiving the source of this energy in objective and psychical terms. Thus, Freud explains the pro-

37. Althusser, "Contradiction and Overdetermination," in *For Marx,* 128.

38. Sigmund Freud, *Beyond the Pleasure Principle,* XVIII, 25, 26, (emphasis added). See Freud, "Au delà du principe du plaisir," in *Essais de psychanalyse.* The passage in French runs as follows: "On peut supposer qu'en passant d'un élément à un autre, l'excitation doit vaincre une résistance et que c'est à la diminution de la résistance qu'on doit rattacher la trace durable laissée par l'excitation (*trajet frayé*); on aboutirait ainsi à la conclusion qu'aucune résistance de ce genre n'est à vaincre dans le système C. où le passage d'un élément à un autre se ferait librement" (p. 35, emphasis added). Freud already introduces this term in his conclusion to *The Interpretation of Dreams,* where he works through the material that he will develop in *Beyond the Pleasure Principle.* The key passage in *The Interpretation of Dreams* occurs two pages before the passage on the essential unknown nature of psychic reality which Breton included at the opening to *Les Vases communicants.* "Ideas, thoughts and psychical structures in general must never be regarded as localized in organic elements of the nervous system but rather, as one might say, *between* them, where resistances and facilitations [*Bahnungen*] provide the corresponding correlates." Freud, *The Interpretation of Dreams,* V, 611.

cess of facilitation by modeling psychical experience on a simple living organism's reaction to external stimuli. "Let us picture a living organism in its most simplified possible form as an undifferentiated vesicle of a substance that is susceptible to stimulation. Then the surface turned towards the external world will from its very situation be differentiated and will serve as an organ for receiving stimuli." [39] Freud proceeds to relocate this most simplified possible living organism within the complexities of the human psyche. Nonetheless, it is significant that he appeals to a model for how external forces mark the interior of an organism to discuss purely psychic energy. This appeal indicates his text's more general hesitation over whether the source of psychic trauma is objective or psychic, a hesitation exemplified by the fact that he initiates his entire discussion of psychic trauma with reference to a trauma purely objective in origin. The trauma is the effect of combat on men in the trenches during the First World War. Freud also points out that it is difficult to ascertain whether the source of the subject's trauma is external or internal. He writes of "a tendency to treat them [internal excitations] as though they were acting, not from the inside, but from the outside, so that it may be possible to bring the shield against stimuli into operation as a means of defense against them. This is the origin of *projection,* which is destined to play such a large part in the causation of pathological processes." [40] We have already seen Breton's interest in other moments in Freud evincing a similar uncertainty, notably Freud's analysis of the source of the uncanny and his discussion of the alterity of unconscious forces in the passage from *The Interpretation of Dreams* Breton cites at the opening to *Communicating Vessels.*

Putting together the Marxist and psychoanalytic pieces: Breton's modern materialism construes chance as the meeting between the material determination that Marxism sees operative in historical processes and the overdetermination that psychoanalysis sees constructing the subject. To describe the shape of this meeting, Breton looks to Freud. It takes the form of *frayage,* as Freud's alien forces breaking through the subject's protective shell become partly objective in nature. At the same time Breton looks to Engels to explain why this meeting occurs. In this context he is particularly interested in Engels's speculations on some kind of unconscious operative both in the objective and psychic domains.

---

39. Freud, *Beyond the Pleasure Principle,* XVIII, 26.
40. Freud, *Beyond the Pleasure Principle,* XVIII, 29.

LA TROUVAILLE (THE LUCKY FIND);
LE HASARD OBJECTIF (OBJECTIVE CHANCE);
LE TROUBLE (THE SURREALIST UNCANNY)

A discussion of modern materialism would not be complete without noting several other of its privileged concepts pervaded by Breton's interest in reconciling Engels and Freud. The first concept is the *trouvaille,* the lucky find that, like the encounter, chance, and the dream, fascinates Breton from his time as a Dada. Breton appropriates the term from Apollinaire's "Lundi rue Christine" (Monday rue Christine), invoking it initially in high Dada fashion as an example of the aesthetic fertility inhering in the accidents of chance. "Starting with 'Lundi rue Christine,'" Breton writes in his 1917 homage to Guillaume Apollinaire, "Guillaume Apollinaire could not be turned away from his goal: the reinvention of poetry" (*OC,* 211). Breton then cites the following lines:

> Lose
> But really lose
> To leave room for the lucky find. (*OC,* 211)

By the time the *trouvaille* assumes its place in Breton's full-blown surrealist theory of subjectivity, it has become an encounter whose undeniably objective component fascinates Breton. Unlike the dream, where the dialectical balance is broken to the benefit of the subject, the *trouvaille* is a piece of the objective world which mysteriously attracts the subject. The *trouvaille* can be a phrase that appears to Breton endowed with a life of its own; it can also be an object, a reified encounter, as his numerous *trouvailles* at flea markets make clear. The *trouvaille* thus holds a charged place in modern materialism's ambition to break down the distinction between libidinal energy and the objective world. If Breton can reveal this indisputable piece of objective reality to be charged with psychic energy, his claims to the existence of an overdetermined psychic and material unconscious become all the more persuasive.

Repeatedly Breton hypothesizes that the appeal of the *trouvaille* derives from its power to embody the subject's desire. The *trouvaille,* Breton suggests, brings the subject a solution to a question the subject could not formulate as such. "It is a matter in such a case, in fact, of a solution which is always in excess, a solution certainly rigorously fitting and yet very superior to the need. The image, such as it is produced in automatic writing, has always constituted for me a perfect example of this," Breton observes (*AF,* 21; *ML,* 13). He writes of the *trouvaille* in general, "artistic, scientific, philosophic, or of as minimal a use as could be desired": "In it alone can we recognize the marvelous precipitate of desire. It alone has the power to enlarge the universe, causing it to relinquish some of its opacity" (*AF*, 21; *ML*, 13; *AF*, 21–22; *ML*, 13–14). Indeed, Breton endows the power of the *trouvaille* to undo repression with therapeutic force. "*The finding [trouvaille] of an object serves here exactly the same purpose as the dream, in the sense that it frees the individual from paralyzing affective scruples, comforts him and makes him understand that the obstacle he might have thought unsurmountable is overcome,*" Breton claims in *Mad Love*, giving a footnote to his discussion of the dream in *Communicating Vessels* (*AF*, 44; *ML*, 32).

The repressed energy that Breton hypothesizes at the source of the *trouvaille*'s appeal varies from case to case. At the flea market in *Nadja* Breton stumbles on a volume of Rimbaud that belongs to the book's only avowed revolutionary, Fanny Beznos. The object attracts him because it exemplifies an avant-garde version of the unchaining that Breton investigates throughout the text. This *trouvaille*, then, is a piece of the objective world manifesting forces that, while subjective, can hardly be called repressed. In addition, at the flea market, Breton stumbles across a "sort of irregular, white, shellacked half-cylinder" which "after examining . . . thoroughly, I had to admit was only some kind of statistical device, operating three-dimensionally and recording the population of a city in such and such a year, though all this makes it no more readable to me" (*OC*, 676; *N*, 52). While Breton does not provide an explanation for his attraction to this mysterious object, the object touches on concerns thematized throughout the text. It poses the problem of how to render vividly (in three dimensions) contemporary urban reality in other than realist fashion. In addition, the object raises the question of the value of representation as statistical compilation, the task, that is, that the French Communist Party set for Breton.

When Breton goes to the flea market with Giacommeti in *Mad Love*, in contrast, he discusses *trouvailles* whose appeal derives from properly psychoanalytic factors. In the sculpted wooden spoon in the shape of a slipper, in the eerie war mask from the Argonne, Breton and Giacometti find manifested the conjunction of their intersubjective desires. Like the *trouvailles* in *Nadja*, these objects lure the strolling surrealist artists by manifesting desires that while unacknowledged are not repressed in the strong psychoanalytic sense. "This more or less conscious desire . . . *based on typical shared preoccupations,*" Breton writes of the forces determining his discovery with Giacommeti (*AF*, 45; *ML*, 32).[41]

Such desires are not only different from the desires manifested by the *trouvailles* in *Nadja* but differ from the unconscious libidinal realm that Breton suggests to structure the encounter at other moments. Breton goes on to link such desires to the repressed forces revealed by the encounter in general, using the *trouvaille* to stress the wide range of affective impulses that it can make manifest. Thus, he concludes, "Friendship and love on the level of the individual, as on the level of the social ties created by the community of sufferings and the convergence of demands, are alone capable of favoring this sudden dazzling combination of phenomena which belong to independent causal series" (*AF*, 51; *ML*, 35). Breton here returns to a central problem of his modern materialism: In what precisely does this repressed realm of forces constituting the subject consist? How does its construction resemble/ differ from Freudian repression? What are the content of the forces here at issue? Different encounters suggest different possibilities and French theory will have to wait for answers until Deleuze and Guattari dismantle the subject/object dichotomy in their own materialist psychology.

Breton's uncertainty as to the composition of the repressed forces structuring the encounter presides over an additional term important to the conceptual cluster of modern materialism. This term is *le hasard objectif*, "objective chance," used by Breton when he is discussing chance in its modern materialist form. In *Communicating Vessels* Breton states that he chooses the term because it comes from Engels's vocabulary of modern materialism. Breton writes, "There is no perceptible relation between a certain letter that arrives for you from Switzerland and a certain preoccupation you might have had around the time this letter was written. But isn't that making the notion of causality absolute in a regrettable way? Isn't it taking too lightly Engels's words: 'Causality can only be understood as it is linked with the category of objective chance, a form of manifestation of necessity'?" (*V*, 110; *CV*, 91–92). It is curious, however, that when Breton returns to the term in *Mad Love*, its materialist component seems to fade. For here Breton uses the term not to suggest that obscured objective forces are at issue in chance but rather that chance makes manifest repressed desire. Speaking of the importance of analyzing experiences that "have seemed . . . fleeting and obscure among all others," Breton proposes

41. I follow Caws's translation of this passage verbatim.

that there the subject will find the powers of "objective chance," or, in other terms, the structuring force of desire: "There . . . all the logical principles, having been routed, will bring to meet him the powers of *objective chance* which make a mockery of plausibility. Everything humans might want to know is written upon this screen in phosphorescent letters, in letters of *desire*" (*AF*, 127; *ML*, 87). Just what Breton means by desire vacillates markedly. He uses the term in a fashion ranging from the alien Freudian libido to some more conscious feeling of sexual love.

When Breton names the surrealist sensation associated with the encounter, he provides one more term in the vocabulary of modern materialism. The sensation is the uncanny shiver provoked by *Nadja*'s odd collection of events, a sensation, however, that Breton did not distinguish with a name of its own in this text. In *Mad Love* Breton baptizes the disturbing uneasiness provoked by the encounter *le trouble*, a term he has already used when he discusses disturbances of the waking state in the *Manifesto of Surrealism*. Considering the "suggestions which come to it [the waking mind] from the depths of that dark night" of the unconscious, Breton writes: "This idea, this woman *disturb* [*trouble*] it, they tend to make it less severe. What they do is isolate the mind for a second from its solvent and spirit it to heaven, as the beautiful precipitate it can be, that it is. When all else fails, it then calls upon chance, a divinity even more obscure than the others to whom it ascribes all its aberrations" (*M*, 13).

In *Mad Love* Breton analyzes the content of that *trouble* in high psychoanalytic terms. He describes it as the Freudian uncanny, an experience in which the subject's sexual repressions are momentarily undone. "Although I never manage to exhaust by analysis all the elements of this disquiet [*trouble*]—*it must in fact come from my most profound repressions*—what I know of it persuades me that there *sexuality* alone presides," Breton writes of the source of the *trouble* provoked by an aesthetic object. "It is really as if I had been lost and someone had suddenly come to give me some news about myself" (*AF*, 13; *ML*, 8–9; emphasis added). *Trouble* as the sensation produced by the return of what has been repressed: Breton provides a more elegant translation of the Freudian *unheimlich* than the cumbersome "inquiétante étrangeté" of French psychoanalysis. Once again, however, we may ask what has become of the collective component that determines this *trouble* so visible not only in the micronarratives comprising *Nadja* but also in *Mad Love*'s subsequent definition of chance.

While Breton is clearly uncertain as to the content of the unconscious forces revealed in the encounter, there is a marked consistency in the content of his oscillation. He hesitates between constructing the forces as imbricated material-psychic forces and construing them as the forces of "desire" deriving from a repressed libidinal realm. His oscillation, occurring even in the space of a page, is fundamental to his description of these forces. Breton proposes his modern materialist definition of chance on page 23 of *Mad Love*. One page later he locates the source of chance in repressed desire alone, sacrificing external necessity altogether. He writes:

> My most enduring ambition will have been to disengage this unknown character [of the encounter] both from some of the facts of my life which at first glance seem the most trivial as well as from the most meaningful. I think I have succeeded in establishing that they both share a common denominator situated in the mind of man, and which is none other than his *desire*. What I have wanted to do above all is to show the precautions and ruses which desire, in search of its object, employs as it tacks in the preconscious waters, and, once this object is discovered, the means (stupefying until some new order) it uses to make it known by consciousness. (*AF*, 37; *ML*, 24–25)

Might Breton's oscillations be resolved chronologically? The section emphasizing the libidinal content to the unconscious follows his modern materialist discussion of the *trouvaille*. It was first published in *Minotaure*, number 7, in 1935 and narrates an uncanny evening promenade when all events seem to be the product of the individual's repressed desire. On "the night of the sunflower," Breton meets and falls in love with a woman of whom, he discovers, he has unknowingly dreamed for eleven years (*ML*, 67). Revealing the power of a subject's unconscious desire to produce external events, the night of the sunflower seems to illustrate Breton's dearest surrealist wish: the power of individual psychic activity to change the world. If previously Breton hesitated between a modern materialist and a psychoanalytic account of repressed forces, could this hesitation have derived from his hesitations over whether surrealism should have any dealings with the revolution? And might "the night of the sunflower" constitute Breton's rejection of the Marxist elements to his thought?

Biographical factors support such a hypothesis. For June 1935, when *Minotaure* published "the night of the sunflower," also marks the moment when Breton's troubled relation with the French Communist Party came to an end, when he was excluded from the International Congress of Writers for the Defense of Culture held in Paris.[42] It is plausible that Breton abandons modern materialism for some more properly psychoanalytic account of subjectivity at the same time. As my chapter 6 shows, however, the principles of modern materialism continue to permeate *Mad Love*'s seemingly most subjective experience, the night of the sunflower. This permeation is, moreover, consistent with Breton's own account of the matter. According to Henri Béhar, he portrays himself as still defending modern materialism to Trotsky in 1938.

> The most serious divergence [between Breton and Trotsky] . . . concerns objective chance, where . . . Trotsky is afraid of a drift towards mysticism: "Comrade Breton, I am not at all clear about your interest in phenomena of objective chance. Yes, I know that Engels appealed to this notion, but I wonder if, in your case, something different is at work, I am not sure that you are not trying to keep [his hands here draw a small space in the air] a little window open on the beyond . . ." Breton has not finished justifying himself when his interlocutor starts up again: "I am not convinced. And moreover, you wrote somewhere . . . oh, yes, that these phenomena had for you a disquieting character." "Excuse me," Breton answers, "I have written: disquieting in the present stage of knowledge [*AF*, 32; *ML*, 24], would you like us to verify this?" Trotsky gets up rather nervously, takes several steps, and comes back to him: "If you said . . . in the present stage of knowledge— I do not see anything more to take up, I withdraw my objection." [43]

TUCHÉ AND MISRECOGNITION: MODERN MATERIALISM, LACAN, ALTHUSSER

The imaginary is that which tends to become real.
                                                                —Breton

In chapter 2, I asserted that Althusser was helpful in illuminating Benjamin's interest in psychoanalysis because Althusser's own Marxism was marked by the modern materialism also important to Benjamin. To conclude my discussion of the tenets of modern materialism, I want to examine the details of that debt. Such an examination, however, necessitates a detour through the writings of another celebrated

---

42. He was, however, to remain preoccupied with the social possibilities of Marxism. Thus, after Breton first met with Trotsky in Mexico in 1938, Trotsky wrote to *Partisan Review* (I am translating from the French of Henri Béhar's *André Breton*): "André Breton, the recognized head of surrealism, is now in Mexico. As you certainly know, on the level of art as well as politics, he is not only independent of Stalinism but completely hostile to it. He has sincere sympathies for the Fourth International" (Béhar, *André Breton*, 312).
43. Béhar, *André Breton*, 313.

member of the French theoretical avant-garde, Jacques Lacan, whose historical link to surrealism is well-known.[44]

Now Althusser makes no secret of his debt to Lacan. Notably, he gives a Lacanian genealogy to his concepts of structural causality and ideological interpellation. For economy of argument, my discussion focuses on Lacan's role in transmitting modern materialism to the second of these key Althusserian concepts. The surrealist content to interpellation can be intimated from Althusser's description of it in "Ideology and Ideological State Apparatuses" as recognition producing a small jolt reminiscent of the surrealist encounter. "It is indeed a peculiarity of ideology that it imposes (without appearing to do so, since these are 'obviousnesses') obviousnesses as obviousnesses, which we cannot *fail to recognize* and before which we have the inevitable and natural reaction of crying out (aloud or in the 'still, small voice of conscience'): 'That's obvious! That's right! That's true!'"[45] In what might seem like a divergence from the surrealist encounter, however, Althusser goes on to point out that such recognition is also misrecognition: "The reality in question in this mechanism, the reality which is necessarily *ignored* (*méconnue*) in the very forms of recognition (ideology = misrecognition/ ignorance) is indeed, in the last resort, the reproduction of the relations of production and of the relations deriving from them."[46]

Althusser makes the Lacanian contribution to his formulation of interpellation explicit when he compares the ideological subject to Lacan's imaginary subject. To describe this subject he refers to one Lacan essay in particular, Lacan's parable for the formation of the imaginary subject in "The Mirror Stage." But to make evident the contribution of modern materialism to Althusser I want rather to pursue the intermediary of another Lacanian discussion fundamental to this account, although its contribution is less widely acknowledged. I refer to Lacan's exposition of the *tuché,* the "real as encounter [*rencontre*]."[47] "What we have in the discovery of psycho-analysis is an encounter [*rencontre*], an essential encounter—an appointment to which we are always called with a real that eludes us," Lacan writes of the essential

44. Lacan cut his intellectual teeth in the surrealist milieu, publishing extracts from his doctoral dissertation on paranoia in the first issue of *Minotaure* (1933). For more on Lacan's links to both high and renegade surrealism, see Macey's *Lacan in Contexts.*
45. Althusser, "Ideology and Ideological State Apparatuses," in *Lenin and Philosophy,* 172.
46. Althusser, "Ideology and Ideological State Apparatuses," in *Lenin and Philosophy,* 182–183.
47. Jacques Lacan, "Tuché and Automaton," in *The Four Fundamental Concepts of Psycho-Analysis,* 55.

encounter that he identifies as *tuché*.[48] A similar failed meeting with
the real is at issue in Althusser's moment of "recognition (ideology =
misrecognition/ignorance)" when the subject both takes its place in the
"reproduction of the relations of production and of the relations deriving from them" and mistakes the nature of this place, casting it in
"imaginary" terms.[49]

Lacan develops the notion of the *tuché* in the first section of *The
Four Fundamental Concepts of Psycho-Analysis*, "The Unconscious
and Repetition." And from his first words of his first seminar Lacan
places the section under surrealism's sign. Opening with a poem by Aragon on the surrealist imaginative encounter, Lacan also compares the
methodology of psychoanalysis to practices of surrealist aesthetic composition. "Personally, I have never regarded myself as a researcher
[*chercheur*]," Lacan asserts, and he goes on to describe his methods
with a statement from Picasso bearing witness to this artist's own close
ties to surrealism.[50] "As Picasso once said, to the shocked surprise
of those around him—*I do not seek, I find* [*Je ne cherche pas, je
trouve*]."[51]

For Lacan the unconscious is the greatest find of psychoanalysis, or,
as he also calls it, the great *trouvaille*. Lacan describes how the unconscious appears initially in obscure psychic manifestations that block the
daily experience of reality: "In the dream, in parapraxis, in the flash of
wit—what is it that strikes one first? It is the sense of impediment to
be found in all of them."[52] But this block, psychoanalysis goes on to
discover, is rather the opening to another scene: "What occurs, what
is produced in this gap in the strong sense of the term *to produce*, presents itself as *the lucky find* [*la trouvaille*].[53] It is in this way that the
Freudian exploration first encounters [*rencontre*] what occurs in the
unconscious. Lucky find [*trouvaille*] that is at the same time solution,"
writes Lacan.[54]

48. Lacan, "Tuché and Automaton," in *The Four Fundamental Concepts*, 53.
49. Althusser, "Ideology and Ideological State Apparatuses," in *Lenin and Philosophy*, 182–183.
50. Lacan, "Excommunication," in *The Four Fundamental Concepts*, 7.
51. Lacan, "Excommunication," in *The Four Fundamental Concepts*, 7.
52. Lacan, "The Freudian Unconscious and Ours," in *The Four Fundamental Concepts*, 25.
53. I have modified Sheridan's translation of *trouvaille* as "discovery" in order to
bring out the links between Lacan's vocabulary and surrealism. For the French original,
see Jacques Lacan, *Le Seminaire, Livre XI, Les quatre concepts fondamentaux de la
psychanalyse*, 27.
54. Lacan, "The Freudian Unconscious and Ours," in *The Four Fundamental Concepts*, 25. I modify Sheridan's text not only to emphasize Lacan's surrealist vocabulary

When Lacan describes the Freudian unconscious, he employs a term familiar from modern materialism, the *trouvaille,* very much in the spirit of Breton. He uses it to describe some seemingly alterior manifestation that is in fact invested with unconscious libidinal content. And Lacan echoes the tenets of modern materialism not only in using this term but in framing the nature of the unconscious as lucky find. "It is in this way that the Freudian exploration first encounters [*rencontre*] what occurs in the unconscious. Lucky find [*trouvaille*] that is at the same time solution," writes Lacan.[55] When Breton writes of the ability of the *trouvaille* to reveal repressed forces, he too describes it as solution: "It is a matter in such a case, in fact, of a solution which is always in excess, a solution certainly rigorously fitting and yet very superior to the need" (*AF,* 21; *ML,* 13). This statement displays yet one more link between Breton's exposition of the *trouvaille* and Lacan's discussion of how the *trouvaille* of the unconscious resolves the subject's difficulties. Like Breton, Lacan suggests that the *trouvaille* brings to the subject a solution in excess of his need: "It [*la trouvaille*] has that indefinable something that touches us, that peculiar accent that Theodor Reik has brought out so admirably—only brought out, for Freud certainly noted it before him—namely, *surprise,* that by which the subject feels himself overcome, by which he finds both more and less than he expected—but, in any case, it is, in relation to what he expected, of exceptional value."[56]

I do not juxtapose Breton and Lacan only to underline the modern materialist source of Lacan's interest in the radically alterior quality of the psychoanalytic real. I also want to draw attention to the extent to which Lacan's difficult syntax is marked by the recalcitrant theoretical exposition of Breton. Althusser, moreover, explains Lacan's difficulty by according it an avant-garde lineage:

> Hence the contained passion and passionate contention of Lacan's language, unable to live or survive except in a state of alert and accusation: the language of a man of the besieged vanguard, condemned by the crushing strength of the threatened structures and corporations to forestall their

but also his Bretonian syntax. Sheridan translates the second sentence of this quote: "This discovery is, at the same time, a solution." For the French original, see Lacan, *Les quatre concepts,* 27.

55. Lacan, "The Freudian Unconscious and Ours," in *The Four Fundamental Concepts,* 25.

56. Lacan, "The Freudian Unconscious and Ours," in *The Four Fundamental Concepts,* 25.

57. Louis Althusser, "Freud and Lacan," in *Lenin and Philosophy,* 203.

blows, or at least to feint a response to them before they are delivered, thus discouraging the opponents from crushing him beneath their assault.[57]

When Lacan picks up the surrealist vocabulary of *trouvaille*, he does so to make a point crucial to Breton's modern materialist discussion from its inception: that psychic reality can exhibit an alterity beyond what we habitually consider the domain of subjective experience. Throughout the remaining seminars in the first section of *The Four Fundamental Concepts of Psycho-Analysis*, "The Unconscious and Repetition," Lacan will return to the vocabulary of modern materialism when he makes this claim. He refers, for example, to the Freudian notion of trauma so important for Breton using the modern materialist vocabulary of the encounter. Trauma is recast in surrealist terms, not only as an encounter but as an "essential encounter" ("capital" is the term Breton and Eluard used when they inquired about the determining power of the encounter in the survey published in *Minotaure*, numbers 3–4). "What we have in the discovery of psycho-analysis is an encounter [*rencontre*], an essential encounter—an appointment to which we are always called with a real that eludes us," Lacan writes of the impossible encounter with the real responsible for giving the subject its distinctive form.[58]

In addition, Lacan sounds most surrealist when he speculates about the objective content of the psychoanalytic real revealed in the encounter. He pursues this speculation by raising an issue familiar from modern materialism's discussion of what kind of material-psychic overdetermination may produce the encounter: On what interpretation of chance does such an encounter depend? Lacan baptizes his notion of the chance at issue in these experiences in antique terms that seem to take him away from the tenets of modern materialism. He turns to the fourth and fifth books of Aristotle's *Physics*, where Aristotle uses the terms *tuché* and *automaton*, which, Lacan tells us, "are incorrectly translated as *chance* and *fortune*."[59] From the improper translations as chance and luck, Lacan claims, he returns these terms to their more proper meanings, which he suggests as close to notions elaborated by Freud. "First, the *tuché*, which we have borrowed, as I told you last time, from Aristotle, who uses it in his search for cause. We have translated it as the encounter with the real [*la rencontre du réel*]. The real is beyond the *automaton*, the return, the coming-back

---

58. Lacan, "Tuché and Automaton," in *The Four Fundamental Concepts*, 53.
59. Lacan, "Of the Network of Signifiers," in *The Four Fundamental Concepts*, 52.

[*la revenue*], the insistence of the signs, by which we see ourselves governed by the pleasure principle. The real is that which always lies behind the *automaton*." [60]

Nonetheless, modern materialist traces persist even in Lacan's Aristotelian exposition of chance. These traces are visible when Lacan returns to the fact that some weird material form of overdetermination seems at work in what is generally considered an experience with purely psychic reality, the experience of the dream. Lacan's seminar from February 12, 1964 moves from *Beyond the Pleasure Principle* to one of Freud's dream narratives in *The Interpretation of Dreams,* the dream of the father watching over his dead son. When Freud interprets this dream, he defines a second motive to the dream besides the fulfillment of wishes, the motive of prolonging sleep. To prolong sleep against what, Lacan asks: "*What is it that wakes the sleeper?* Is it not, *in* the dream, another reality?" [61] This is the reality of desire that is simultaneously the reality of loss, a reality, that is to say, where the opposition between material and psychic no longer holds: "Desire manifests itself in the dream by the loss expressed in an image at the most cruel point of the object." [62] Lacan, that is to say, considers a collapse between external events and psychic reality resembling the encounter so important to Breton. When Lacan defines the reality manifested in this obscure collapse, he uses a Bretonian term. Lacan writes, "The real may be represented by the accident, the noise, the small element of reality [*peu-de-réalité*], which is evidence that we are not dreaming. But, on the other hand, this reality is not so small, for what wakes us is the other reality hidden behind the lack of that which takes the place of representation—this, says Freud, is the *Trieb*." [63] The discussion of the "peu-de-réalité" that is simultaneously not so small because it gives access to a reality that can never be represented in positive terms is reminiscent of Breton's "Introduction au discours sur le peu de réalité" with its interest in dislocating the "boundaries of the *so-called real*" for the reality always elsewhere. [64]

Lacan also invokes the surrealist view of the other reality at issue in uncanny chance by prefacing his discussion of the "peu-de-réalité" with an allusion to Breton's *Manifesto of Surrealism*. He speaks of a dream caused by "knocking at my door just before I actually awoke. With

60. Lacan, "Tuché and Automaton," in *The Four Fundamental Concepts,* 53–54.
61. Lacan, "Tuché and Automaton," in *The Four Fundamental Concepts,* 58.
62. Lacan, "Tuché and Automaton," in *The Four Fundamental Concepts,* 59.
63. Lacan, "Tuché and Automaton," in *The Four Fundamental Concepts,* 60.
64. André Breton, "Introduction au discours sur le peu de réalité," in *Point du jour,* 25 (emphasis added).

this impatient knocking [*coups*] I had already formed a dream, a dream that manifested to me something other than this knocking," and Lacan goes on to compare awakening [*le coup de réveil*] to a knocking of its own.[65] In doing so he alludes to and modifies an experience recounted by Breton in the *Manifesto* to introduce the way in which the surrealist subject is called by that other reality within everyday life: "One evening, therefore, before I fell asleep, I perceived . . . a phrase, if I may be so bold, *which was knocking at the window*" (M, 21). When Althusser describes the moment of ideological recognition, he makes it vivid by appealing to the experience both Lacan and Breton use to describe contact with the hidden unconscious reality constructing the subject. Althusser cites an experience of knocking, when a friend knocks "on our door and we ask, through the door, the question 'Who's there?', answer (since 'it's obvious') 'It's me'. And we recognize that 'it is him', or 'her'. We open the door, and 'it's true, it really was she who was there.'"[66]

If Lacan echoes Breton's modern materialist encounter in his exposition of the uncanny meeting with the psychoanalytic real, he also modifies it substantially. What is most important to note is that Lacan's understanding of the encounter contrasts both with Breton's suggestion that the encounter foreshadows some future moment of surrealist revolution and with Breton's general representation of this experience in highly positive terms. For Lacan the subject's essential encounter is a meeting that has already occurred and occurred badly. But Lacan's explanation of the negative nature of the essential encounter could be used to explain the fundamentally unsatisfying nature of the surrealist encounter palpable even through Breton's highly affirmative rhetoric. No surrealist encounter ever quite fulfills the promise that it held. At no moment does the subject get more than a glimmer of supposedly eman-

---

65. Lacan, "Tuché and Automaton," in *The Four Fundamental Concepts*, 56.
66. Althusser, "Ideology and Ideological State Apparatuses," in *Lenin and Philosophy*, 172. For an illuminating discussion of the relation between Lacan and Althusser around the problem of interpellation, see Slavoj Žižek's *The Sublime Object of Ideology*, a text that both takes its title from a surrealist-inspired film and bears an illustration from Max Ernst's *Une Semaine de Bonté* on its cover. Žižek assesses the Real revealed in the father's dream of the burning child as follows: "The thing that he encounters in the dream, the reality of his desire, the Lacanian Real . . . is more terrifying than so-called external reality itself," and Žižek explains: "It is exactly the same with ideology. Ideology is not a dreamlike illusion that we build to escape insupportable reality; in its basic dimension it is a fantasy-construction which serves as a support for our 'reality' itself: an 'illusion' which structures our effective, real, social relations and thereby masks some insupportable, real, impossible kernel (conceptualized by Ernesto Laclau and Chantal Mouffe as 'antagonism': a traumatic social division which cannot be symbolized)." See Slavoj Žižek, *The Sublime Object of Ideology*, 45.

cipatory unconscious reality or discover an end to the metonymical substitution of desire; the experience of recognition is always also an experience of misrecognition. The sequel to the ending of *Nadja* encapsulates the fate of all surrealist encounters: "All I know is that this substitution of persons stops with you, because nothing can be substituted for you," writes Breton in his conclusion to the text, giving closure by suggesting that he has finally had the encounter to end all encounters (*OC, 752; N,* 158).[67] To discover that substitution continues to operate following this encounter, however, one need only open the subsequent works of the Parisian prose trilogy. "What, speaking of the function of desire, I have designated as *manque-à-être,* a 'want-to be,'" Lacan writes of the real that is revealed in "an appointment to which we are always called with a real that eludes us."[68] Lacan's notion of the fundamental lack revealed in the encounter sums up the progressive discovery of Breton's haunting subject across his prose trilogy.

One more similarity between Breton and Lacan on the problem of the encounter deserves mention: Lacan opposes his notion of the *tuché* to an orthodox Marxist notion of praxis. Lacan opens his seminar of February 12 with the following statement:

> I wish to stress here that, at first sight, psychoanalysis seems to lead in the direction of idealism.
>
> God knows that it has been reproached enough for this—it reduces the experience, some say, that urges us to find in the hard supports of conflict, struggle, even of the exploitation of man by man, the reasons for our deficiencies—it leads to an ontology of the tendencies, which it regards as primitive, internal, already given by the condition of the subject.
>
> We have only to consider the course of this experience from its first steps to see, on the contrary, that it in no way allows us to accept some such aphorism as *life is a dream.* No praxis is more oriented towards that which, at the heart of experience, is the kernel of the real than psycho-analysis.[69]

"Struggle," "exploitation of man by man," "praxis": Lacan summons up orthodox Marxism by employing its hard-hitting vocabulary as he directs his interest in the psychoanalytic real against the same vision of praxis so problematic for Breton. Lacan appeals too to a similar aspect of Freud's thought to answer charges that psychoanalysis is lost in idealism. He asserts the materiality of the psychoanalytic real by focusing not only on Freud's discussion of dreams but also by discussing Freud on trauma, an experience when the subject visibly enters into

67. I follow Howard's translation of this passage verbatim.
68. Lacan, "Of the Subject of Certainty," in *The Four Fundamental Concepts,* 29. Lacan, "Tuché and Automaton," in *The Four Fundamental Concepts,* 53.
69. Lacan, "Tuché and Automaton," in *The Four Fundamental Concepts,* 53.

contact with some alien real. "Is it not remarkable," he asks in the middle of this seminar focusing on Freud's fundamental text of trauma, *Beyond the Pleasure Principle,* "that, at the origin of the analytic experience, the real should have presented itself in the form of that which is *unassimilable* in it—in the form of the trauma, determining all that follows?" [70]

Lacan sets forth the constitution of the realm where material and psychic overdetermination collapse with much greater depth and coherence than Breton. For Lacan the factors of material overdetermination become the symbolic order that Lacan terms the Other, as Lacan's *tuché* situates the subject at the meeting between psychic drives and the symbolic order: "I say somewhere that *the unconscious is the discourse of the Other,*" writes Lacan in a subsequent seminar.[71] "Now, the discourse of the Other that is to be realized, that of the unconscious, is not beyond the closure, it is *outside.*" [72] Certainly, Lacan's interest in the unconscious nature of the symbolic order has intimate links to the privileged formative and performative power that surrealism accords language, Breton's "after you, my beautiful language" from the "Introduction au discours sur le peu de réalité." [73] Nonetheless, Lacan has suppressed the Marxist vocabulary in which Breton talks of the external determination at issue in the collapse of psychic and objective causality; it is no longer a question, as in *Mad Love,* of viewing chance as the moment when Engels's forces of objective necessity mark the subject's unconscious.

When Althusser incorporates the *tuché* into his notion of ideological recognition, he both displaces Lacan's Other toward a Marxist version of material determination and, following Lacan, recasts this determination in psychoanalytic terms as overdetermination. For Althusser ideological recognition is a fundamental (imaginary) misrecognition of unconscious forces, but, unlike Lacan, he construes the unconscious not only in symbolic-libidinal but also in economic terms. In such displacement, however, Althusser returns the *tuché* to the theoretical concerns at its source. Like a divining rod, Althusser recognizes the Marxist contribution implicit in the concept that Lacan proposes to seize the material content of the psychoanalytic real: the contribution of Breton's encounter reconciling Engels and Freud.

70. Lacan, "Tuché and Automaton," in *The Four Fundamental Concepts,* 55.
71. Lacan, "Presence of the Analyst," in *The Four Fundamental Concepts,* 131.
72. Lacan, "Presence of the Analyst," in *The Four Fundamental Concepts,* 131.
73. Breton, "Introduction au discours sur le peu de réalité," in *Point du jour,* 23. See David Macey, *Lacan in Contexts,* for a discussion of this link.

CHAPTER 6

The *Rencontre Capitale*

The mechanism of waiting (I know that well). To
be generalized indefinitely.

                                 —*Breton*

THE NIGHT OF THE SUNFLOWER

On May 29, 1934 Breton has an uncanny *rencontre* with a beautiful
woman whom he meets in an area of Paris reminiscent of his favorite
sites in *Nadja*: "this liveliest and, at times, most disquieting part of
Montmartre" (*AF,* 65; *ML,* 43).[1] The two arrange a late-night rendez-
vous at the well-known Café des Oiseaux and set out from there in the
early hours of the morning to wander the Parisian streets. Although
Breton is madly attracted to his companion, he is already involved in
a relationship with another woman, and he uses his walk to engage in
intense self-examination. Should he overturn his life for this "*scandalously* beautiful" woman, he wonders, and by the time that he has
wandered with her from Montmartre to the nighttime market at Les
Halles, he decides against it (*AF,* 63; *ML,* 41).[2]

But suddenly reaching the heart of Paris, "the *quartier* of la Cité,"
Breton has an experience of troubling dizziness which leads him to
change his mind. Why his vertigo has this effect is something the narrative does not make clear. All Breton states is that it may have to do
with the cradle of Paris in which his promenade occurs: "I succumb to
the wonderful dizziness that these places perhaps inspire in me" (*AF,*
73; *ML,* 47). While critics attentive to Breton's interest in alchemy have

1. I follow Caws's translation of this passage verbatim.
2. Again, I follow Caws verbatim.

pointed to the importance of the Tour Saint-Jacques in producing Breton's sudden euphoria it is, in fact, the Hôtel de Ville that directly precipitates Breton's inexplicable alteration.[3] And if, lacking any visible reason for the power of Paris to unleash such dizziness, we turn to *Nadja*'s treatment of the Parisian uncanny, we see that the *quartier* of the Cité is filled with some well-known ghosts. A few lines from the 1925 *Paris et ses environs* suffice to recall the Hôtel de Ville's historical significance: "Let us recall the storms that thundered there during the revolutionary assemblies of the Commune of Paris, Robespierre who futilely sought asylum there on 9 Thermidor, and was reduced to committing suicide without succeeding in this either. And all the revolutions of the nineteenth century having there their *dénouement* and their triumph."[4] As in *Nadja,* ghosts of civil insurrection and specifically class struggle are associated with this disturbing site.

As in *Nadja* too traces of these ghosts are obliquely visible in the details preceding this uncanny moment rending the fabric of everyday life. Having already explored Breton's oblique method of evoking an unstated Parisian past in detail, I give only one example from *Mad Love.* Prior to his vertigo, Breton discusses the Tour Saint-Jacques, which takes him, with the metonymic displacement familiar from Freudian dream logic, to a poem that he wrote on the tower comparing it to a sunflower. *Tournesol* is French for both sunflower and litmus paper:

> The very change from blue to red which constitutes the specific property of the reactive-sunflower can doubtless be justified by analogy with the distinctive colors of Paris whose cradle this quarter of the Cité is, of Paris which is expressed here in a quite specifically organic and *essential* way by its Hôtel de Ville, which we leave on our left as we walk towards the Latin Quarter. I succumb to the wonderful dizziness that these places perhaps inspire in me, places where everything I will have best known began. I have, suddenly, disposed of the previous representations which had just been threatening to subjugate me. . . . Let this curtain of shadows be lifted and let me be led fearlessly towards the light! (*AF,* 70–73; *ML,* 47–49)

The English translation renders the profoundly ambiguous first lines of this passage in overly clear fashion. When Breton explains his fascination with the colors of the city of Paris evoked by the litmus paper,

---

3. On the significance of alchemical history for Breton, see Balakian's *André Breton,* Jean Gaulmier's "Remarques sur le thème de Paris chez André Breton," and Inez Hedges's *Languages of Revolt.*
4. Bournon and Dauzat, *Paris et ses environs,* 35–36.

he employs a tortured, opaque language full of double negatives and qualifying statements. The original French reads: "Il n'est pas jusqu'au virement du bleu au rouge en quoi réside la propriété spécifique du tournesol-réactif dont le rappel ne soit sans doute justifié par analogie avec les couleurs distinctives de Paris" (*AF*, 70). Such language is typical of Breton's haunting writing, which functions to undercut the explanations it puts forth. "Doubtless" the transformation of the litmus paper is not only justified by its comparison to the colors of Paris, for the transformation of blue to red in the context of Parisian history is one with a more explicitly political significance. Breton is fascinated here, as at *Nadja*'s place Dauphine, by the color adopted by radical revolutionaries.

Although *Nadja* and *Mad Love* share a collective Parisian uncanny, its structure and content in each work take a somewhat different cast. In *Nadja*'s uncanny encounters the subject's personal concerns focus on the problem of social revolution and these concerns are not repressed. Contacting a mixture of libidinal and political forces in his strolls with the bohemian Nadja, Breton is interested in the social application of the bohemian powers unchained. In *Mad Love* the effaced collective ghosts unleash Breton's own sentimental energies that have been held in check. When Breton calls the Hôtel de Ville the *heart* of Paris, beating "throughout the stroll, as we have seen, in unison with mine," he draws attention to the Parisian ghosts' imbrication in the subject's sentimental life (*AF*, 94; *ML*, 64).[5]

The affect surrounding Breton's own "encounter of capital importance" in *Mad Love* also differs from *Nadja*'s uncanny experiences (*AF*, 27; *ML*, 19). In *Nadja*, the strange encounters heighten the *trouble* of the surrealist subject, who never quite uncovers the "it" tracked throughout the text. On the night of the sunflower, in contrast, the collapse of the heart of Paris into the heart of the *flâneur* dispels Breton's fear. Breton stresses the positive power of the ghosts on this night to free him from the past or at least from the constraining presence of his own past. "I have, suddenly, disposed of the previous representations which had just been threatening to restrain me," he declares positively. "I feel myself freed from those ties that made me still believe in the impossibility, in the realm of affect, of getting rid of my character of yesterday" (*AF*, 73; *ML*, 47–49). Tomorrow is in no way determined by today, Breton decides: "Tomorrow will be *other* . . . it is mysteri-

5. I follow Caws's translation here verbatim.

ously, entirely torn from yesterday" (*AF, 69; ML, 47*). The ghosts serve precisely the therapeutic psychic function that Breton accords to the *trouvaille*: "*The finding of an object serves here exactly the same purpose as the dream, in the sense that it frees the individual from paralyzing affective scruples, comforts him and makes him understand that the obstacle he might have thought unsurmountable is overcome*" (*AF, 44; ML, 32*).

THE AXIAL FLOWER AND
THE PRAXIS OF DESIRE

A happy ending thus results from *Mad Love*'s Parisian phantomatic therapy: the insurrectional ghosts of Paris free Breton to live out his desire and he gets the girl. But Breton also devotes such space to representing this event because it justifies assumptions crucial to his modern materialist view of activity with socially transformative potential. The night of the sunflower validates one of the great dreams of surrealist praxis, that repressed desire does not simply manifest itself through the events of the external world but in fact *produces* them.

Breton's meeting with the beautiful woman and his meeting with Paris are not the only uncanny encounters that lend the night of the sunflower such "capital importance" in *Mad Love*. Getting up on "one of the first mornings following this long night walk in Paris," Breton recalls a fragment from one of his 1923 automatic poems, "Sunflower," which he had not looked at for many years (*AF, 77; ML, 53*).[6] Rereading this poem, he discovers that it describes his experience with the scandalously beautiful woman eleven years before the event occurred, although in 1923, this experience was represented in the disfigured and condensed form typical of material under repression.

To demonstrate the correspondence between the 1923 poem and 1934 event, Breton has recourse to Freudian techniques of dream analysis, even laying out his discussion in the typographical layout familiar from Freud's writings on dreams. Breaking the poem down into discrete fragments, Breton employs italics to designate the text produced through the processes of repression. Like Freud too Breton follows the fragment with a paragraph or two explaining how this text of repression manifests unconscious concerns. Here as elsewhere, however, Breton gives his invocation of psychoanalysis a modern materialist

6. I follow Caws's translation of this phrase verbatim.

twist. For Freud the repressed text is the retrospective manifestation of earlier psychic disturbances. For Breton, in contrast, the text of repression masks objectively verifiable events that occur many years later. "I say that there isn't anything in this poem of 1923 that did not announce the most important thing that was to happen to me in 1934" (*AF*, 95; *ML*, 65).

Such correspondence endows Breton's night of the sunflower with more than personal significance. While political revolutionaries found Breton's practical interest in the unconscious highly dubious, the night of the sunflower demonstrates that unconscious forces seep through objective reality in deferred and hidden fashion, their effect only evident many years later, after their subterranean work is complete. Strangely, in *Communicating Vessels* Breton enunciates his faith in the subterranean effectiveness of surrealist unchaining by using a trope that prefigures his experience on the night of the sunflower with uncanny prescience. When Breton attacks the teleological view of revolutionary activity admitted by the French Communist Party, he writes:

> Who knows if it is not fitting that there should be shaped, in the most tormented periods and even against their will, the solitude of a few beings whose role is to avoid letting perish that which should have a fleeting existence only in a corner of the hothouse, in order to find much later its place at the center of the new order, thus marking with a *flower* [emphasis added] absolutely and simply present because *true*—a flower in some way *axial in relation to time*—that tomorrow should conjugate itself all the more closely with yesterday for having to break in a more decisive manner with it? (*V*, 159; *CV*, 137–138)[7]

Breton's flower turns with what Benjamin would call "a secret heliotropism" "toward the sun which is rising in the sky of history."[8] Breton concludes the night of the sunflower by explicitly brandishing his narrative against the French Communist Party:

> I have insisted, especially in *Les Vases communicants*, on the fact that self-analysis alone is, in many cases, capable of *exhausting* the content of dreams,

7. In French this difficult Bretonian sentence runs:

Qui sait s'il ne convient point qu'aux époques les plus tourmentées se creuse ainsi malgré eux la solitude de quelques êtres, dont le rôle est d'éviter que périsse ce qui ne doit subsister passagèrement que dans un coin de serre, pour trouver beaucoup plus tard sa place au centre du nouvel ordre, marquant ainsi d'une fleur absolument et simplement présente, parce que *vraie*, d'une fleur en quelque sorte *axiale par rapport au temps*, que demain doit se conjuguer d'autant plus étroitement avec hier qu'il doit rompre d'une manière plus décisive avec lui? (*V*, 159)

8. Benjamin, "Theses on the Philosophy of History," in *I*, 255. The parallel between Breton's and Benjamin's figurations of historical process remains to be explored.

and that this analysis, if it is thorough enough, leaves none of the *residue* that might permit us to attribute a transcendental character to oneiric activity. On the other hand, it seems to me that I deviated too quickly when I had to explain that, similarly, self-analysis could sometimes exhaust the content of real events, to the point of making them depend entirely on the least directed prior activity of the mind. The concern that I had, on the revolutionary level, not to cut myself off from practical action, perhaps kept me from pushing my thought to its limits, given the difficulty of making most of the revolutionaries *of that period* share such a dialectically rigorous point of view. Not having for all that been able to pass over to practical action, I feel today no scruples in returning to it, all the more *since I think this time I have at my disposal a far more conclusive document than the one I relied on then* [emphasis added]. I say that there isn't anything in this poem of 1923 that did not announce the most important thing that was to happen to me in 1934. (*AF*, 94–95; *ML*, 64–65)

"Turn, earth [*sol*]," Breton writes of the vertigo that he experiences on the night of the sunflower, describing the transformation that his encounter with the beautiful woman works on his own life as the earth moving or, as it is also called, a revolution (*AF*, 73; *ML*, 49).

LYRIC BEHAVIOR AND THE APPLE'S OTHER HALF

In his chapter devoted to the night of the sunflower Breton accompanies his demonstration that unconscious forces can change the world with a call for "*lyric behavior*," most obviously love and poetry (*AF*, 77; *ML*, 53).[9] He justifies his interest in this behavior with a modern materialist breakdown of the material/ideal distinction. He writes:

It is only by making evident the intimate relation linking the two terms *real* and *imaginary* that I hope to deal a new blow to the distinction, which seems to me less and less well founded, between the subjective and the objective. It is only from the meditation that can be brought to bear on this relationship that I ask if the idea of *causality* doesn't come out completely in disarray. It is only, finally, by underlining the continuous and perfect coincidence of two series of facts considered—until a new order—as rigorously independent, that I intend to justify and advocate more and more choice of a *lyric behavior*. (*AF*, 77; *ML*, 53)

But at moments Breton's praise of that most exemplary of lyric behaviors, mad love, comes uncomfortably close to the bourgeois ideology that his modern materialism attacks. This is the case, for example, when Breton backs up his praise with appeal to the two fathers of

9. I follow Caws's translation of this phrase verbatim.

modern materialism in *Mad Love*'s chapter five. There Breton quotes Engels and Freud asserting that individual sex-love, particularly monogamy, contributes to cultural progress. In doing so, however, he appeals to moments when these thinkers preserve bourgeois ideology intact in unreflected form, advancing views of history and morality that modern materialism questions elsewhere. Breton cites Engles on monogamous love as a tool of "moral progress," and Freud on sexual love as contributing to "cultural progress." Yet more disturbing, Breton seems to follow the example of Engels and Freud in his praise of their texts: "These two testimonies [of Engels and Freud], which present a conception, less and less frivolous, of love as a fundamental principle for moral as well as cultural progress, would seem to me by themselves of such a nature as to give poetic activity a major role as a tried and tested means to fix the perceptible and moving world on a single being as well as a permanent force of anticipation" (*AF,* 113; *ML,* 77). Breton's praise of love here falls back into the commonplaces of bourgeois morality even more quickly than the avant-garde unchaining proposed by *Nadja.* The domain of individual sentimental relations has long functioned in bourgeois society as compensation for economic, political, and other social inequalities, cited by bourgeois thinkers throughout the nineteenth century as the place where these inequalities are to be remedied.

But Breton's rather reactionary praise of the social potential of individual love is less straightforward than it seems. If the night of the sunflower fulfills Breton's dream concerning the practical social power of desire, Breton's text also questions this power at the very moment that its surrealist hero puts it forth. Through such questioning Breton can be read as exposing the ideological dimension to his notion of mad love and, more generally, the socially transformative power that he proposes for lyric behavior. This reading reconciles Breton's praise of love with modern materialism in less than emancipatory fashion. Pessimistic utopianism is, however, a fundamental surrealist stance from the founding hyperbole of the *Manifesto of Surrealism*: "It is in quest of this surreality that I am going, certain not to find it but too unmindful of my death not to calculate to some slight degree the joys of its possession" (*M,* 14). "The spirit of *demoralization* has elected domicile," Breton writes of the imagined surrealist brotherhood that the *Manifesto* sets up in a *château* (*M,* 17).

Breton's haunting writing is among the tactics that undercut his hyperbolic praise of mad love on the night of the sunflower. Here, as throughout his prose exposition, Breton uses ambiguity, hyperbole, and the multiplication of qualifying statements to blur the clarity of his assertions. Breton's previously cited opaque sentence framing the power of Paris to change his heart exemplifies this practice. While Breton asserts the power of his mad love to bring about a new order, its arrival in fact never comes. "Let this curtain of shadows be lifted and let me be led fearlessly toward the light! Turn, earth [*sol*]," Breton states, but he uses the subjunctive tense of longing, with no indication that his command is accomplished (*AF,* 73; *ML,* 49). The promenade, moreover, ends not in the promised light of day, but only the "morning twilight" [10] (*AF,* 75; *ML,* 51). One more "demoralizing" strategy on the night of the sunflower is reminiscent of *Nadja*: the ambiguous messages of the collective ghosts summoned up. The ghosts that initiate Breton's sentimental revolution are those of insurrectional failure (albeit spectacular) rather than success, as Breton once more confronts his readers with surrealism's ambivalent relation to the revolutionary tradition that Benjamin so aptly terms the clearance sale of revolution. Breton calls attention to this feature of the ghosts by the curious term that he chooses to designate the Hôtel de Ville. The adjective "organic" is inaccurate in a socially significant way; rather than an organic part of the Parisian cradle, the Hôtel de Ville is a structure designed to give that illusion. Torched by the Commune in 1871 during the last days of street fighting, the Hôtel de Ville was largely destroyed. One of the first gestures of the new bourgeois republic was to build this structure to look as if it had stood for hundreds of years, thereby effacing any visual reminder of the Commune's recent challenge to bourgeois rule. As Freud comments on screen memories: "Strong forces from later life have been at work on the capacity of childhood experiences for being remembered," leaving "not the genuine memory-trace but a later revision of it, a revision which may have been subjected to the influences of a variety of later psychical forces." [11]

When Breton calls the Hôtel de Ville "organic," there is a substantial gap between his adjective and the reality to which it applies. The nonorganic condition of the Hôtel de Ville exemplifies, moreover, the generally nonorganic condition of the entire cradle of Paris which produces Breton's vertigo. This condition results, as in the case of the Hôtel de Ville, from the area's failed revolutionary past. As the administrative

10. This word is *crépuscule* in French; Breton will name the daughter he conceives with the heroine of the night of the sunflower *Aube,* dawn.
11. Freud, *The Psychopathology of Everyday Life,* VI, 47–48.

center of Paris and an area with a large working-class population, the *quartier* of the Cité was a site of much of the revolutionary activity that repeatedly erupted in the capital city in the years 1789–1851. Consequently, when Haussmann sought to gentrify central Paris, this was the area that he most profoundly changed.[12] Seeking to displace its working-class population, Haussmann sought to efface even its potential to recall details from its revolutionary past. As Louis Chevalier puts it: "Destroying the old quarter of the Cité to the point of effacing it completely from the map of Paris, Haussmann will destroy much more than a heap of broken-down houses and criminals' haunts. . . . He will destroy the very images that this quarter evoked, provoked, and which were attached to it in the memory of the people of Paris."[13] After the destruction of the Hôtel de Ville by the Paris Commune, the Tour Saint-Jacques remained one of the few fragments of the pre-Haussmannized past left in this area. Does its link to pre-Haussmannized Paris contribute to the power that Breton accords it on his promenade? Such, at least, is the conclusion suggested by the phrase Breton uses to describe the tower. "The world's great monument to the unrevealed," Breton calls the Tour, echoing Victor Hugo's description of the Tour Saint-Jacques in *Notre-Dame de Paris* as that Parisian structure "which poses to new Paris the riddle of the old" (*AF*, 69; *ML*, 47).[14]

But perhaps the most definitive indication that the night of the sunflower may be less than a jubilant praise of the praxis of desire is the

12. David Pinkney describes Haussmann's reconstruction of the right bank near the Seine as follows: "Between 1851 and 1856 the demolitions for the Central Markets and for the Rue de Rivoli forced thousands from the crowded quarters just north of the river. The population of the Arcis quarter at the eastern end of the Rue de Rivoli fell from nearly 12,000 in 1851 to fewer than 4,000 in 1856." David Pinkney, *Napoleon III and the Rebuilding of Paris*, 165. Pinkney writes of the Ile de la Cité, where Breton ends his promenade:

> On the Ile de la Cité Haussmann did not quite achieve his ambition of demolishing every private building on the island and making it the exclusive preserve of law, religion, and medicine, but he came very close to it. In all of old Paris no other area of comparable size was so completely altered by new or remodeled buildings. In 1850, aside from the Cathedral, the Palace of Justice, and two buildings of the Public Relief Administration, the island was covered with a mass of old houses into which crowded more than 14,000 residents, making it one of the worst slums of Paris. In 1870 only two small triangles of houses remained, one between the cathedral and the north branch of the river and the other opposite the new west front of the Palace of Justice, and but a few hundred people made their homes on the Island. (p. 87)

Anthony Sutcliffe states that from 1852 to 1855, 293 houses were demolished around the Tour Saint-Jacques to make way for a public garden. Anthony Sutcliffe, *The Autumn of Central Paris*, 126.

13. Chevalier, *Classes laborieuses et Classes dangereuses*, 183.

14. Hugo, *Notre-Dame de Paris*, 152.

haunting presence of the prostitute in Breton's representation of mad love. In the Marxist theory important to Breton, the prostitute is a figure used to expose the praise of monogamy as bourgeois ideology masking the unsatisfactory content of sexual and sentimental life in capitalist society.[15] Breton's other discussions of the vicissitudes of love in capitalist society make clear that he was well aware of the prostitute's Marxist significance.

The prostitute is used in this fashion in a text cited by Breton both in *Communicating Vessels* and *Mad Love*: Engels's *The Origin of the Family, Private Property, and the State*. Breton alludes to Engels's text throughout his discussion of sentimental relations, although not always in the same way. In *Communicating Vessels* Breton's allusions serve to bolster a Marxist critique of love. Proclaiming that "human love must be rebuilt, like the rest," he calls for a transformation of the social order which will permit "the accession," as he puts it,

> to love and to everything else worthwhile in life by this new generation announced by Engels: "a generation of men who never in their lives will have had to purchase with money, or any social power, a woman's surrender [*l'abandon d'une femme*]; and a generation of women who will never have needed to give themselves to a man for any other reason than real love, nor to refuse themselves to their lover from fear of the economic consequences." (*V*, 136–137; *CV*, 116–117)

In the statement cited by Breton, Engels asserts the impossibility of satisfactory sentimental-sexual relations in current society because women are socially subordinate to men. Relations between the sexes are consequently not based on what Engels calls "real love" but rather constitute economics and politics by other means. Prostitution is the activity that Engels uses to characterize sexual relations in this society, whether legally sanctioned or practiced on the sidewalks of the night. Engels, indeed, points out that prostitution and the legally sanctioned marriage that Victorian culture opposes to it are not only surprisingly similar but also interdependent. Based on financial interest rather than "sex love," monogamous marriage is a form of prostitution that forces men to purchase sexual favors elsewhere: "At the side of the husband who embellishes his existence with hetaerism stands the neglected wife.

15. Following the ambiguously misogynist lead of Baudelaire, Benjamin was interested in the prostitute as an embodiment of distinctive features of modernity as well as for her privileged link to the commodity. On the first aspect of Benjamin's interest in the prostitute, see Janet Wolff, "The Invisible *Flâneuse*," in *The Problems of Modernity*, ed. Andrew Benjamin. Buck-Morss discusses the relationship of the prostitute to the commodity in *The Dialectics of Seeing*.

And one cannot have one side of this contradiction without the other, any more than a man has a whole apple in his hand after eating half." [16]

But while in *Communicating Vessels* Breton concurs with Engels in proposing current sentimental-sexual relations as deformed by unsatisfactory material conditions, he appeals to *The Origin of the Family* in rather different fashion in *Mad Love*. Here he not only uses Engels against the general sense of Engels's argument but cites a passage from Engels which, when taken in context, in fact contradicts the point that Breton invokes it to make. "Once private property has been abolished," Breton writes in support of his argument on the socially transformative potential of *current* monogamous love, " 'we can reasonably affirm,' declares Engels, 'that *far from disappearing, monogamy will rather be realized for the first time*' " (*AF,* 112; *ML,* 77). The Engels passage to which Breton refers is, however, less than affirmative about the future existence of monogamy and decidedly negative about the current existence of monogamy as a socially improving force. "Having arisen from economic causes, will monogamy then disappear when these causes disappear," asks Engels, and he continues:

> One might answer, not without reason: far from disappearing, it will on the contrary begin to be realized completely. For with the transformation of the means of production into social property there will disappear also wage labor, the proletariat, and therefore the necessity for a certain—statistically calculable—number of women to surrender themselves for money. Prostitution disappears; monogamy, instead of collapsing, at last becomes a reality—also for men.
>
> In any case, therefore, the position of the men will be very much altered. But the position of women, of *all* women, also undergoes significant change . . . have we not seen that in the modern world monogamy and prostitution are indeed contradictions but inseparable contradictions, poles of the same state of society? Can prostitution disappear without dragging monogamy with it into the abyss? [17]

At the moment that Breton uses Engels to support the positive value of his current experience of monogamy, he quotes from Engels linking monogamy and prostitution in bourgeois society as the apple's two halves.[18] Dropping any mention of the context of Engels's statement, Breton provides negative confirmation of his awareness of the conflict between the text he invokes and the argument he uses it to make.

16. Friedrich Engels, *The Origin of the Family, Private Property, and the State,* 98.
17. Engels, *The Origin of the Family,* 106–107.
18. In the subsequent paragraph Engels complicates the matter further by introducing another factor into the equation which is also of interest to Breton: what Engels calls individual sex-love.

Breton's strolling surrealist is, moreover, uncomfortably close to "the husband who embellishes his existence with hetaerism": "At the side of the husband who embellishes his existence with hetaerism stands the neglected wife," Engels declares. On this evening Breton casts himself as a man who has momentarily deserted "the irreproachable being who had spent the time preceding this by my side" to take in Paris by night with a woman whom he describes with multiple, but oblique, allusions to prostitution (*AF*, 85; *ML*, 59).[19] These references, it should be stressed, conflict with the biographical details on which Breton's narration was based. Breton's stroll with a woman in Paris is modeled on his meeting with the painter Jacqueline Lamba, who became his second wife. But Breton makes no mention of the scandalously beautiful woman's artistic career in his narrative. Rather, he situates her in the lineage of bohemian women running throughout his Parisian trilogy, women whose activities as prostitutes the other works are not reluctant to expose.

PARIS BY NIGHT

When Breton meets the "all-powerful coordinator of the night of the sunflower," she resembles the other bohemian women who fill the pages of his trilogy (*AF*, 97; *ML*, 67). Nadja made no mystery of the means she would use to support herself if Breton did not give her money, and neither did the licentious Parisette of *Communicating Vessels*: "She was charming, moreover, and used a freedom of language that delighted me, as good as Juliette's in the marvelous book by Sade. . . . I accompanied her to Meudon, where, she confided to me, an old man under the influence of her charms was waiting for her" (*V*, 115–116; *CV*, 97). Like Parisette, the "all powerful coordinator" is a dancer in a nightclub, and, like Parisette, she is in a café writing a letter when Breton meets her. In addition, "*scandalously* beautiful," the text endows her with a bohemian lineage. When Breton first meets her, he compares her to a fern "in the ruins of . . . a splendid fourteenth-century French town today abandoned to gypsies [*bohémiens*]" (*AF*, 62; *ML*, 41).[20] He also links her to "ancient Egypt," a realm perhaps associated in *Communicating Vessels* with prostitution when Breton mentions "the extraordinary nostalgia always invoked in me, from the age of thirteen or fourteen, by violet eyes of the kind that had fascinated me in a woman who had

19. I follow Caws's translation here verbatim.
20. I follow Caws's translation here verbatim.

to work the sidewalk at the corner of the Rue Réaumur and Rue de Palestro. I was, I remember so well, with my father. Never again . . . did I find myself in front of such a *sphinx*" (*V*, 120; *CV*, 101; emphasis added).

The social connotations of the Parisian spaces in which Breton pursues the scandalously beautiful woman evoke the activity of prostitution as well. Breton not only meets her in Montmartre, the 1934 capital of Parisian prostitution, but meets her in "this liveliest and, at times, most *disquieting* [*la plus trouble*] part of Montmartre," as he qualifies the area with an adjective recalling the illicit commerce for which Montmartre of the time was famed (*AF*, 65; *ML*, 43; emphasis added).[21] Breton strengthens the social importance he accords to this area when he specifies the night-spot where he meets this woman later that evening, the Café des Oiseaux. Its well-known contemporary ambiance, unmentioned by Breton, is described by Chevalier: "Sitting at tables, the bourgeoisie out on the town, from this quarter or elsewhere. At the counter, the people of the night, from La Chapelle and from Barbès who stop a moment to have a drink on their way to Pigalle."[22] When Breton and the beautiful woman go out for their promenade, they continue to visit Paris by night. They proceed to Les Halles, a recognized site of prostitution, largely because of its late-night central market. Breton once more underlines the social importance he accords this area by the locale he suggests as typical of it, the Chien qui fume. While Breton fails to describe its clientele, the *Pleasure Guide to Paris* supplements his lacuna:

> Thus, on leaving the *Grappe d'Or*, take the *rue des Halles*, already beginning to wake up, to go and eat oysters or onion-soup at the *Restaurant du Chien qui fume*, rue du Pont-Neuf, corner of rue Berger.
> At three in the morning, the ground-floor, the small saloons on the first floor, and private rooms are all full of supper.
> The very motley ensemble is most interesting. The lady in evening-dress is side by side with the young workgirl or the hatless prostitute.[23]

Breton's failure to describe the late-night aspect of this spot might be attributed to an aesthetic *parti pris*, surrealism's "case against the realist attitude."[24] But Breton shows no reluctance about giving social

21. I follow Caws's translation here verbatim.
22. Louis Chevalier, *Montmartre du plaisir et du crime*, 370.
23. *Pleasure Guide to Paris*, 129.
24. Breton, *Manifesto*, in *M*, 6. I modify the translation's rendering of *réaliste* as "realistic." See *OC*, 313.

details of other sorts. If, discussing "the tiny streets of Les Halles," he does not mention the streetwalking for which it is known, he does comment on the fact that

> it becomes too hard to walk side by side among the trucks in this increasing noise, which mounts like the sea towards the immense appetite of the next day. My gaze and some magnificent white, red, and green cubes of the first vegetables of the season slide unfortunately upon the sidewalk, gleaming with horrendous garbage. It is also the hour when bands of revelers begin to pour out in this region to finish the night in some celebrated greasy spoon, *sounding in the vigorous rhythms of honest work the black, equivocal, and gauzy note of evening clothes, furs, and silks.* (AF, 68; ML, 45; emphasis added)[25]

The streets of Les Halles are peopled by "equivocal" members of the bourgeoisie who resemble the bourgeois clientele of the Café des Oiseaux and the Chien qui fume, but they appear next to "honest" workers (rather than hatless prostitutes) who fill "the immense appetite of the next day."

Oblique evocations of prostitution extend to the area where Breton and the scandalously beautiful woman finish their promenade. Despite its tranquil air, the cradle of Paris was, until its reconstruction by Baron Haussmann, not only a site of Parisian revolution but also the center of Parisian prostitution and crime. Breton demonstrates his interest in this past by alluding to a celebrated text by Hugo which preserves this area's now effaced bohemian form. In fact, references to Hugo's novel punctuate Breton's entire description of the area, as the phrase "the cradle of Paris" itself demonstrates. "Paris was born," writes Hugo in the chapter "A Bird's Eye View of Paris," "as is known, on this old Île de la Cité which has the shape of a cradle."[26] Hugo's text not only describes the Cité's long-ago character as an area of pleasure and crime but puts its medieval past in relation to its nineteenth-century bohemian state.[27]

25. I use here Caws's translation verbatim.

26. Hugo, *Notre-Dame*, 139. Hugo's phrase was dear to subsequent writers of Parisian guidebooks who maintain that Hugo himself took it from a prior tradition of Parisian guides.

27. While a possible second literary allusion to the nineteenth-century Paris of prostitution and crime is too vague to argue for, Breton's route through the cradle of Paris, crossing from the right bank to the Ile de la Cité across the Pont-au-Change, retraces the steps that open Eugène Sue's *Les Mystères de Paris,* an allusion Breton perhaps reinforces by ending his stroll in the Marché aux Fleurs dear to Sue's heroine, Fleur-de-Marie, where he compares his own companion to a flower. Sue's text opens with the following description of Breton's route: "Le 13 décembre 1838, par une soirée pluvieuse et froide, un

Breton thus simultaneously invokes and avoids the prostitute in the episode functioning as his primary piece of evidence for the social potential of monogamous love, as he represents her with strategies familiar from Freudian descriptions of the manifestation of repressed material. Might this representation be interpreted as strategic, a way for Breton to problematize the vision of love he is putting forth? As we have seen, Breton knew the Marxist literature viewing monogamous love as a construct of bourgeois ideology, the apple's other half of hetaerism. That Breton would simulate a text of repression is consistent with his previous practice. From surrealism's earliest forays into automatic writing, Breton simulates the texts of psychic turmoil studied by psychoanalysis. He not only produces texts resembling dreams and narrates uncanny experiences but in *The Immaculate Conception* goes so far as to imitate the discourse of those afflicted with "mental deficiency," "acute mania," "general paralysis," "interpretative delirium," and "dementia praecox."

Strategic or not, on the night of the sunflower the surrealist revolutionary, far from escaping the impasse of *Nadja,* plunges back in it, embroiled even more deeply than before. *Nadja* ends with Breton's hero acutely conscious of the contradictions between his articulated revolutionary aspirations and his class position, a contradiction he could not resolve in positive form. When Breton reformulates the relation between prostitute and surrealist revolutionary on the night of the sunflower, however, the surrealist hero loses what limited mastery over this impasse he previously possessed. Unable to recognize the contradictions of his position, the hero of *Mad Love*'s fourth chapter instead enacts them unconsciously; his situation, once poignant, is now painful beyond poignancy. Freud tells us that repression arises from contradiction and conflict too great to be surmounted, the sense of a "helpless and hopeless deadlock." [28] Freud writes:

> The satisfaction of an instinct which is under repression would be quite possible, and further . . . such a satisfaction would be pleasurable in itself; but it would be irreconcilable with other claims and intentions. It would, therefore, cause pleasure in one place and unpleasure in another. It has consequently become a condition for repression that the motive force of un-

---

homme . . . traversa le Pont-au-Change et s'enfonça dans la Cité, dédale de rues obscures, étroites, tortueuses, qui s'étend depuis le Palais-de-Justice jusqu'à Notre-Dame." Eugène Sue, *Les Mystères de Paris,* I, 5.

28. Sigmund Freud, "Remembering, Repeating and Working-Through," XII, 150.

pleasure shall have acquired more strength than the pleasure obtained from satisfaction.[29]

"*Chance is the form of manifestation of exterior necessity which traces [se fraie] its path in the human unconscious*" (*AF*, 31; *ML*, 23): If the night of the sunflower reveals the imbrication of psychic and material reality constituting the surrealist subject, it does so in a less positive fashion than Breton's exultant rhetoric leads the reader to expect. Exterior necessity turns out to be the constraints of the surrealist hero's class position, which emerge in what Breton represents as the fulfillment of his unconscious desires. The eruption of the repressed is not liberation, but rather, as Althusser following Lacan would frame it, the repetition of an encounter with a traumatic social real that has already occurred and occurred badly and that Breton's surrealist hero moreover repeats in encounter after encounter of his Parisian prose trilogy. But if this reading of the "capital" encounter dismantles Breton's assertion of lyric behavior as social praxis, such dismantling simultaneously confirms Breton's vision of the subject as overdetermined by an unconscious defined in social, historical, and libidinal terms. *Precisely* the moment making visible the class horizon limiting Breton's claims for surrealist praxis constitutes Breton's most important contribution to the sixties and seventies French theoretical avant-garde.

"IT IS DIFFICULT TO PROVE THAT THIS IS REALLY SO"

Before we leave Breton's proposed model for surrealist praxis in *Mad Love*, it remains to stress one last way in which the night of the sunflower dismantles the notion of social intervention it purports to confirm. I have in mind the curious ineffectiveness of the unconscious desire revealed. While Breton calls attention to the invisible workings of the unconscious forces, these workings are manifest only retrospectively, after they erupt from the realm of repression into conscious view. In their retrospective verifiability, the forces unleashed by surrealist efforts continue to resemble the unconscious forces studied by Freud. Discussing the access that analysis has to repressed material, Freud writes: "The transformation is achieved, but often only partially: portions of the old mechanisms remain untouched by the work of analysis. It is

29. Sigmund Freud, "Repression," XIV, 147.

difficult to prove that this is really so; *for we have no other way of judging what happens but by the outcome which we are trying to explain.*" [30]

Freud hence refuses the predictive power of analysis, for only when repressed material disturbs existing order can its presence be discerned. In clinical terms the patient and analyst must have visible evidence of insecure repressions before they can work to replace them, and "if an instinctual conflict is not a currently active one, is not manifesting itself, we cannot influence it even by analysis." [31] Similarly, in Breton's surrealist scenario for disruption, the social significance of any gesture can only be known retrospectively, at some unspecified moment when the unconscious succeeds in erupting to conscious view. On the night of the sunflower, for example, Breton discovers the power of unconscious desire that has worked in subterranean fashion for at least eleven years. Such a form of social transformation is not so much an alternative to orthodox Marxist praxis as at the farthest remove from any pragmatic program of social change. Unconscious forces can either be accessible to consciousness or working to social effect, but not both at the same time. That Breton saw this paradox as fundamental to the surrealist attempt to harness unconscious desire is suggested by its repeated confirmation throughout his texts. *Communicating Vessels,* in particular, is devoted to Breton's repeated discovery that the desire accessible to his consciousness has little to do with the sort of unconscious forces at work on the night of the sunflower.

Breton situates this demonstration within the arena of purely personal rather than political concerns. He spends much of *Communicating Vessels* trying to produce a woman who will fulfill his dreams, and at the opening of *Mad Love* gives an almost comical enumeration of his failures:

> So that, in order to have a woman appear, I have seen myself opening a door, shutting it, opening it again—when I had noticed that it was not enough to slip a thin blade into a book chosen at random, after having postulated that such and such a line on the left page or the right should have informed me more or less indirectly about her dispositions, confirming her immediate arrival or her nonarrival—then starting to displace the objects, setting them in strange positions relative to each other, and so on. (*AF,* 22–23; *ML,* 15) [32]

Breton's attempts to use his desire to produce the future start to resemble a shaggy-dog story, and he gives the punchline in an explanation

30. Sigmund Freud, "Analysis Terminable and Interminable," XXIII, 229 (emphasis added).

31. Freud, "Analysis Terminable and Interminable," XXIII, 231.

32. I follow Caws's translation of this passage verbatim.

of these events in *Mad Love*. "Self-analysis," Breton declares, "could
sometimes exhaust the content of real events, to the point of making
them depend entirely on the least directed *prior* activity of the mind"
(*AF*, 94; *ML*, 64–65; emphasis added). This statement grants transformative social power to surrealist activity by stripping it of the practical
application that initially constituted its appeal. The value of any gesture can only be known retrospectively, through a procedure of "self-
analysis," as surrealism's efforts at social transformation are split between blind efforts to unleash the power of the unconscious and
conscious reconstruction attempting to isolate its prior subterranean
workings.

"ANDRÉ BRETON, HE SAID,
PASS(ES) ON (BY)"

Surrealism, this tiny footbridge above the abyss, cannot be
edged with guard-rails.

—Breton

When Breton designates his own heart in the Paris of the night of
the sunflower, he identifies it with the statue of arguably the first Parisian bourgeois insurgent, Etienne Marcel, who in the fourteenth century defended the interests of the Parisians against royalty both inside
and outside the city: "The statue of Etienne Marcel, flanking one of
the façades of the Hôtel de Ville, doubtless designates in the poem the
heart of Paris, beating throughout the stroll, as we have seen, in unison
with mine" (*AF*, 94; *ML*, 64).[33] When Breton mentioned the statue in
1923, he placed this silent effigy next to a minuscule, but powerful
voice:

> I am the plaything of no sensual power
> And yet the cricket singing in the ashen hair
> One evening near the statue of Etienne Marcel
> Gave me a knowing look
> André Breton it said pass(es) on (by) [*passe*]. (*AF*, 81; *ML*, 56)

Who is the cricket, what does he say? Breton provides an interpretation
in 1934 with the help of Lautréamont: "'It was Maldoror! Magnetizing the flourishing capitals, with a pernicious fluid, he induces in them
a lethargic state where they are incapable of keeping up their guard, as
they should'" (*AF*, 93; *ML*, 64).[34] The cricket instructing Breton in

33. I follow here Caws's translation verbatim.
34. I cite here Caws's translation verbatim.

front of the effigy of the bourgeois revolutionary is Lautréamont, that Marx of the purely conceptual realm: "Just as Marx's forecasts and predictions—as far as almost all the external events which have transpired since his death are concerned—have proved to be accurate[!], I can see nothing which would invalidate a single word of Lautréamont's with respect to events of interest only to the mind."[35] Breton interprets the message of the cricket as an incitement to surrealist unchaining, which he links to the seemingly liberating experience of mad love: "It is too clear, in any case, that the cricket, in the poem as in life, intervenes to take away all my doubts" (*AF*, 93–94; *ML*, 64). "Too clear," writes Breton, drawing our attention to just how unclear the cricket's message is: "André Breton he said pass(es) on (by)." Lacking the punctuation which would fix its meaning, the message is only ambiguous. Breton, he says, passes by. Or perhaps the imperative: Breton, pass on? Does Breton need the cricket's command to detach him from the statue of Etienne Marcel? And if so, does he heed it? We, in any case, leave him posed ambiguously between the monument to a practical but long-dead bourgeois revolutionary and the mouthpiece of a bohemian poet magnetizing flourishing capitals.

35. *Second Manifesto of Surrealism*, in M, 156.

CHAPTER 7

Benjamin Reading the *Rencontre*

ONE-WAY STREET: AGAINST THE LAND OF DREAM

Benjamin produced *One-Way Street* during his intoxication with the heroic phase of surrealism and placed it under the movement's sign. "It was in Paris that I found the form for that notebook, which I sent you some samples from a long time ago, very prematurely," he wrote to Hugo von Hoffmansthal in 1927.[1] The text's composition from the debris of contemporary experience is paramount among its surrealist features, as is its preoccupation with "the street . . . the only field of valid experience" (OC, 716; N, 113).[2] In addition, *One-Way Street* narrates dreams, presents its material through unexpected juxtaposition, and does homage to Aragon's *The Paris Peasant*, the surrealist prose narrative of Parisian wandering which Benjamin was later to place at the scene of his project's inception: "There stands at its [the arcades project's] beginning Aragon—*Le Paysan de Paris*," Benjamin wrote in 1935, "which, evenings in bed, I could never read for more than two or three pages because my heartbeat would become so strong that I would have to put the book down."[3] Notably, in "Stamp Shop" Benjamin reworks Aragon's description of a stamp store in *The Paris Peasant*

1. Benjamin to Hugo von Hoffmansthal, Pardigon, 5 June 1927, B, I, 446.
2. Benjamin used this phrase as epigraph for the surrealist-inspired "Marseilles" (R, 131).
3. Walter Benjamin to Theodor Adorno, Paris, 31 May 1935, B, II, 662–663.

into historical commentary on the stamp as an expression of nineteenth-century European imperialism and nationalism.

But while multiple features of *One-Way Street* recall surrealism, a polemic against the movement also runs through the text. From its second fragment Benjamin defiantly criticizes those who seek to efface the boundary between dream and waking life. "For only from the far bank, from broad daylight, may dream be recalled with impunity," Benjamin observes in "Breakfast Room" (*OWS*, 46). Consistent with this stance, Benjamin treats the dream along standard Freudian lines. He does not seek to bring the disruptive energy of the dream into waking life but rather, through dream analysis, to gain insight into the content of subjective experience under late capitalism. In "No. 113," the fragment following "Breakfast Room," for example, Benjamin introduces the first dream, which he narrates in "Cellar," with a comment on the subject's diminished experience of some sort of sacred in private life: "We have long forgotten the ritual by which the house of our life was erected" (*OWS*, 46).

Benjamin's attack on the surrealist use of the dream is visible in the very title he gives the collection of dream analyses including "Cellar." "No. 113" was the name of a notorious gambling den in the arcades of the Palais-Royal, represented in an 1815 watercolor, "La Sortie du Numéro 113" (fig. 15). But in placing his discussion of dream in the Palais-Royal, Benjamin does not only pay homage to the dream space of surrealism. The eighteenth-century Palais-Royal is constructed somewhat differently from the nineteenth-century arcades dear to Aragon. While in the nineteenth-century arcades the shops open onto another interior hall, in the eighteenth-century arcades the buildings open onto the street.[4] The architectural difference between the eighteenth- and nineteenth-century arcades serves to figure Benjamin's distance from the surrealist treatment of dream. The nineteenth-century arcade is both an architectural structure produced by the historical period when, as Benjamin states in the *Passagen-Werk*, a dream-sleep came over Europe and a space lit by various forms of half-light, the artificial light of gas lamps and diffused natural light as it appears when filtered through opaque glass (fig. 16).[5] It is thus a space ruled by the form of light which traditional epistemology uses to figure mental delusion. Benjamin's

4. Johann Friedrich Geist discusses the history of the Parisian arcade in *Arcades: The History of a Building Type*.

5. See Sieburth's "Benjamin the Scrivener" in Smith et al., *Benjamin*, for a discussion of Benjamin's epistemological application of the light filtering through the arcades.

15.   Georg Emanuel Opiz. *Leaving Number 113 (La Sortie du Numéro 113)*.
Courtesy of the Bibliothèque Nationale.

16. Anonymous. *Théâtre des Variétés*, Passage des Panoramas. Courtesy of the Musée Carnavalet.

dreamer, in contrast, emerges into an arcade that is not only the product of the Enlightenment period but that belongs to the world outside. He examines his dreams by the natural light that traditional epistemology associates with critical reason and with the objective state of things as they are. As Benjamin states in the *Passagen-Werk*'s epistemological Konvolut N: "Setting off the slant of this work against Aragon: whereas Aragon persistently remains in the realm of dreams, here it is a question of finding the constellation of awakening" (N 1, 9).

A closer look at Opiz's "La Sortie du Numéro 113" reveals Benjamin's passing reference, in characteristically Benjaminian fashion, to be an emblem of great complexity. The 1815 representation of No. 113 makes clear that its preferred hours of business were nocturnal. Rather than emerging into natural light, Benjamin's dreamer wakes to a site of nighttime decadence, where illicit commerce in sex and money is illuminated by the artificial light associated with mental aberration. The state of the eighteenth-century arcades in this painting encapsulates in visual terms a critical problem advanced throughout the Parisian production cycle, from *One-Way Street* to Benjamin's theoretical discussion of ideology as dream. How is critical demystification to be practiced in late capitalist society where all viewpoints are saturated by the phantasmagorical experience of commodity fetishism? "Fools lament the decay of criticism [*Kritik*]," Benjamin writes in *One-Way Street*'s much-quoted "This Space for Rent" (*OWS*, 89). "For its day is long past. Criticism is a matter of correct distancing. It was at home in a world where perspectives and prospects counted and where it was still possible to take a standpoint. Now things press too closely on human society" (*OWS*, 89).

One-Way Street also takes its distance from surrealism in what might seem like its most obvious nod to the movement's practices, the use of dreamlike juxtapositions to produce the arresting descriptions Benjamin will conceptualize as the dialectical image. In "Marseilles, Cathedral," for example, Benjamin constructs "the Marseilles religious railway station [*Religionsbahnhof*]," fusing the practices of commerce and religion which bourgeois ideology relegates to differing spheres (*OWS*, 82). But Benjamin does not present this image as a surrealist would, a *fait accompli* mysteriously surging forth from some unconscious source that must be deduced retrospectively. Rather, the image concludes a section in which Benjamin engages in the dialectical interweaving of the attributes of nineteenth-century commerce and religion. First enumerating the ways in which the Marseilles cathedral resembles a railway station, Benjamin then reverses subject and predicate to demonstrate how the commerce practiced there is its own kind of religion. Only after visibly knitting together these two seemingly disparate activities does Benjamin finally come up with the "Marseilles religious railway station," a striking but thoroughly intelligible synthesis more resembling Eisensteinian montage than the transformations of the surrealist image (*OWS*, 82). In *Pariser Passagen I,* written around the time that *One-Way Street* was published, Benjamin makes explicit his equation of such juxtaposition with the dialectical processes of thought:

> arcades and railway station: yes / arcades and church:
> yes / church and railway station: Marseilles /
> posters and arcades: yes / posters and buildings / no /
> posters and [x]: open /
> conclusion: erotic magic / time / perspectives /
> dialectical turn-overs [*Umschlagen*] (commodity-type) (*PW,* 995)

Most extensively, *One-Way Street* takes on the inheritance of surrealism in a prime piece of polemic on writerly method, the opening section of "Post No Bills." Entitled "The Writer's Technique in Thirteen Theses," this section refutes one of surrealism's most celebrated formulations of its practice, the *Manifesto of Surrealism*'s "Secrets of the Magical Surrealist Art," with point-by-point thoroughness. From their title Benjamin's theses pose writing as technique against the language of illumination and initiation that Breton employs. In keeping with this stance Benjamin consistently turns an ironic discourse valorizing askesis and reason against Breton's capricious and elusive praise of unconscious inspiration. To Breton's "Put yourself in as passive, or receptive, a state of mind as you can," Benjamin answers, "Keep your pen aloof from inspiration, which it will then attract with magnetic power" (*M,* 29; *OWS,* 65). Benjamin continues: "The more circumspectly you delay writing down an idea, the more maturely developed it will be on surrendering itself," as he opposes Breton's "Write quickly, without any preconceived subject, fast enough so that you will not remember what you're writing and be tempted to reread what you have written" (*OWS,* 65; *M,* 29–30). To Breton's "Go on as long as you like," Benjamin responds: "Never stop writing because you have run out of ideas" (*M,* 30; *OWS,* 65). And so the theses proceed to their closing formulation on the work as "the death mask of its conception," which opposes the *Manifesto*'s closing section, "*Against death*" (*OWS,* 65). "Surrealism will usher you into death, which is a secret society. It will glove your hand, burying therein the profound M with which the

word Memory begins," Breton writes, asserting the power of aesthetic
activity to introduce its initiates into some sort of mystical, transcen-
dant state, while Benjamin dwells rather on the frozen, mournful quality of the finished product (*M*, 32).

Benjamin sums up his distance from surrealism in *One-Way Street*'s
rewriting of the most celebrated surrealist figure for poetic composition,
Lautréamont's fortuitous encounter of an umbrella and a sewing machine on a dissection table. In "Polyclinic" Benjamin constructs the field
of writerly operation both in medical terms and as a space dear to Parisian intellectuals, as an operating table that is also the marble-topped
table of a café. Within this amphitheater, however, Benjamin brings together neither randomly juxtaposed objects (the Dada Lautréamont),
nor seemingly chance juxtapositions that are, in fact, the products of
unconscious activity (the surrealist Lautréamont). Rather, he places
there his conscious thoughts, which he considers with the distanced
stance and techniques of optical analysis familiar to scientific method.
"The author lays his idea on the marble table of the café. Lengthy meditation, for he makes use of the time before the arrival of his glass, the
lens through which he examines the patient" (*OWS*, 88).

While Benjamin found *One-Way Street*'s form in Paris, he directs
much of its content against heroic surrealism's dreamlike apotheosis of
contemporary urban reality. Not for Benjamin Aragon's pipestore display enacting memories of a night with a German prostitute on the
Rhine in *The Paris Peasant* or the hallucinatory fusion of subject and
object into an imaginary landscape closing Breton's *Soluble Fish*:

> Only one mediocre book has been written about celebrated escapes. What
> you must know is that beneath all the windows that you may take a notion
> to jump out of, amiable imps hold out the sad sheet of love by the four car-
> dinal points. My inspection had lasted only a few seconds, and I knew what
> I wanted to know. The walls of Paris, what is more, had been covered with
> posters showing a man masked with a black domino, holding in his left hand
> the key of the fields: this man was myself.[6]

Rather than a collection of surrealist experiences, *One-Way Street* assumes toward surrealism the stance articulated in Benjamin's letters of
the time. Here is the philosophical Fortinbras, that young prince from
a neighboring country "of unimproved mettle hot and full."[7] Armed
with the two-edged sword of dialectical reason, he enters into battle

---

6. Breton, *Soluble Fish*, in *M*, 109.
7. William Shakespeare, *Hamlet*, in *The Riverside Shakespeare*, I, i, 96.

against surrealism's haunted Hamlet, lost in ghosts, dreams, and the seductions of aesthetic representation.

SHOCK IN *ONE-WAY STREET:* THE ROUTE OF MARXISM

In *One-Way Street* the philosophical Fortinbras is above all concerned with demystifying the realm of contemporary commerce (*Verkehr*) which Marx posed as constitutive of social relations in *The German Ideology*.[8] Benjamin's text represents this *Verkehr* as ultimately unsatisfying in one of two opposing ways. At moments, the subject draws near the objective dimension but experiences no contact with it, remaining rather enclosed in his own imaginings (I use the masculine pronoun pointedly; the hero of Benjamin's accounts of modern life is, with a few notable exceptions, male). At other moments, however, *One-Way Street* represents an encounter between subject and objective dimension when a transformative contact takes place. But in this contact the subject does not touch an objective dimension in any process of ongoing, harmonious, and mutually influential exchange. Rather, the objective dimension pierces the subject in a momentary illumination that Benjamin often describes in violent terms, at times threatening the subject's destruction in the process.

The two-edged problematic content that Benjamin accords the encounter between subject and the forces of the exterior world is evident in the diverse forms of social traffic that the text represents. While Benjamin designates contemporary contact with texts using a term that he employs elsewhere to designate a sacred experience of writing, "die Schrift," the contemporary subject accedes to "die Schrift" in *One-Way Street* only in a violent and unpleasant way. The last refuge of "die Schrift" is the typography of advertising: "Writing [*die Schrift*], having found in the printed book a refuge in which to lead an autonomous existence, is pitilessly dragged out onto the street by advertisements and subjected to the brutal heteronomies of economic chaos. This is the hard schooling of its new form" (*OWS*, 62).[9] Such writing assaults the subject rather than touching him gently and allows him no way to

8. Marx uses the term here to describe that commerce both necessary for production and "again determined by production." See Marx and Engels, *The German Ideology*, 42–43.

9. I modify here Jephcott and Shorter's translation of the opening of the first sentence which runs: "Printing, having found in the book a refuge etc." For the German original, see *GS*, IV, 1, 103.

penetrate the book in a moment of harmonious exchange: "Before a contemporary finds his way clear to opening a book, his eyes have been exposed to such a blizzard of changing, colorful, conflicting letters that the chances of his penetrating the archaic stillness of the book are slight" (*OWS*, 62).[10] Similarly, in Kafkaesque fashion, the object world at once forces itself on the attention of the subject and flees from him: "Now things press too closely on human society," but also, "The objects of daily use gently but insistently repel us" (*OWS*, 89; *OWS*, 58). General social relations too are pervaded by "a curious paradox: people have only the narrowest private interest in mind when they act, yet they are at the same time more than ever determined in their behavior by the instincts of the mass. And more than ever mass instincts have become confused and estranged from life" (*OWS*, 55).

Contact as failed or contact as a violent, one-way street: the two sides of contemporary experience represented in *One-Way Street* provide the nucleus of the experiences that Benjamin's later work on Baudelaire will develop into the opposition between *Erlebnis* and *Chock*. Failed contact becomes the *Erlebnis,* sterilized for memory, while violent contact becomes the experience of shock, that moment when the shock defense fails and excessive stimuli mark the subject's unprepared unconscious. *One-Way Street* also resembles the later essay in opposing these two forms of contemporary contact to a form of contact that Benjamin calls *Erfahrung,* a term that, as Wolin has argued, constitutes a privileged crossroads throughout Benjamin's thought.[11] Despite the widely diverging theoretical paradigms from which Benjamin draws at differing points in his career, Wolin suggests that a common thread links the history of the concept's articulation.[12] The theory of experience "seeks to recapture a sense of wholeness, an integral

10. I have modified Jephcott and Shorter's translation of "*Zeitgenosse*" as "child of our times." For the German, see *GS*, IV, 1, 103.

11. See Wolin, *Walter Benjamin, An Aesthetic of Redemption,* as well as "Experience and Materialism in Benjamin's *Passagenwerk*," in Smith et al., *Benjamin.* In this latter essay Wolin divides Benjamin's theory of experience into three moments: "monad (*Trauerspiel* book), dialectical image (Arcades Project), and *Jetztzeit,* or Now-time ('Theses on the Philosophy of History')" (p. 212). Michael Löwy's discussion of experience in *Walter Benjamin et Paris,* "Walter Benjamin critique du progrès: A la recherche de l'expérience perdue," is also helpful in clarifying the wide battery of conceptual paradigms informing Benjamin's use of this term (pp. 629–637).

12. That Benjamin had not abandoned his interest in the linguistic side to *Erfahrung* at the moment he incorporated it in a Marxist theoretical paradigm is demonstrated by the term's only use in the first draft of the arcades project, when Benjamin continues to associate it with the power of sacred language. "Because similarity is the organon of experience, it means that the name can only be recognized in contexts of experience," Benjamin writes (*PW*, 1038).

sense, which had been eclipsed owing to the omnipresence of historical fragmentation."[13]

Wolin's statement well applies to Benjamin's use of the term in *One-Way Street*. For this text opposes the failed or violent contemporary contact with the objective dimension to a harmonious exchange between subjective and objective dimensions situated both in an individual and collective past. In the "magic experience [*Erfahrung*]" of child's play, the child transforms the "horror of apartments" into an animated world (*OWS*, 74, 48). The child both becomes himself a part of it, "something floating and white, a ghost," and masters it with his imaginative techniques, as "shaman" or "engineer" (*OWS*, 74).[14] The child reading, too, has a gentle and mutually transformative experience of the text that Benjamin, pursuing the meteorological metaphor he used to describe the adult's more painful contact with "die Schrift," turns to snowy wandering, rewriting Goethe's "Elf King" in the process. The reading child is carried off to a realm made at once of his own imaginings and the stories that he reads, but he returns enriched, rather than disappearing into it entirely: "For a week you were wholly given up to the soft drift of the text, that surrounded you as secretly, densely, and unceasingly as snowflakes. You entered it with limitless trust. The peacefulness of the book that enticed you further and further! Its contents did not much matter. For you were reading at a time when you still made up stories in bed" (*OWS*, 71).

Benjamin suggests a similar form of interchange accessible to the adult subject in preindustrial, pre-Enlightenment society. "Nothing distinguishes the ancient from the modern man so much," writes Benjamin in the text's final section, "To the Planetarium," "as the former's absorption in a cosmic experience [*Erfahrung*] scarcely known to later periods" (*OWS*, 103). "Rausch," intoxication, Benjamin terms ancient *Erfahrung* as well, in order to stress the effacement of subject and object poles that the experience entailed: "The ancients' intercourse with the cosmos had been different, the ecstatic trance [*im Rausche*]. For it is in this experience [*Erfahrung*] alone that we gain certain knowledge of what is nearest to us and what is remotest to us, and never of one without the other" (*OWS*, 103).

13. Wolin, "Experience and Materialism," in Smith et al., *Benjamin*, 213.
14. I modify Jephcott and Shorter's translation of "magische Erfahrung" as "magic discovery." See *GS*, IV, 1, 116. See Buck-Morss's *Dialectics of Seeing* for a more extensive discussion of the importance that Benjamin accorded to children's ways of renewing the world. On this question, see also the work of Jack Zipes, as, for example, "Walter Benjamin, Children's Literature, and the Children's Public Sphere: An Introduction to New Trends in West and East Germany."

Antique *Erfahrung* opposed to contemporary experience where the possibility for harmonious fusion between the subject and the cosmos has been lost: Benjamin will define *Erfahrung* in similar fashion in his later work on shock, aura, and Baudelaire. Nonetheless, significant differences exist between the two moments of his thought. Thus, the first work in the Parisian production cycle does not consistently give either aspect of contemporary experience the negative valorization that it will later receive. At moments Benjamin represents the subject's remaining within the compass of his imaginings as something sweet: "Few things are more characteristic of the Northerner than that, when in love, he must above all and at all costs be alone with himself, must first contemplate, enjoy his feeling in solitude" (*OWS*, 70).[15] So too Benjamin associates the violent form in which the subject encounters forces external to him with desirable events: "Gifts must affect the receiver to the point of shock" (*OWS*, 71).

One difference between Benjamin's early and later representation of the subject's contact with the cosmos is crucial to my argument. In *One-Way Street* Benjamin does not yet invoke psychoanalytic notions to theorize the forces structuring contemporary subjective experience. Rather, he characterizes these forces in predominantly Marxist terms. Thus in an experience that might be called proto-*Chock* Benjamin translates the speculative Hegelian opposition between subject and object into the realm of history, using it to characterize the relation between contemporary subject and material processes. Thus too throughout the text Benjamin describes the experience of ideological distortion with appeal to the key Marxist concepts of reification, alienation, and commodity fetishism (see in particular "Imperial Panorama," "Fire Alarm," "Attested Auditor of Books," "This Space for Rent," "Betting Office," and "To The Planetarium").[16] *One-Way Street* suggests that contemporary contact with the forces structuring experience takes such violent form because existing material conditions produce ideological effects veiling the subject's ability to encounter the material world. In order for the world to emerge as it really is, material processes must somehow penetrate the ideological veil (throughout *One-Way Street* Benjamin uses Marxism's figuration of ideological mystification as deluded vision).

The dedication of *One-Way Street* calls attention to a specific conflu-

15. I modify the translation's "Nordic man" to "Northerner." See *GS*, IV, 1, 111.
16. Löwy points out that there exists a Weberian component to Benjamin's conception of the decline of *Erfahrung* as well. See Löwy, "Walter Benjamin critique du progrès," in *Walter Benjamin et Paris*, 632.

ence of practical and theoretical Marxism informing its social analysis. "This street is named Asja Lacis Street after her who as an engineer cut it through the author," Benjamin writes (*OWS*, 45). When Benjamin describes Lacis's effect on him in the language of urban renovation, he recalls the Haussmannization of Paris discussed throughout his Parisian production cycle. But if Benjamin's language here recalls Haussmann's project, his *percées* work to opposing political end. The engineer responsible for the laying of *One-Way Street* was a Latvian bolshevist, theater director, and assistant to Brecht.

Benjamin's letters describe how he grew seriously interested in Marxism during his 1924 sojourn on Capri, when he and Lacis sat around with Ernst Bloch reading *History and Class Consciousness* and discussing the practical and theoretical applications of Marxism.[17] "Since my stay here, the political praxis of Communism . . . appears to me in another light than ever before," he wrote to Scholem on September 16, 1924.[18] Benjamin's Lukácsian construction of the violent way in which the contemporary subject encounters objective reality is perhaps most visible in a section that Benjamin drafted while still on Capri, the extensive analysis of contemporary conditions entitled "Imperial Panorama" in the completed work. At the time Benjamin called this text "Descriptive Analysis of German Decay." Benjamin's publication plans for this text make his interest in a revolutionary Marxism evident. The analysis was "supposed to appear this winter in the Moscow 'Red Guard.'"[19]

In figuring his powerful encounter with Lacis as urban renovation, Benjamin represents this experience as one more example of proto-*Chock*. During the reconstruction of a city long-standing structures are broken through, foundations torn up, well-trodden paths altered or destroyed. Throughout *One-Way Street* Benjamin's encounters with his "Riga Friend" retain this violent and transformative/destructive character.[20] In "Ordnance," he writes: "But of the two of us I had to be, at

17. Benjamin made the acquaintance of Lacis when he was vacationing on Capri in the summer of 1924. He speaks of her as "one of the most outstanding women that I have met." Benjamin, letter to Gershom Scholem, Capri, 7 July 1924, in *B*, I, 351.
18. Benjamin, letter to Scholem, Capri, 16 September 1924, in *B*, I, 355.
19. Benjamin to Scholem, 16 September 1924, in *B*, I, 355. Following Benjamin's editor, Buck-Morss has distinguished between four versions of this text elaborated between 1923 and 1928, which Buck-Morss sees documenting Benjamin's growing interest in Marxism. Buck-Morss comments: "What becomes evident through this procedure is how much—or, rather, how little—Benjamin needed to change the text in order to incorporate a Marxist orientation (and thus how close he was already in 1923 to that orientation—or, rather, how his loose interpretation of Marxism allowed it to fit his previous thinking)" (*DS*, 378–379 n.).
20. Lacis did live in Riga, and Benjamin visited her there in November 1925.

any price, the first to see the other. For had she touched me with the match of her eyes, I should have gone up like a magazine" (*OWS*, 69). That Benjamin frames his dedication as a moment of proto-*Chock* indicates the importance of this form of experience to the concerns of *One-Way Street*. That he repeatedly frames his own crucial encounter with theory and love in this fashion indicates that he not only views proto-*Chock* negatively but also values it as an experience disrupting ideological distortion.

When *One-Way Street* seeks to define the shape taken by praxis in contemporary alienated conditions, proto-*Chock* hence provides its core. Most obviously, *One-Way Street* incorporates proto-*Chock* when it describes praxis in the aesthetic realm. When Benjamin discusses the decline of the experience of reading, he speculates that advertising and cinematic technology offer experiences of proto-*Chock* which may open to the artist new powers of social intervention: "With the foundation of an international moving script they [poets] will renew their authority in the life of peoples" (*OWS*, 63). But at the conclusion to *One-Way Street* Benjamin extends his speculations on the practical appropriation of proto-*Chock* to the everyday subject's experience of the world. Benjamin concludes *One-Way Street* by dissolving his text's opposition between proto-*Chock* and *Erfahrung,* asking whether violent contemporary contact with external reality may in fact be the precursor of a form of *Erfahrung* not yet recognized as such. Might not proto-*Chock*, Benjamin asks, constitute the convulsions accompanying the birth of a new construction of the cosmos and the subject, and one, notably, where the cosmos comes to include the forces of second nature? Benjamin writes:

> Men as a species completed their development thousands of years ago; but mankind as a species is just beginning his. . . . One need recall only the experience of velocities by virtue of which mankind is now preparing to embark on incalculable journeys into the interior of time, to encounter there rhythms from which the sick shall draw strength as they did earlier on high mountains or at Southern seas. The "Lunaparks" are a prefiguration of sanatoria. The paroxysm of genuine cosmic experience is not tied to that tiny fragment of nature that we are accustomed to call "Nature." In the nights of annihilation of the last war the frame of mankind was shaken by a feeling that resembled the bliss of the epileptic. And the revolts that followed it were the first attempt of mankind to bring the new body under its control. (*OWS*, 104)

Once this cosmos is firmly in place, Benjamin suggests, what we now experience as violent shock will be revealed in all its therapeutic force.

Restoring lost *Erfahrung* in a final cataclysmic about-turn despite its previous decline, Benjamin displays an ambivalence concerning the nature of historical process which will run throughout his Parisian production cycle. More or less committed to historical materialism, the cycle gives an account of experience using its terms: the decline in experience results from the "rise" of technology, as well as the "rise" of capitalism and the "rise" of the commodity form. Nonetheless, as Hansen has observed and as the conclusion to *One-Way Street* illustrates, "the historical-materialist trajectory of decline" is "endebted to the temporality of Jewish Messianism . . . defined by the trajectory of Fall and Redemption."[21] In this schema most visible in Benjamin's thinking before his turn to Marxism, catastrophe substitutes for decline, and Benjamin gives the moment of catastrophe an "always already" character that helps account for its appeal to deconstructive readers. As Wohlfarth notably has detailed, Benjamin will explicitly invoke the apocalyptic temporality of Jewish messianism throughout his writings following his turn to Marxism to express a number of complex concerns.[22] Their overlap with the factors stimulating his turn to modern materialism is relevant to the current context. Like psychoanalysis, redemptive schemas provide sophisticated alternative models of temporal process to the linear account of history often regulating the mechanical dialectics of vulgar Marxism, encoded in such favorite phrases as the "rise."

THE RESTORATION OF *ERFAHRUNG*: SURREALISM'S "PROFANE ILLUMINATION"

Keep the entrance clear day and night
  —traffic directive on Berggasse 19
     (Freud's apartment building
     in Vienna)

21. Hansen, "Benjamin, Cinema, and Experience," 190. Hansen describes the persistence of redemptive schemas in Benjamin's notion of aura: "Benjamin leaves no doubt that, being contingent upon the social conditions of perception, the experience of aura is irrevocably in decline, precipitated by the effects of industrial modes of production, information, transportation and urbanization, especially an alienating division of labor and the proliferation of shock sensations. Yet only in the process of disintegration can the aura be recognized, can it be registered as a qualitative component of (past) experience" (p. 189). She also points out that redemption from loss is a concern of Benjamin's drawing him to surrealism: "To Benjamin, the Surrealists signalled the possibility of such a redemptive turn by their efforts to overcome the esoteric, isolating aspect of inspiration, to give the auratic promise of happiness a public and secular meaning—to make it a 'profane illumination'" (p. 193).
22. See, notably, Wohlfarth's "On the Messianic Structure of Walter Benjamin's Last Reflections."

What had at first seemed chance [*Zufall*] then
became uncanny [*unheimlich*] . . . the shock
[*Chock*] I then experienced must be felt by the
reader of *Nadja*.
                              —Benjamin, "Surrealism"

Benjamin returns to the concept of *Erfahrung* in the next published
work that his letters signal as important to the Parisian production cycle, the 1929 essay on surrealism which Benjamin described to Scholem
as "an opaque folding screen standing before the arcades project." [23] In
"Surrealism," however, Benjamin uses the term to designate practices
that are no longer situated in a lost collective or individual past but
rather are anchored in the present.

> This is not the place to give an exact definition of surrealist experience
> [*Erfahrung*]. But anyone who has perceived that the writings of this circle
> are not literature but something else—demonstrations, watchwords, docu-
> ments, bluffs, forgeries if you will, but at any rate not literature—will also
> know, for the same reason, that the writings are concerned literally with ex-
> periences [*Erfahrungen*], not with theories and still less with phantasms. And
> these experiences are by no means limited to dreams, hours of hashish eat-
> ing, or opium smoking. It is a cardinal error to believe that, of "surrealist
> experiences," we know only the religious ecstasies or the ecstasies of drugs.
> (*R*, 179)

"Erfahrungen," Benjamin terms contemporary surrealist explorations,
also characterizing them with the term that "To the Planetarium" used
to describe an ancient ritual relation to the cosmos preceding "an optical connection to the universe" (*OWS*, 103). These experiences are
"Rausch," intoxication, and Benjamin speaks of the "loosening of the
self by intoxication," which is the "fruitful, living experience that allowed these people to step outside the domain of intoxication" (*R*,
179).

Benjamin's surrealism essay differs markedly from *One-Way Street*
in suggesting that the privileged experience of *Erfahrung* and its accompanying affect of *Rausch* have not been lost in the contemporary world.
This *Erfahrung*, however, seems to be different enough from past experiences to warrant a name of its own. "The true, creative overcoming
of religious illumination certainly does not lie in narcotics," writes Benjamin. "It resides in a *profane illumination* [*Erleuchtung*], a materialist,
anthropological inspiration, to which hashish, opium, or whatever else

23. Benjamin, letter to Scholem, Berlin, 14 February 1929, in *B*, II, 489.

can give an introductory lesson" (*R*, 179).²⁴ The profane illumination does not have the plenitude of lost antique *Erfahrung*; as its very designation indicates, Benjamin accords it features of *One-Way Street*'s experience in decline. In terming these moments "illumination," Benjamin employs the luminous language that characterized the sudden and piercing proto-*Chock* of subject and object dimension in his earlier text.²⁵ Consistent with this language, the profane illumination is a momentary transfiguration rather than an experience of ongoing and harmonious exchange. Further linking the profane illumination to *One-Way Street*'s proto-*Chock* is the fact that Benjamin figures its loosening of the self in terms associated with violence and pain, albeit both possibly incurred in the curative process. "In the world's structure dream loosens individuality like a bad tooth," Benjamin writes (*R*, 179). But while the "profane illumination" shares features of degraded experience, the "Surrealism" essay has nonetheless taken back the charged terms *Erfahrung* and *Rausch* from the past or future to locate them squarely in the present. Why does Benjamin perform this relocation through reading the surrealist movement? What aspect of surrealism does he value; and might his interest in surrealism help explain why lost *Erfahrung* has been to some measure refound?

"Surrealism" broaches the concept of the profane illumination by lauding the collective experiments from what Benjamin calls the movement's heroic phase. But when Benjamin defines the "profane illumination," he turns away from these experiments, examining surrealist prose narratives instead. He suggests that the "writings that proclaim it [the profane illumination] most powerfully" are "Aragon's incomparable *Paysan de Paris* and Breton's *Nadja*" (*R*, 179). Benjamin goes on to isolate the qualities of the profane illumination through reading these two most celebrated surrealist narratives, although surprisingly he performs no close analysis of his beloved *The Paris Peasant*. "Leaving aside Aragon's *Passage de l'Opéra*," Benjamin writes, and gives instead specifics from "Breton's book [*Nadja*] [which] illustrates well a number of the basic characteristics of this 'profane illumination'" (*R*, 182, 180).²⁶

24. I modify Jephcott's translation by changing "materialistic" to "materialist." For the German original, see *GS*, II, 1, 297.

25. Benjamin uses here the luminous language found in surrealism's descriptions of its momentary, unexpected, and transfiguring image juxtapositions and encounters.

26. *Nadja* appeared at the moment when what Benjamin defines as the heroic phase of surrealism was drawing to a close. The text was published in its entirety by Gallimard at the end of May 1928, although portions of it had already been excerpted in reviews of 1927 and 1928. The complete prologue was published under the title "*Nadja*/First

What are the basic characteristics of the profane illumination that *Nadja* illustrates? From Benjamin's first example, he investigates the commerce between objective and subjective dimension at issue in *One-Way Street*. Benjamin shows interest in the nature of *Nadja*'s autobiographical gesture: that it is a narrative in which Breton's imaginative self-representation and the facts of his social existence meet. *Nadja* is "'a book with a banging door,'" Benjamin writes, echoing Breton, and also, "*Nadja* has achieved the true, creative synthesis between the art novel and the *roman-à-clef*" (*R*, 180). Benjamin focuses on one form of commerce between subject and exterior forces which he deems particularly important: the uncanny encounters that *Nadja* narrates, particularly the encounters between Breton and Nadja. "Ecstasy," "intoxication," "transport," Benjamin writes of these encounters, qualifying them with the ecstatic language that *One-Way Street* used to describe antique cosmic *Erfahrung*.

But if Benjamin gives center stage to a traffic between subject and external forces reminiscent of *One-Way Street,* "Surrealism" portrays the structure of this traffic in a rather different way. In *One-Way Street* Benjamin describes an encounter where the shock comes from the violent and direct fashion in which external forces mark the subject. Similarly, in "To the Planetarium" the electric effect of the power of the cosmos on the subject is at issue; in "Ordnance" Benjamin experienced the transformative power of the Riga friend. In the description of the profane illumination in "Surrealism," in contrast, the transfiguration is produced by a *third* realm opened through the subject's encounter with some mysterious exterior force. In *Nadja*'s moments of profane illumination, Benjamin tells us, Breton "is closer to the things that Nadja is close to than to her" (*R*, 181). "What are these things," Benjamin proceeds to ask of the hidden realm opened in *Nadja*'s uncanny encounters (*R*, 181). When Benjamin answers this question, he makes use of the psychoanalytic structure of the *rencontre* to modify *One-Way Street*'s binary and Marxist description of subject-object *Verkehr*.

In his first answer Benjamin casts the hidden realm within the horizon of a Marxist project for social change. Benjamin writes, "The relation of these things to revolution—no one can have a more exact concept of it than these authors," and he associates the things with

---

Part" in the review *Commerce*, XIII, Autumn 1927, and the central narrative of Breton and Nadja's uncanny contact with the Parisian dead on the place Dauphine was published in *La Révolution surréaliste*, no. 11. "Thus," Bonnet tells us, "the attention of a discriminating public was drawn to this book before it appeared" (*OC*, 1495).

"revolutionary energies" as well (*R*, 181). But in a substantial modification of his conclusion to *One-Way Street* Benjamin does not define this
energy in orthodox Marxist terms. The encounter does not unleash the
energy of the proletariat or of technology. Rather, it unleashes a source
of revolutionary energy deriving from the past. Sliding from a consideration of Breton's practice in *Nadja* to a more general consideration of
surrealism, Benjamin writes:

> It [surrealism] can boast an extraordinary discovery. It was the first to per-
> ceive the revolutionary energies that appear in the "outmoded," in the first
> iron constructions, the first factory building, the earliest photos, the objects
> that have begun to be extinct, grand pianos, the dresses of five years ago,
> fashionable restaurants when the vogue has begun to ebb from them. The
> relation of these things to revolution—no one can have a more exact concept
> of it than these authors. No one before these visionaries and augurs per-
> ceived how destitution—not only social but architectonic, the poverty of
> interiors, enslaved and enslaving objects—can suddenly turn over [*umschla-
> gen*] into revolutionary nihilism. (*R*, 181–182)[27]

Benjamin here connects the revolutionary energy unleashed by the surrealist with the detritus of industrial-capitalist society. In addition, Benjamin suggests *Nadja*'s encounter as deriving energy from contact with
the occulted but unlaid dead. Benjamin continues: "The trick by which
this world of things is mastered—it is more proper to speak of a trick
than a method—consists in the substitution of a political for a historical
view of the past. 'Open, graves, you, the dead of the picture galleries,
corpses behind screens, in palaces, castles, and monasteries'" (*R*, 182).
When Benjamin reads *Nadja* to isolate the revolutionary potential of
surrealism, he thus discovers no orthodox Marxist schema for social
change. Rather, he comes upon the disruptive energy of the past and
decay refused by Marxism from the more nineteenth-century progressive moments of Marx himself: "The social revolution of the nineteenth
century cannot draw its poetry from the past, but only from the future,"
Marx comments in *The Eighteenth Brumaire*.[28] Benjamin goes on to
identify the structure of collective life permitting the past to work in
the present by appropriating the psychoanalytic rhetoric of Breton's
modern materialism. Benjamin writes: "Nadja is an exponent of these
masses and of what inspires them to revolution: 'The great living,
sonorous unconsciousness that inspires my only convincing acts, in the

---

27. Jephcott translates "umschlagen" as "be transformed." I also modify Jephcott's
translation of the first two sentences which runs, "He [Breton] can boast an extraordinary
discovery. He was etc." See *GS*, II, 1, 299.
28. Marx, *The Eighteenth Brumaire*, 18.

scnsc that I always want to prove that it commands forever everything that is mine'" (R, 183).[29] In this statement Benjamin structures Nadja's transfiguring experiences of profane illumination as contact with some form of unconscious realm as well as (his more orthodox Marxist side) with the revolutionary power of the proletariat.

In the paragraph following his reading of *Nadja,* Benjamin makes explicit his interest in applying *Nadja*'s modern materialist structure of subjectivity to his more general discussion of the subject's interchange with the "cosmos" in modern life. "The surrealists' Paris, too, is a 'little universe,'" he writes. "That is to say, in the larger one, the cosmos, things look no different. There, too, are crossroads [*carrefours*] where ghostly signals flash from the traffic [*Verkehr*], and inconceivable analogies and connections between events are the order of the day" (R, 183). If the terms *cosmos* and *traffic* are familiar from *One-Way Street,* *Nadja*'s encounters have worked a substantive difference in Benjamin's description of the structure of the traffic. It is no longer a question, as in *One-Way Street,* of the violent encounter between subjective and objective forces; rather, in the moment of violent encounter, the subject contacts a ghostly third realm hidden from daily sight.

From *Nadja*'s uncanny encounters, I am suggesting, Benjamin takes the notion that there exists a domain structuring modern experience *other* than the subject and object realms at issue in *One-Way Street.* The nature of this domain is certainly far from clear; as we have seen, Benjamin will speculate on its content not only in the surrealism essay but throughout the remaining years of the Parisian production cycle. My concern here is to emphasize the importance of Breton's modern materialism in calling *it* into being. The Marxist-psychoanalytic content to *Nadja*'s uncanny encounters enables Benjamin to articulate a notion of contemporary *Verkehr* in other than dialectical terms.

In doing so, the modern materialist encounter directly contributes to Benjamin's restoration of contemporary possibilities for *Erfahrung.*

29. Is it significant that Benjamin garbles *Nadja* in the process? Benjamin here puts a quotation in Nadja's mouth that in fact belongs to Breton; he also gets the quotation slightly wrong. "La grande inconscience vive et sonore qui m'inspire mes seuls actes probants dans le sens où toujours je veux prouver, qu'elle dispose à tout jamais de tout ce qui *est à moi*" runs the French in the German original. See *GS,* II, 2, 301 (emphasis added). This statement is made by Breton's narrator and in the 1928 edition of *Nadja* available to Benjamin when he wrote the essay in 1929 runs as follows: "Que la grande inconscience vive et sonore qui m'inspire mes seuls actes probants dans le sens où toujours je veux prouver, dispose à tout jamais de tout ce qui *est moi* [Let the great living sonorous unconsciousness that inspires my only convincing acts in the sense that I always want to prove command forever everything that is *me*]." André Breton, *Nadja* (Paris: Gallimard, 1928), 206 (emphasis added).

When *One-Way Street* construes *Verkehr* as the exchange between damaging objective forces and damaged subjectivity, it confronts the problem of where, in such degraded conditions, recuperative energy is to be found. Benjamin's answer to this question in *One-Way Street* is dialectical: he investigates how degraded *Verkehr* may contain the forces of its own sublation. Throughout the text Benjamin has represented technology in Lukácsian fashion, as resulting in the subject's increasingly alienated experience of the object world. But in "To the Planetarium" Benjamin points out that because technology itself sublates the subject/object distinction (there is some slippage when he translates the subject-object opposition into social terms), it contains the potential to disrupt the experiential distress it has caused. "In technology a *physis* is being organized through which mankind's contact with the cosmos takes a new and different form from that which it had in nations and families," Benjamin writes, and he treats the revolutionary potential of the proletariat in similar fashion.

In "Surrealism," in contrast, Benjamin uses the psychoanalytic structure of *Nadja*'s uncanny *rencontre* to open a reservoir within damaged life. Luna Parks and proletarian revolts give way to the contacting of an ambiguously unconscious realm permeating objective and subjective reality.

THE PROFANE ILLUMINATION
AND THE IMAGE SPHERE

When Benjamin subsequently elaborates his vision of materialist historiography, he develops the power inhering in the third realm in the direction of *Nadja*'s unlaid ghosts. Breton's search for "it [*cela*]" will turn to Benjamin's search for the "'*Now of recognizability*,'" in which things put on their *true—surrealist—face*" (N 3a, 3, emphasis added). This vision of praxis is, however, nowhere visible in "Surrealism," which rather models praxis on vanguard aesthetic activity.

Looking to the aesthetic avant-garde as a model for social change, "Surrealism" seems to reiterate the vision of praxis found in *One-Way Street*. But, in fact, the praise of the avant-garde in this essay makes evident Benjamin's move away from the prior text's Marxist content. In *One-Way Street* Benjamin evinces interest in the avant-garde because it provides a model for his dialectical notion of praxis, notably in its disruptive use of technology. Benjamin dwells on Mallarmé as "the first to incorporate the graphic tensions of the advertisement in the typographical layout [*Schriftbild*]" citing also "the typographical experiments [*Schriftversuchen*] later undertaken by the Dadas" (*OWS*, 61).[30] While in "Surrealism" Benjamin continues to look to avant-garde practices, he now formulates their appeal in other than dialectical terms. They are *Erfahrungen,* he suggests, opening up hidden reality underlying daily subject/object commerce. "It is as magical experiments with words, not as artistic dabbling, that we must understand the passionate phonetic and graphical transformational games that have run through the whole literature of the avant-garde for the past fifteen years, whether it is called Futurism, Dadaism, or Surrealism" (*R*, 184).

When Benjamin concludes "Surrealism," he explicitly underlines the distance his reading of surrealism has taken his notion of praxis from *One-Way Street*. He does so by rewriting "To the Planetarium" to displace this earlier text's dialectical model of *Verkehr*. "In technology a *physis* is being organized through which mankind's contact with the cosmos takes a new and different form from that which it had in nations and families," proclaimed the concluding section (*OWS*, 104). When Benjamin concludes "Surrealism," revolutionary energy no longer inheres in the sublation of the opposition between mankind and cosmos, be it the forces of technology or the proletariat. Rather, the energy is transferred from technology to representation into what Benjamin calls the image sphere: "The *physis* that is being organized for it [the collective] in technology can, through all its political and factual reality, only be produced in *that image sphere in which profane illumination makes us feel at home*" (*R*, 192, emphasis added).[31] True, Benjamin then returns to technology, stipulating it as the site where body and image rather than mankind and cosmos meet. But even this return demonstrates the extent to which the dialectical paradigm ruling *One-Way Street* has broken down in "Surrealism." The terms to be put into relation proliferate (technology, image sphere, collective body), and when Benjamin describes revolutionary energy, he employs the somatic rhetoric of stimulus found in psychoanalytic accounts of trauma: "Only when in technology body and image so interpenetrate that all revolutionary tension becomes bodily collective innervation, and all the bodily innervations of the collective become revolutionary discharge, has reality transcended itself to the extent demanded by the *Communist Man-*

---

30. Jephcott and Shorter translate "Schriftbild" as "printed page." See *GS*, IV, 1, 102.
31. I substitute "makes us feel at home" for Jephcott's "initiates." See *GS*, II, 1, 310.

ifesto. For the moment, only the surrealists have understood its present commands" (*R*, 192).

Benjamin's notion of the image (*Bild*) in the service of praxis will go on to have a celebrated career: as the dialectical image. Recognizing its surrealist component helps clarify critical disputes concerning the practices of representation at stake in this term. The meanings of *Bild* point both toward the linguistic paradigm of tropes and to the visual paradigm of pictorial representation, and, as Shierry Weber Nicholsen has noted, Benjamin's readers characteristically pursue Benjamin's *Bild* practice in either one or the other of its two directions.[32] For surrealism, however, the image designates a form of representation in which the distinction between visual and verbal itself breaks down. In the image surrealism seeks to approximate the representations where unconscious processes come to expression, even if it understands these processes in less than orthodox psychoanalytic terms. In this kind of representation, as Freud's *Interpretation of Dreams* makes amply clear, the difference between visual and verbal modes of signification is ultimately inconsequential. "It" is a question of another form of relation whose elaboration has been central to the work of such theoreticians as Lacan. The surrealist content of Benjamin's notion of the image hence confirms the *rapprochement* of the dialectical image with nonsensuous correspondences proposed in chapter 2.[33]

Consonant with its modern materialist source, the "Surrealism" essay hypothesizes that the hidden reality revealed in the image sphere constitutes subjectivity in other than libidinal terms. Benjamin describes the image sphere as "the sphere, in a word, in which political materialism and physical nature share the inner man, the psyche, the individual, or whatever else we wish to throw to them, with dialectical justice, so that no limb remains unrent" (*R*, 192). Terming the dissolution

---

32. See Shierry Weber Nicholsen's review of *The Dialectics of Seeing*, by Susan Buck-Morss, *On Walter Benjamin*, ed. Smith, and *Benjamin—Philosophy, Aesthetics, History*, by Smith et al.

33. Benjamin, however, does not explicitly refer to the most celebrated codification of the surrealist image, found in Breton's *Manifesto of Surrealism*. Rather, he refers to Aragon's further elaboration of the image in the 1928 *Traité du style*, and particularly Aragon's attack on the metaphor as opposed to the image: "Oh, who will tell the evil wrought by metaphors, the wrongs of the word Analogy, the crushing weight of Baudelairean *correspondances*." Louis Aragon, *Traité du style*, 51. In its dependence on pre-existing notions of resemblance, Aragon suggests, the metaphor cannot help but reproduce the accepted order of things. When Aragon asserts the disruptive power of the surrealist image, he stresses its destructive force. "Poetry is in essence stormy, and each image should produce a cataclysm. It's got to burn!" writes Aragon, using the language of fire/light common to surrealism's exposition of the image (p. 140).

of the subject worked by the image sphere dialectical, Benjamin makes evident his continued allegiance to Marxist method, although he in fact increasingly diverges from dialectics understood in Marxist terms. The content of the forces rending subjectivity have Marxist overtones as well: political materialism and physical nature. In the remainder of the Parisian production cycle, however, the content of the hidden realm becomes increasingly modern materialist, including occulted economic, symbolic, and libidinal collective forces, both from the present and the past.

At the moment Benjamin is publishing his observations on surrealism, he is already allying the image with the dense temporality of modern materialism behind the essay's opaque screen. "On the dialectical image. Time is involved in it," he states in *Pariser Passagen I*, composed around the same time that he wrote "Surrealism" (*PW*, 1037).

> It is already involved with the dialectic in Hegel. This Hegelian dialectic, however, has a concept of time that is only properly historical [*historische*] if not psychological—mental time. He does not yet have a notion of the differential of time, in which alone the dialectical image is real ... The temporal moment in the dialectical image can be entirely established only through confrontation with another concept. This concept is the "Now of recognizability." (*PW*, 1037–1038)

Benjamin thus concludes this fragment by allying the dialectical image with the moment when things take on their true—surrealist—face.

TOWARD A POLITICIZED HISTORIOGRAPHY: BRETON'S TRICK

Benjamin writes: "The trick by which this world of things is mastered—it is more proper to speak of a trick than a method—consists in the substitution of a political for a historical view of the past" (*R*, 182). When Benjamin discusses *Nadja*'s great living unconscious, he puts his finger on the conceptual turn essential to surrealism's trick. In transposing a psychoanalytic model for individual memory to the contemporary subject's contact with the collective past, Breton finds the beginnings of a theoretical justification for eliminating the separation of past and present.[34] In psychoanalysis the past that matters has a curiously liv-

---

34. In *Beyond the Pleasure Principle* Freud writes: "As a result of certain psychoanalytic discoveries, we are to-day in a position to embark on a discussion of the Kantian theorem that time and space are 'necessary forms of thought.'" Freud, *Beyond the Pleasure Principle*, XVIII, 28.

ing presence, determining the present yet hidden from its view. It can remain a subterranean, suspended force for years, ready to erupt at any moment when, for a multiplicity of reasons, the repression may crumble.

In *Nadja* Breton's transposition of individual to historical memory is, as Benjamin rightly observes, a trick, for Breton performs the transposition without theoretical justification. But Benjamin too makes use of this trick. Throughout the *Passagen-Werk* Benjamin speculates on the political potential of historiography by casting historical process in psychoanalytic terms. Having already discussed this use of psychoanalytic vocabulary as it pertains to the notion of a collective dream, let me recall here just one example. In an early entry from Konvolut K devoted to dreams, Benjamin approaches the political appropriation of the past by conceptualizing nineteenth-century social processes according to a psychoanalytic scenario of repression:

> The condition of the consciousness that is multiply patterned, and checkered with sleep and waking needs only to be transferred from the individual to the collective. Naturally, much is internal to it which would be external to the individual, architectures, fashions, yes, even weather are in the interior of the collective what organ sensations, the feeling of sickness or health are in the interior of the individual. And they are, like digestion and breathing, natural processes as long as they remain in an unconscious, unformed dreamshape. They stand in the circulation of the eternal same, until the collective *takes possession of them in politics and they become history*. (*PW*, 492, emphasis added)

In his application of psychoanalytic vocabulary to objective history, Benjamin allies the everyday life of the past with some kind of unconscious realm. Appealing to Freud's notion that the unconscious is eternal, he uses the concept to describe how ideology holds sway over this past. Under the rule of ideology, the everyday life of the past cannot be perceived as political, as part of historical process.[35] Benjamin thus here casts the political dimension to historiography as its ability to draw the everyday past from the eternal realm of ideology into the temporally articulated field of history. Particularly reminiscent of surrealism is his speculation that no great divide exists between waking and sleeping states.

---

35. "Our proposition: ideology has no history, can and must . . . be related directly to Freud's proposition that the *unconscious is eternal*," writes Althusser in "Ideology and Ideological State Apparatuses," in *Lenin and Philosophy,* 161.

As we have seen, Benjamin does not only use Breton's trick, but strives to give it a conceptual base, even if this effort is less than successful. My point here is that successful or not, Benjamin finds Breton's transposition endowed with substantial methodological suggestiveness. Throughout the *Passagen-Werk* Benjamin reflects on how historiography is endowed with socially transformative force by casting historical process in psychoanalytic terms.

Benjamin makes use of surrealism, then, not only for its shocklike aesthetics but also because the movement provides a conceptual paradigm with the potential to explain *why* these shocklike aesthetics work to political effect. And the centrality of Breton's trick to Benjamin's politicized notion of historiography may explain why Benjamin uses *Nadja* rather than his acknowledged favorite, *The Paris Peasant,* to explicate the profane illumination. While Aragon's text performs a dreamlike transfiguration on the arcades, *The Paris Peasant* operates this transfiguration as subjective hallucination which Aragon is careful not to collapse into the objective realm.[36] Even in such an extensive hallucination as the transfiguration of the cane store window into an evocation of a prostitute from his past, Aragon does not leave the reader uncertain as to where this hallucination occurs. He introduces it with exclamations such as "What was my surprise," signaling to the reader that something different from the preceding minutely detailed description of the cane store window is about to occur.[37] And by commenting throughout his description on the divergence between this transfiguration and his habitual experience of external reality, Aragon emphasizes the distinction between the window's imaginative transfiguration and its objective state. Concluding by providing a psychological explanation

36. When Wolin explains why Benjamin turns to surrealism to elaborate the profane illumination, he singles out Benjamin's appropriation of the magical mood created when surrealist chance erupts:

Like religious illumination, profane illumination captures the powers of spiritual intoxication in order to produce a "revelation," a vision or insight which transcends the prosaic state of empirical reality; yet it produces this vision in an *immanent* manner, while remaining within the bounds of possible experience, and without recourse to otherworldly dogmas. Benjamin clearly has in mind the intoxicating, trancelike effect induced by surrealist "romances" . . . in which the streets of Paris, the most seemingly commonplace locations and objects, are transformed into a phantasmagorical wonderland of chance encounters and surprise, where the monotony of convention is burst asunder by the powers of *l'hasard* [sic] *objectif.* After traversing these enchanted landscapes, could life ever again be experienced with the same complacency and indolence as before? (Wolin, *Walter Benjamin,* 132)

37. Louis Aragon, *Le Paysan de Paris,* 30.

of the external transformation that he witnesses, Aragon makes the imaginative content of this transformation definitive. "A meerschaum pipe which represented a siren" provoked the sudden memory of a prostitute that he once knew on the Rhine.[38] Aragon's text also does not provide a psychoanalytic alternative to the linear progress of nineteenth-century history. Rather, it is precisely Aragon's linear notion of history that endows with urgency his project to document a way of life about to disappear.

The difference in Benjamin's interest in Breton and Aragon also explains an apparent paradox in Benjamin's representation of his interest in surrealism: Benjamin's simultaneous association of his Now of historiographical recuperation with the surrealist face of things and his positing of historiography as an antidote to surrealism's dwelling in the land of dreams. "Setting off the slant of this work against Aragon: whereas Aragon persistently remains in the realm of dreams, here it is a question of finding the constellation of awakening. . . . Of course, that can only happen through the awakening of a not yet conscious knowledge of what has gone before" (N 1, 9).[39] When Benjamin condemns the movement for dwelling in the land of dreams, he alludes to Aragon's practice in *The Paris Peasant,* specifically naming Aragon in the context of this condemnation. When Benjamin in the same Konvolut speaks of the Now of recognizability as the surrealist face of things, he uses the term *surrealist* (such use is common) to designate the practices of the movement's Pope. This now becomes the moment of uncanny recognition structuring the modern materialist encounter.

"To encompass both Breton and Le Corbusier—that would mean drawing the spirit of present-day France like a bow, and shooting knowledge to the heart of the moment," Benjamin declares in Konvolut N (N 1a, 5). While Le Corbusier's modernist utopias propose avantgarde intervention in social processes as future-oriented construction,

38. Aragon, *Le Paysan de Paris,* 33. When Benjamin sums up Aragon's stance in relation to the objective world in an outtake from "Paris, the Capital of the Nineteenth Century," he links Aragon's practice to the techniques of photography, a medium where the relation of subject to object is bridged but not dissolved: "technique of Aragon compared with the technique of photography" (*PW,* 1208).

39. The end of Hafrey and Sieburth's translation of this fragment runs ". . . the awakening of a knowledge not yet conscious of what has gone before." Tiedemann draws attention to Benjamin's mistrust of surrealism's artificial paradises, which applies above all to the *early* surrealist practices of intoxication designed to *épater le bourgeois:* "Benjamin knew that this motif of awakening separated him from the surrealists. . . . For the early surrealists, both dream and reality would unravel to a dreamed, unreal Reality, from which no way led back to contemporary praxis and its demands." Tiedemann, "Dialectics at a Standstill," in *On Walter Benjamin,* ed. Smith, 270.

Breton's translation of psychoanalysis from the individual to the collective opens the possibility for conceptualizing the fertilization of socially transformative practice by the past.

THE AFTERLIFE OF "SURREALISM"

If, as Benjamin asserts, the essay "Surrealism" stands before the *Passagen-Werk* like an opaque screen, the modern materialist structure of the profane illumination appears as an important figure traced on it. But while Breton's Parisian *rencontre* informs Benjamin's Now of historiographical recognition, the visibility of this link is effaced as Benjamin's work on the arcades project proceeds. By the final celebrated "Theses on the Philosophy of History," Benjamin has dropped any explicit reference to the uncanny surrealist encounter, also suppressing his representation of historical process in psychoanalytic terms. While this essay does rely on a view of history as forgetting, Benjamin grounds the view in an appeal to Nietzsche. And when he explains why historiography takes on political power in such a situation, he appeals to messianic Judaism and above all to Marxism. The past has become "oppressed" in the barbaric cultural march of the ruling classes, Benjamin states, writing:

> To articulate the past historically does not mean to recognize it 'the way it really was' (Ranke). It means to seize hold of a memory as it flashes up at a moment of danger. Historical materialism wishes to retain that image of the past which unexpectedly appears to the historical subject at the moment of danger.[40] The danger affects both the content of the tradition and its receivers. The same threat hangs over both: that of becoming *a tool of the ruling classes*. (I, 255, emphasis added)

Benjamin's rejection of surrealism may derive in part from its ultimately rather pessimistic conclusions (which it shares with psychoanalysis) about the possibility of gaining access to the hidden third sphere: no encounter ever fulfills the promise it holds. True, a utopian thread visible already in the movement's heroic beginnings runs through the failures of surrealist praxis, but this thread becomes increasingly frayed, while messianic redemption provides a more durable image of the hopefulness of those without hope. In addition, Benjamin may prefer explicit allusion to Jewish paradigms of redemption given the

40. Zohn's translation of this sentence runs: "Historical materialism wishes to retain that image of the past which unexpectedly appeals to man singled out by history at a moment of danger." For the German, see *GS*, I, 2, 695.

"moment of danger" framing his later formulations of historiographical recuperation (*I,* 255). Nonetheless, there is evident conceptual continuity between Benjamin's 1940 representation of historiography seizing "a *memory* as it *flashes* up at a moment of danger," and Benjamin's earlier alliance of the Now of historiographical recuperation with the surrealist encounter (*I,* 255, emphasis added).[41] In addition, Benjamin continues to formulate his own historiographical method throughout the thirties in terms crucial to Breton's uncanny encounter even when the encounter is not a visible presence.

This is the case, for example, when Benjamin represents his historiographical method as ragpicking. Wohlfarth has persuasively argued that this representation owes much to Baudelaire.[42] But it also owes something to Breton's psychoanalytically informed fascination with the power of debris. The Baudelairean ragpicker poet seeks aesthetic finds above all, as is visible in the constellation of poems that Wohlfarth uses to show Baudelaire's linking of the ragpicker and the poet, notably "Le Vin des chiffoniers" (Ragpicker's Wine) and "Le Soleil" (The Sun). In "Le Soleil," when the poet stumbles like the drunken ragpicker from "Le Vin des chiffoniers," he runs across unexpected solutions to aesthetic problems: "Stumbling on words like cobblestones / Sometimes bumping into lines dreamed of for a long time."[43] For Baudelaire the ragpicker's yield lacks an explicitly historical content. This content however, is found in Breton's representation of the attraction of the *trouvaille,* as his visits to the flea market well illustrate. Breton values debris not only for its aesthetic fertility but also for its relation to obscured history, and above all for its ability to make manifest repressed forces from both a collective and individual past. Benjamin's *Lumpen*-historiographer thus more resembles Breton's flea-market ragpicker on the hunt for the *trouvaille* than the drunken, stumbling ragpicker poet portrayed by Baudelaire. This debt might also be put in terms of Breton's own intense relation to Baudelaire: Benjamin's notion of the historiographer as ragpicker owes something to Breton's modern materialist updating of Baudelaire.

Benjamin's interest in Breton's modern materialist updating of Baudelaire is visible as well in Benjamin's representation of his his-

41. Wohlfarth likens the state of historiographical emergency in the "Theses" to the *Bildraum* of "Surrealism" where the alarm clock rings sixty seconds a minute. See Wohlfarth, "On the Messianic Structure of Walter Benjamin's Last Reflections," 157.

42. See Wohlfarth's "Et Cetera? The Historian as Chiffonier." The essay was first published in *Walter Benjamin et Paris* and subsequently translated/modified in *New German Critique.*

43. Baudelaire, *Oeuvres complètes,* I, 83.

toriographical method as *flânerie*. For while this *flânerie* is often compared to Baudelairean *flânerie* (a comparison initiated by Benjamin himself), in fact Benjamin's promenade more resembles the haunted wandering of Breton's surrealist subject on the track of "it [*cela*]" (*OC*, 663; *N*, 32). "The solitary and pensive stroller draws a peculiar intoxication from this universal communion," Baudelaire writes in his seminal piece on *flânerie*, "Les Foules," positing *flânerie* as the contact between self and the feverish life of the city streets. Baudelaire continues: "He who easily marries the crowd knows feverish pleasures which will be eternally unavailable to the egotist, locked up like a chest and the lazy person, shut up like a mollusk. He adopts as his own all professions, all joys and all miseries that circumstances present to him."[44] Breton, in contrast, strolls through an empty Paris, where the contact with objective reality does not open him to the living crowd. Rather, he turns from this crowd in a gesture of frustration ("No, it was not yet these who would be found ready to make the Revolution"), meeting at this moment Nadja, who initiates him into the unseen crowd of "the dead": "Where only two or three couples are at this moment disappearing into the shadows, she seems to see a crowd. 'And the dead, the dead!'" (*OC*, 683; *N*, 64; *OC*, 695; *N*, 83). True, in *Nadja*'s central promenade Breton echoes a specific Baudelairean moment of *flânerie* contacting the past, "Le Cygne." But this representation of the *flâneur* is isolated in Baudelaire's poetry; the contact is far more often between poet and the living city.

When Benjamin describes his own vision of *flânerie*, he too sees a promenade into the past: "The street leads the strolling person into a vanished time," he writes (*PW*, 524). And when Benjamin describes the availability of the past that he encounters in this promenade, he also has recourse to the language of the unconscious and ghosts. While "in the clear light of day the labyrinth of houses of the city resembles consciousness" (*PW*, 135), Benjamin seeks the places where, as in *Nadja*, the solid facades of the city give way to the ghosts that they obscure: the "walk that we make through the arcades; that, too, is fundamentally this sort of walk through a haunted house, where the doors give way and the walls yield" (*PW*, 516).[45] The ghostly quality that Benja-

44. Baudelaire, *Oeuvres complètes*, I, 291. Baudelaire here echoes Balzac's discussion of *flânerie* in "Facino Cane."
45. "In ancient Greece," Benjamin writes, "sites were designated, which led down into the underworld. Our waking existence is also a country, where hidden sites lead down into the underworld, full of inconspicuous spots into which dreams run" (*PW*, 135).

min ascribes to the Paris that he haunts extends from its diverse places
to its names: "the name of the 'Château d'Eau,' an earlier fountain that
is long since gone, still haunts diverse *arrondissements,*" writes Benjamin at the opening to the Konvolut entitled "The Streets of Paris"
(*PW,* 643).

The Bretonian character of Benjamin's ghostly psychoanalytic stroll
through Paris is particularly evident in Benjamin's fascination with the
gates of the city, a fascination Winfried Menninghaus has elaborated
when discussing Benjamin's interest in the threshold. One type of structure, Menninghaus points out, "make[s] this notion of threshold particularly intelligible": "the city gates and triumphal arches." [46] If the
arcades dear to Benjamin are *the* Aragonian space of *flânerie,* Breton
designates the Porte Saint-Denis as the locus where "it" will happen.
Leading the subject back into the past while simultaneously promising
a redemptive future that does not quite live up to its allure, *Nadja*'s
"very beautiful and very useless Porte Saint-Denis" works a collapse of
linear historical temporality that permeates Benjamin's later notion of
a politically charged historiography.

In addition, I wonder if modern materialist imagery does not extend
to Benjamin's figuration for his nonorthodox Marxist notion of historical process in his final essay. I have in mind the flower following the
sun of history, an image Benjamin uses to differentiate his redemptive
yet politicized notion of history from the deterministic and teleological
view of history held by the Social Democrats. Attacking the mechanistic
schema of social progress assumed by the Social Democrats, Benjamin
writes: "They [the refined and spiritual things] have retroactive force
and will constantly call in question every victory, past and present, of
the rulers. As flowers turn toward the sun, by dint of a secret heliotropism the past strives to turn toward the sun which is rising in the
sky of history" (*I,* 255). In this passage Benjamin echoes Nietzsche on
historical process, rewriting the fragment "Historia abscondita" from
The Gay Science: "Every great human being exerts a retroactive force:
for his sake, all of history is placed in the balance again and a thousand
secrets of the past crawl out of their hiding places—into *his* sun [*Sonne*].
There is no way of telling what may yet become part of history. Perhaps
the past is still essentially undiscovered! So many retroactive forces are

---

46. Winfried Menninghaus, "Walter Benjamin's Theory of Myth" in *On Walter Benjamin,* ed. Smith, 307. I have translated the sentence from Menninghaus's "Science des
Seuils" in *Walter Benjamin et Paris,* 540–541, which uses slightly different terminology
from the essay as it appears in *On Walter Benjamin.*

still needed!" [47] When Benjamin transforms Nietzsche's figure for the individual's power to illuminate the past into a sun of collective history, however, he expresses the heliotropic movement that Nietzsche ascribes to the past with a figure that is not found in Nietzsche: the figure of the flower. And this is precisely the figure that Breton uses when he reworks the same Nietzsche fragment in writings published throughout the 1930s. [48]

In *Communicating Vessels* Breton couches his challenge to teleological and narrowly defined revolutionary activity by appealing to a notion of history similar to that formulated by Nietzsche, and Breton represents this notion of history with a similar figure, describing a flower that follows a secret historical sun. [49] For Breton it is the sun of a new order that has not yet arrived; against the French Communist Party, we saw him write:

> Who knows if it is not fitting that there should be shaped, in the most tormented periods and even against their will, the solitude of a few beings whose role is to avoid letting perish that which should have a fleeting existence only in a corner of the hothouse, in order to find much later its place at the center of the new order, thus marking with a *flower* [emphasis added] absolutely and simply present because *true*—a flower in some way *axial in relation to time*—that tomorrow should conjugate itself all the more closely with yesterday for having to break in a more decisive manner with it? (V, 159; CV, 137–138)

("In order for a part of the past to be touched by actuality, there must be no continuity between them," Benjamin asserts in Konvolut N [N 7, 7].) Breton elaborates his description of nonlinear history with the conceit of a flower following an alternative sun yet more extensively in *Mad Love*. He entitles the poem that exemplifies the subterranean future forces at work in the present "Tournesol" (Sunflower); he also uses the figure of the sunflower to describe the uncanny fashion in which the past persists in the present. Following his 1923 poem, he

47. Friedrich Nietzsche, *The Gay Science*, 104. Kaufmann translates "Sonne" as "sunshine."
48. Bataille uses the figure of a plant turned toward the sky but with "its obscene-looking roots" in "the earth" to attack Breton for idealism in "The 'Old Mole' and the Prefix *Sur*." In *Visions of Excess*, 36. For Bataille's own version of the heliotrope, see, for example, "The Language of Flowers" and "The Solar Anus," also in *Visions of Excess*.
49. If I previously insisted on the similarity between Breton's view of the retroactive forces at work in history and Freud's account of historical process, it should be noted that Freud was himself a good reader of Nietzsche.

applies this image to the Tour Saint-Jacques, a fragment from the past whose disruptive and mysterious persistence in the present he discusses:

> You showed me, in passing, the Tour Saint-Jacques under its pale veil of scaffolding, rendering it for years now even more the world's great monument to the unrevealed. You knew how I loved that tower: yet I see again now a whole violent existence forming around it to include us, to contain the desperate in its cloudy gallop around us:
>
> > In Paris the Tour Saint-Jacques swaying
> > Like a sunflower [*tournesol*] . . . (*AF*, 69; *ML*, 47)

Breton's promenade ends with the figure of a second flower that, like his "tournesol," fulfills its name by turning toward a sun that Breton associates with the past. "Soon it will be June, and the *heliotrope* bends its thousands of crests over the round black mirrors of the wet earth," Breton writes (*AF*, 74; *ML*, 49). The heliotropes at the flower market open toward Breton's future by gesturing toward the past, gazing down at the dark earth from which they spring rather than up at the sun toward which they grow.

The multiple sunflowers of the night thus justify Breton's assertions concerning the secret sun of historical process in *Communicating Vessels*. Marginal flowers take their place at the center of a new order; the present shows itself shot through with chips of an as yet unconscious future both radically ripped from yesterday and conjugated closely with it, composed of forces already at work in the past. Whether Benjamin took his sunflower from Breton or not, both thinkers use a similar figure to similar ends.

Breton differs from Benjamin, of course, in the theoretical models that he explicitly invokes to produce his nonlinear view of historical process. He modifies Marxism with appeal to a psychoanalytic disruption of linear temporality, whereas Benjamin makes a great show of borrowing from the apocalyptic schema of messianic Judaism. Nonetheless, I wonder if the difference between Benjamin's messianism and surrealism's psychoanalysis is as great as it first appears. I cannot help reading the last lines of the "Theses on the Philosophy of History" as Benjamin's unorthodox Marxist revision of the lines with which Freud concluded his *Interpretation of Dreams*. Freud writes:

> And the value of dreams for giving us knowledge of the future? There is of course no question of that. It would be truer to say instead that they give us knowledge of the past. For dreams are derived from the past in every sense. Nevertheless the ancient belief that dreams foretell the future is not

wholly devoid of truth. By picturing our wishes as fulfilled, dreams are after all leading us into the future. But this future, which the dreamer pictures as the present, has been moulded by his indestructible wish into a perfect likeness of the past.[50]

While Benjamin too ends his "Theses" with the question of the relation between remembering the past and transforming the future, he introduces the possibility of a radical severing of past and future which is simultaneously their joint conjugation.

We know that the Jews were prohibited from investigating the future. The Torah and the prayers instruct them in remembrance, however. This stripped the future of its magic, to which all those succumb who turn to the soothsayers for enlightenment. This does not imply, however, that for the Jews the future turned into homogeneous, empty time. For every second of time was the strait gate through which the Messiah might enter. (*I*, 264)

"ON SOME MOTIFS IN BAUDELAIRE" I:
CHOCK AND THE MODERN SUBJECT

Benjamin's Parisian production cycle does not simply elaborate the uncanny modern materialist encounter in recuperative fashion as the Now of recognizability essential to historiography. Benjamin also incorporates the encounter into his discussion of the subject's more equivocal contact with contemporary reality, the experience identified as *Chock* in Benjamin's late work on Baudelaire. This incorporation is visible in the essay where the concept comes to its full-blown expression, the 1939 "On Some Motifs in Baudelaire." The essay, moreover, is the only work in which Benjamin names the concept as such.[51]

To explain how the modern materialist encounter informs *Chock*, however, it is necessary to proceed in somewhat indirect fashion. While Benjamin himself puts forth a direct lineage leading from the surrealist *rencontre* to the profane illumination to the Now of historiographical recognition, he nowhere explicitly models his late *Chock* on Breton. Rather, an unstated similarity is at issue, most visible in Benjamin's modern materialist reading of Baudelaire. To articulate the notion of *Chock* Benjamin uses a Marxist-psychoanalytic theoretical apparatus

50. Freud, *The Interpretation of Dreams*, V, 621.
51. The concept of *Chock* is absent in Benjamin's first draft of the Baudelaire project, the 1938 "The Paris of the Second Empire in Baudelaire" included in *Charles Baudelaire: A Lyric Poet in the Era of High Capitalism*. There, Benjamin casts the contact between modern subject and material processes of determination in predominantly Marxist terms.

which sometimes sits rather uneasily on the poetry to which it is applied. This uneasy relationship can be explained by the fact that at these moments Benjamin is rather describing Breton's modern materialist translation of Baudelaire's *Tableaux parisiens* into the Parisian encounter than the *Tableaux* themselves.

Benjamin began "On Some Motifs in Baudelaire" in February 1939 and sent it off to the Institute for Social Research in July of that same year.[52] From the essay's opening section Benjamin is preoccupied with the structure of contemporary experience already at issue in the Parisian production cycle's opening work. While "On Some Motifs in Baudelaire" takes Baudelaire's poetry as its central subject, the essay poses this poetry at the watershed of a general historical transformation. There has been a "change in the structure of . . . experience [*Erfahrung*]," Benjamin hypothesizes from the text's opening section, and the first part of his work is devoted to characterizing this change.[53]

Features of Benjamin's interest in the history of *Erfahrung* have remained constant across the eleven years separating "On Some Motifs in Baudelaire" from *One-Way Street*. Like *One-Way Street*, this late work presents *Erfahrung* in contemporary life as a degraded form of the full *Erfahrung* that reigns in a nonalienated, precapitalist world: "Where there is experience [*Erfahrung*] in the strict sense of the word," Benjamin writes in 1939, "certain contents of the individual past combine with material of the collective past" (*I*, 159). In 1939 the moment of piercing encounter and its alternative, when contact is rather failed than violent, finally receive a name of their own: to *Chock* the essay opposes *Erlebnis*.[54] Nonetheless, substantial differences exist between the representations of *Erfahrung* and shock in each work deriving in part from Benjamin's passage through modern materialism. In 1939 Benjamin modifies his earlier binary model for subject/object interchange with appeal to a hidden third realm theorized both in psychoanalytic and Marxist terms.

Benjamin edges toward a psychoanalytic model of subjectivity when

52. See Benjamin, *GS*, I, 3, 1064.

53. "Motifs," in *I*, 156. For this section I will indicate quotations from the essay by page numbers in parentheses in my text. My discussion owes a great deal to Wohlfarth's previously mentioned essay on the ragpicker as well as to Wolin's reading of "On Some Motifs in Baudelaire" in his *Walter Benjamin*.

54. Benjamin qualifies *Chock* both as *Erfahrung* and *Erlebnis* in this text. He writes, for example, "Baudelaire placed the shock experience [*Chockerfahrung*] at the very center of his artistic work" (*I*, 163) but also Baudelaire "indicated the price for which the sensation of the modern age may be had: the disintegration of the aura in the experience of shock [*Chockerlebnis*]" (*I*, 194). See *GS*, I, 2, 616, and *GS*, I, 2, 653.

he characterizes the mediation between subject and cosmos obtaining before the decline of *Erfahrung*. "Experience [*Erfahrung*]," Benjamin writes of this precapitalist *Erfahrung*, "is indeed a matter of tradition, in collective existence as well as private life. It is less the product of facts firmly anchored in memory than a convergence in memory of accumulated and frequently not conscious data" (*I, 157*).[55] But if Benjamin suggests that the exchange between individual and tradition is not conscious, he means by this a state differing substantially from the unconscious described by Freud. This state knows no painful repression, no unbridgeable bar separating the subject from alien components of its experience which it cannot admit to have occurred. In addition, this state is composed of both collective and individual memories, with no great distinction drawn between them.

Benjamin only turns to the psychoanalytic topography of consciousness when he describes how subjectivity responds to the transformations that modernity works on the material world. In terms reminiscent of *One-Way Street,* "On Some Motifs in Baudelaire" allies the rise of capitalism with the unleashing of new technological forces endowed with the ability to destroy the individual. In such a situation, Benjamin posits, the subject can no longer afford the easygoing exchange with the cosmos that it enjoyed before. Rather, it erects defenses against this external world as a tactic of self-preservation: "The greater the share of the shock factor in particular impressions, the more constantly consciousness has to be alert as a screen against stimuli; the more efficiently it does so, the less do these impressions enter experience (*Erfahrung*), the more they fulfill the concept of *Erlebnis*" (*I, 163*).[56]

Following the Freudian model for trauma, Benjamin hence suggests that the only unmediated contact between subject and material reality is a disastrous one; a destructive assault on the subject's unprepared unconscious similar to the assault at the origin of traumatic neuroses. Benjamin finds this form of experience represented in Baudelaire:

55. I modify Zohn's translation of "nicht bewußten Daten" as "unconscious data." For the German original, see *GS*, I, 2, 608.

56. I modify Zohn's translation of the closing clause of this sentence which runs, "tending to remain in the sphere of a certain hour in one's life (*Erlebnis*)." Given Benjamin's materialist explanation for the development of repression, it is appropriate that he elaborates it with the psychic topography that Freud develops in *Beyond the Pleasure Principle*. As Wohlfarth observes, *Beyond the Pleasure Principle* is a work in which Freud models the psychic topography of repression on the subject's response to the destructive forces of second nature. Wohlfarth writes: "Freud's biological model, itself prompted by the study of war trauma and accident neurosis, clearly acquires special relevance." Wohlfarth, "On the Messianic Structure of Walter Benjamin's Last Reflections," 165.

Without reflection there would be nothing but the sudden start, usually the sensation of fright which, according to Freud, confirms the failure of the shock defense. Baudelaire has portrayed this condition in a harsh image. He speaks of a duel in which the artist, just before being beaten, screams in fright. This duel is the creative process itself. Thus Baudelaire placed the shock experience [*Chockerfahrung*] at the very center of his artistic work. (*I*, 163)

As Wolin observes, "Benjamin detects a remarkable confirmation of Freud's theory concerning the shock-preventative function of consciousness in Baudelaire's characterization of poetic creation."[57] The rather grim twist that such a Marxist-psychoanalytic account of modern subjectivity gives to the project of lyric poetry is particularly important for Benjamin. If lyric poetry, as the Romantics have it, reports on the exchange between subject and cosmos, the only moment when the modern subject contacts the cosmos is the disastrous moment when the subject's shock defenses are destroyed, the *Chock* Benjamin's late essay sometimes qualifies as *Erfahrung* and sometimes as *Erlebnis*. Baudelaire, Benjamin writes, "indicated the price for which the sensation of modernity may be had: the disintegration of the aura in the experience of shock [*Chockerlebnis*].[58] He paid dearly for consenting to this disintegration—but it is the law of his poetry, which shines in the sky of the Second Empire as 'a star without atmosphere'" (*I*, 194).[59]

"ON SOME MOTIFS IN BAUDELAIRE" II:
CHOCK AND THE POETRY OF BAUDELAIRE

Benjamin's formulation of *Chock* is indisputably powerful and is one of his concepts which has been most influential outside of literary studies. But to what extent is it applicable to the work of Baudelaire? To explore this question, I return to Baudelaire's representation of modern subjectivity. How well does it in fact correspond to Benjamin's description of this representation as shock?

57. Wolin, *Walter Benjamin*, 230.
58. I substitute "the sensation of modernity" for Zohn's "the sensation of the modern age." See *GS*, I, 2, 653.
59. In suggesting that the shocks of modern life produce Baudelaire's poetry, Benjamin both appropriates and modifies a commonplace from Baudelaire criticism. That Baudelaire's poetry makes use of shock tactics in its formal practices had been observed by many of his readers familiar to Benjamin, as Benjamin's observations in "On Some Motifs" as well as his notes in the Baudelaire Konvolut make evident. But Benjamin muses in this Konvolut: "The motif of shock does not only play into the aesthetic theory of Baudelaire as a maxim of prosody. Rather, the same motif is at work when Baudelaire makes Poe's theory on the significance of surprise in the art work his own" (*PW*, 484).

Benjamin isolates the traumatic encounter with the crowd as the material experience with perhaps the most formative power for Baudelaire. "Of all the experiences [*Erfahrungen*] which made his life what it was," Benjamin writes, "Baudelaire singled out his having been jostled by the crowd as the decisive, unique experience" (*I*, 193). Benjamin reiterates this notion in the conclusion to the essay, which proposes the urban crowd as the material disaster that Baudelaire's poetry attempts to set right: "Baudelaire battled the crowd—with the impotent rage of someone fighting the rain or the wind. This is the nature of something lived through (*Erlebnis*) to which Baudelaire has given the weight of an experience (*Erfahrung*)" (*I*, 193–194).

When Benjamin considers how this decisive experience makes its way into Baudelaire's poetry, he follows the psychoanalytic model for traumatic response found in *Beyond the Pleasure Principle*. He asserts that Baudelaire cannot bring the crowd to direct representation but rather occults it, much as the neurotic represses a formative psychical trauma. Benjamin writes: "This crowd, of whose existence Baudelaire is always aware, has not served as the model for any of his works, but it is imprinted on his creativity as a hidden figure, just as it constitutes the figure concealed in the fragment quoted before" (Benjamin refers here to a statement from the dedication of *Paris Spleen* where Baudelaire links his method of prose composition to the "numberless interconnecting relationships" of the city) (*I*, 165). And again: "The masses had become so much a part of Baudelaire's interior that one will look in vain for a portrayal [*Schilderung*] of them. So his most important subjects are hardly ever encountered in descriptive form" (*I*, 167).[60]

But Benjamin's argument for Baudelaire's elision of the crowd runs into difficulty on several fronts. First, it does not quite characterize Baudelaire's relation to the crowd, which, while undeniably problematic, is by no means suppressed. Far from "hidden" or "a part of Baudelaire's interior," the crowd fills Baudelaire's writings, notably the prose pieces of *Paris Spleen*. In these texts the streets of Paris overflow with the "hubbub" and "din" of "a big city," and this collection includes a prose poem entitled "Les Foules" (Crowds).[61] Much of "Les Veuves" (Widows) is also devoted to establishing contrasts between different kinds of crowds. In this prose poem Baudelaire portrays an old lady

---

60. Zohn translates the first sentence of this quote as follows: "The masses had become so much a part of Baudelaire that it is rare to find a description of them in his work." See *GS*, I, 2, 621.

61. Baudelaire, *Oeuvres complètes*, I, 279.

under "one of those skies, from which a *crowd* of regrets and memories
come down," sitting "to the side in a garden, to hear, far from the
crowd, one of those concerts where regimental music gratifies the Parisian people." [62] Baudelaire then passes from the old lady, far from the
crowd and assailed by her crowd of memories, to "a *crowd* of pariahs
who press around the edges of a public concert space." [63]

That Baudelaire did not always represent the crowd as hidden is a
fact of which Benjamin was very much aware less than a year before.
In the 1938 "The Paris of the Second Empire in Baudelaire," as in 1939,
Benjamin senses something unrepresentable in Baudelaire's treatment of
the crowd. He identifies this unrepresentable aspect, however, in more
orthodox Marxist terms. There Benjamin writes: "The deepest fascination of this spectacle lay in the fact that as it intoxicated him it did not
blind him to the horrible social reality. He remained conscious of it,
though only in the way in which intoxicated people are 'still' aware of
reality. That is why in Baudelaire the big city almost never finds expression in the direct presentation of its inhabitants." [64] Only occasionally,
Benjamin goes on to tell us, does the phantasmagoria of the crowd dis-
sipate to reveal the class struggle it obscures: "Only when this veil tears
and reveals to the *flâneur* 'one of the populous squares . . . which are
empty during street fighting' does he, too, get an unobstructed view of
the big city" (*CB,* 60). In 1938, Benjamin suggests that Baudelaire is
unable to bring to representation the social specificity of the crowd and
the collective historical processes in which it is involved. Contrasting
Baudelaire and Hugo on the crowd, Benjamin writes: "To Baudelaire
the crowd never was a stimulus to cast the plummet of his thought
down into the depths of the world" (*CB,* 61).

Benjamin revises this assessment in 1939 in a fashion consonant with
psychoanalysis. The crowd becomes repressed, and the moment tearing
the ideological veil becomes the notion of trauma advanced in *Beyond
the Pleasure Principle.* Nonetheless, even in 1939 Benjamin remains uncertain as to just how the decisively important urban crowd does *not*
appear. The crowd is the "*hidden* figure," we have seen him assert, and
also: "The masses had become so much a part of Baudelaire's interior
that one will look in vain for a portrayal [*Schilderung*] of them. So his
most important subjects are hardly ever encountered in descriptive

62. Baudelaire, *Oeuvres complètes,* I, 293 (emphasis added).
63. Baudelaire, *Oeuvres complètes,* I, 293 (emphasis added).
64. Benjamin, "The Paris of the Second Empire," in *Charles Baudelaire: A Lyric Poet
in the Era of High Capitalism,* 59. The volume will subsequently be abbreviated as *CB.*

form" (*I*, 165, emphasis added; *I*, 167). But are these two modes of invisibility the same? While the first phrase posits a psychological scenario linked throughout the essay to the paradigm of repression, the second sentence suggests the crowd as absent in a fashion more consistent with Benjamin's 1938 reading of Baudelaire: the crowd is not portrayed according to the descriptive strategies of social realism. Benjamin appeals once again to Hugo to support such a distinction: "It is futile to search in *Les Fleurs du mal* or in *Spleen de Paris* for any counterpart to the paintings of the city which Victor Hugo did with such mastery" (*I*, 168).[65] Benjamin's 1939 uncertainty as to whether the crowd is repressed or represented in nonrealist fashion pervades his essay: several sentences later he returns to his hypothesis that the crowds are conspicuously absent: "In *Tableaux parisiens* the secret presence of a crowd is demonstrable almost everywhere. When Baudelaire takes the dawn as his theme, the deserted streets emanate something of that 'silence of a throng' which Hugo senses in nocturnal Paris" (*I*, 168).

Another problematic aspect of Benjamin's argument is the rhetorical torsion it displays. In order to find his account of Parisian shock in the writings of Baudelaire, Benjamin must sometimes suppress the context from which he cites and engage in a bit of slippage among Baudelaire's texts. The passage where Benjamin describes Baudelaire's bringing the shock experience to vivid representation exemplifies this torsion:

> Without reflection there would be nothing but the sudden start, usually the sensation of fright which, according to Freud, confirms the failure of the shock defense. Baudelaire has portrayed this condition in a harsh image. He speaks of a duel in which the artist, just before being beaten, screams in fright. This duel is the creative process itself. Thus Baudelaire placed the shock experience [*Chockerfahrung*] at the very center of his artistic work. (*I*, 163)

65. Zohn renders "Gemälden" as "portrayals." See *GS*, I, 2, 621. In the *Passagen-Werk* fragment M 16, 1 Benjamin does find an early example of Baudelaire's engaging in a detailed description of the crowd: "Description of the crowd in Baudelaire, to compare with that of Poe:

> Le ruisseau, lit funèbre où s'en vont les dégoûts
> Charrie en bouillonnant le secret des égouts;
> Il bat chaque maison de son flot délétère,
> Court jaunir de limon la Seine qu'il altère,
> Et présente sa vague aux genoux du passant.
> Chacun, nous coudoyant sur le trottoir glissant,
> Egoïste et brutal, passe et nous éclabousse,
> Ou, pour courir plus vite, en s'éloignant nous pousse.
> Partout fange, déluge, obscurité du ciel:
> Noir tableau qu'eût rêvé le noir Ezéchiel!" (*PW*, 559)

Benjamin reads this image as an apt representation of *Chock* and goes on, with the help of "Le Soleil" and *Paris Spleen*'s "À Arsène Houssaye," to link the image of the fencer to the poet encountering the urban crowd: "We may discern the image of the fencer in it; the blows he deals are designed to open a path through the crowd for him" (*I*, 165). But to do so Benjamin must suppress the context in which Baudelaire proposes the figure of the artist crying out in fright. For if Baudelaire describes a moment akin to Freud's failure of the shock defense, Baudelaire situates this experience within the lineage of a more Romantic experience of the sublime than Benjamin here allows. The passage comes from "The *Confiteor* of the Artist," which concludes: "Oh! is it necessary to suffer eternally or eternally to flee the beautiful? Nature, sorceress without mercy, always victorious rival, leave me! Stop tempting my desires and my pride. *The study of the beautiful* is a duel where the artist cries out in fright before being beaten." [66] At the moment that Baudelaire visibly represents the shock experience, he thus gives it a speculative source, making it the result of a confrontation between the self and metaphysical Nature in the study of beauty rather than the subject's encounter with the overwhelming practical forces of modern life.[67] Moreover, Benjamin fails to explain why Baudelaire describes the shock experience as resulting from metaphysical forces rather than the urban sublime. This is not to deny that Benjamin's reading of Baudelaire could be used to explain the metaphysical source Baudelaire ascribes to shock, that this source could be viewed as a displacement of contemporary urban experience. But such explanation does not dispel Benjamin's failure to articulate the difference between Baudelaire's representation of shock and his own reading of it; Benjamin also fails to cite the crucial Baudelaire passage directly.

There is thus some slippage in Benjamin's use of psychoanalytic concepts to describe how Baudelaire brings the crowd to representation. The explanation for this slippage lies in Benjamin's materialist-psychoanalytic model of shock which does not precisely describe the Baudelairean sublime. The model does, however, characterize Breton's updating of this sublime into the modern materialist encounter extremely well. Breton's prose narratives obsessively replay a moment of shock

66. Baudelaire, *Oeuvres complètes*, I, 278–279 (emphasis added).
67. A similar metaphysico-aesthetic origin to shock is visible in other metaphors of the artist-fencer which Benjamin allies with the experience of the Parisian crowd. Thus Baudelaire describes Constantin Guys dueling in artistic isolation, as Guys struggles with the "nature" that is both resistant material and his own imagination to bring forth his vision: "La fantasmagorie a été extraite de la nature." See Baudelaire, *Oeuvres complètes*, II, 694.

threatening the integrity of the subject—and Breton, unlike Baudelaire, resolutely situates that moment in the arena of urban experience. Here, consonant with Benjamin's account of shock, the surrealist subject's self-sufficiency crumbles in the face of some irresistible external force.

The link between Baudelaire's representation of Paris and the Paris of modern materialist shock is also one that Breton himself repeatedly makes. We have seen Breton open *Nadja* by associating the uncanny encounter central to his prose trilogy with the Baudelaire of "Les Sept Vieillards." And Breton's fascination with the gaze of a strange woman encountered on the street is prominent in *Nadja*'s opening enumeration of uncanny encounters: "Nantes: perhaps with Paris the only city in France where I feel that something worthwhile can happen to me, where certain looks burn for their own sake with too much fire (I noticed this only last year, the time it took to cross Nantes by car and see that woman—a workingwoman, I think, accompanied by a man—raise her eyes: I should have stopped)" (*OC*, 658–661; *N*, 28). Breton's debt to "A une passante" emerges most notably in his first meeting with Nadja: "I had just crossed this intersection whose name I forget or don't know, there, in front of a church. Suddenly, perhaps still ten feet away, coming from the opposite direction, I see a young woman, very poorly dressed, who also sees me or has seen me. She walks head high, unlike all the other passerbys [*passants*]" (*OC*, 683; *N*, 64). In both experiences Breton's rendition of "A une passante" is closer to Benjaminian shock than is Baudelaire's original poem. In Baudelaire's poem the shock of the encounter between lyric poet and Parisian muse is aesthetically fertile in a fashion strengthening the poet's self: "Fugitive beauté / Dont le regard m'a fait soudainement renaître," Baudelaire writes in the tercets redeeming the experience narrated in the quatrains.[68] In Breton's shocking encounters with women, above all Nadja, in contrast, an unconscious force is released which threatens to perform the dissolution of the lyric subject altogether. Indeed, given the extent to which Breton devotes his prose trilogy to reworking the erotic Baudelairean encounter with the unknown passerby by attempting to prolong it in narrative, one wonders at the literary site where Benjamin finds the "late" residue of "A une passante" (*I*, 170). Multiple experiences in *Nadja* (to say nothing of *Communicating Vessels* and *Mad Love*) are closer to Benjamin's description of shock than is the glance of Proust's Albertine locked up in Marcel's apartment.

68. Baudelaire, *Oeuvres complètes*, I, 93. A literal translation of these lines runs: "Fleeting beauty / Whose look made me suddenly be reborn."

Benjamin's Baudelaire parrying the shocks of Parisian urban reality
and failing in a moment that both destroys the lyric subject and is aesthetically fertile is, I am suggesting, a better reading of Breton in search
of "it" than of Baudelaire's own *flânerie*. This reading is all the better
because it allows us to articulate an aspect of the urban surrealist sublime that Breton's own writings obscure. While Breton often presents
his Parisian encounters in positive terms, Benjamin's account of *Chock*
makes clear the objective terror that such a violent version of subjective
experience has at its source. "One could say," writes Benjamin of Baudelaire in "Central Park," "happiness sent its shudder through him"
("CP," 34). One could say this even more appropriately of Breton's
encounter than of the Baudelairean *correspondances*.

I wonder if the contribution of modern materialism to Benjamin's
later elaboration of *Chock* extends beyond Breton's practice of the
uncanny encounter to its theorization. I am struck by the similarities
between Benjamin's notion of modern subjectivity as constituted by a
traumatic shock that is both psychic and material in origin and the
modern materialist elaboration of the construction of subjectivity in
Mad Love. True, when Benjamin discusses *Beyond the Pleasure Principle* in late fragments from the *Passagen-Werk,* he refers to its explica-
tion by Reik. Nonetheless, the resemblance between Benjamin's Freudian description of shock trauma and Breton's late theorization of the
encounter is remarkable. "*Chance is the form of manifestation of exterior necessity which traces [se fraie] its path in the human unconscious*
(boldly trying to interpret and to reconcile Engels and Freud on this
point)" (*AF*, 31; *ML*, 23). In this central modern materialist formulation Breton represents the encounter decisive to the surrealist subject
as a moment when material forces overwhelm the shock defenses and
mark the subject's unconscious.

In this context it is striking that Breton alludes to Baudelaire not only
in his narratives of Parisian encounters but also in his attempts to explain why these encounters occur. This allusion is visible, for example,
in Breton's discussion of objective chance in *Mad Love*. There Breton
associates the uncanny moment of surrealist chance with the power of
the surrealist image, which he formulates as *shock*: "Such images,
whose best examples are found in Lautréamont, are endowed with a
persuasive strength rigorously proportional to the violence of the initial
shock they produced" (*AF*, 129; *ML*, 88, emphasis added).[69] Breton
then associates this shock with Baudelaire's poetry, an association also

69. I follow Caws's translation here verbatim.

found in Benjamin's discussion of existing critical commonplaces concerning the jarring effect of Baudelaire's style. Breton displaces these critical commonplaces in similar fashion. Like Benjamin, he finds shock not only in Baudelaire's poetic technique but also in Baudelaire's representation of experience. Like Benjamin too, he likens this shock to the psychoanalytic understanding of the moment when the repression containing unconscious libidinal forces comes undone. In a passage making Baudelaire the precursor of psychoanalytic discussions of the libido, Breton writes:

> Desire, the only motive of the world, desire, the only rigor humans must be acquainted with, where could I be better situated to adore it than on the inside of the cloud? The forms that the clouds take, from the ground, in the eyes of man, are in no way random; they are augural. If a good part of modern psychology tends to stress that fact, I am all the more certain that Baudelaire sensed its coming in that stanza of "The Voyage," where the last line, while loading them with meaning, echoes the first three in such a disturbing [*troublante*] fashion: "The richest cities, the greatest landscapes / Never held the mysterious allure / Of those that chance makes with the clouds / And our desire would let us have no peace!" (*AF*, 129; *ML*, 88)

The importance of Breton's later work to Benjamin's notion of shock cannot be proved. But such a link is historically plausible, and not only because Adorno directed Benjamin's attention to *Communicating Vessels*. While Benjamin does not mention *Mad Love,* there is an excellent chance he laid his hands on its chapters when they first appeared. As the *Passagen-Werk* citations make clear, Benjamin was a reader of the contemporary periodicals where *Mad Love* was first published in article form, notably *Minotaure.*[70]

At the moment that Benjamin was working on "On Some Motifs on Baudelaire," in March 1939, he went to an opening of Gisèle Freund's photography at Adrienne Monnier's bookstore, where he met the all-powerful arranger of the night of the sunflower, Jacqueline Breton.[71] Breton too was there, and if Benjamin did not talk with him, he certainly had the chance to meet his representation. For Freund projected Breton's image on the wall in the principal event of the evening, a panoramic slide show presenting her portraits of the major figures on the contemporary Parisian intellectual scene.

70. *Mad Love*'s chapter 2 on the *rencontre* appeared first as a survey in *Minotaure,* nos. 3–4; chapter 1 on convulsive beauty appeared in *Minotaure,* no. 5; chapter 4 on the *rencontre capitale* of the night of the sunflower in *Minotaure,* no. 7; and chapter 5 on Tenerife in *Minotaure,* no. 8. Chapter 3, on the *trouvaille,* appeared in *Documents* in June 1934.

71. Gary Smith drew my attention to this encounter.

17. *Robertson's Phantasmagoria in the Cour des Capucines* (*La Fantasmagorie de Robertson dans la Cour des Capucines*).

CHAPTER 8

Le Diable à Paris

Benjamin's Phantasmagoria

Why should the nineteenth century . . . be the century of
spiritism?

—Benjamin, *Passagen-Werk*

Curious comment of Engels on "social forces": "Once their
nature has been understood, they can be turned from
daemonic rulers into willing servants in the associated
producers' hands." (!)

—Benjamin, *Passagen-Werk*

THE FRENCH MARX

My study has considered Benjamin's interest in a twentieth-century
French Marx influential to this day. But there is also a second French
Marx crucial to Benjamin, not Marxism in its 20th-century French
manifestation but rather Marx himself in France. "This investigation . . . becomes important for Marxism in two ways," Benjamin asserts of the *Passagen-Werk*'s methodological goals in an early fragment
from Konvolut N (N 1a, 7). "First, it will explore the way the environment from which Marx's teaching arose influenced the latter through
its expressive character, and not just through its causal relationships;
and secondly, it will show those features that Marxism shares with the
expressive character of the material products that are contemporary
with it" (N 1a, 7).

While Benjamin's subsequent theoretical discussion did not develop
these ambitions, they remain a visible if unarticulated concern of the
Passagen-Werk to the end. As concluding gesture, I want to underline
their presence; I do so from a sense of their high methodological stakes.
In asking how Marx's teachings are a product of Marx's time, Benjamin
dissolves the suprahistorical status of conceptual categories into the history they are used to seize. He thus pursues the need to establish a
dialectical relation between theory and its historical object. As end-
point, such investigation seeks a historically nuanced Marxism, capable

simultaneously of analyzing nineteenth-century commodity culture and of articulating its own implication in the culture it seeks to explain. It is a project whose completion we still await.

I confine myself here to the principal expressive environment at issue in the *Passagen-Werk*. This is "Paris, then, the old university of philosophy (*absit omen!*) and the new capital of the new world," as Marx put it in the famous 1843 letter, a city on which Marx wrote extensively and of which Marx was briefly a resident as well.[1] Benjamin's interest in the expressive character of mid-nineteenth century Paris informing Marx's writings saturates the *Passagen-Werk*'s Konvoluts. Benjamin cites copiously from Marx and Engels's political, economic, and polemical writings on Paris. In the Konvolut entitled "Social Movement," he suggests the "influence of Romanticism on political phraseology" as a topic for investigation (*PW*, 865). In this same Konvolut he repeatedly juxtaposes literary representations of Parisian insurrection with its representations by Marx and Engels. And he includes fragments on Marx and Engels's sojourn in the city, like the following observation by Paul Lafargue in Konvolut D: "Engels told me how in 1848 in Paris in the Café de la Régence, one of the first centers of the revolution of 1789, Marx for the first time put forth to him the economic determinism of his theory of a materialist conception of history" (*PW*, 164). Benjamin's interest in Marx in Paris also surfaces briefly in the essay "Eduard Fuchs, Collector and Historian." This essay not only formulates a materialist program for cultural critique but brings up the issue of "the image of France that lived in Marx and Engels": "the scene of three great revolutions, the home of exiles, the wellspring of utopian socialism, the fatherland of the tyrant-haters Quinet and Michelet, the earth in which the Communards lie buried" (*OWS*, 371).

The following discussion, however, focuses not on the *Passagen-Werk* but rather on the 1938 "The Paris of the Second Empire in Baudelaire." It does so in allegiance to Benjamin's critical imperative of rescue. This "now infamous" text, as Buck-Morss observes, is among the most "highly criticized" of Benjamin's works (*DS*, 205). Notably, it is criticized, to borrow Adorno's phrasing, for "crassly and roughly . . . confront[ing] the Baudelairean world of forms with the necessities of life" (*AP*, 129). But recognizing Benjamin's interest in what Marx shares with the expressive character of nineteenth-century Paris places the essay's crass confrontations in a more favorable light. Benjamin

1. Marx, letter to Ruge, in *The Marx-Engels Reader*, 12.

does not only here bring together materialist theory with the work of Baudelaire in order to reduce Baudelaire to an illustration of Marx. In addition, he asks how Marx and Baudelaire are implicated in the same Parisian rhetorical milieu.

The second half of this chapter pursues Benjamin's interest in the expressive environment informing Marx's theory beyond Benjamin's explicit discussion. It does so through reawakening the nineteenth-century Parisian history buried in a Marxist term that Benjamin increasingly uses to characterize ideological projection in his late work on the arcades project: the *phantasmagoria*. In nineteenth-century usage this term designated both a form of magic lantern show and a psychological experience when the distinction between subject and objective conditions breaks down. Reawakening the nineteenth-century life of the phantasmagoria reveals one explanation for Marx's borrowing from the Parisian rhetorical milieu dear to Baudelaire. This milieu provides him with figures for concepts he seeks to articulate but cannot produce from within the Enlightenment horizon of his thought. In addition, reawakening the phantasmagoria allows us to answer a question raised in my second chapter. Why, when Benjamin rewrites the 1935 "Paris, the Capital of the Nineteenth Century" in 1939, does he drop the dream language, describing ideological transposition exclusively as phantasmagorical?

ON SOME MOTIFS IN BAUDELAIRE AND MARX I: *THE EIGHTEENTH BRUMAIRE AS TABLEAUX PARISIENS*

Benjamin cites Marx frequently when analyzing nineteenth-century Parisian culture, most obviously because Marx's theory explains the material factors shaping its products so well. Indeed, the Frankfurt School's major objection to Benjamin's use of Marx in this context is that Marx works *too* well. Benjamin shows the products of "the remoter realms of the superstructure" to be marked by emerging industrial capitalism, they charge, at the expense of the products' aesthetic complexity (*OWS*, 368). This was certainly Adorno's assessment of "The Paris of the Second Empire in Baudelaire," written during the summer and autumn of 1938 and then sent off for his perusal.

Adorno's opinion was consistent throughout his highly critical response to the essay. "Unless I am very much mistaken," Adorno wrote in his letter of November 1938, "your dialectic lacks one thing: mediation. Throughout your text there is a tendency to relate the pragmatic contents of Baudelaire's work directly to adjacent features in the social history of his time, preferably economic features. I have in mind the passage about the duty on wine, certain statements about the barricades." [2] If Adorno's judgment is correct, Benjamin's practice in this work is strange. It conflicts with Benjamin's previously discussed methodological comments on the complex relations obtaining between aesthetic production and social conditions. It also conflicts with Benjamin's general characterization of his methodological aspirations in reading Baudelaire. "The historical projection of the experiences which underlie the *Fleurs du mal* is what this study should offer" is how Benjamin couched his goal in the fragments of "Central Park" ("CP," 43). The spatial terms Benjamin uses to suggest the relation of the *Fleurs du mal* to its age could lead us to suspect him of vulgar determinism: experiences are cast as the base supporting the superstructure of Baudelaire's work. But, as Wohlfarth has shown, Benjamin's statements on his methodological goals in the Baudelaire Konvolut reveal that he views the relation of Baudelaire to contemporary social conditions in a more complex way. [3] "What I have in mind is to show Baudelaire as he lies embedded in the nineteenth century. The imprint that he has left behind upon it must stand out as clearly and as untouched as that of a stone that is one day rolled from its place after having lain there for decades" Benjamin writes in Konvolut J (*PW*, 405). Here Benjamin employs a figure for the relation between Baudelaire and his time consonant with his overdetermined notion of base-superstructure relations advanced in other contexts. Benjamin asks not only how Baudelaire is shaped by his age but how he shapes it and shapes as well the landscape of the age as it now appears to us. It is important that Benjamin describes this relation with a metaphor that modifies a vulgar Marxist model for base-superstructure relations in the spirit of surrealism. Rather than constructing the relation of Baudelaire to the nineteenth century using the tropes of visual reflection common to functional accounts of base-superstructure relations, Benjamin uses the rhetoric of contact familiar from surrealist accounts of overdetermination.

Benjamin's theory and practice have no obligation to coincide. But when Benjamin responded to Adorno's November 1938 letter, he made clear that establishing a direct and deterministic link between Parisian cultural products and material forces was not his aim. Without denying

2. Theodor Adorno to Walter Benjamin, New York, 10 November 1938, *AP*, 128.
3. See Wohlfarth's "Et Cetera? The Historian as Chiffonier."

Adorno's charge that his work engaged in "a wide-eyed presentation of mere facts," Benjamin suggested that this presentation must be understood as part of a larger project (*AP*, 129).[4] It was an absent theoretical construction, Benjamin intimated, which would provide the framework in which his riveting use of the detail might be both preserved and superseded: "The missing theoretical transparency to which you rightly refer is by no means a *necessary* consequence of the philological procedure prevailing in this section. I am more inclined to see it as the result of the fact that this procedure has not been designated as such. This deficiency may be traced in part to the daring attempt to write the second part of the book before the first" (*AP*, 138).[5]

Where and what is the missing theory? As so often with Benjamin, the critic confronts a situation resembling one of Benjamin's own favorite figures for critical practice. Contemplating a shattered landscape, she is challenged to perform the *tikkun* which Benjamin saw as the task of the translator and the materialist historiographer alike. I want now to bring Benjamin's interest in the historicity of Marx's own theoretical project to the critical mosaic around "The Paris of the Second Empire in Baudelaire."

From its opening sentences "The Paris of the Second Empire in Baudelaire" links Baudelaire to "the necessities of [Parisian] life" by relying on Marx's analysis of nineteenth-century commodity culture. And throughout the essay Benjamin certainly applies Marx to Baudelaire in the manner that provoked Adorno's critique. From his discussion of bohemians and conspirators to his analysis of the effects

4. As Buck-Morss states, "In 1937 Benjamin conceived of a separate book on Baudelaire" (*DS*, 205). Benjamin told Scholem that this work was to provide a "miniature model" of the arcades project in a letter dated April 14, 1938 (*B*, II, 748). To what extent this statement is valid constitutes the subject of some critical dispute. See Tiedemann's "Baudelaire, Zeuge gegen die Bürgerklasse," in *Charles Baudelaire*, for details on the Baudelaire project. See also Michel Espagne and Michael Werner's "Les Manuscrits parisiens de Walter Benjamin et le Passagen-Werk," in *Walter Benjamin et Paris*, as well as Buck-Morss's discussion of the matter in *DS*, 205ff.

5. Benjamin characterized the relations between the three parts of the project somewhat differently in a letter to Horkheimer from the time of the essay's composition, written from Copenhagen and dated 28 September 1938. There he proposed the existing essay as a second section situated between a missing first and third part. Terming the unwritten first part the thesis, he suggested it as a "problematic of aesthetic theory" (*B*, II, 774). To this section he opposed the existing second part as antithesis, an "interpretation of the poet from the standpoint of social critique" (*B*, II, 774). A third part entitled "The Commodity as Poetic Object" was to perform the synthesis "in which form in the material contexts should come as decisively into its right as it did as a problem in the first section" (*B*, II, 774). On the missing parts of the study, see also Tiedemann's "Baudelaire, Zeuge gegen die Bürgerklasse," and Lloyd Spencer's "Introduction to 'Central Park,'" 29.

of industrial production and commodification on the literary marketplace and on the conception of the artist, Benjamin sees Baudelaire as reproducing Marx's delineation of nineteenth-century industrial capitalism in poetic form. Benjamin writes of the supernatural language found in Baudelaire's evocation of the barricades: "Baudelaire does not say farewell to the city without invoking its barricades; he remembers its 'magic cobblestones which rise up to form fortresses'. These stones, to be sure, are 'magic' because Baudelaire's poem says nothing about the hands which set them in motion" (*CB*, 15). Benjamin here explains Baudelaire's use of magic vocabulary by appealing to the explanation for the nineteenth-century supernatural that Marx gives in *Capital*. The magic is that of commodity fetishism, a situation in which social relations between men take on the phantasmagorical form of relations between things. In similar fashion Benjamin will explain the behavior of the man of letters on the boulevard as embodying Marx's labor theory of value: "He behaved as if he had learned from Marx that the value of a commodity is determined by the working time socially necessary to produce it" (*CB*, 29).

But to read Benjamin's juxtapositions of Marx and Baudelaire in "The Paris of the Second Empire in Baudelaire" in this way alone is to consider only the more visible half of the story. Using Marx's writings to analyze nineteenth-century Parisian culture, Benjamin also investigates how these writings exemplify the culture they explain. This investigation emerges most often in the text's first section, "La Bohème." Benjamin reads "the litany entitled 'Abel et Cain' " in following fashion:

> Cain . . . appears as the founder of a race, and this race can be none other than the proletariat. In 1838 Granier de Cassagnac published his *Histoire des classes ouvrières et des classes bourgeoises*. This work claimed to give the origin of the proletarians; they form a class of subhumans which has come into being by crossing robbers with prostitutes. Did Baudelaire know these speculations? It is easily possible. What is certain is that Marx, who hailed Granier de Cassagnac as "the thinker" of Bonapartist reaction, had encountered them. *Capital* parried this racial theory by developing the concept of a "race of peculiar commodity-owners," by which was meant the proletariat. (*CB*, 22)

I cite at length to stress that Benjamin does more than employ Marx for documentation of fact. Situating Baudelaire's representations fusing class struggle with diabolical and racial motifs in an arena of contemporary Parisian discussion on the proletariat, Benjamin asks how *Capital* bathes in the same rhetorical milieu saturating the work of Baudelaire.

This question persists through many of the textual juxtapositions in
"La Bohème." Benjamin raises it most often when reading Marx's writings on Paris, notably *The Eighteenth Brumaire*.[6] Benjamin shows, for
example, that both writers respond not only to conservative discourse
on the proletariat as *classes dangereuses* but to the socially engaged
avant-garde art that enjoyed great prestige under the July Monarchy.
Stressing the importance of one of its practitioners, Pierre Dupont, for
Baudelaire and Marx, Benjamin initiates this discussion by reflecting on
Barbey d'Aurevilly's comparison of Dupont to Cain.[7]

> This characterization expresses exactly what gave Baudelaire solidarity with
> Dupont. Like Cain, Dupont had "gone to the cities" and turned away from
> the idyllic. . . . When the achievements of the Revolution were lost, one after
> another, Dupont wrote his *Chant du vote*. There are few things in the polit-
> ical literature of the time that are a match to its refrain. It is a leaf of that
> laurel which Karl Marx claimed for the "threateningly dark brows" of the
> June fighters.
>
> > Fais voir, en déjouant la ruse
> > O Républicain! à ces pervers
> > Ta grande face de Méduse . . . (*CB, 25–26*)

As in the preceding example, Benjamin does not here invoke Marx to
describe the reality to which Baudelaire gives aesthetic form. Rather,
he implicates Baudelaire and Marx in a common rhetorical figuration
of class struggle, one where diabolical themes are again employed.[8]
Benjamin also juxtaposes Baudelaire's politically charged satanism to
the polemical flourishes surrounding Marx on the disorders of liberal-
republican politics in the Second Republic. Benjamin begins: "Baudelaire was thoroughly familiar with this dual aspect of Satan. To him,
Satan spoke not only for the upper crust but for the lower classes as
well" (*CB*, 24). He proceeds to liken Baudelaire's representation of
Satan in nineteenth-century Paris to a passage from *The Eighteenth
Brumaire*:

> Marx could hardly have wished for a better reader of the following lines
> from the *Eighteenth Brumaire*: "When the Puritans complained at the Coun-
> cil of Constance about the wicked lives of the popes . . . Cardinal Pierre

6. Benjamin more often appeals to *Capital* in explanatory and factual fashion.
7. Does Benjamin's discussion on the relation between Baudelaire and Pierre Dupont
also dialogue with Breton's comments on the subject in *Minotaure* no. 6 (Winter, 1935)?
Benjamin cites at length from Breton's "La grande actualité poétique" in Konvolut D,
"Literary History, Hugo" (see *PW*, 904–905).
8. On the prevalence of castration and petrification imagery around the revolution
of 1848, see Neil Hertz's "Medusa's Head: Male Hysteria under Political Pressure," in
The End of the Line.

d'Ailly thundered at them: 'Only the devil incarnate can save the Catholic church and you demand angels.' Thus the French bourgeoisie cried after the *coup d'état*: 'Only the head of the Society of the Tenth of December can save bourgeois society! Only theft can save property, perjury can save religion, bastardy the family, and disorder, order.'" (*CB*, 24–25)

Here it is not the factual status of Satan in the nineteenth century that is at issue but rather the fact that Baudelaire and Marx belong to a Parisian rhetorical milieu that describes class conflict in satanic terms. Or rather, it is the factual status of Satan in nineteenth-century Paris if the "wide-eyed presentation of mere facts" includes rhetorical facts.

Such passages on the rhetorical constructions common to Marx and Baudelaire are Benjamin exploring *not* how Marx's concepts explain the workings of nineteenth-century Paris *but rather* how the "expressive character" of the Parisian environment shapes Marx's thought. The preceding example makes clear what an open conception of expression Benjamin holds. Benjamin constructs the expressive character of the Parisian environment with appeal to aesthetic products, certainly, but also with appeal to representations across the ideological spectrum cutting through the boundaries of institutionally separated genres. Thus, Benjamin juxtaposes Marx and Baudelaire's rhetoric fusing diabolical issues and class struggle to examples of this rhetoric in conservative sociology on the proletariat and in avant-garde art, in historical discussions of Blanqui, in Vigny's poetry, in the domination of the ruling class as it is depicted by Barthélmy.

How are these nongenre-specific Parisian expressive units that Benjamin isolates to be designated? They might be called *motifs,* borrowing the term used by Benjamin himself throughout his late work on Baudelaire. The *motif* designates a recurring representational unit, whether formal or thematic, within one representation and across representations as well. "Form in the material contexts should come as decisively into its right as it did as a problem in the first section," Benjamin wrote to Horkheimer on the function of the Baudelaire project's unwritten third section "synthesizing" parts one and two (*B*, II, 774). "Form in the material contexts": this ambiguous phrase could be read as designating the material context of the form. But it could also be read as designating the material existence of form at issue in Benjamin's concept of the Parisian motif.

In his textual juxtapositions of Baudelaire and Marx, Benjamin thus accumulates a sort of nineteenth-century Parisian fact for which Adorno's reading of his essay makes no room. When Adorno charges

Benjamin with brutally confronting "the social history of his [Baude-laire's] time, preferably economic," with "the Baudelairean world of forms," he does not recognize Benjamin's interest in how social facts manifest themselves primarily in the world of forms, in a world of forms that is not aesthetic but rather the realm of social fact (*AP*, 128, 129). Indeed, Adorno's failure to recognize the representational nature of the facts at stake in "The Paris of the Second Empire in Baudelaire" is visible in many of his individual objections to the essay. This is the case, for example, with Adorno's response to Benjamin's discussion of Baudelaire's wine poems. "The direct inference from the duty on wine to *L'Ame du Vin* imputes to phenomena precisely that kind of spon-taneity, palpability and density which they have lost in capitalism," Adorno wrote (*AP*, 129). But Benjamin in fact initiates discussion by considering how "motifs which appear in this poem were being publicly discussed" (*CB*, 17). He asks, that is, not how Baudelaire's work repro-duces existing material conditions but rather how it inscribes reactions to material conditions in current representational circulation. The new title Benjamin gave the essay when he revised it to answer Adorno's ob-jections emphasizes the representational status of the facts he is out to seize: "On Some *Motifs* in Baudelaire."

That Benjamin juxtaposes Marx and Baudelaire to show how Baude-laire's poetry inscribes economic and political conditions and to ex-amine both these writers' implication in a common discursive milieu is not inconsistent. Rather, these approaches comprise the two faces of Benjamin's dialectical interest in the relation between theory and its historical object. As the reception of "The Paris of the Second Empire in Baudelaire" has made clear, however, when Benjamin simply pre-sents these faces without explanation, he obscures his project's his-toricizing side. Within the Marxist tradition that Benjamin addresses, it requires some theoretical, if not polemical, dynamite to dislodge Marx's texts from their habitual status as authoritative analyses of nineteenth-century reality, as transparent access to "the social history of his [Baudelaire's] time, preferably economic" (Adorno, *AP*, 128).

Benjamin's exploration of Marx's implication in contemporary Pari-sian rhetorical formations is less visible in the subsequent sections of "The Paris of the Second Empire in Baudelaire," the second section entitled "The *Flâneur*," which deals with the rise of literature as com-modity as well as with the urbanization of Paris, and the third section entitled "Modernity [*Die Moderne*]," on the accompanying transfor-mation that these conditions work on the later nineteenth-century understanding of the artist and the social situation of the work of art. More often, these sections invoke Marx's texts as windows onto material processes, notably for *Capital*'s unraveling of the commodity form. Benjamin provides an example of such use in his reading of Baudelaire's "Crowds." In this celebrated prose poem, Benjamin suggests, Baudelaire represents the voice of "the fetish itself with which Baudelaire's sensitive nature resonated so powerfully; that empathy with inorganic things which was one of his sources of inspiration" (*CB*, 55).

But Benjamin's interest in what Marx's writings share with the expressive character of nineteenth-century Paris nonetheless remains visible. Benjamin appends, for example, the following footnote to his discussion of Poe's demonic representation of the urban metropolis:

> The image of America which Marx had seems to be of the same stuff as Poe's description. He emphasizes the "feverishly youthful pace of material production" in the States and blames this very pace for the fact that there was "neither time nor opportunity . . . to abolish the old spirit world" (Marx, *Der achzehnte Brumaire des Louis Bonaparte*, op. cit., p. 30). In Poe there is something demonic even about the physiognomy of the businessmen. Baudelaire describes how as darkness descends "the harmful demons" awaken in the air "sluggish as a bunch of businessmen" (I, 108). This passage in "Le Crépuscule du soir" may have been inspired by Poe's text. (*CB*, 52)

Juxtaposing Marx and Baudelaire as readers of Poe, Benjamin places Marx in the lineage of an American writer who played an important role in shaping the mid-nineteenth century Parisian expressive environment. In particular, Poe's work informed the nineteenth-century French tradition of *l'art pour l'art* that the methodological addendum of "The Paris of the Second Empire in Baudelaire" describes as crucial to understanding Baudelaire. "The tradition of Baudelaire's works is a very short one, but it already bears historical scars which must be of interest to critical observers," Benjamin writes of Baudelaire's relation to *l'art pour l'art* (*CB*, 104).[9]

9. In linking Marx to Baudelaire's Poe, Benjamin thus pursues another statement from the methodological addendum, a prescription against vulgar Marxism which he formulates in his own reading of the master: "It is an illusion of vulgar Marxism that the social function of a material or intellectual product can be determined without reference to the circumstances and the bearers of its tradition" (*CB*, 104). The methodological addendum also, however, uses Marx in inverse fashion, to explain the material factors dictating the prestige accorded to the theory of *l'art pour l'art*. This theory, Benjamin speculates, assumed decisive importance around 1852, at a moment Marx "recollects" in *The Eighteenth Brumaire*: when the bourgeoisie sought to "take its 'cause' from the hands of the writers and poets" (*CB*, 106).

ON SOME MOTIFS IN BAUDELAIRE AND MARX II:
ALLEGORY AND THE COMMODITY FORM

When Benjamin described the relation of the final section of the Baudelaire project to "The Paris of the Second Empire in Baudelaire" to Max Horkheimer, he wrote that "the second [section] brings the data required" for a "resolution" to the problem of Baudelaire as allegorist (*B*, II, 774). I have suggested that this data is in part Benjamin's delineation of the expressive character of the Parisian environment, and the title that Benjamin formulated for the projected third section confirms this suggestion. He proposed "The Commodity as Poetic Object," linking the two terms with an ambiguous "as" that allows the phrase to be read in several ways (*B*, II, 774). To show how the commodity comes to representation in the poetic object is an orthodox materialist ambition and it is a central component in Benjamin's work. But the "as" can also be read as Benjamin comparing the commodity to the poetic object. This comparison is extremely suggestive because of the ambiguity of the terms themselves. First, what is the objecthood of poetry that interests Benjamin? Does "poetic object" designate the text as material commodity for sale in the marketplace or as aesthetic object? In the latter case, how can one liken the commodity to the poetic object; does this juxtaposition transform the commodity into an aesthetic form? And second, what does Benjamin understand by "commodity" itself; does the term refer to the phenomenal object or could it refer to the Marxist conceptual category of the commodity as well? If so, could Benjamin's title designate his interest in the resemblance between the concept of the commodity and a poetic work? Without trying to resolve these ambiguities, let me only stress that they fall within the parameters of current discussion. They raise not only the orthodox Marxist question of how the poetic object inscribes the commodity but also the problem of what Marx's conceptualization of the commodity may share with expressive and here specifically aesthetic forms.

In an earlier letter to Horkheimer, from April 16, 1938, Benjamin designated more precisely the kind of poetic object whose link to the commodity was at issue in his Baudelaire project. "The third part treats the commodity as the fulfillment of the allegorical outlook in Baudelaire," Benjamin suggests (*B*, II, 752). That Benjamin's word "fulfillment" is vague is key, pointing to the complex fashion (never fully resolved) in which he understood the relation between the commodity and allegory. The phrase can, of course, be read to designate Benjamin's

interest in Baudelairean allegory as an inscription of commodity exchange. But it also can be read as designating Benjamin's interest in the
commodity as allegorical form, his construction of Marx as an allegorist on a par with Baudelaire.

To argue Benjamin's attention to Marx as allegorist would be an immense task. The argument requires passage through untheorized fragments evincing Benjamin's historicizing and specifically aesthetic interest in Marx. In addition, it would confront two complex, related issues: (1) Benjamin's understanding of Baudelairean allegory, and
specifically what Benjamin considered the central problem confronting
his Baudelaire work: why "an attitude which, in appearance at least,
is as out of keeping with its time as that of allegory takes pride of place
in the poetic work of the century?" ("CP," 46); and (2) the *Passagen-
Werk*'s understanding of Marx's discussion of the commodity. Such
exploration would, however, be greatly facilitated by the work of Buck-
Morss. *The Dialectics of Seeing* explores Benjamin's formulation of the
link between the commodity and Baudelairean allegory from a materialist viewpoint in illuminating detail.[10]

While a consideration of Marx as allegorist is beyond the bounds
of my study, the remainder of this chapter approaches the problem
obliquely. Discussing how Benjamin's increasingly frequent late characterization of ideology as phantasmagoria may derive from the figurative potential of the term's lively nineteenth-century life, I show the
phantasmagoria as one instance of the nineteenth-century diabolical.
And in doing so I pursue, albeit indirectly, the allegorical component
to Marx's notion of the commodity form. A diabolical world of ghosts
and specters is not only at issue in Marx's phantasmagorical rhetoric
for commodity fetishism but is also central to allegory, or at least to
the baroque allegorical lineage of interest to Benjamin.[11]

10. Buck-Morss points out that allegory captures the abstract yet material existence
of the commodity, its phantom-like objectivity, its inorganic form yet erotic appeal, its
implication in the fragmentation of social processes, and its intimate links to the problem
of the new and decay. See *The Dialectics of Seeing,* notably pp. 179ff. In addition, Buck-
Morss links the literary inscription of the commodity in Baudelairean allegory to Benjamin's interest in it as a model for his own dialectical image. On this subject, too, see
Lloyd Spencer, "Allegory in the World of the Commodity." See also Wohlfarth's discussion of the importance of Baudelairean allegory for Benjamin in both the French and
English versions of "Et Cetera? The Historian as Chiffonier."

11. In *The Origin of German Tragic Drama,* Benjamin mentions the affinity between
the German baroque and the nineteenth-century fantastic. He cites Borinski differentiating between the didactic and Christian moralizing aims of medieval allegory and the mystical and supernatural interest of baroque allegory:

"Medieval allegory is Christian and didactic—in the mystic and natural-historical respect the baroque is descended from antiquity . . . And thanks to the mediation of an

FROM DREAM TO PHANTASMAGORIA:
THE TRANSFORMATION OF
BENJAMIN'S PARISIAN RESUMÉS

In the famous Hornberg letter Adorno noticed Benjamin's fascination with the phantasmagoria. "Of course, a great definition and theory
of phantasmagoria belong on p. 165f," Adorno commented, pushing
his friend to expand this evocative figure in a conceptual direction (*AP*,
116–117). When Benjamin rewrote the 1935 essay in March 1939, he
seems to have paid Adorno's suggestion some heed.[12] "Paris, Capitale
du XIXème siècle"[13] opens with a new methodological introduction
where the phantasmagoria assumes conceptual pride of place:

> Our inquiry proposes to show how, as a consequence of this reifying rep-
> resentation of civilization, the new forms of life and the new creations of a
> fundamentally economic and technological nature that we owe to the last
> century enter into the universe of a phantasmagoria. These creations un-
> dergo this "illumination" not only in a theoretical manner, by an ideological
> transposition, but also in the immediacy of perceptible presence. They man-
> ifest themselves as phantasmagorias. (*PW*, 60–61)

This passage proposes the phantasmagoria as the concept defining the
appearance of the nineteenth century's material products when they un-
dergo "ideological transposition." Or, as Benjamin also put it in the
Passagen-Werk fragment concluding the Konvolut on Marx written
around this time: "The image that it [the commodity-producing soci-
ety] ... produces of itself, and that it is wont to label its culture, corresponds to the concept of the phantasmagoria" (*PW*, 822).[14]

The increased methodological importance accorded to the phantasmagoria is but one of many differences between the 1935 and 1939 exposés. As Buck-Morss points out, the 1939 exposé is written "in a lucid,
descriptive style, with a totally new introduction and conclusion, in
which the dream theory is strikingly absent."[15] Consonant with this ob-

---

anchorite of the same name (in E. T. A. Hoffmann's *Die Serapionsbrüder*), the antique
painter who was picked out from Pliny's much discussed passage on decorative painting as the classic of the grotesque, the 'balcony-painter' Serapion, has also been used
in literature as the personification of the subterranean-fantastic, the occult-spectral."
Benjamin, *The Origin of German Tragic Drama*, 171 (abbreviated hereafter as *OGTD*).

12. He rewrote the essay in French at Horkheimer's instigation "to interest Frank
Altschul, a New York banker who was active as a patron" (*PW*, 1255).

13. In the remainder of my text I have designated the 1935 essay with its German
title and the 1939 essay with its French title in order to avoid their confusion.

14. Buck-Morss dates this fragment from the final period of Benjamin's *Passagen-
Werk*, between January 1938 and May 1940 (*DS*, 51).

15. Buck-Morss, "Benjamin's *Passagen-Werk*: Redeeming Mass Culture for the Revolution," 238. In *The Dialectics of Seeing* she reformulates the significant alterations

servation, in 1939 Benjamin abandons a constellation of concepts related to the dream. A glance at the revised Fourier section makes clear that he does away with a discussion of the wish image, the collective unconscious, and the dialectical image. In dropping the dream vocabulary that Adorno found suspect, "Paris, Capitale du XIXème siècle" seems to analyze the ideological products of nineteenth-century Paris in more rigorously Marxist terms. Allegory is presented as the aesthetic equivalent of the commodity; in addition, Benjamin no longer suggests Fourier's utopia as a wish image but rather follows Marx in characterizing Fourier as "the only man next to Hegel who penetrated the fundamental mediocrity of the petty bourgeois" (*PW*, 64). Benjamin also abandons the section entitled "Daguerre, or the Panoramas," which describes how the new nineteenth-century visual technologies of the panorama and photography express the nineteenth-century's "new feeling about life" (*R*, 150). For my purposes, however, the most important transformation is the rise in importance of the phantasmagoria, which I understand as the obverse of Benjamin's turn away from the ideological dream.

Throughout the 1939 essay Benjamin employs the phantasmagoria in a fashion consonant with his conceptualization of the term in his added methodological introduction. At these moments Benjamin seems to echo his untheorized use of the term in 1935. Both the 1935 and 1939 exposés suggest the crowd as "the veil through which the familiar city lures the *flâneur* like a phantasmagoria" (*R*, 156). Both exposés cast the Universal Exhibitions and the department stores, the freedom of the proletariat and the interior in phantasmagorical terms. But the 1939 exposé also applies the term to products of the superstructure which Benjamin did not identify as phantasmagorical in 1935. To some extent

---

somewhat differently. She considers them "the addition of a new introduction and conclusion based on the texts of Blanqui, as well as 'extensive changes' in 'Fourier' and 'Louis Philippe'" (*DS*, 209). Buck-Morss's assessment of the matter in *The Dialectics of Seeing* occurs when she debates with Espagne and Werner's "Les Manuscrits parisiens de Walter Benjamin et le *Passagen-Werk*" on whether Benjamin transformed his theoretical position significantly in the last years of his life.

In line with their thesis of a "failed" *Passagen-Werk*, Espagne and Werner argue that Benjamin's work on the Baudelaire "book," subsequently reflected in the substantive changes of the 1939 exposé (—which also included the addition of a new introduction and conclusion based on the texts of Blanqui, as well as "extensive changes" in "Fourier" and "Louis Philippe,"—) represented a fundamental shift in the philosophical conception of the project, leading to internal contradictions so serious that they threatened to undermine the entire edifice. They refer specifically to the contradiction between the "continuous phenomenology of the commodity form" and the "discontinuity implied by the dialectical image." The crucial point is that this ambivalence was not *new* (*DS*, 209).

this difference is quantitative: when Benjamin adds an extended discussion of Baudelaire's "Les Sept Vieillards" as "une fantasmagorie angoissante," he uses the term much as in the examples cited above (*PW*, 71). But when Benjamin describes Fourier's *phalanstère* as a phantasmagorical hallucination, it becomes clear that the difference is qualitative as well: "The *phalanstère* is a city made from arcades. In this 'city of arcades' the construction of the engineer takes on a phantasmagorical character" (*PW*, 63–64). Benjamin here applies the qualification phantasmagoria to ideological products he previously designated as wish images, dream.

In 1939, then, Benjamin seems to abandon his 1935 distinction between ideological products in touch with the collective unconscious containing recuperative potential, the wish images, and those that are pure mystification, the phantasmagorias. Rather, all ideological products become phantasmagorias in a shift that could be surmised to stem from Benjamin's new view of ideology as solely an experience of mystification. But the essay's conclusion places this shift in a somewhat different light. The 1935 essay ended with Benjamin's interest in demystifying the ideological transpositions of nineteenth-century Paris. He couched this demystification as an experience of awakening, the moment when the dream image is recuperated as dialectical image: "The utilization of dream elements in waking is the textbook example of dialectical thinking" (*R*, 162). If the 1939 essay too concludes by calling for demystification, it accords this power to the phantasmagoria itself. Auguste Blanqui's *Eternité par les Astres* is "a last phantasmagoria of cosmic character, that implicitly includes the most acerbic critique of all the others," writes Benjamin (*PW*, 75). Transforming the 1935 opposition between dream image and dialectical image into the difference between mystifying and (critically) illuminating phantasmagorias, Benjamin suggests the last phantasmagoria as the form by which phantasmagorical delusion may be undone. Why does the phantasmagoria have such a seemingly contradictory trajectory in 1939? An answer to this question will emerge from regrounding the term in the nineteenth-century Paris that produced it.

"THE IMMEDIACY OF PERCEPTIBLE PRESENCE": ROBERTSON'S PHANTASMAGORIA

While Marx's use of the phantasmagoria explains why Benjamin applies the term to the nineteenth century's "ideological transposition" of "new creations of a fundamentally economic and technological na-

ture," it does not explain why Benjamin describes this experience as an
"'illumination'" of "perceptible presence" (*PW*, 60). True, ideological
transposition does accord human creations a strange sort of perceptible
presence, but this presence hardly seems illuminating, either in a literal
or a figurative sense. Benjamin, however, provides an alternative way
to understand the illuminations of phantasmagorical manifestation in
the *Passagen-Werk* fragment that opens Konvolut Q, "Panorama," a
section devoted to popular nineteenth-century visual spectacles:

> There were panoramas, dioramas, cosmoramas, diaphanoramas, navalo-
> ramas, pleoramas (πλεω I travel by sea, boating), *phantoscope*, phantasma-
> parastasias, *phantasmagorical experiences* and phantasmaparastatic ones,
> picturesque trips in a room, georamas; optical picturesques, cineoramas,
> phanoramas, stereoramas, cycloramas, dramatic panorama. (*PW*, 655, em-
> phasis added)

One among these spectacles, the "phantasmagorical experience," or
phantasmagoria, as it was also called, was literally illuminating. A mov-
able magic lantern called a phantoscope, it projected for its spectators
a parade of ghosts.

"An engraving advertising *Fabrication d'instruments de précision
J Molteni et Cie, 62 Rue du Château d'Eau* speaks—after 1856!—
among other things of 'instruments of Phantasmagoria, Polyoramas,
Dioramas, etc.,'" Benjamin notes as he peruses the representations collected in the Bibliothèque Nationale's Cabinet des Estampes (*PW*,
663). That Benjamin puts an exclamation point after 1856 indicates his
familiarity with the spectacle's history. The phantasmagoria was invented in the late 1790s by the Belgian "doctor-aeronaut," Etienne-
Gaspard Robertson.[16] It enjoyed the greatest vogue in the hands of its
creator, with accounts of Robertson's popular performances proliferating in newspapers of the time (fig. 17).

These accounts suggest that the original phantasmagoria exemplified
the nineteenth-century Parisian ideological representations of interest to
Benjamin. A 1798 spectacle reviewed in *L'Ami des Lois* opened with

---

16. For my discussion of Robertson's phantasmagoria I rely on Etienne-Gaspard
Robertson, *Mémoires récréatifs, scientifiques et anecdotiques du physicien-aéronaute
E.-G. Robertson* and on information from G.-M. Coissac's *Histoire du Cinématographe*.
The subject is also treated extensively in Max Milner's invaluable *La Fantasmagorie*. In
addition, see Terry Castle's article on the evolution of the concept of the phantasmagoria
in the nineteenth century, which provides information on the phantasmagoria not found
in Coissac or Milner. I have relied to some extent on Castle's translations of accounts of
Robertson's spectacles; see Terry Castle, "Phantasmagoria: Spectral Technology and the
Metaphorics of Modern Reverie."

Robertson's answer to a member of the audience who demanded to see the ghost of Marat:

> "Because I have not been able to re-establish the cult of Marat in an official newspaper, I'd at least like to see his shade."
>
> Robertson pours onto a lighted brazier two glasses of blood, a bottle of vitriol, 12 drops of brandy, and two copies of the newspaper *Hommes-Libres*. Right away, a small, livid ghost gradually begins to appear, armed with a dagger and wearing a red cap. The man with bristling hair recognizes it to be Marat; he wants to kiss it, the ghost makes a terrifying grimace and disappears.[17]

On this night the phantasmagorian also called before his spectators less horrifying ghosts, the mythic founder of the Swiss republic, William Tell, who appeared "with republican pride," the ghosts of Virgil and Voltaire, as well as the ghost of a Parisian dandy's gallant adventure:

> A young dandy begs for the appearance of a woman whom he tenderly loved, and shows her portrait in miniature to the phantasmagorian, who throws onto the burner some sparrow feathers, a few grains of phosphorus, and a dozen butterflies. Soon, a woman is to be perceived, her breast uncovered, her hair streaming, gazing steadily at her young friend with a tender and sorrowful smile.
>
> A serious man sitting next to me cries, in carrying his hand to his forehead: "Oh my God! I think that's my wife," and he slips out, fearing that it is no longer a ghost.[18]

Robertson's performance proceeded to reach the following spectacular climax:

> "Citizens and gentlemen," said Robertson, "until now I have only shown to you one shade at a time; my art is not limited to these trifles, they are only the prelude to the *savoir-faire* of your humble servant. I can show to kindly men the crowd of shades who, during their life, have been helped by them; reciprocally, I can make the shades of evil men's victims parade before them."
>
> Robertson was invited to this test by almost unanimous cheers. Two individuals alone were against it; but their opposition only irritated the desires of those gathered.
>
> Immediately the phantasmagorian throws onto the brazier the reports of May 31, those pertaining to the massacres at the prisons of Aix, Marseilles and Tarascon, a collection of denunciations and decrees, a list of suspects, the collection of judgments of the Revolutionary Court, a bundle of demagogic and aristocratic newspapers, a copy of the *Réveil du Peuple*; then he pronounces with emphasis the magic words: *Conspirator, humanity,*

17. *L'Ami des Lois*, 28 March 1798, quoted in Robertson, *Mémoires*, I, 216–217.
18. Robertson, *Mémoires*, I, 217.

terrorist, justice, Jacobin, public safety, exaggerated, alarmist, hoarder, Girondin, Moderate, Orleanist. One sees groups covered with bloody veils instantly rising up; they surround, they press the two individuals who had refused to give in to the general wish, and who, frightened by this terrible spectacle, run out of the room hastily giving horrible howls . . . [sic] One was Barrère [sic], the other Chambon [sic].[19]

The recent history haunting Robertson's phantasmagoria resembles the class conflict informing the nineteenth-century Parisian cultural products studied by Benjamin. And Robertson performs on this history a transformation exemplifying the ideological transposition of material reality which Benjamin understands these cultural products to perform. Robertson turns the bloody events of class warfare into aesthetic apparitions, fantastic nightmares of an evening's entertainment that also includes the diversion of attractive young women. Divested of their material reality, these historical figures are more than entertaining. Robertson helps them to *entrer dans la légende,* integrating them into the pantheon of " the phantasmagoria of 'cultural history,' " where they play the role of evil demons to the proud hero who founds Swiss bourgeois liberty. Robertson's representation thus seeks to exorcize the demonic power of the revolutionary memories haunting Parisian imagination, an exorcism the journalist Poultier-Delmotte well understands when he personifies it in the flight of two ex-members of the Committee for Public Safety, Cambon and Barère. What better synecdoche for the ideological transposition worked by " the phantasmagoria of 'cultural history' " and " the phantasmagoria of civilization" than the phantasmagoria itself?

Once the original meaning of the phantasmagoria, as magic lantern show, is restored, aspects of this meaning become visible in Benjamin's specific descriptions of ideological transposition in 1939. These aspects are, moreover, not found in the term's usage in 1935. Both the 1935 and 1939 works suggest the Universal Exhibition to open up "a phantasmagoria that people enter to be distracted" (R, 152).[20] But in 1935 Benjamin's descriptions of these manifestations is vague: "The phantasmagoria of capitalist culture reaches its most brilliant display in the Universal Exhibition of 1867" (R, 153). In 1939, in contrast, Benjamin turns the exhibition into a spectacle of modern technology where the nineteenth-century viewer enters into contact with fantastic apparitions: "A balcony in cast iron would represent at the Universal Exhi-

19. Robertson, *Mémoires*, I, 218–220.
20. I substitute "distracted" for Jephcott's "amused." See *PW*, 50.

bition the ring of Saturn and those who made their way along it would
see themselves caught up in a phantasmagoria where they felt themselves transformed into inhabitants of Saturn," Benjamin writes (*PW*,
66). Similarly, the technological phantasmagoria is palpable in the more
sensuous way in which the 1939 essay describes the *flâneur*'s experience
of the crowd. While in both essays the crowd is the agitated veil through
which the *flâneur* perceives the city, in 1939 Benjamin goes on to describe the transformed city landscape in terms likening it to the shim-
mering images of a magic lantern show: "This phantasmagoria, where
it appears sometimes as a landscape, sometimes as a room" (*PW*, 70).

PHANTASMAGORIA AS THE
AFTERLIFE OF ALLEGORY

The linguistic content of Robertson's spectacle may contain a second
attraction for Benjamin. The term *phantasmagoria* was coined by
Robertson in 1797 to describe his ghostly performances, although the
etymology of his neologism is unclear. Littré proposes: "E. φάντασμα
apparition (see *ghost)*, and ἀγορεύω, speak: to speak to the ghosts, to
call the ghosts." [21] *Le Robert,* in contrast, suggests: "from the Greek
phantasma 'ghost', and *agoreuein* 'to speak in public', under the infl.
of *allegory* (⟶) Phantasm); for Guiraud, 'popular hybrid' of *fantasme*
and *gourer, agourer* 'to fool.'" [22] While Littré's etymology expresses
Robertson's procedure, the principal etymology offered by *Le Robert*
is more significant for Benjamin. Describing phantasmagoria as modeled on allegory, the dictionary links this term to Benjamin's privileged metaconcept in *The Origin of German Tragic Drama*. Indeed, the
1939 exposé explicitly suggests the phantasmagorical transformations
worked by the commodity structure on objects as the nineteenth-
century equivalent to seventeenth-century allegory. Benjamin writes:
"To the singular debasement of things by their meaning, which is characteristic of seventeenth-century allegory, corresponds the singular debasement of things by their price as commodities" (*PW*, 71). This
sentence substantially modifies the translation of allegory into the nineteenth century that Benjamin proposed in 1935: "As in the seventeenth
century the canon of dialectical imagery came to be allegory, in the
nineteenth it is novelty" (*R*, 158).

21. Emile Littré, *Dictionnaire de la langue française*, III, 1407.
22. Paul Robert, *Dictionnaire alphabétique et analogique de la langue française*, IV,
404.

The supposition that Benjamin's interest in the phantasmagoria stems partially from the term's etymological relation to allegory is supported by Benjamin's repeated statements linking the *Passagen-Werk* to his earlier study. When Benjamin writes to Scholem of his newly conceived arcades project, he describes this project as a Parisian *Tragic Drama*: "When I have finished the work with which I am occupied at the moment, carefully, provisionally . . . then the *One-Way Street* production cycle will be closed for me in the same way that the tragic drama book brought the Germanist one to a close. The profane motifs of *One-Way Street* will parade by there in a hellish intensification" (*B,* I, 455). Granting the phantasmagoria a place of honor in his hellish parade, Benjamin privileges a term whose etymology not only links the arcades project to *The Origin of German Tragic Drama* but expresses an important difference between the worlds that the German and the French production cycles study. The etymology of allegory can be read to mean, among other things, speaking other (*allos*) within the *agora,* a word that identifies the marketplace as well as the public place. True to its etymology, seventeenth-century allegory remains for Benjamin within the marketplace but it also indicates an alternative to it. The fallen aspect taken by the sacred in the realm of the profane, allegory points toward the sacred and hence toward a possible theological redemption of secular history. The etymology of allegory implying the possibility of redemption contrasts with the etymology of phantasmagoria, allegory's demonic doppelgänger. Constructed from *phantasma* and *agoreuein* instead of *allos* and *agoreuein,* allegory substitutes ghosts for the *allos* signifying allegory's transcendence. Consonant with this etymological transformation, Benjamin understands the nineteenth-century commodity landscape as one where no escape from the marketplace is possible. It is a space where the transcendence of the authentically supernatural has turned to a demonic rooted in the processes of market exchange.

Benjamin already contrasts the permanently fallen phantasmagoria with provisionally fallen allegory in the final pages of *The Origin of German Tragic Drama*. Describing the experience of transcendence underwriting the ruins of allegory, he writes:

> In God's world the allegorist awakens. . . . Allegory, of course, thereby loses everything that was most peculiar to it: the secret, privileged knowledge, the arbitrary rule in the realm of dead objects, the supposed infinity of a world without hope. All this vanishes with this *one* about-turn, in which the immersion of allegory has to clear away the final *phantasmagoria* of the objec-

tive and, left entirely to its own devices, re-discovers itself, not playfully in the earthly world of things, but seriously under the eyes of heaven. (*OGTD*, 232; emphasis added)

It is noteworthy that the details of Robertson's phantasmagoria suggest that the first phantasmagorian understood his ghosts as the permanently fallen avatars of the temporarily fallen baroque. Robertson's spectacle often ended with the topos of the *memento mori* dear to the allegorical imagination. Robertson pronounced the following admonition: "You who have perhaps smiled at my experiments, beauties who have experienced a few moments terror . . . this is the fate that is reserved for you, this is what you will be one day. Remember the phantasmagoria," and he then displayed the "skeleton of a young woman standing on a pedestal." [23] Although related to the allegorical memento mori, Robertson's final gesture diverges from the final allegorical use of this topos as it is described by Benjamin. While Robertson turns enchantment to death, the final moment of allegory turns death to eternal life, a transformation Benjamin exemplifies by citing from the baroque dramatist Lohenstein: "Yea, when the Highest comes to reap the harvest from the graveyard, then I, a death's head, will be an angel's countenance" (*OGTD*, 232).

In his *Mémoires* Robertson makes explicit that his phantasmagoria belongs to a world in which the possibility for authentically supernatural transcendence has been lost. He recounts his interest in the supernatural investigations of the seventeenth-century Jesuit, Athenasius Kircher, who was not so coincidentally the inventor of the magic lantern.[24] Robertson writes: "Father Kircher, it is said, believed in the devil; too bad, the example could be contagious, for Father Kircher was endowed with such great knowledge that many people would be

23. Robertson, *Mémoires*, I, 284.

24. The technological history of the phantasmagoria thus links it to allegory, for Milner makes the point that the representational universe of Kircher's magic lantern was exemplary of the baroque. In the *Ars magna lucis et umbrae*, Milner tells us, Kircher gives spectacular descriptions of all the artificially constructed illusions made possible with the play of mirrors: "How to give access inside a small box to the sight of gardens stretching out to infinity or fabulous treasures, or cities with amazing architecture. More complex mechanisms transform the spectator's head into the head of an animal or a monster. If mirrors line the sides of the room, he will have the impression of walking in air, or head down." Milner continues: "It would not be wrong to see there a manifestation of the baroque aesthetic with its glorification of appearances, its taste for *trompe-l'oeil* and metamorphoses and its appeal to the powers of illusion to transfigure a universe which it is a question of wresting from opacity and weight. The vogue which anamorphs enjoyed at the same time is doubtless related to the same tendencies." Milner, *La Fantasmagorie*, 15, 16.

tempted to think that if he believed in the devil, he had good reasons for this." [25] Robertson's attempts to imitate the occult knowledge of Kircher soon reveal to him, however, the divide separating the late eighteenth from the seventeenth century. He invents the phantasmagoria, he goes on to tell us, as consolation for this divide: "The devil refusing to communicate to me the science of producing wonders, I set myself to producing devils, and my wand had only to move to force the whole infernal procession to see the light." [26] Turning to technology as an imperfect substitute for the authentically supernatural, Robertson associates the phantasmagoria with the disappearance of the religious demonic. But he maintains an ambiguous relation to the rationality the Enlightenment puts in its place. For in continuing simultaneously to link his technological creation to some sort of supernatural power, Robertson indicates his recognition of the demonic potential of human invention.[27] His phantasmagoria thus well expresses Benjamin's Marxist understanding of the supernatural power at work in ideological transposition, which is man-made rather than theological in origin.

That Benjamin's interest in the phantasmagoria derives in part from its suitability, as a magic lantern show, to figure nineteenth-century ideological projection is consistent with Benjamin's treatment of the technology of visual representation throughout his Parisian production cycle. Repeatedly, Benjamin evinces interest in the relation between a historical period's visual technology and its structures of understanding. Thus, he writes in *Pariser Passagen I*: "Careful investigation in what relation the optics of the myriorama stands to the time of modernity,

---

25. Robertson, *Mémoires*, I, 143–144.

26. Robertson, *Mémoires*, I, 145.

27. On the ambiguous ideological agenda of Robertson's phantasmagoria, Milner writes: "We find, then, in the spectacles proposed by Robertson the mind which presided over the *expériences récréatives* [entertaining experiments] of the *cabinets de physique* [physical laboratories], as well as a certain fascination with everything that transforms usual perception of the universe. But this mind is placed in the service of an ambiguous ideology, tightly linked to the time when he began his activities." Milner goes on to stress that Robertson is a "convinced propagandist of the philosophy of the Enlightenment, animated by the desire to unmask the 'deceit of the priests' and to denounce false marvels." Milner, *La Fantasmagorie*, 17. Castle concurs:

> The specter-shows of the late eighteenth and early nineteenth centuries, we will find, mediated oddly between rational and irrational imperatives. Producers of phantasmagorias often claimed, somewhat disingenuously, that the new entertainment would serve the cause of public enlightenment by exposing the frauds of charlatans and supposed ghost-seers. Ancient superstition would be eradicated when everyone realized that so-called apparitions were in fact only optical illusions . . . But the pretense of pedagogy quickly gave way when the phantasmagoria itself began, for clever illusionists were careful never to reveal exactly how their own bizarre, sometimes frightening apparitions were produced. Everything was done, quite shamelessly, to intensify the supernatural effect. (Castle, "Phantasmagoria," 30)

the newest. They are certainly attributed to this world as the basic coordinates" (*PW*, 1011). Here Benjamin makes evident his concern to historicize the traditional epistemological equation of seeing and knowing.

It would be instructive to examine the multiple stereoscopes, magic lanterns, panoramas, dioramas, myrioramas, georamas, mechanical spectacles, mirrors, photographs, advertisements, and descriptions of cinematic projection littering Benjamin's Parisian production cycle in light of Benjamin's historicizing approach to a visual rhetoric of understanding. In the context of considering the phantasmagoria, let me only suggest that this approach could be used to explain why the 1939 "Paris, Capitale du XIXème siècle" abandons the 1935 section entitled "Daguerre, or the Panoramas." Although we could conclude that Benjamin turns away from photography because he has already devoted a substantial essay to the subject, he seems to have no qualms about retaining a large section on Baudelaire, on whom he has also already written extensively. Rather, it seems to me that Benjamin's abandonment of photography and the panorama is a consequence of the increased power he accords the phantasmagoria to figure nineteenth-century understanding. While in 1935 Benjamin toys with both photography and the panorama as vivid expressions of the nineteenth century's "new feeling about life," in 1939 he has settled on the phantasmagoria as *the* visual mastertrope emblematizing this feeling (*R*, 150). He hence relegates alternative forms of visual representation to a distinctly subordinate place.

IN THE CAMERA OBSCURA OF IDEOLOGY

"Concerning the doctrine of the ideological superstructure," Benjamin writes in a key passage from Konvolut K:

> At first it seems as if Marx here wanted only to establish a causal relation between superstructure and base. But the observation that the ideologies of the superstructure reflect the relations in a false and distorted manner already goes beyond this. The question is, namely: if the base somehow determines the superstructure in the material of thought and experience, but this determination is not one of simple *reflection*, how is it then to be characterized, leaving aside the question of the cause for its emergence? As its *expression*. The superstructure is the expression of the base. (*PW*, 495, emphasis added)

We have discussed at length the reasons why Benjamin objects to Marx's mimetic description of base-superstructure relations. Of interest here is the Marxist figuration of ideology which provokes Benjamin's attack. When Benjamin takes Marx's description of ideology to task, he challenges a representation of ideology common to historical vulgar naturalism. This is ideology as the inverted reflection of the real world, a topos inaugurated by a celebrated comparison from the early Marx: "If in all ideology men and their circumstances appear upside-down as in a *camera obscura* . . ."[28] Sarah Kofman has explained the contradictions in which this figure catches Marx, asserting the derivative status of ideology but not its autonomy and "impl[ying] nostalgia for clear, transparent, and luminous knowledge" that Marx's notion of scientific construction refuses.[29] Sensitive to these contradictions, most twentieth-century theorists attacking reductive accounts of base-superstructure relations take apart the figure in some way. Benjamin is no exception. In the passage from Konvolut K he points out that Marx's description of ideological distortion already gives ideological work more autonomy than his figure suggests. In keeping with his interest in modern materialism, when Benjamin suggests the need to devise new figures for this experience, he turns to the model of the dream.

But Benjamin has dropped discussion of the dream by 1939. If Benjamin rather figures ideological experience as phantasmagoria, it may be because the original phantasmagoria, besides its other attractions, functions in the field of Marxist polemic. Representing ideological transposition as the projection of a magic lantern show, Benjamin finds a figure that both links him to the Marxist tradition of the camera obscura and expresses his distance from this tradition. The technology of Robertson's phantasmagoria modifies the Renaissance technology of the camera obscura in a fashion aptly expressing Benjamin's challenge to the way in which "historical vulgar naturalism" understands ideological representation (N 2, 6). While, like "historical vulgar naturalism," the camera obscura mechanically reverses the world out there in the darkened chamber of thought, the magic lantern of the phantasmagoria inverts painted slides that are themselves artistic products (figs. 18 and 19). It thus does not project a *reflection* of the objective world but rather the objective world's *expression,* its representation as it is mediated through imaginative subjective processes. As Kofman writes on *Capital*'s use of fantastic language, "Ideology is not the reflection of real relations but rather that of a world already transformed, enchanted."[30]

28. Marx and Engels, *The German Ideology,* 47.
29. Sarah Kofman, *Camera obscura de l'idéologie,* 33.
30. Kofman, *Camera obscura,* 25.

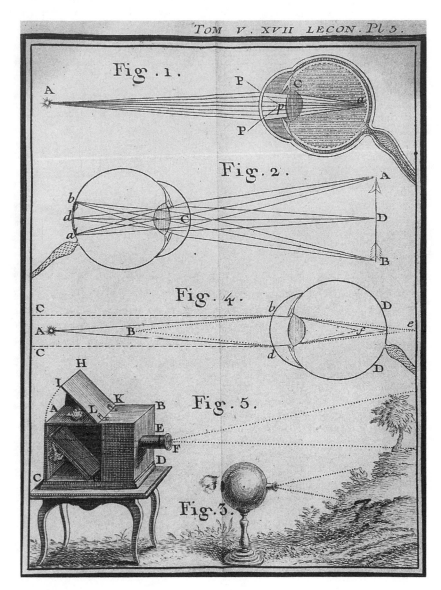

18.   Camera Obscura. In *Leçons de Physique,* by Jean-Antoine Nollet.

The aesthetic effect of the phantasmagoria also more closely resembles the subjective experience of ideological transposition of interest to Benjamin. While the camera obscura does not attempt to fool its audience into mistaking its two-dimensional inversions of reality for the outside world, the phantasmagoria makes every effort to reinforce the spectral

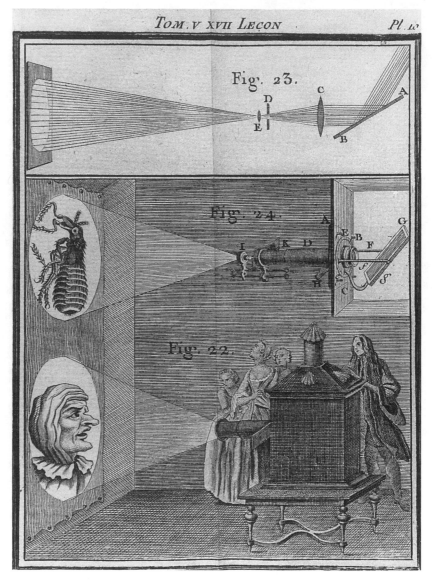

19. Magic Lantern. In *Leçons de Physique,* by Jean-Antoine Nollet.

reality of its illusionary projections. Robertson's phantasmagoria indeed captures not only the nonreflective transformation that Benjamin works on Marxist representations of ideology but also the content of Benjamin's own relation to these representations. The forerunner of the magic lantern, the camera obscura provided the optical principles this later technology refined.

MENTAL ALCHEMY

A yet additional appeal of the phantasmagoria for Benjamin may be the term's animated nineteenth-century psychological life. If the phantasmagoria originated as a nineteenth-century visual spectacle, Max Milner observes that in early nineteenth-century France "the word 'phantasmagoria' was exceptionally successful."[31] In its figurative usage, Milner suggests, the term came to designate a specifically nineteenth-century form of "mental alchemy":

> Confronting an imagination of reproduction, to which an aesthetic based on *mimesis* gave all its attention not without suspecting it of possible deformation or lie, or a creative imagination tending to substitute for the real world a different world that is, however, ordered according to the same laws, *a new form of imagination* [emphasis added] starts to gain prominence, which assumes the opening of an interior space, an "other stage," in which images are projected, undergo metamorphoses, and follow one another with the violation of logic found in dreams, and which constitutes both a route of access toward the depths where interior and exterior being, desire and reality, have relations other than in everyday life, and a fearful power.[32]

For both Milner and Castle this psychological experience simultaneously derives from Enlightenment thought and performs its critique. While based on the transcendent power that the Enlightenment accords the human subject, the phantasmagoria characterizes an experience challenging the fundamentally rational nature of the subject as well as the Cartesian divide that the Enlightenment draws between subject and objective world.

When Benjamin describes the psychological nature of ideological transposition in his 1939 exposé, he uses the phantasmagoria in the term's strong nineteenth-century psychological sense. This use is visible notably in Benjamin's added sentences at the end of the second part of the Baudelaire section (D) discussing "Les Sept Vieillards." Benjamin writes of this poem, whose original title was, as Benjamin observes in the Baudelaire Konvolut, "Fantômes parisiens" (*PW*, 488): "It is there that an anguishing phantasmagoria shows itself at the heart of *flânerie*. Baudelaire developed it with great force in the 'Sept Vieillards'" (*PW*, 71). Benjamin thus applies the term to a poem celebrated as an explo-

31. Milner, *La Fantasmagorie*, 23.
32. Milner, *La Fantasmagorie*, 23 (emphasis added). Castle too underlines the fact that the nineteenth century used the phantasmagoria to designate a new vision of imagination: "What such statements articulated, at bottom, was a new conception of the daemonic or irrational nature of thought." Castle, "Phantasmagoria," 58.

ration of the new mental fields that Milner suggests the phantasmagoria to designate. The poem's closing lines are celebrated, above all, on that monstrous moment when the subject's ability to differentiate reason from hallucination, objective from subjective experience, breaks down: "Vainement ma raison voulait prendre la barre / . . . Et mon âme dansait, dansait, vieille gabarre / Sans mâts, sur une mer monstrueuse et sans bords!" [33]

When Benjamin abandons a dream description of ideology in 1939, the term he substitutes instead still seems to contain the potential to figure his psychoanalytic modification of ideology. Describing ideology with a term from Marx's own text—phantasmagorical—Benjamin couches it as a nonrational psychological activity with affinity to psychological material of prime interest to Freud; we have already seen Breton place Baudelaire's "fantasmagorie angoissante," "Les Sept Vieillards," in the lineage of the Freudian uncanny. Interestingly, the close link of the world of phantasmagorical projection to the world of dream was evident even in the phantasmagoria's first technological manifestation. In an article cited by Robertson in his memoirs, Sébastien Mercier describes the world that the new spectacle opens up:

> "I would rather see hell than total destruction. Demons frighten me less than the mute horror of the naked abyss. Another world is at Robertson's.
> There, things are as they are dreamed each night. The dream! Who has excavated the dream? You sleep: the divine rod strikes you or mercy consoles you. It is in the dream that we live, it is there that our soul takes pleasure with all its authority over nature." [34]

"PASSIONS WITHOUT TRUTHS": MARX'S PHANTASMAGORIA

In an earlier, more general book on the French diabolical, Milner isolates several historical concerns this late eighteenth to mid-nineteenth century motif inscribes. *Le Diable dans la littérature française de Cazotte à Baudelaire* suggests the diabolical as a response to the supernatural powers unleashed by revolutionary class conflict as well as an expression of the fascination and fear inspired by the demonic power of reason manifested in technological innovation. [35] Milner's discussion

33. Baudelaire, "Les Sept Vieillards," *Oeuvres complètes*, I, 88.
34. Robertson, *Mémoires*, I, 306.
35. See *Le Diable dans la littérature française de Cazotte à Baudelaire*, particularly the chapter entitled "Le diable et la Révolution." Similarly, Philippe Muray observes, "It is the Revolution which gives 'the Evil One' renewed contemporaneity." See Philippe

provides one explanation for Marx's decision to figure ideology in phantasmagorical terms. When *The Eighteenth Brumaire* qualifies the ideological constructions of the Second Republic as phantasmagorical, it applies the term to a situation of ideological transposition resulting from the pressures of class conflict. So too when Marx describes the phantomlike objectivity of commodity fetishism as phantasmagorical, he characterizes an experience arising from the expansion of the commodity structure to all social relations, a process that reaches its apogee in industrial capitalism.

In the current context, however, I mention Milner's historicization of the French diabolical to pursue another aspect of this historicization which is illuminating for Marx.[36] Among the contemporary concerns

---

Muray, *Le 19ᵉ siècle à travers les âges,* 648. Robertson's show too displays the historical and economic concerns that Milner suggests at stake in the Parisian diabolical. His spectacle represents revolutionary class struggle and makes evident that Robertson and his audience were fascinated by the power of optical technology.

I wonder if Milner's general discussion of the diabolical also provides an explanation for the lack of interest in the term in Germany. Milner suggests that the phantasmagoria is a specifically Parisian form of mental hallucination, observing that the phantasmagoria does not figure prominently in German Romantic accounts of similar experiences of subjectivity. Showing the German interest in the figurative power of visual technologies including the magic lantern, the telescope, the microscope, and the mirror, Milner observes that the mirror "is the most suited to signify the ambivalent powers of artistic imagination" in German Romanticism. Milner, *La Fantasmagorie,* 34. At the time that the phantasmagoria enjoyed its greatest appeal in France, Germany was still preindustrial, predominantly agricultural, with a more feudal social organization than France. The social struggles which the phantasmagoria links with psychological delusion are thus not yet its concern. Confirming this suggestion would be the success obtained by the technological and psychological phantasmagoria when exported across the Channel to a country preoccupied with the social problems of the Industrial Revolution. While the phantasmagoria originated in France, as Castle observes, "it met with—if possible—an even more enthusiastic reception" in England, both in its technological and psychological use. Castle, "Phantasmagoria," 37. There the term was used to describe a hallucinatory form of subjective activity associated both with the marvels of industrial creation and the terrors of class conflict, particularly as this conflict was spectacularly played out in France. Castle cites the "description of the storming of the Bastille, as seen through the eyes of the Jacobin leader Thuriot" from Thomas Carlyle's 1837 *French Revolution*:

> But outwards, behold, O Thuriot, how the multitude flows on, welling through every street: tocsin furiously pealing, all drums beating the *générale*: the Suburb Saint-Antoine rolling hitherward wholly, as one man! Such vision (spectral yet real) thou, O Thuriot, as from thy Mount of Vision, beholdest in this moment: prophetic of what other *Phantasmagories* [emphasis added], and loud-gibbering Spectral Realities, which thou yet beholdest not, but shalt! (Castle, "Phantasmagoria," 26)

She also cites Carlyle on "the terrible days of Prairial [when] the red-shirted crowd of condemned 'flit' toward the guillotine—a 'red baleful Phantasmagory, towards the land of Phantoms.'" Castle, "Phantasmagoria," 27.

36. A full discussion of Marx's interest in the demonic needs to take account of Marx's fondness for the German fantastic born out of Faust's Brocken, and notably for E. T. A. Hoffmann, an inclination S. S. Prawer discusses in *Karl Marx and World Liter-*

brought to representation in the Parisian diabolical, Milner includes a psychological challenge to Enlightenment rationality from within a horizon of Enlightenment thought—we have already seen him pursue the issue in his later discussion of the phantasmagoria (as does Castle). I would suggest that a similar historically specific concern is at issue in Marx's frequent casting of ideology not only in phantasmagorical but more generally in diabolical terms. I make this suggestion to give one example of the potential application of Benjamin's ambition to re-awaken the expressive environment from which Marx's teachings arose. Multiple theoreticians in the history of Marxism have lamented that the bulk of Marx's discussion of ideology is composed of rhetorical flourishes, with no extensive theoretical exposition of its own. Recalling the nineteenth-century epistemological concerns at stake in Marx's diabolical rhetoric reveals this rhetoric as more than ornament to a conceptual discussion that Marx forgot to provide. Rather, Marx's rhetorical displays constitute symptomatic expressions of conceptual contradictions that he can neither articulate nor resolve.

As Benjamin suggests, Marx frames what is arguably his major text on ideology, *The Eighteenth Brumaire,* as a representation of a haunted Parisian universe of spirits, ghosts, demonic projections, and black magic.[37] Let me give just a few more examples of this text's fondness for diabolical rhetoric, palpable from Marx's mention of history as a collective nightmare on the first page. There are Marx's phantasmagorical descriptions of Louis Bonaparte abolishing, among other things, "*liberté, égalité, fraternité* and the second Sunday in May 1852—all has

---

ature. According to Eleanor Marx, Marx used to spin out fantastic tales himself "in the manner of E. T. A. Hoffmann . . . from week to week, from month to month":

> ". . . Hans Röckle himself was a Hoffmann-like magician, who kept a toy-shop, and who was always 'hard up.' His shop was full of the most wonderful things—of wooden men and women, giants and dwarfs, kings and queens, workmen and masters, animals and birds as numerous as Noah got into the Ark, tables and chairs, carriages, boxes of all sorts and sizes. And though he was a magician, Hans could never meet his obligations either to the devil or the butcher, and was therefore—much against the grain—constantly obliged to sell his toys to the devil. These then went through wonderful adventures—always ending in a return to Hans Röckle's shop."

Quoted from *Marx and Engels on Literature and Art,* eds. L. Baxandall and S. Morawski (St. Louis, Milwaukee, 1973), 147, in Prawer, *Karl Marx and World Literature,* 393–394.

37. More evidently, he frames *The Eighteenth Brumaire* as a meditation on history as theater. Andrew Parker provides an acute discussion of the significance of Marx's use of theatrical rhetoric in the *Brumaire* in "Unthinking Sex: Marx, Engels and the Scene of Writing."

vanished like a phantasmagoria before the spell of a man whom even his enemies do not make out to be a sorcerer," and his description of the bourgeoisie's fear of working class revolt as the "'red specter,' continually conjured up and exorcised by the counter-revolutionaries."[38] It is not "Circe, by means of black magic" but rather the bourgeoisie's attempt to negotiate the contradictions of its class position which "has distorted that work of art, the bourgeois republic, into a monstrous shape."[39] The text's diabolical rhetoric continues through to its final paragraph describing Bonaparte's artful response to his difficult situation throughout the years of revolutionary turbulence: "Driven by the contradictory demands of his situation and being at the same time, like a conjurer, under the necessity of keeping the public gaze fixed on himself . . . Bonaparte throws the entire bourgeois economy into confusion, violates everything that seemed inviolable to the Revolution of 1848, makes some tolerant of revolution, others desirous of revolution, and produces actual anarchy in the name of order."[40]

When *The Eighteenth Brumaire* describes ideology in diabolical terms, it designates a challenge to Enlightenment subjectivity in keeping with the nineteenth-century epistemological use of this rhetoric. Marx uses such rhetoric to characterize an experience in which the individual subject not only becomes confused in his/her ability to distinguish between objectivity and subjectivity, desire and reality, but is threatened with the loss of this ability altogether. For in *The Eighteenth Brumaire* Marx explains ideological distortion as a response to the conflicts and contradictions of class struggle from which no individual subject in class society is immune.[41] The vision of ideology advanced in this text potentially constitutes all social subjects as ideological subjects, denying what Benjamin would call the distance necessary for Enlightenment critique. But the radical post-Enlightenment content to Marx's notion of ideology here simultaneously conflicts with *The Eighteenth Brumaire*'s representation of ideology as temporary mystification to be dispelled by the rational subject engaging in dialectical analysis. *The Eighteenth Brumaire* also contrasts the mystified conditions of bour-

---

38. Marx, *The Eighteenth Brumaire*, 20, 44.
39. Marx, *The Eighteenth Brumaire*, 119.
40. Marx, *The Eighteenth Brumaire*, 135.
41. In Marx's use of the diabolical, the nineteenth-century epistemological significance of this rhetoric thus reinforces its nineteenth-century social use previously mentioned: to designate the fact that class conflict appears endowed with a man-made supernatural power.

geois revolutions with the ruthless critique and self-critique characterizing the proletarian revolution Marx propounds: "Proletarian revolutions, like those of the nineteenth century, criticize themselves
constantly." [42]

In *The Eighteenth Brumaire*, I am arguing, Marx simultaneously formulates a notion of ideological representation challenging the possibility of Enlightenment rationality and insists on this rationality as the tool
cutting through the delusions of ideological thought. That he couches
the post-Enlightenment aspect to his understanding of ideology in
figurative form results from his attempt to circumvent the theoretical
impasse produced by this contradiction. Althusser is eloquent on Marx's
use of figurative language at a moment of theoretical impasse. Considering Marx's use of the metaphor of inversion to describe his relation
to Hegel, Althusser writes: "An interrogation of the inversion metaphor shows that it cannot itself think itself, and hence that it both
points to a real but absent problem, a real but absent question outside
itself, and to the conceptual emptiness or ambiguity corresponding to
this absence, the *absence of a concept behind a word*." [43] A similar process is at issue in Marx's diabolical representations of ideological work.
Unable to conceptualize the subject's necessary implication in ideology
because it would contradict his Enlightenment understanding of critique, Marx employs figurative language to indicate a challenge he can
neither articulate nor dismiss.

No passage better demonstrates that Marx turns to diabolical
rhetoric when he seeks to conceptualize the post-Enlightenment nature
of ideology than a paragraph where Marx discusses how the class conflicts of Second Republic France cause the distinction between ideological projection and reality to dissolve. "The period that we have before
us comprises the most motley mixture of crying contradictions," Marx
states, and he proceeds to enumerate these contradictions, which culmi-
nate in the breakdown of the concept of the material event itself. [44]
"Passions without truths, truths without passion; heroes without heroic deeds, history without events," he states. [45] Marx concludes by
figuring this situation in phantasmagorical terms. He describes Second
Republic Paris as a world where men themselves take on the quality of
projections in ghostly optical technology, appearing as figures in a

42. Marx, *The Eighteenth Brumaire*, 19.
43. Althusser and Balibar, *Reading Capital*, 33.
44. Marx, *The Eighteenth Brumaire*, 43.
45. Marx, *The Eighteenth Brumaire*, 43.

magic lantern show or the *ombres chinoises*: "If any section of history has been painted grey on grey, it is this. Men and events appear as inverted Schlemihls, as shadows that have lost their bodies." [46] These may be "only" figures of speech. But they are also, to echo *The Eighteenth Brumaire*, figures where the content goes beyond the phrase.

WHY NOT ALLEGORY?

The extent of Benjamin's familiarity with the historical phantasmagoria, although difficult to determine, does not alter my fundamental premise: Benjamin privileges phantasmagoria as the *Passagen-Werk*'s potential allegory. A term taken from the time and place under consideration, the phantasmagoria is sufficiently polyvalent to designate (1) the nineteenth-century Parisian cultural products working ideological transposition, (2) Benjamin's principal theoretical apparatus in analyzing this transposition, (3) the psychological content of the experience of ideological transposition, (4) the social causes of such transposition, and (5) the relation of Benjamin's Parisian production cycle to his work on the German baroque. But at this point, it may be asked: What has happened to allegory? In the context of discussing Baudelaire, Benjamin draws multiple links between allegory and the commodity form. In addition, he links allegory to his own recuperative critical procedure, notably the dialectical image. Would these links not indicate Benjamin's interest in transferring his privileged metaconcept from his earlier work on the German baroque to the *Passagen-Werk*?

Why not allegory indeed? Benjamin never approached a problem from only one side. But in the 1939 exposé Benjamin specifically elected phantasmagoria as the term designating the form of representation under investigation in his work: "Our inquiry proposes to show how as a consequence of this reifying representation of civilization, the new forms of life and the new creations of a fundamentally economic and technological nature that we owe to the last century enter into the universe of a phantasmagoria" (*PW*, 60). This selection may derive from the marked conflict between salient features of allegory and the nineteenth-century universe of phantasmagorical perception that the *Passagen-Werk* describes.

In his work on the German baroque Benjamin suggests that allegory responds to specifically seventeenth-century social conflicts, notably the

46. Marx, *The Eighteenth Brumaire*, 44.

decline of faith and the struggle between absolute monarchs and feudal princes at issue in the Thirty Years War. Allegory is thus not an expressive form with evident links to the principal material concerns of nineteenth-century Paris: the flowering of urban industrial capitalism and the struggle among the declining aristocracy, the bourgeoisie risen to a position of mastery, the emerging proletariat, and the disgruntled peasantry, a situation that was the legacy of the French Revolution.[47] In addition, while Benjamin links allegory to a crisis of faith, he stresses that allegory remains oriented toward a theological notion of transcendence and an authentically superhuman form of the demonic. Once again, this situation is very different from the man-made demonic producing the ideological transpositions of Paris, capital of the nineteenth century. Finally, the difficulty with which allegory seizes the psychological content of ideological transposition is important. Benjamin opposes allegory not only to the Romantic concept of the symbol but to Romantic notions more generally, notably to the Romantic notion of the imagination. "'Fantasy', the creative faculty as conceived by the moderns, was unknown as the criterion of a spiritual hierarchy" (*OGTD*, 179). The contrast between Romantic accounts of psychological activity and allegory extends from the emblem's production to its reception. Insisting on the "absence of . . . radiance" of allegory, Benjamin makes its ruins work an almost Brechtian demystification on the glitter of Renaissance representation (*OGTD*, 180). These qualities, however, do not describe the palpable illusions of nineteenth-century ideological transposition. "It is a hallucination—not an allegory—which this poem gives us," Claude Pichois writes of Baudelaire's "Les Sept Vieillards."[48] Reading this poem as "an anguishing phantasmagoria," Benjamin seems to agree.

If allegory describes the *form* of the commodity, then, it cannot grasp the spectral yet extraordinarily palpable way in which the commodity form *appears*.[49] One might counter that while the phantasmagoria

47. In the *Passagen-Werk* Benjamin uses Marx to designate material processes informing the allegorical emblem in the baroque period. See J 78, 4, on the link between the division of labor and the fragmentation of the baroque emblem. Benjamin writes: "The 'interruption,' that according to Marx characterizes the individual stages of this work process, could stretch out unforseeably long during the age of the Thirty Years' War, that halted production now here now there. The real triumph of baroque emblematics, where the death's head is the most important pawn, consisted in including the human himself in this process" (*PW*, 462–463). I thank Martin Reichert for this translation.

48. Pichois, notes to Baudelaire, *Oeuvres complètes*, I, 1011.

49. On this question see the paragraphs surrounding Buck-Morss's discussion of Espagne and Werner in her *DS*, 209.

figures the palpable experience of objective transfiguration at issue in ideological transposition, it cannot seize the demystification of this transposition that is one of Benjamin's central aims. Might Benjamin be constructing here an opposition between Phantasmagoria and Allegory modeled on the Baudelairean couple of *Idéal* and *Spleen* (or *correspondances* and allegory)? I prefer, however, to dissolve this opposition altogether. The (critically) illuminating phantasmagoria is a late avatar of Benjamin's interest in a critique of ideology modeled on therapeutic practices, heir to the profane illumination and the dialectical image that is a dream image.

"A LAST PHANTASMAGORIA": FROM DIALECTICAL FÉERIE TO BENJAMIN'S BROCKEN

Benjamin concludes his 1939 exposé by designating as phantasmagorical an ideological product that is critical of ideology. He calls Blanqui's *Eternité par les Astres* a "last phantasmagoria" that "implicitly includes the most acerbic critique of all the others" (*PW*, 75). Why does he use the term in a fashion that is opposed to his use of it in the essay's previous sections? The polyvalence of the phantasmagoria in the realm of ideological mystification is clear enough, but what aspect of this concept suits it to designate practices of ideological critique?

The answer to this question lies as much in Benjamin's post-Enlightenment understanding of cultural critique as in the phantasmagoria itself. From the inception of the Parisian production cycle Benjamin states that Enlightenment critical procedures no longer function in today's world.[50] With all experience saturated by the phantasmagorical power of the commodity, even the cultural critic cannot achieve the distanced and multidimensional relation to his/her object necessary for rational thought. "Criticism is a matter of correct distancing," we remember from "This Space for Rent" in *One-Way Street* (*OWS*, 89). "It was at home in a world where perspectives and prospects counted and where it was still possible to take a standpoint. Now things press too closely on human society. The 'unclouded', 'innocent' eye has become a lie" (*OWS*, 89). Rational demystification can hence no longer be the critic's task. Rather, the critic must seek some form of activity using his/her immersion in the very objects of study to productive end.

Throughout *Profane Illumination* we have seen Benjamin speculate

50. See "Imperial Panorama" in *One-Way Street*.

diversely on the most adequate form of critical thought in such a situation. In *One-Way Street* Benjamin suggests that it is a question of seizing the forces destroying the distinction between subject and object to recuperative/disruptive end. If, as Lukács explains, these forces have paradoxically produced in the subject an increasing sense of distance from the objective dimension, the question for Benjamin becomes how to use these forces to disrupt their own ideological effect. We have seen Benjamin turn to surrealism for psychoanalytic methods of expressing forces that determine the subject and the situation but from which the subject has no distance. And we have seen Benjamin's effort to seize Marx's immersion in the society that Marx simultaneously describes. Benjamin's much discussed unorthodox strategies of critical writing constitute another approach to the problem, as he plays with rhetorical and poetic effects to incite all manner of irrational states: fascination, enchantment, melancholy, frustration, distraction.[51] True, the Enlightenment version of "critique" articulated in *One-Way Street* does not entirely disappear from Benjamin's writings, particularly when he turns to assessing aesthetic products. In the essay on surrealism Benjamin's initial stance seems to take measured and rational advantage of the perspective distance affords: "The German observer is not standing at the head of the stream. That is his opportunity. He is in the valley. He can gauge the energies of the movement" (*R*, 177). But by the end of the essay Benjamin has shed his stance as distanced observer, engaging in his own hyperbolic assessments of revolutionary praxis in the surrealist image zone.

When Benjamin uses the phantasmagoria to designate commodity culture's acerbic critique, he attempts to solve a problem *accompanying* his post-Enlightenment displacement of critical activity: how to represent critical thought when its traditional metaphysical figuration breaks down. The ocular rhetoric traditionally used by metaphysics to express critical knowledge is prime among the figurative schemas Benjamin's understanding of critique renders problematic. Following traditional metaphysics, Enlightenment discourse maps its opposition between

51. On the subject of Benjamin's fascination with fascination, Abbas remarks: "Benjamin's criticism is an affective criticism, a criticism of affectivity both in its rejection of sentimentality and stupor and in its use of fascination. And if we remember Marx's still pertinent remark that 'the cultivation of the five senses is the work of all previous history' [a place in the 1844 Manuscripts to which Benjamin himself refers], it becomes clear that a genuine affective criticism like Benjamin's can only be historically grounded." Abbas, "On Fascination: Walter Benjamin's Images," 61. For an argument concerning Benjamin's politicized use of style, see, for example, Terry Eagleton's *Walter Benjamin*.

valid rational and mystified nonrational thought on the field of physical vision. Figuring rational thought as the natural vision of natural objects, it figures mystified thought in opposing terms, either as technologically aided vision or as a technologically produced show (the procession in Plato's cave is the first phantasmagoria). Indeed, Benjamin himself figures rational thought by employing the visual tropes of Enlightenment discourse, as the previously quoted passage from *One-Way Street* makes clear. But these tropes cannot encompass the concept of contemporary critical activity which his Parisian production cycle puts forth. A form of thinking that falls on neither side of the reason/illusion binary opposition, Benjamin's critical activity transgresses not only a conceptual opposition fundamental to Enlightenment epistemology but also the physical practices that Enlightenment discourse invokes to infuse its concepts with life.

In order to express his understanding of contemporary critical activity, Benjamin must hence devise figures of his own. And from Benjamin's earliest descriptions of the arcades project, he casts his post-Enlightenment representation of nineteenth-century Paris in phantasmagorical terms. Thus, Benjamin describes his work to Scholem as a ghostly procession: "The profane motifs . . . will parade by there in a hellish intensification" (*B*, I, 455).[52] In this letter too Benjamin gives the *Passagen-Werk* a provisional title that explicitly indentifies it with a supernatural spectacle invented by the time and place under study. "Parisian arcades. A dialectical *féerie*" (*B*, I, 455). While the fairy-tale aspects of Benjamin's interest in *féerie* have been amply discussed, the word's specifically nineteenth-century meaning needs to be made clear. *Féerie* was a term introduced in 1823 Paris to designate a theatrical spectacle "where supernatural characters appear . . . and which requires considerable theatrical means," notably mechanical ones.[53] All the mode during the middle part of the century, these productions led Flaubert to comment: "Along with suckling pig, the *féerie* is the heaviest thing that I know of."[54] Benjamin points to this meaning of the term in citations accumulated in an early fragment from Konvolut Y, "Photography," on the question of "Feenstücke" [*Féerie*]: "So in 'Parisiens à Londres' (1866), for example, the exhibition of English industry is brought on stage, and there illustrated with a display of naked beauties, that evidently just trace their lineage to *allegory* and poetic

---

52. *Theory* derives from a Greek word meaning spectacle as well as viewing.
53. *Le Robert*, IV, 444.
54. *Le Robert*, IV, 444.

invention" (*PW*, 825, emphasis added). It is fitting that Georges Méliès, one of the pioneers of cinema, got his start producing a version of the magic lantern show where the *féerie* met the phantasmagoria. In the late 1880s Méliès "became a skillful producer of imaginative sketches combining the romantic, spectacular, and absurd—'genre féerique et fantasmagorique,' Méliès called it, suggesting a lingering persistence of the Robertson tradition."[55]

The *féerie* tempted Benjamin not only for its degraded link to allegory, as it transformed the allegorical stage props of ruin into cumbersome technology, but also for the nineteenth-century historical conditions it inscribed. Like phantasmagoria, the term was employed to characterize the marvelous aspect of industrial production. In the early section of Konvolut Q, Benjamin quotes from Eugène Buret's 1840 *De la misère des classes laborieuses en France et en Angleterre* on industrial manufacture as a *féerie*. "The most fantastic creations of the *féerie* are just about brought into being under our eyes . . . each day in our factories marvels are produced as great as those which Doctor Faustus produced with his magic book" (*PW*, 826). ·

That Benjamin does not long privilege the *féerie* as figure for his own project of Parisian representation derives perhaps from the term's lack of sufficient resonance in the theoretical sphere. Soon abandoning *féerie*, Benjamin experiments with the figurative potential of multiple nineteenth- and twentieth-century technologically produced visual spectacles. These technologies are the same as those he uses to figure ideological illusions: stereoscopes, magic lanterns, panoramas, dioramas, mechanical spectacles, mirrors, and photographs. In Konvolut N he declares: "Pedagogic side of this undertaking: 'To train our image-making faculty to look *stereoscopically* and dimensionally into the depths of the shadows of history'" (N 1, 8, emphasis added). The phantasmagoria is a late example of such experimentation.

Most often Benjamin compares his practice to the cinema: "Method of this project: literary montage. I need say nothing. Only show (*zeigen*)," he writes in the methodological Konvolut N (N 1a, 8).[56] The preference of the Parisian production cycle for this figuration of critical activity only supports my suggestion for the cycle's late use of the phantasmagoria to similar ends. A form of visual representation which played a role in the development of cinema (in the process of figuring

55. Erik Barnouw, *The Magician and the Cinema*, 46.
56. I substitute "to show" for Hafrey and Sieburth's "to exhibit."

out how to use the magic lantern to phantasmagorical effect, Robertson made it easily portable), the phantasmagoria proceeds through the principle of juxtaposition underwriting cinematic montage.

Multiple aspects of the original phantasmagorical performance foreshadow Benjamin's understanding of the critical gesture. Robertson relies not only on montage but also on humor, mystery, and fascination, all effects whose critical potential Benjamin explores. And Robertson's spectacle treats illusion in a fashion recalling Benjamin's interest in critical enchantment. On the purpose of Robertson's spectacle, Milner writes: "He means to make his invention help to educate the people." [57] To some extent this education appeals to reason. Showing supernatural beings to be the products of human ingenuity, Robertson seeks to convince his audience that supernatural beings are only a mystified effect of human invention. At the same time, however, Robertson devotes great attention to endowing his fanciful creations with the illusion of independent life. Milner points out that Robertson justified this procedure by citing his spectacle's didactic end. Robertson thought he would contribute more effectively to a project of enlightenment with his enchanting spectacle than through using the tools of the rational method whose cause he serves. Milner continues: "He means to make his invention help to educate the people, who will only slowly be touched by the book and the newspaper, while a direct presentation of supposedly supernatural phenomena would readily be convincing. It is in this role of educator that he boasts of himself in the prospectus that he publishes to introduce his show." [58]

It remains to mention one last advantage of the technological phantasmagoria in the realm of critique: its power to figure the revision that Benjamin's critical illumination works on an orthodox Marxist notion of critical activity. We return to Marx's camera obscura but view it from the other side.

Marx's camera obscura represents both ideology and critical knowledge in standard Enlightenment terms. Opposing the darkened space of ideological illusion to the sun-filled landscape of reality, Marx's Enlightenment figuration for knowledge well emblematizes Marx's faith in the illuminating power of rational critique (even if the metaphor entails some slippage, as Kofman points out, around whether this knowledge is immediate or constructed: the sun shines both on the natural

57. Milner, *La Fantasmagorie*, 17.
58. Milner, *La Fantasmagorie*, 17–18.

world of "real" men and the Western metaphysical tradition of philosophical construction). But for Benjamin Marx's phantasmagorical conception of ideology renders both Marx's (and Marxism's) Enlightenment conception and figuration of critical activity questionable.

In designating ideological critique with Marx's term for ideological transposition, phantasmagoria, Benjamin thus invokes a post-Enlightenment moment in Marx to correct the Enlightenment understanding of *Kritik* that Marx simultaneously displays. In doing so Benjamin stumbles on a technological figure for critical knowledge which corrects the Enlightenment figuration of the critic's task proposed by Marx's camera obscura. The last phantasmagoria turns the world as it exists outside the camera obscura to artificial show. Unable to seek access to the sun-filled real, the critic remedies enclosure in the cave of ideology by producing technological spectacles herself.

When the phantasmagoria represents a situation nowhere visible as such, it provides a form of imaging resembling that at issue in the dialectical image. I have suggested that an important dimension of the dialectical image is its transgression of traditional representational boundaries. That the phantasmagorical show transgresses these boundaries further suits it to inherit the dialectical image's epistemological task. From its inception with Robertson, this show brought magic lantern projection together with verbal utterances, sound effects, music, smoke, incense, mirrors, and audience participation. At the center of the spectacle stood the phantasmagorian's phantascope, which projects with a medium of illumination that itself encapsulates Benjamin's post-Enlightenment challenge to Marx. The fire kindled in the phantoscope transforms the unfiltered natural light of rational understanding into an energy somewhere between nature and art. Stolen by Prometheus for man, this light of the gods is also the first technology.

To propose Benjamin as a phantasmagorian? The ghost of Adorno, making a terrifying grimace, appears: "You need not fear that I shall suggest that in your study phantasmagoria should survive unmediated or that the study itself should assume a phantasmagorical character." [59] And: "Your idea of providing in the *Baudelaire* a model for the *Arcades* study was something I took very seriously, and I approached the satanic scene much as Faust approached the phantasmagoria of the Brocken

59. Adorno to Benjamin, New York, 10 November 1938, in *AP*, 127. I modify Zohn's translation of "phantasmagorischen Charakter" as "phantasmagoric character." For the German, see *B*, II, 784.

mountain, when he thought that many a riddle would now be solved. May I be excused for having had to give myself Mephistopheles' reply that many a riddle poses itself anew?" (*AP*, 126–127). But what if the untheorized montage of Parisian facts in "The Paris of the Second Empire in Baudelaire" were Benjamin at work constructing a Brocken of his own? When Benjamin defended himself against Adorno, he suggested that the phantasmagoria had been "integrated into the construction" of his study rather than described.[60]

"Gretel once said in jest that you are an inhabitant of the cave-like depths of your Arcades, and that you shrink from finishing your study because you are afraid of having to leave what you have built," Adorno also told Benjamin in this letter, exhorting him to emerge from the cave of representation and bring his project into the light of day (*AP*, 131). But Benjamin refused Adorno's description of his critical route as emergence from a darkened cave into a natural space where things appear as they really are. "Theory . . . breaks like a single ray of light into an artificially darkened chamber," Benjamin countered, placing his spectators, and possibly himself, in the camera obscura where phantasmagorical projection occurs (*AP*, 135).

If Adorno repeatedly demands the "explosion of . . . [the] phantasmagoria," it is perhaps because this grand inquisitor of rationality scents the challenge to his own activity implied by Benjamin's fondness for the term.[61] Benjamin does not mystify material reality in his phantasmagoria, but he does not exactly demystify it either. Rather, material reality becomes one more representation in his magic theater, part of a ghostly conceptual parade. Adorno may bristle. And Benjamin is not much easier with the phantasmagoria's enchanting possibility. Forced to employ such procedures because demystifying criticism no longer works, Benjamin hopes for an end to the world of phantasmagorical vision. When Benjamin conceives of criticism as profane illumination, however, he does not just mourn criticism's decline. Admitting criticism's commerce with irrational forces, he draws attention to criticism's power both to locate contemporary demons and to press them into positive epistemological, aesthetic and political service.

"The world dominated by its phantasmagorias, is—to use Baudelaire's expression—modernity," writes Benjamin in the conclusion to "Paris, Capitale du XIXème siècle" (*PW*, 77). If Benjamin is one of mo-

---

60. Benjamin to Adorno, Paris, 9 December 1938, *AP*, 138.
61. Adorno, Hornberg letter, in *AP*, 113.

20. Frontispiece to *Le Diable à Paris*.

dernity's more acerbic critics, he remains indisputably preoccupied with its defining concerns. As do we. Surveying the ruins of postmodernism, we are confronted with proliferating representations instead of the reality that produced them, or rather, the distinction between reality and representation no longer quite describes the shadowy yet acutely perceptible landscape of our own Gothic world. Such realization, however, in no way dispels, indeed it rather exacerbates, the need for concrete material practice. I too am not easy with Benjamin's critical phantasmagoria, suspicious of the mystifying ends to which its enchantment can be put. But perhaps this very danger indicates its vitality.

Bibliography

Abbas, Ackbar. "On Fascination: Walter Benjamin's Images." In *New German Critique,* no. 48, Fall 1989, 43–62.

Adorno, Theodor Wiesengrund. "Benjamins 'Einbahnstraße.'" In *Über Walter Benjamin.* Frankfurt: Suhrkamp, 1968, 55–61.

Aesthetics and Politics. London: New Left Books, 1979.

Althusser, Louis. *For Marx.* Trans. Ben Brewster. London: New Left Books, 1977.

————. *Lenin and Philosophy.* Trans. Ben Brewster. London: Monthly Review Press, 1971.

Althusser, Louis, and Etienne Balibar. *Reading Capital.* Trans. Ben Brewster. London: Verso, 1979.

The American Guide to Paris. London: Paul Brewster, 1925.

Aragon, Louis. *Le Paysan de Paris.* Paris: Gallimard, 1966.

————. *Traité du style.* Paris: Gallimard, 1983.

Archives du surréalisme, vol. 1: *Bureau de recherches surréalistes.* Paris: Gallimard, 1988.

L'Art de circuler dans Paris. Paris, 1922.

Balakian, Anna. *André Breton, Magus of Surrealism.* New York: Oxford University Press, 1971.

Balzac, Honoré de. "Facino Cane," vol. 6, 46–48, in *Oeuvres illustrées de Balzac,* 8 vols. Paris: Marescq et Co., 1852.

Banquart, Marie-Claire. *Paris des Surréalistes.* Paris: Seghers, 1971.

Barnouw, Erik. *The Magician and the Cinema.* New York: Oxford University Press, 1981.

Barthes, Roland. *Camera Lucida.* Trans. Richard Howard. New York: Farrar, Straus and Giroux, 1985.

———. *La Chambre claire*. Paris: Editions de l'Etoile, Gallimard, Le Seuil, 1980.

Bataille, Georges. *Visions of Excess*. Ed. Allan Stoekl. Minneapolis: University of Minnesota Press, 1985.

Baudelaire, Charles. *Oeuvres complètes*. 2 vols. Paris: Gallimard, Bibliothèque de la Pléiade, 1975.

Beaujour, Michel. *Miroirs d'encre*. Paris: Seuil, 1980.

———. "Qu'est-ce que *Nadja*?" In *La Nouvelle Revue Française*, 15th year, no. 172, April 1967, 780–799.

Becker, Lucille F. *Louis Aragon*. New York: Twayne, 1971.

Bedel, Jean. *Les Puces ont cent ans*. Cany-Barville: La Côte des Antiquités, 1985.

Béhar, Henri. *André Breton*. Paris: Calmann-Lévy, 1990.

Benjamin, Andrew, ed. *The Problems of Modernity*. New York: Routledge, 1989.

Benjamin, Walter. *Briefe*. 2 vols. Frankfurt: Suhrkamp, 1966.

———. "Central Park." Trans. Lloyd Spencer. In *New German Critique*, no. 34, Winter 1985, 32–58.

———. *Charles Baudelaire*. Frankfurt: Suhrkamp, 1974.

———. *Charles Baudelaire: A Lyric Poet in the Era of High Capitalism*. Trans. Harry Zohn. London: New Left Books, 1973.

———. *Gesammelte Schriften*. 7 vols. Frankfurt: Suhrkamp, 1972–1989.

———. *Illuminations*. Ed. Hannah Arendt. Trans. Harry Zohn. New York: Schocken Books, 1969.

———. "N [Re the Theory of Knowledge, Theory of Progress]." Trans. Leigh Hafrey and Richard Sieburth. In Gary Smith et al., *Benjamin—Philosophy, Aesthetics, History*. Chicago: University of Chicago Press, 1989.

———. *One-Way Street and Other Writings*. Trans. Edmund Jephcott and Kingsley Shorter. London: New Left Books, 1979.

———. *The Origin of German Tragic Drama*. Trans. John Osborne. London: New Left Books, 1977.

———. *Das Passagen-Werk*. 2 vols. Frankfurt: Suhrkamp, 1983.

———. *Reflections*. Ed. Peter Demetz. Trans. Edmund Jephcott. New York: Harcourt Brace Jovanovich, 1978.

Billy, André. *Paris vieux et neuf*. 2 vols. Paris: Eugène Rey, 1909.

Bloch, Ernst. *Heritage of Our Times*. Trans. Neville and Stephen Plaice. Berkeley and Los Angeles: University of California Press, 1990.

Bonnet, Marguerite. *André Breton: Naissance de l'aventure surréaliste*. Paris: José Corti, 1975.

Bournon, Fernand, and Albert Dauzat. *Paris et ses environs*. Paris: Librairie Larousse, 1925.

Breton, André. *L'Amour fou*. Paris: Gallimard, 1982.

———. *La Clé des champs*. Paris: Editions du Sagittaire, 1953.

———. *Communicating Vessels*. Trans. Mary Ann Caws and Geoffrey T. Harris. Lincoln: University of Nebraska Press, 1990.

———. *Mad Love*. Trans. Mary Ann Caws. Lincoln: University of Nebraska Press, 1987.

——. *Manifestoes of Surrealism.* Trans. Richard Seaver and Helen R. Lane. Ann Arbor: University of Michigan Press, 1986.

——. *Nadja.* Paris: Gallimard, 1928.

——. *Nadja.* Trans. Richard Howard. New York: Grove Press, 1960.

——. *Oeuvres complètes,* vol. 1. Paris: Gallimard, Bibliothèque de la Pléiade, 1988.

——. *Point du jour.* Paris: Gallimard, 1977.

——. *Les Vases communicants.* Paris: Gallimard, 1981.

Breton, André, and Paul Gluard. "140 réponses à l'enquête sur la rencontre." *Minotaure,* nos. 3–4, December 1933, 101–116.

Brooks, Peter. *Reading for the Plot.* New York: Knopf, 1984.

Buci-Glucksmann, Christine. *La Raison baroque de Baudelaire à Benjamin.* Paris: Galilée, 1984.

Buck-Morss, Susan. "Benjamin's Passagen-Werk: Redeeming Mass Culture for the Revolution." In *New German Critique,* no. 29, Spring-Summer 1983.

——. *The Dialectics of Seeing.* Cambridge: MIT Press, 1989.

——. *The Origin of Negative Dialectics.* New York: The Free Press, Macmillan, 1977.

Bürger, Peter. *Der französische Surrealismus.* Frankfurt: Athenäum, 1971.

Cain, Georges. *Coins de Paris.* Paris: Flammarion, 1907.

Camhi, Leslie. "Extended Boundaries." In *Art in America,* February 1992, 39–43.

Carrouges, Michel. *André Breton and the Basic Concepts of Surrealism.* Trans. M. Prendergast. University: University of Alabama Press, 1974.

Castle, Terry. "Phantasmagoria: Spectral Technology and the Metaphorics of Modern Reverie." In *Critical Inquiry,* vol. 15, no. 1, Autumn 1988, 27–61.

Caws, Mary Ann. *André Breton.* New York: Twayne, 1971.

Caws, Mary Ann, et al. *Surrealism and Women.* Cambridge: MIT Press, 1991.

Certeau, Michel de. *Arts de faire.* Paris: Union Générale d'Editions, Collection 10/18, 1980.

——. *Heterologies.* Trans. Brian Massumi. Minneapolis: University of Minnesota Press, 1986.

Chevalier, Louis. *Classes laborieuses et Classes dangereuses.* Paris: Hachette, 1984.

——. *Montmartre du plaisir et du crime.* Paris: Robert Laffont, 1980.

Citron, Pierre. *La Poésie de Paris dans la littérature française de Rousseau à Baudelaire.* 2 vols. Paris: Editions de Minuit, 1961.

Cixous, Hélène. "The Laugh of the Medusa." In *New French Feminisms,* ed. Elaine Marks and Isabelle de Courtivron, 245–264. New York: Schocken Books, 1981.

Clébert, Jean-Paul. "Traces de Nadja." *Revue des Sciences Humaines,* no. 184, October–December 1981, 79–93.

Clej, Alina. "Phantoms of the *opera*: Notes Towards a Theory of Surrealist Confession—The Case of Breton." In *MLN,* vol. 104, no. 4, September 1989, 819–844.

Coissac, G.-M. *Histoire du Cinématographe.* Paris: Editions du "Cinéopse," 1925.

Corbin, Alain. *Les Filles de noce.* Paris: Aubier Montaigne, 1978.

Dada/Surrealism, no. 17 (special issue devoted to André Breton). Ed. Anna Balakian and Rudolf Kuenzli. 1989.

Darys, Jacques. *Comment et où s'amuser à Paris.* Paris: Editions du Couvre-feu, n.d.

Deleuze, Gilles, and Félix Guattari. *Anti-Oedipus.* Trans. Robert Hurley, Mark Seem, and Helen R. Lane. New York: Viking Press, 1977.

Derrida, Jacques. "Différance." In *Margins of Philosophy,* pp. 3–27. Trans. Alan Bass. Chicago: University of Chicago Press, 1982.

Le Diable à Paris. 2 vols. Paris: Hetzel, 1868.

Dubois, Philippe. "Le Corps et ses fantômes." *La Recherche Photographique,* October 1986, 41–50.

Eagleton, Terry. *Walter Benjamin or Towards a Revolutionary Criticism.* London: Verso, 1985.

Engels, Friedrich. *Herr Eugen Dühring's Revolution in Science (Anti-Dühring).* Trans. Emile Burns. New York: International Publishers, 1966.

———. *Ludwig Feuerbach and the Outcome of Classical German Philosophy.* New York: International Publishers, 1934.

———. *The Origin of the Family, Private Property, and the State.* London: Penguin Books, 1985.

———. *Socialism: Utopian and Scientific.* Peking: Foreign Languages Press, 1975.

Evenson, Norma. *Paris: A Century of Change, 1878–1978.* New Haven: Yale University Press, 1979.

Fegdal, Charles. *Dans notre vieux Paris.* Paris: Librairie Stock, Delamain, Boutelleau et Cie, 1934.

———. *La Fleur des curiositez de Paris.* Paris: Editions de la Revue Contemporaine, 1921.

Freud, Sigmund. "Analysis of a Phobia in a Five-year-Old Boy" (1909). In *The Standard Edition of the Complete Psychological Works of Sigmund Freud,* ed. James Strachey, X. London: Hogarth Press, 1953–74.

———. "Analysis Terminable and Interminable" (1937). In *The Standard Edition,* XXIII.

———. *Au delà du principe du plaisir.* In *Essais de psychanalyse.* Trans. S. Jankélévitch. Paris: Payot, 1927.

———. *Beyond the Pleasure Principle* (1920). In *The Standard Edition,* XVIII.

———. "Constructions in Analysis" (1937). In *The Standard Edition,* XXIII.

———. "The Dynamics of Transference" (1912). In *The Standard Edition,* XII.

———. *The Interpretation of Dreams* (1900). In *The Standard Edition,* IV–V.

———. *Letters of Sigmund Freud.* Ed. Ernst Freud. New York: Basic Books, 1960.

———. *The Psychopathology of Everyday Life* (1901). In *The Standard Edition,* VI.

———. "Remembering, Repeating and Working-Through" (1914). In *The Standard Edition,* XII.

———. "Repression" (1915). In *The Standard Edition,* XIV.

———. "The 'Uncanny'" (1919). In *The Standard Edition,* XVII.

Frichet, Henry. *Paris et ses merveilles*. Paris: Maison L. Guilmin, 1925.

Furnkäs, Joseph. "La 'voie à sens unique' weimarienne de Walter Benjamin." In *Weimar ou l'explosion de la modernité*. Ed. Gérard Raulet. Paris: Editions Anthropos, 1984.

―――. *Surrealismus als Erkenntnis*. Stuttgart: Metzler, 1988.

Furet, François. *Marx et la Révolution française*. Paris: Flammarion, 1986.

Gaulmier, Jean. "Remarques sur le thème de Paris chez André Breton." In *Les Critiques de notre temps et Breton*, ed. Marguerite Bonnet, 130–138. Paris: Garnier, 1974.

Geist, Johann Friedrich. *Arcades: The History of a Building Type*. Trans. Jane O. Newman and John H. Smith. Cambridge, Mass.: MIT Press, 1985.

Gindine, Yvette. *Aragon, prosateur surréaliste*. Geneva: Droz, 1966.

Les Grands Boulevards. Paris: Paris-Musées, 1985.

Grossberg, Lawrence, and Cary Nelson, eds. *Marxism and the Interpretation of Culture*. Urbana: University of Illinois Press, 1988.

Le Guide historique et anecdotique de Paris. Paris: Editions Argo, 1929.

Guide de Paris mystérieux. Paris: Tchou, 1966.

Les Guides Bleus: Paris et ses environs. Paris: Hachette, 1924.

Hansen, Miriam. "Benjamin, Cinema, and Experience: 'The Blue Flower in the Land of Technology.'" In *New German Critique*, no. 40, Winter 1987, 179–224.

Haverkamp, Anselm. "Notes on the 'Dialectical Image' (How Deconstructive Is It?)" In *Diacritics,* Winter 1992.

Hector-Hogier. *Paris à la fourchette: Curiosités parisiennes*. Paris: Honoré Champion, 1906, 3d series.

Hedges, Inez. *Languages of Revolt*. Durham, N.C.: Duke University Press, 1983.

Henny, Charles. *Guide de Paris, abrégé esthétique et pratique avec un plan*. Paris: Librairie Fischbacher, 1923.

Hertz, Neil. "Medusa's Head: Male Hysteria under Political Pressure." In *The End of the Line*, 161–193. New York: Columbia University Press, 1985.

Hollier, Denis, ed. *The College of Sociology (1937–39)*. Trans. Besty Wing. Minneapolis: University of Minnesota Press, 1988.

Holly, Michael Ann. "Past Looking." In *Critical Inquiry*, vol. 16, no. 2, Winter 1990, 371–395.

Hugo, Victor. *Notre-Dame de Paris*. Paris: Garnier-Flammarion, 1967.

Jameson, Fredric. *Marxism and Form*. Princeton, N.J.: Princeton University Press, 1971.

Jay, Martin. "The Disenchantment of the Eye: Surrealism and the Crisis of Ocularcentrism." In *Visual Anthropology Review*, vol. 7, no. 1, Spring 1991, 15–38.

―――. *Marxism and Totality*. Berkeley and Los Angeles: University of California Press, 1984.

Jennings, Michael. *Dialectical Images: Walter Benjamin's Theory of Literary Criticism*. Ithaca, N.Y.: Cornell University Press, 1987.

Kofman, Sarah. *Camera obscura de l'idéologie*. Paris: Galilée, 1973.

Krauss, Rosalind. "Nightwalkers." In *Art Journal,* Spring 1981, 33–38.

Krauss, Rosalind, and Jane Livingston, eds. *L'Amour fou: Photography and Surrealism.* New York: Abbeville Press, 1985.

Lacan, Jacques. *Le Séminaire XI, Les quatre concepts fondamentaux de la psychanalyse.* Paris: Seuil, 1973.

———. *The Four Fundamental Concepts of Psycho-Analysis.* Trans. Alan Sheridan. New York: W. W. Norton, 1981.

Laclau, Ernesto, and Chantal Mouffe. *Hegemony and Socialist Strategy.* London: Verso, 1985.

Leiris, Michel. *L'Age d'homme.* Paris: Gallimard, 1979.

Lenk, Elizabeth. *Der springende Narziss.* Munich: Rogner and Bernhard, 1971.

Lewis, Helena. *The Politics of Surrealism.* New York: Paragon House, 1988.

Littré, Emile. *Dictionnaire de la langue française.* 7 vols. Paris: Jean-Jacques Pauvert, 1956.

Lukács, Georg. *History and Class Consciousness.* Trans. Rodney Livingstone. Cambridge, Mass.: MIT Press, 1983.

Macey, David. *Lacan in Contexts.* London: Verso, 1988.

Marx, Karl. *Capital.* Trans. Samuel Moore and Edward Aveling. New York: Modern Library, 1906.

———. *Economic and Philosophic Manuscripts of 1844.* Trans. Martin Milligan. New York: International Publishers, 1964.

———. *The Eighteenth Brumaire of Louis Bonaparte.* New York: International Publishers, 1963.

———. *The Holy Family.* Trans. Richard Dixon and Clemens Dutt. Moscow: Progress Publishers, 1975.

Marx, Karl, and Friedrich Engels. *The German Ideology: Part One, With Selections from Parts Two and Three and Supplementary Texts.* Ed. C. J. Arthur. New York: International Publishers, 1976.

———. *Manifesto of the Communist Party.* New York: International Publishers, 1971.

———. *The Marx-Engels Reader.* Ed. Robert Tucker. New York: W. W. Norton, 1972.

Milner, Max. *La Fantasmagorie.* Paris: Presses Universitaires de France, 1982.

———. *Le Diable dans la littérature française de Cazotte à Baudelaire.* 2 vols. Paris: José Corti, 1960.

Montorgueil, Georges. *Paris au hasard.* Paris: Printed for Henri Beraldi, 1895.

Muray, Philippe. *Le 19ᵉ Siècle à travers les âges.* Paris: Denoël, 1984.

Nicholsen, Shierry Weber. Review of *The Dialectics of Seeing, On Walter Benjamin* and *Benjamin—Philosophy, Asthetics, History.* In *New German Critique,* no. 51, Fall 1990, 179–188.

Nietzsche, Friedrich. *The Gay Science.* New York: Random House, 1974.

On Bataille. Yale French Studies, no. 78.

On Walter Benjamin. Ed. Gary Smith. Cambridge, Mass.: MIT Press, 1988.

Parker, Andrew. "Unthinking Sex: Marx, Engels and the Scene of Writing." In *Social Text,* no. 29, 28–45.

Paris-Guide: Le Guide de la vie à Paris. Paris: Les Editions G. Crès et Compagnie, 1925.

Pinkney, David. *Napoleon III and the Rebuilding of Paris.* Princeton, N.J.: Princeton University Press, 1958.

Pleasure Guide to Paris. Paris: Management, 53 Quai des Grands Augustins, 1927.

Prawer, S. S. *Karl Marx and World Literature.* Oxford: Clarendon Press, 1976.

Pynchon, Thomas. *Gravity's Rainbow.* New York: Viking, 1973.

Robert, Paul. *Dictionnaire alphabétique et analogique de la langue française.* 9 vols. Paris: Le Robert, 1985.

Robertson, Etienne-Gaspard. *Mémoires récréatifs, scientifiques et anecdotiques du physicien-aéronaute E.-G. Robertson.* 2 vols. Paris: 1831.

Rousseau, Jean-Jacques. *Les Confessions.* In *Oeuvres complètes,* vol. 1. Paris: Gallimard, Bibliothèque de la Pléiade, 1986.

Seigel, Jerrold. *Bohemian Paris: Culture, Politics, and the Boundaries of Bourgeois Life, 1830–1930.* New York: Viking, 1986.

Shakespeare, William. *Hamlet.* In *The Riverside Shakespeare,* 1135–1197. Boston: Houghton Mifflin, 1974.

Schikaneder, Emmanuel. Libretto to *The Magic Flute.* Trans. Robert Jordan. New York: Capital Records, 1974.

Smith, Gary, et al. *Benjamin—Philosophy, Aesthetics, History.* Chicago: University of Chicago Press, 1989.

Spencer, Lloyd. "Allegory in the World of the Commodity: The Importance of 'Central Park.'" In *New German Critique* 34, Winter 1985, 59–77.

———. "Introduction to 'Central Park.'" In *New German Critique* 34, Winter 1985, 28–31.

Stallybrass, Peter. "Marx and Heterogeneity: Thinking the Lumpenproletariat." In *Representations,* no. 31, Summer 1990, 69–95.

Sue, Eugène. *Les Mystères de Paris.* Paris: Gosselin, 1843.

Suleiman, Susan. *Subversive Intent: Gender, Politics, and the Avant-Garde.* Cambridge: Harvard University Press, 1990.

Suleiman, Susan, ed. *The Female Body in Western Culture.* Cambridge, Mass.: Harvard University Press, 1986.

Le Surréalisme au service de la révolution. Paris: Editions Jean-Michel Place, 1976.

Sutcliffe, Anthony. *The Autumn of Central Paris.* London: Edward Arnold, 1970.

Tison-Braun, Micheline. *La Crise de l'humanisme.* 2 vols. Paris: Librairie Nizet, 1967.

Veuillot, Louis. *Les Odeurs de Paris.* Paris: Le Livre Catholique, 1914.

Walter Benjamin et Paris. Ed. Heinz Wisman. Paris: Cerf, 1986.

Warnod, André. *Les Plaisirs de la rue.* Paris: L'Edition Française Illustrée, 1928.

Wohlfarth, Irving. "Et Cetera? The Historian as Chiffonier." In *New German Critique,* no. 39, 1986, 143–168.

———. "Re-fusing Theology. Some First Responses to Walter Benjamin's Arcades Project." In *New German Critique,* no. 39, 1986, 3–24.

———. "On the Messianic Structure of Walter Benjamin's Last Reflections." In *Glyph,* no. 3, 148–212.

Wolin, Richard. *Walter Benjamin, An Aesthetic of Redemption.* New York: Columbia University Press, 1982.

Wollen, Peter. "The Situationist International." In *New Left Review* 174, March/April 1989, 67–95.

Zipes, Jack. "Walter Benjamin, Children's Literature, and the Children's Public Sphere: An Introduction to New Trends in West and East Germany." *The Germanic Review,* vol. LXIII, no. 1, Winter 1988, 2–5.

Žižek, Slavoj. *The Sublime Object of Ideology.* London: Verso, 1989.

Index

Designer: U.C. Press Staff
Compositor: Prestige Typography
Text: 10/13 Sabon
Display: Sabon
Printer: Braun-Brumfield, Inc.
Binder: Braun-Brumfield, Inc.